Photoshop® CS
TIMESAVING TECHNIQUES
FOR
DUMMIES®

Photoshop® CS
TIMESAVING TECHNIQUES
FOR
DUMMIES®

by Phyllis Davis

Wiley Publishing, Inc.

Photoshop® CS Timesaving Techniques For Dummies®

Published by
Wiley Publishing, Inc.
909 Third Avenue
New York, NY 10022
www.wiley.com

WILEY

About the Author

Phyllis Davis is a writer, graphics and Web designer, teacher, and graphics software expert. Her professional design credits include many books, fine art posters, and advertisements.

In addition to *Photoshop CS Timesaving Techniques For Dummies*, Phyllis is also the co-author of *Photoshop CS For Dummies*, and the author of *The GIMP: Visual QuickStart Guide* (Peachpit Press), *CorelDraw: Visual QuickStart Guide* (Peachpit Press), and many other highly regarded books about graphic design and photo-manipulation software.

When she isn't writing and designing books and creating Web sites, Phyllis can be found developing and teaching computer courses, digging in her garden with her husband, Harold, and playing with her wonderful boys, Julian and Nicholas.

Dedication

For Harold, the love of my life.

Author's Acknowledgments

Many thanks go out to Bob Woerner and Matt Wagner for entrusting me with this great project. I also owe a huge debt of gratitude to Nicole Sholly, Rebecca Senninger, and Virginia Sanders, who untwisted my gnarled sentences and made sense of the nonsensical. Dennis Cohen caught my technical blunders and gently nudged me in the right direction. Thanks, Dennis!

Many of the beautiful photographs in this book were created by my husband, Harold Davis. These photographs are copyright © Harold Davis and are used with his permission.

Publisher's Acknowledgments

We're proud of this book; please send us your comments through our online registration form located at www.dummies.com/register/.

Some of the people who helped bring this book to market include the following:

Acquisitions, Editorial, and Media Development

Associate Project Editor: Nicole Sholly

Acquisitions Editor: Bob Woerner

Copy Editors: Rebecca Senninger, Virginia Sanders

Technical Editor: Dennis R. Cohen

Editorial Manager: Kevin Kirschner

Senior Permissions Editor: Carmen Krikorian

Media Development Specialist: Travis Silvers

Media Development Manager: Laura VanWinkle

Media Development Supervisor: Richard Graves

Editorial Assistant: Amanda Foxworth

Cartoons: Rich Tennant (www.the5thwave.com)

Production

Project Coordinator: Courtney MacIntyre

Layout and Graphics: Lauren Goddard, Joyce Haughey, Stephanie D. Jumper, Michael Kruzil, Heather Ryan, Jacque Schneider, Melanee Wolven

Proofreaders: Laura Albert, Vicki Broyles, Andy Hollandbeck, Carl Pierce, Dwight Ramsey, Brian H. Walls

Indexer: Sherry Massey

Publishing and Editorial for Technology Dummies

Richard Swadley, Vice President and Executive Group Publisher

Andy Cummings, Vice President and Publisher

Mary C. Corder, Editorial Director

Publishing for Consumer Dummies

Diane Graves Steele, Vice President and Publisher

Joyce Pepple, Acquisitions Director

Composition Services

Gerry Fahey, Vice President of Production Services

Debbie Stailey, Director of Composition Services

Contents at a Glance

Table of Contents

Introduction

Welcome to the incredible world of Photoshop! I use this program every day and it never ceases to amaze me. Photoshop is like one of those "learn a new word every day" calendars. I always discover something new about Photoshop every time I use it, even if it's just a keyboard shortcut that makes things go quicker or a different approach to solving a sticky problem.

Photoshop CS Timesaving Techniques For Dummies is jam packed with ideas and information. Whether you're familiar with Photoshop and want to find out more or you know a lot about Photoshop and you're looking for new ideas, these pages have something for everyone.

Saving Time with This Book

Photoshop CS Timesaving Techniques For Dummies focuses on high-payoff techniques that help you get the job done. Although a technique may take time when you first use it, after you've got the steps under your belt, it saves you time down the road.

This book gets to the point in a hurry with an easy-to-use, two-column format and step-by-step instructions that speed you through the tasks you need to do. I don't spend any time on extra talk or irrelevant explanations. The 64 techniques zero in on key Photoshop features that you can use to work faster and smarter, not harder.

In *Photoshop CS Timesaving Techniques For Dummies,* you can find out how to

- **Bam! Take your skills up a notch:** You're already familiar with the basics of using Photoshop. Now use this book to take your skills to the next level.

- **Customize the Photoshop workspace to meet your needs:** Spending some upfront time customizing the workspace helps you work more proficiently and saves you time later on.

✔ **Tame time-consuming tasks:** Do you need to perform the same command over and over? Don't drive yourself batty; make it easy by creating a custom keyboard shortcut or action. From there, you can quickly batch process files by using the custom action. Let Photoshop do the work for you — you're in the driver's seat.

✔ **Print your projects right the first time:** Printing at home or in the office can be a frustrating process. Preparing images for high-end commercial presses can be a nightmare — but it doesn't have to be that way. Wake up, sit back, and have a latte. This book shows you the ins and outs of printing one step at a time.

✔ **Create tool presets:** If you're working under a deadline, you don't need to be fiddling with tool settings. Create the tool settings you need at the beginning of a project and save them in a custom library. Then you'll have the tools that you need with the right settings anytime.

✔ **Expand Photoshop's capabilities:** Installing plug-ins, third-party software, or downloading tool presets or actions from the Web can save you oodles of time. If you need to do something in Photoshop, chances are that someone has done it before. Where relevant, I list Web sites that you can go to and third-party software products that you can use to find the solutions that you need.

Basic Assumptions

Here's where I get silly and start making assumptions about you even though I've never met you. The following are some of my basic assumptions about you, dear reader:

✔ **You have a Mac or Windows computer.** You are familiar with the computer, and you can navigate around through dialog boxes and menus without getting hung up.

✔ **Your computer is running Photoshop.** Although this book was written for Photoshop CS, you *can* use this book if you're working with a previous

version of Photoshop. Bear in mind, however, that if you aren't running Photoshop CS, some of the features that I explain here might not be available to you. For instance, the History palette, which I use in Techniques 7 and 25, was introduced in Photoshop version 6. Layer Comps, which I discuss in Technique 16, were introduced with CS.

 If you're using a previous version, you can find out what your version includes (and what it doesn't) by choosing Help➪Photoshop. Click the Index link and then click the letter P. Scroll down the list of P topics until you reach Photoshop Format. Click the link next to About(1).

✔ **You have a good basic knowledge of Photoshop and want to find out more.** What does this mean? Well, this book doesn't hold your hand and tell you to choose File➪Save when you need to save something. Instead, it takes you step by step through some very cool effects, showing you just what you need to do. And, after you've done something once, the second time is certainly easier and faster.

Conventions Used in This Book

I'm not too conventional (what writer/Photoshop artist/scuba diver/tap dancer is?), so I'm not a great one for setting conventions. However, to get us all on a level playing field, I came up with a few items for consistency. They include:

✔ **Command keys:** You press the command keys in combinations to activate commands — Shift, Ctrl, and Alt for Windows, and Shift, ⌘, Alt, and Control for Mac. When using control keys in this book, I list the Windows version first followed by a backslash and then the Mac version. So, if I tell you to copy a layer with command keys, it appears like this: Ctrl+J/⌘+J.

✔ **Drop-down lists versus pop-up menus:** Menus that appear when a button or arrow is clicked are known as drop-down lists in Windows and pop-up menus on the Mac. Instead of bogging you down with terminology throughout the book and writing "Choose the Widget item from the drop-down list/pop-up menu," I made a blanket decision to call this feature a drop-down list. After all, these menus do appear to drop down more often than they pop up.

✔ **New terms are italicized:** When I introduce a new term or concept, it first appears in *italics*. After the italics is a quick definition explaining exactly what the italicized term means.

✔ **Filenames, paths, and Web addresses are set in monospace font:** For instance, the Adobe Web site is `www.adobe.com`. My e-mail address is `photoshop@bearhome.com`.

How This Book Is Organized

To save you time, this book is organized into *techniques* (short sections, usually four to eight pages long) that show you how to use a specific Photoshop feature or create a cool effect.

This book is laid out in an easy-to-read, two-column format that's full of figures to speed you through the steps. No unnecessary fluff — just the steps, straight and simple.

 Because this book is so nice and wide (and a bit floppy), make space on your desk to lay it out flat. Crack the binding a bit if you have to. That way, you can see exactly what you're doing without pages flipping unexpectedly or the book sliding off a pile.

You can work through the book from front to back if you want to or you can just dive right into the technique of your choice. Either way works just fine. Whenever I mention a concept that I don't cover in depth in that technique, I provide a cross-reference to another technique that gives you more information. If you need to find something specific, look through the Table of Contents or scan the Index.

The Cheat Sheet at the beginning of the book lists the most commonly needed features with a quick reference to the technique that shows you how to make it happen. Also included are important keyboard shortcuts and references to techniques that show you how to save time by automating repetitive tasks. Tear out the Cheat Sheet, use a highlighter to mark the features most important to you, and then tape it on your wall. Use it and abuse it — the Cheat Sheet is there to help you find things fast.

The sixteen-page color section shows several techniques as they progress from step to step. Look at the Color Insert to get a taste of what you can accomplish with this book. If you see a finished image or idea that you really like, turn to that technique, open an image, and create your own masterpiece!

The walled city of Isengard has seven levels, and three rings of power were given to the elves, but this book needs ten parts to accomplish its task.

Part I: Making Photoshop Work for You

Get organized and get ready to be creative! The techniques in this part show you how you can customize Photoshop to tailor it to your needs. Create custom keyboard shortcuts, organize and rank your image files, set up a color management system, work with tool presets, and batch process your files. Everything that you need to save you time while performing repetitive tasks is here.

Part II: Getting Images Into and Out of Photoshop

Peripheral devices such as digital cameras, scanners, tablets, and printers can make even the most savvy computer users tear their hair out at times. Take a look at the techniques in this part to avoid pitfalls when scanning images, using a digital camera, setting up a tablet, using a printer, or getting your files ready for high-end offset printing.

Part III: Using Layers to Save Time, Protect Your Work, and Create Cool Images

Layers are one of the fundamental building blocks in Photoshop. You can't create great images without 'em. The techniques in this part show you how to manage and organize layers and create layer comps. You find out how to use all those great layer features: using blending modes; setting opacity; performing transformations; adding special effects such as drop shadows, bevels, embossing; and much more.

Part IV: Painting and Coloring to Enhance Your Images

If you've ever felt daunted by painting in the real world, Photoshop can open doors to your painterly imagination that you never thought possible. The techniques in this part show you how to create custom brushes, create an oil painting by using a photograph, apply color from one image to another, recolor images by using gradients, and even paint backward in time.

Part V: Restoring and Retouching Images for Quick, Beautiful Results

Everyone loves a beautiful photograph, but few photos fall under the beautiful category. Usually, something is a bit off — perhaps the color isn't quite right, little Susie's eyes look like something from *Fright Night,* or Uncle George's schnoz is just way too big. You can fix these problems in a flash with Photoshop. The techniques in this part deal with fixing problems, recoloring with photo filters to enhance tones, creating and colorizing black and white images, and stitching photos together to create fantastic panoramas or photomontages. With only a few clicks of the mouse, you can turn a boring daytime scene with ordinary lighting into a mysterious sunset photo with beautiful twilight tones.

Part VI: Amazing Fast Filter Effects

When I say amazing effects, I mean it! Some of the techniques create subtle results, and other results are downright wild. Sharpen your images or blur for emphasis. Create beautiful watercolors, make images look like pressed tin, or create a lovely sketch. Be your own Andy Warhol and create photo silkscreens to rival the Campbell's Soup series. When you're finished creating your masterpieces, add frames or special edges to really customize your work.

Part VII: Super Type Effects

Type doesn't just have to be flat, boring, one-dimensional letters on a page. Create type by using nothing but shadows, use layer masks to create type cut-outs, melt metal, drip lava, and wiggle with jelly. The techniques in this part show you how to create super type, super fast.

Part VIII: Transforming Images Using Channels and Masks (It's not as hard as you think!)

Layer masks are one of the great Photoshop features that I use everyday. Find out how to make layers fade in or out, use masks to hide portions of a layer, and group layers into clipping masks.

Often ignored or just plain forgotten, channels are essential in the Photoshop artist's arsenal of talents. Take a look at the techniques in this part to find out what really makes channels tick, how to use them, and how to get better results when recoloring and applying filters.

Part IX: Creating Flashy, Professional Web Graphics

Web graphics are easy and fun to create. Even if your family Web site has a "mom and pop" feel, you can create great graphics with Photoshop and Image-Ready, Photoshop's sister program. You can teach your old graphics new tricks by making them roll over or run across a page. I even show you how to add hotspots for users to click. The techniques in this section help you create super Web graphics, save them, and preview them in your favorite browser.

Part X: The Scary (Or Fun) Stuff

Have you ever wondered if there's more to Photoshop than meets the eye? (Actually, who needs to wonder? We all know it has a lot under the hood.) The techniques in this part show you how to extend Photoshop's capabilities by installing plug-ins, loading tool and brush libraries, and using third-party software within Photoshop to make your images even more spectacular.

About the Color Insert and the Web Site

This book comes with a Color Insert and a companion Web site. Because the book is printed in black and white, I've chosen certain images from the techniques so that you can see the colorful results. At the Web site, you can find links to great Photoshop sites and jpeg images from the Color Insert. If you want to follow along and experiment with the techniques featured in the Color Insert, go to www.dummies.com/go/ photoshopcstt and download the images.

Icons Used in This Book

As you use this book, you're sure to run across some icons sprinkled in the margins. Each icon has a purpose, which I define here:

 This handy little icon marks interesting tidbits that can save you time, tell you how to do something faster, or just generally help speed things up. When you're working in Photoshop, editing and manipulating images can take lots of time. (I can't even remember how many times I've looked at the clock and realized that

two hours have just gone by in what felt like two minutes.) These handy hints help speed you on your way.

 When I have an interesting idea, or a special feature is worth mentioning, I use this icon. Tips can explain how to use an alternative method or point the way to something helpful.

 This icon is like the string tied around your finger — without the numbness and blue skin tone. You don't need to memorize the info marked with this icon. However, try to remember that this icon indicates a special Photoshop feature that you may need to know for future endeavors.

 I hate being worried or feeling pressured, so I don't want to pass anything on to you. I use this icon — which serves to protect you from file damage or worse — only when it's *really, really* necessary. There's no need to get uptight about stuff, so you don't see this icon very often. (I think I use it only three or four times in the whole book.) Photoshop and your computer are there for you (not the other way around). If you make a mistake or get frustrated, you can just leave the computer and come back after a cappuccino — the computer will still be there waiting ever so patiently for you.

Where to Go from Here

If you think this book is worth its weight in salt or if you just want to gab with the publisher, you can contact the *For Dummies* folks at www.dummies.com. Click the Contact Us link to find out where you can send your comments and suggestions.

You can contact Phyllis at photoshop@bearhome.com with any questions or comments. I can't promise to answer everything that comes my way — what with two children, a third on the way, and a ridiculous writing and teaching schedule — but I'll do my best! I will certainly include any good suggestions or tips in the next edition of this book.

So, fire up your computer, launch Photoshop, grab some handy images, and have fun! (*Having fun is very important!*) Discover a topic that you know nothing about, put a mustache on Aunt Marge, or create an "oil painting" — with Photoshop and *Photoshop CS Timesaving Techniques For Dummies,* the sky's the limit!

Part I

Making Photoshop Work for You

The 5th Wave   By Rich Tennant

WIRED HOME OF THE FUTURE

"I'm setting preferences – do you want Oriental or Persian carpets in the living room?"

Technique 1

Organizing Image Files and Managing Projects

Save Time By

- ✔ Maintaining projects
- ✔ Navigating the File Browser
- ✔ Organizing your images
- ✔ Adding virtual notes and voice messages

Before you start a project, take a few minutes to get organized. This may seem like a waste of time — you're excited and you want to get started — but a little organization now goes a long way in helping you work smarter, not harder.

Some projects can consist of one or two image files, while other projects can be made up of hundreds. Even if you don't think you'll end up with a ton of image files, many projects created in Photoshop CS and Image-Ready, Photoshop's sister program, end up involving literally hundreds of files. How do you organize all this?

Thankfully, Photoshop CS comes with a great organizing tool, the File Browser. The File Browser is more than just a window showing thumbnails of your image files. It is a pretty complete *asset management* system that you can use to, well, manage your *assets* (image files). With the File Browser, you can create a folder system to organize image files, search for images using thumbnails, move and rename images, flag and rank images, and much more. This technique covers the ins and outs of how to use the File Browser and includes tips for organizing image folders to help your workflow.

In addition, this technique shows you how to add virtual sticky notes or vocal annotations to an image and gives you a few tips about which image files you should save and which ones you should discard.

Managing Your Projects

If you take a few minutes to organize folders and files before embarking upon a project, you'll be more organized, be able to find the image files you want to work on, and reduce the possibility of deleting files that may be important.

When I start on a project, I create a master folder that contains all the folders and files for that project. Usually, I give this folder a name that refers to the project and helps me find it quickly (especially when I arrive at the computer in the morning bleary-eyed because my little son has kept me up all night!).

Inside this master folder are more folders that divide the project into parts. For instance, if I'm working on a new series of images that I've scanned, I create one Scans folder that contains the original scanned images, another Working folder that contains all the files I'm working on, and a third Finished folder that contains only completed image files. I never save over any of the original scanned images in the Scan folder; instead I save a copy in the Working folder. That way, if I make a huge, tremendous mistake, I always have the original available.

This is only one way to go about it. You can have folders within a Working folder that are dated so that you know what you were working on when; you can also divide up a project by its pieces — if you're working on a brochure, for example, you could have Front Flap, Panel 1, and Back Flap folders. What I'm suggesting is to take the time to think about your project before you start working on it. Take a good old-fashioned piece of paper and a pen or some 3 x 5 cards and block out the process of your project. If you take the time now to think about what you're creating and how you're going to create it, you save a huge amount of time in the long run.

Deciding which files to discard

Another workflow issue is what I call *housekeeping* — deciding which files are valuable and need to be kept, and which images can head toward the virtual circular file.

Because my computer has a large hard drive, I tend to keep more than I probably should. I always have that lingering thought in the back of my mind, "What if I need that layer mask, or need this technique again?"

My best advice for deciding which images to delete is to carefully consider where your project is heading. Is a particular image file one that you used to test a specific technique that didn't work? Then, fine, delete it. Be careful, though, because after an image file is gone, it's gone. Take a look at Technique 7 for tips about creating backups and snapshots.

Also, if you have a CD-R or CD-RW, you can archive your files on a CD-ROM disc. This saves you precious hard drive space and still saves any files you might want to keep "just in case."

Using the File Browser

The File Browser is your place for one-stop shopping when you need to find image files, open them, save copies, rename them, flag or rank them, and so on. The File Browser is a large window, which you can open by clicking the Toggle File Browser button on the Options bar, choosing File⇨Browse, or pressing Ctrl+Shift+O (the letter)/⌘+Shift+O (the letter).

The File Browser, shown in Figure 1-1, is divided into two sections. Four palettes are on the left side of the window and a Preview pane is on the right:

- The **Folders** palette shows you a branching, hierarchical view of all your folders and files. The tree structure lets you dig around in folders to find your image files.

- The **Preview** palette shows you a thumbnail image that is selected in the Preview pane. If you double-click the preview image in the Preview palette, the image opens.

- The **Metadata** palette displays information about the currently selected image file, including file size, date created, image height and width, resolution, color mode, camera data, and other important info. The Metadata palette also includes a GPS section that you can set to the exact position on the earth where you took the photo (just in case you want to return to the exact spot!).

- The **Keywords** palette displays keywords assigned to an image. You can group and organize images by these keywords.

- The **Preview pane** shows thumbnail previews of the image file types that Photoshop CS supports.

Flag an image

Click to view palette menu | Delete

Preview pane

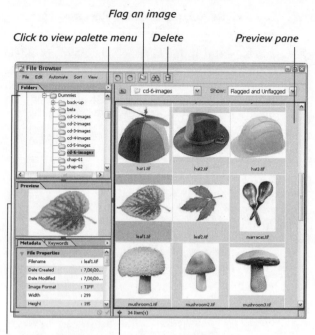

Palettes   Click here to expand the Preview pane

• Figure 1-1: The File Browser makes finding and opening images easy.

File Browser basics

The first step to managing your image files is to understand the basic functionality of the File Browser — opening files, selecting images in the Preview pane, moving files to different folders, and deleting files. Here's a list of the basics:

✔ To **select a file in the Preview pane**, just click the image thumbnail. A larger version of the selected image thumbnail appears in the Preview palette.

✔ To **open a file**, either double-click the image thumbnail in the Preview pane, double-click the image thumbnail in the Preview palette, or select the image in the Preview pane and then choose File➪Open from the File Browser menu.

✔ To **navigate through your folders in the Folders palette**, on a PC click the plus sign next to a folder name to view all the subfolders inside that folder. On a Mac, click the triangle next to a folder name to view the subfolders.

✔ To **move a file to a different folder**, select the image file in the Preview pane, and then drag it to the desired folder in the Folders palette.

✔ To **delete a file**, you can either select it in the Preview pane and then press the Delete key, drag the image from the Preview pane to the trashcan icon at the top of the File Browser window, or right-click/option-click on the thumbnail in the Preview pane and choose the Delete option from the context-sensitive menu.

Renaming individual files

To rename an individual file, click the filename below the thumbnail in the Preview pane. The filename becomes highlighted. Type a new name for the image file, and then click the image thumbnail. When you click the image's filename to rename it, only the filename is selected, not the three-letter file extension that tells Photoshop cs what kind of file it is (such as .tif or .pdf). You must drag over the file extension to change the file type, if you want.

If you're a Mac user and you send files to someone using a PC, remember to add the three-letter file extension to your filenames. You can tell Photoshop to automatically add the extension to the filename when saving the image file. Either press Option+K and then Option+2, or choose Edit➪Preferences➪ File Handling to open the Preferences dialog box. Select the Always option from the Append File Extension drop-down list. In addition, select the Use Lower Case option as well. This ensures compatibility with other platforms, including UNIX, and makes any Web graphics you create work on any platform.

Batch renaming

When you use the Batch Rename command, you can rename the files in the folder where they currently live or move them to a different folder. (*Remember:* Moving files does just that — it moves them to a new folder instead of creating copies.) Also, you can add up to six different additions to each filename, such as a serial number or letter or month/day/year. Follow these steps to rename multiple files at once:

1. **Select the files you want to rename.**

Select a bunch of files from the same folder by holding down Shift (to select consecutive files) or Ctrl/⌘ (to select non-consecutive files) and clicking the files. Or you can choose Edit⇨Select All from the File Browser menu to select an entire folder of images.

2. **Choose Automate⇨Batch Rename from the File Browser menu.**

The Batch Rename dialog box opens, as shown in Figure 1-2.

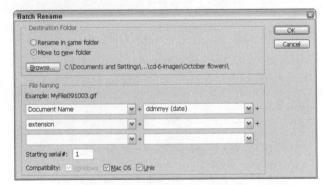

• **Figure 1-2: You select the location of the renamed image files and set how to modify the image filenames in the Batch Rename dialog box.**

3. **Select whether you want to keep the files in the folder where they are currently located or move them to a new folder.**

In the Destination Folder area, select the Rename in Same Folder or the Move to New Folder radio button. Click Browse (Windows) or Choose (Mac) to locate a folder for a different location.

4. **Use the File Naming area to select how you want to rename the files.**

You have the option of appending up to six different file variables with the drop-down menus, such as a serial number or letter, or a date (shown in Figure 1-3). For example, I want the images I selected in Step 1 renamed using the document name + the date + the three-letter file extension. For instance, `Flower.jpg` is renamed `Flower010904.jpg`.

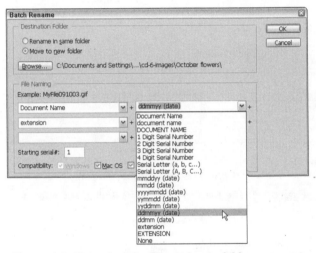

• **Figure 1-3: You select the filenaming variables you want to use with the drop-down lists.**

5. **Select the Compatibility check boxes at the bottom of the Batch Rename dialog box.**

This ensures the files are named so that they work on any computer, no matter what operating system is running.

6. **Click OK.**

Photoshop CS goes to work renaming all the selected files.

Creating a new folder

Creating a new folder for your images with the File Browser is easy. Select the location for the new folder with the Folders palette — this can be a hard drive or another folder (if you select a folder, the new folder appears as a subfolder within the selected folder). Then, either right-click/option-click on the selected folder and choose the New Folder option from the context-sensitive menu or choose File⇨New Folder from the File Browser menu.

 You should know, however, that you can't delete a folder with the File Browser. You have to minimize Photoshop CS and go to the desktop level to do that.

Get Organizing!

Photoshop CS gives you many options to organize your image files — you can rank and flag them, sort images, and add and move images around the File Browser.

Flagging files

If you need to quickly sort through many images (suppose you import 50 photos from a digital camera), flagging images in the File Browser is a quick way to separate the wheat from the chaff.

To flag an image, simply select the image you want to flag in the Preview pane, and then click the Flag icon at the top of the File Browser window. A small flag icon appears at the bottom-right corner of the image thumbnail in the Preview pane. You can view either flagged or unflagged image files by selecting either the Flagged Files or Unflagged Files option or both from the Show drop-down list at the top right of the File Browser window (see Figure 1-4).

Ranking files

Another way to sort files is to rank them. Suppose you flag 20 photo files, and then just view those flagged files, which I discuss in the preceding section. You can also line the images up in a specific order. This is where ranking comes in. Ranking lets you control how to sort images in the File Browser. You can rank one image at a time or give the same rank to several selected images.

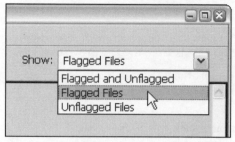

• **Figure 1-4: Use the Show drop-down list to select whether you want to view flagged or unflagged files, or all files.**

To rank images, follow these steps:

1. **Select the image or images you want to rank in the Preview pane.**

   If you want to select more than one image, you can either Shift+click or Ctrl+click/⌘+click the files you want to select.

2. **Right-click/Ctrl+click the selected image and choose the Rank option from the shortcut menu or choose Edit⇨Rank from the File Browser's menu bar.**

   The Rank Files dialog box opens, as shown in Figure 1-5.

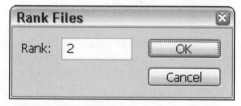

• **Figure 1-5: Rank image files with the Rank Files dialog box.**

3. **Enter numbers and/or letters in the Rank text box.**

   When you sort the files, Photoshop sorts them numerically and/or alphabetically, depending upon what you enter in the Rank text box.

4. Click OK.

To view the image ranks, choose View⇨ Show Rank from the File Browser menu.

To sort the images in the Preview pane by rank, choose Sort⇨Rank.

Sorting images

The File Browser comes with more than a dozen ways you can sort image files. With the Sort menu, you can sort by filename, by image dimensions, resolution, file type, when you created the images, and much more.

To sort a folder of images displayed in the Preview pane, simply click the Sort menu at the top of the File Browser window, and then choose from one of the many options. The images sort and re-sort the way you choose.

Turning the File Browser into a lightbox

When working with 35mm slides on a lightbox, I move the slides around, rearrange them in the order that I need them in, and then place them in a plastic slide page to keep them in that order. You can do the same thing with the File Browser.

To sort images as you do with a lightbox, click the Toggle Expanded View arrows at the bottom of the File Browser, as shown in Figure 1-6. This hides the palettes at the left side of the File Browser and expands the area of the Preview pane.

You can now just drag the image thumbnails around on the virtual lightbox into the order you want to sort them. *Note:* When you drag an image file to a new position, the other files move over to make room, automatically snapping into position.

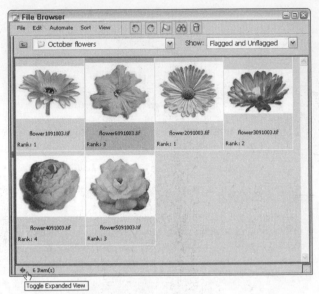

• **Figure 1-6:** The Toggle Expanded View arrows hide the palettes and enlarge the Preview pane.

 Photoshop remembers the positions in which you sort the image files. Even if you close the File Browser and shut down Photoshop, the next time you view that folder of image files using the File Browser, the files will still be in the same positions you left them in. How does Photoshop do this? By creating a special *cache file* that saves all the positioning information.

Adding Notes and Vocal Annotations

Another way to organize a project and help to remember diddly items about an image that you're working on is to add virtual sticky notes to an image or even record a message.

To add a virtual sticky note to an image, follow these steps:

1. **With the image open in Photoshop, select the Notes tool from the Toolbox (or press N on the keyboard).**

2. **Click in the image window.**

A note window appears, as shown in Figure 1-7.

3. **Type your message, and then click the tiny Close box at the upper corner of the note window.**

A small note icon remains in the image window. If you want to open the note, just double-click it. To delete the note, right-click/⌘+click on the note icon and choose the Delete Note option from the context-sensitive menu.

• **Figure 1-7: Adding notes to remind you of something.**

 The small note icon is visible only in the image window when the image is open in Photoshop cs. If you print the image, the icon does not print.

Follow these steps to add a vocal annotation to an image:

1. **With an image open in Photoshop, select the Audio Annotation tool from the Toolbox.**

Remember: You need a microphone plugged into your computer's sound card.

2. **Click anywhere in the image window.**

The Audio Annoation dialog box, shown in Figure 1-8, opens.

• **Figure 1-8: Click Start to begin recording an audio annotation.**

3. **Click Start to begin recording your message.**

4. **When you're finished recording, click Stop.**

A tiny speaker icon appears in the image window. If you want to hear the recorded message, just double-click the icon. To delete the annotation, right-click/⌘+click the speaker icon and choose the Delete Audio Annotation option from the context-sensitive menu.

 The speaker icon is visible only in the image window when the image is open in Photoshop cs. If you print the image, the icon does not print.

Technique 2

Creating Custom Palette Groups and Workspaces

Save Time By

✔ Saving palette locations

✔ Creating palette groups

✔ Selecting palettes for specific tasks

✔ Customizing workspaces

When you open Photoshop CS for the first time (see Figure 2-1), notice that some palettes are arranged along the right side of the program window, some palettes are available in the Palette Well on the Options bar, and, if you open the Window menu, some palettes are not visible at all.

• **Figure 2-1: By default, not all palettes are shown in the Photoshop CS program window.**

As you work on projects, you'll discover that you need to move palettes out of the way in order to see something and access palettes that aren't displayed. In addition, you'll probably find that some palettes display in the program window that you never use. Why have unused palettes taking up valuable screen real estate? Why not customize your working environment so that you can work more efficiently? That's where this technique comes in.

In this technique, you find out how to customize your workspace. You discover how to make Photoshop remember the location of the palettes and Toolbox, so they appear in the same positions every time you launch Photoshop. You find out how to break apart the default *palette groups* and create your own palette groups. Then, you find out how to create *custom workspaces* so that you can retrieve these custom palette groups when you need them for a special project.

Saving Palette Locations

With one simple check box selected, you can tell Photoshop CS to remember the location of your palettes and Toolbox between work sessions. Every time you launch Photoshop, the palettes and Toolbox reappear in the same place you left them as last time (Photoshop considers the Toolbox a palette). In addition, if you create any custom palette groups (as described in the next section), Photoshop remembers those as well.

To save your palette locations, press Ctrl/⌘+K to open the General panel of the Preferences dialog box, as shown in Figure 2-2. Make sure that the Save Palette Locations box is checked, and then click OK.

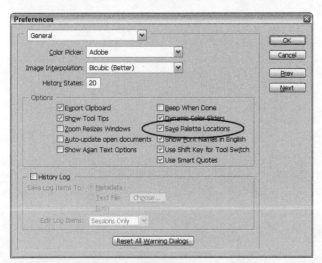

• **Figure 2-2: Select Save Palette Locations in the Preferences dialog box.**

Making Custom Palette Groups

Photoshop CS gives you everything to help you work more efficiently — this includes creating your own palette groups. In Figure 2-3, notice that three palettes are grouped together; this is known as, well, a palette group.

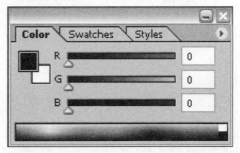

• **Figure 2-3: You can arrange palettes in palette groups.**

Breaking apart palette groups and building custom palette groups based on the type of work you're doing is easy. For instance, if you're doing a lot of painting, creating a custom palette group containing the Brushes, Color, and Tool Presets palettes makes sense.

To separate a palette from its palette group, all you need to do is drag the palette's tab out of the group, as shown in Figure 2-4.

To add a palette to a palette group (making your own custom palette groups), drag a palette's tab onto another palette group.

 Windows users: If you want to keep a palette or palette group displayed in the Photoshop program window but want to recapture some screen real estate, click the Minimize box at the upper right of the palette, as shown in Figure 2-5. When you do, the palette collapses. Mac users can click the tiny green button at the upper left of a palette to toggle between three sizes.

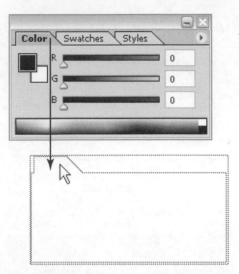

• **Figure 2-4: Drag the palette's tab out of the palette group.**

Click here to minimize palette.

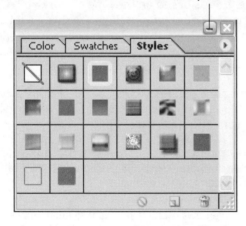

Click here to expand palette.

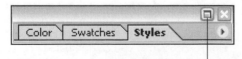

• **Figure 2-5: Click the Minimize box to collapse a palette.**

A few palette group suggestions

You can create custom palette groups to help you work more efficiently depending upon the type of project you are working on. Of course, you can group palettes in any way that works for you, but here are a few suggestions to get you started:

- ✔ If you're doing a project that requires a lot of painting, group the Brushes, Color, and Tool Presets palettes together. Substitute the Swatches palette for the Tool Presets palette for a different variation.

- ✔ If you are working on a text intensive project, open the Character and Paragraph palettes (they are grouped together by default) by choosing either Window⇨Character or Window⇨Paragraph. Then, add the Tool Presets palette to this palette group. Any custom Type tool presets that you create are quickly available. (Take a look at Technique 6 to find out how to create your own tool presets.)

- ✔ If you're creating graphics for the Web in Photoshop's sister program, ImageReady, try out the palette groups that are available when you choose Window⇨Workspace. One palette group helps with *optimizing* graphics files, the other makes creating GIF animations easy. To find out more about these palettes and creating Web graphics using ImageReady, turn to Part IX.

Using the Palette Well

Another place to put palettes that you use all the time is in the Palette Well on the Options bar. By default, the Brushes, Tool Presets, and Comps palettes are docked in the Palette Well, as shown in Figure 2-6.

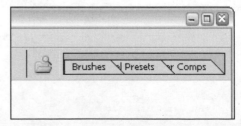

• **Figure 2-6: When you launch Photoshop for the first time, three palettes are docked in the Palette Well.**

If you don't see the Palette Well in the upper-right corner of the Photoshop program window, your monitor's resolution may be the culprit. If your monitor resolution is set to 800 x 600 or less, the Palette Well — and other parts of the program window — are hidden. Raise your monitor resolution to see the entire program window.

You can use the Palette Well to store palettes that you use frequently but want out of the way. To access a palette docked in the Palette Well, simply click the palette's tab and the palette opens.

Removing and adding palettes to the Palette Well works just like removing and adding palettes from palette groups (see the "Making Custom Palette Groups" section). Drag the tab of the palette that you want to remove out of the Palette Well. To add a palette, drag the palette's tab over the Palette Well.

Creating Custom Workspaces

Letting Photoshop automatically remember your palette locations, as described in "Saving Palette Locations," is fine and dandy if you are the only one working on your computer. But, what if other people use your computer and you don't have separate user accounts set up? Suppose that one of them likes to close all the palettes and use them only when she needs them. That could really mess up your workspace. Also, suppose that you are a very creative person and you like to do several different kinds of projects — brochures for Company A, photo retouching for Company B, and creating Web graphics for your own Web site. These different kinds of projects use different palettes. You may want to set up your workspace very differently depending upon the type of work you're doing on a certain day.

Ordinarily, you would have to rearrange palettes and move everything around until you're satisfied and

ready to work. This gets pretty tedious if you are working on one type of project on Monday, but another type of project on Tuesday. However Photoshop takes all the tedium out of setting up workspaces by remembering palette locations for you. To create a custom workspace:

1. **Position and group palettes where you want them, close palettes you don't need, and dock any palettes you would like in the Palette Well.**

2. **Choose Window➪Workspace➪Save Workspace.**

   The Save Workspace dialog box opens, as shown in Figure 2-7.

• **Figure 2-7:** Enter a name for your workspace in the text box, and then click OK.

3. **Type a descriptive name for your custom workspace in the Name text box.**

4. **Click OK.**

Create as many workspaces as you need. When you want to load a workspace, choose Window➪ Workspace and then choose the custom workspace you want to use from the bottom of the Workspace submenu, as shown in Figure 2-8.

If you ever want to delete a workspace, choose Window➪Workspace➪Delete Workspace. Then, select the workspace you want to delete from the drop-down list and click Delete.

 You can also return the palettes to their default Photoshop locations with just a click of the mouse. Choose Window➪Workspace➪ Reset Palette Locations.

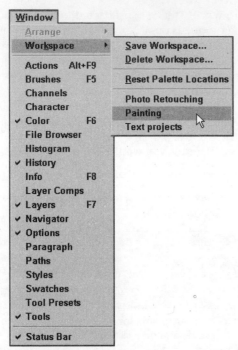

• **Figure 2-8:** Choose a custom workspace from the bottom
of the Workspace submenu.

Technique 3

Assigning Custom Keyboard Shortcuts

Save Time By

- ✔ Creating your own shortcuts that work for you
- ✔ Creating and deleting shortcut sets
- ✔ Printing out a list of shortcuts available in a shortcut set

Using keyboard shortcuts that are easy to remember can increase your productivity, helping you work faster and more efficiently. If you like the keyboard shortcuts you use in other programs, you can customize Photoshop CS to do it your way.

Depending upon the type of work you do, you might like to define several *shortcut sets*. For instance, if you are using several filters over and over, you can assign custom shortcuts that give quick, easy access to those filters. You could save these filter shortcuts in a shortcut set named "Filters." A second shortcut set that you might create, suppose it's named "Color Modes," could include custom shortcuts that quickly convert images from one color mode to another (for instance, from RGB color mode to CMYK color mode). Any time you need one of these shortcut sets, you can quickly load it.

This technique covers how to create custom shortcuts, save them in a shortcut set, and load the shortcut set when you need it. In addition, you find out how to view a complete list of shortcuts available to you in a shortcut set. Finally, you find out how to revert to the standard shortcuts that come with Photoshop, and delete unwanted shortcut sets.

Defining Custom Shortcuts

Creating your own shortcuts is easy. You have to keep some things in mind, though, when creating shortcuts. Photoshop lets you come up with almost any keystroke combination that you can think of, but there are a few rules:

- ✔ Single letter keystrokes such as M or B can be assigned only to tools in the Toolbox.

- ✔ Single digits, such as 1 or 9, cannot be used for shortcuts.

- ✔ You can use any combination of the Shift, Ctrl/⌘, or Alt/Option keys with a letter or number. For instance, you could use Shift+8 or Ctrl+Shift+K/⌘+Shift+K for shortcuts.

✔ Any of the function keys can be used on their own or in combination with the Shift, Ctrl/⌘, or Alt/Option keys.

✔ Any shortcuts assigned by Photoshop to permanent features, such as palettes, cannot be used. For instance, Ctrl+1/⌘+1 is assigned as a shortcut to access the first channel in the Channels palette. You cannot reassign this shortcut.

That said, you can come up with plenty of other combinations. If any shortcuts conflict (a shortcut is in use somewhere else or you create an impossible combination), don't worry! Photoshop tells you what's wrong.

To create your own custom shortcuts, follow these steps:

1. **Choose Edit⇨Keyboard Shortcuts or press Shift+Ctrl+Alt+K/Shift+⌘+Option+K on the keyboard. (You can use your toes if you need to.)**

The Keyboard Shortcuts dialog box shown in Figure 3-1 opens, displaying the currently selected shortcut set.

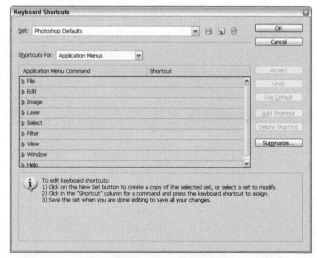

• **Figure 3-1: The Keyboard Shortcuts dialog box opens showing the loaded shortcut set.**

2. **Locate the menu item or tool to which you want to add the shortcut.**

3. **Use the Shortcuts For drop-down list to select the location of the item to which you want to add the shortcuts.**

You can choose from:

▶ **Application Menus:** These are the commands found on the Menu bar at the top of the program window.

▶ **Palette Menus:** These are the commands available with each palette.

▶ **Tools:** These are the tools in the Toolbox.

4. **Select the menu command or tool to which you want to add the custom shortcut.**

If you selected Application Menus or Palette Menus in Step 3, then you need to click the tiny arrow next to a menu or palette category to view the available commands, as shown in Figure 3-2.

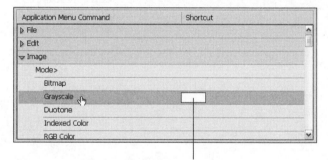

Enter shortcut here

• **Figure 3-2: Click the tiny arrow to access the commands in a menu or palette.**

5. **Enter a custom shortcut in the text box.**

Just enter the combination you want to use in the text box, such as Ctrl+O/⌘+O. If there's a conflict or problem, Photoshop tells you as shown in Figure 3-3.

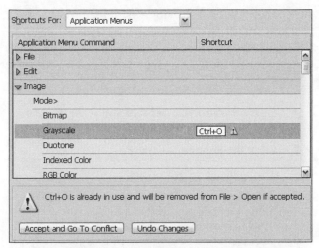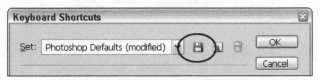

• **Figure 3-3:** If you try to assign a custom shortcut that is unacceptable or creates a conflict, Photoshop tells you.

6. **Accept or cancel the shortcut:**

If the shortcut does not create any conflicts, click Accept to add the shortcut.

If the shortcut creates a conflict and you don't want to use it, click either Undo or Undo Changes.

If the shortcut creates a conflict and you still want to accept it, you can either click Accept to add the change and not view the command that created the conflict or click Accept and Go To Conflict to add the change and view the command that created the conflict.

When you add a custom shortcut, you may notice that (modified) is appended to the currently selected shortcut set name. Any custom shortcuts you create are automatically saved with the currently selected set unless you save them in their own shortcut set.

Saving Shortcut Sets

Say the title of this section 10 times fast! After you create custom shortcuts, you want to save them. You have two options: You can save the new shortcuts with the currently selected shortcut set or save the shortcuts in a new shortcut set.

To save custom shortcuts to the currently selected shortcut set, click the Save Changes to Current Set button, shown in Figure 3-4.

• **Figure 3-4:** Click the Save Changes to Current Set button to add custom shortcuts to the selected set.

To save custom shortcuts to a new shortcut set, follow these steps:

1. **Click the Create New Set button, shown in Figure 3-5.**

• **Figure 3-5:** Click the Create New Set button to make a new shortcut set.

The Save dialog box, shown in Figure 3-6, opens with the appropriate folder location, Keyboard Shortcuts, selected.

2. **Type a name for your shortcut set in the File Name (Windows) or Save As (Mac) text box.**

3. **Click Save.**

The Save dialog box closes and the new set you just created appears selected in the Set drop-down list.

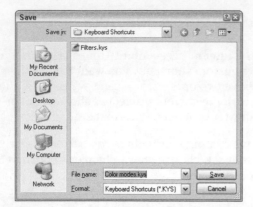

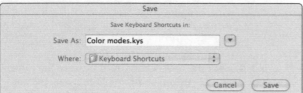

• **Figure 3-6:** Enter the name for your custom shortcut set in the File Name text box (Windows, top) or Save As text box (Mac, bottom).

 After you create a custom shortcut set, you can load it by choosing Edit⇨Keyboard Shortcuts to open the Keyboard Shortcut dialog box. Select the set name from the Set drop-down list, and then click OK to close the dialog box and load the shortcuts.

Viewing a Complete List of Shortcuts

Even with the best intentions — creating shortcuts that you're *sure* you can't forget — things happen. Time passes, you have a new baby in the house (in other words, you're so sleep deprived your brain stops functioning), whatever. Shortcuts can be forgotten.

Photoshop makes retrieving custom shortcuts easy. You can view them on-screen or even print them for quick reference.

1. **Open the Keyboard Shortcuts dialog box by choosing Edit⇨Keyboard Shortcuts.**

2. **Select the shortcut set that you want to view from the Set drop-down list.**

3. **Click the Summarize button.**

   The Save dialog box opens.

4. **Enter a name for the shortcut set in the File Name text box and select a folder where you want to save the list of shortcuts, and then click Save.**

   Photoshop automatically creates an HTM file containing all the keyboard shortcuts assigned to that set and opens the file in your default browser (see Figure 3-7).

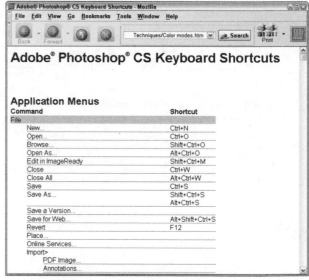

• **Figure 3-7:** The shortcut list automatically opens in your default browser.

From here, you can just give the shortcut list a look over to refresh your memory or use your browser's print feature to print the list as a handy desk reference.

Reverting to Standard Photoshop Shortcuts

If you find that you just can't live without Photoshop's standard shortcut set, getting it back is easy.

Open the Keyboard Shortcuts dialog box by choosing Edit⇨Keyboard Shortcuts, select Photoshop Defaults from the Set drop-down list, and then click OK.

Of course, if you need them, any custom shortcut sets that you create are still available. You can select a custom set from the Set drop-down list in the Keyboard Shortcuts dialog box at any time.

Deleting a Shortcut Set

Moving out, moving up, moving on. For some reason you decide you don't need a particular shortcut set anymore. The project is over and you're sure you'll never have to convert so many images to CMYK again. You're moving to a new job and you don't want to leave *your* custom shortcuts lying around.

Whatever the reason, simply choose Edit⇨Keyboard Shortcuts to open the Keyboard Shortcuts dialog box. Next, use the Set drop-down list to select the shortcut set you want to delete, and then click the Delete Shortcut Set button, shown in Figure 3-8.

• **Figure 3-8:** Click the trashcan to delete the selected shortcut set.

Technique 4

The Last Word about Color Management

Save Time By

- ✔ Calibrating your monitor
- ✔ Setting a color working space
- ✔ Setting color management policies
- ✔ Handling color space conversion

When I travel to different countries, I'm not always lucky enough to speak the language. Over the years I've managed to learn a good deal of Spanish and French, but Danish, Russian, Hindi? Nope. If I want to speak to someone who knows no English (or Spanish or French), I need a language interpreter. A good *color management system* works as a color interpreter. It looks at how color is created by different peripheral devices — such as digital cameras, monitors, and printers — and then translates the color for each device, helping them display (or print) the colors as accurately and consistently as possible.

Why do you need a color management system? Well, have you ever scanned a photograph, opened the scanned image in Photoshop, and then discovered to your dismay that the colors you see on-screen don't look anything like the original photograph? A color management system checks the colors coming in from the scanner and then tells the monitor to match those colors and accurately display them.

If you think that setting up a color management system is difficult, it's not. Here's the secret: All you have to do is adjust the colors of your monitor (or *calibrate* your monitor) to display colors accurately, and then you must tell Photoshop what devices you're using so that it knows how to accurately adjust and standardize the colors from device to device.

This technique deals with color management — a topic that's created lots of confusion over the years. Whenever I talk to Photoshop users, many are puzzled about how the colors on the monitor can differ from a photograph or color printout. Follow through this technique to find out how to set up color management on your computer. First, I discuss why each device handles color so differently. Then, I move on to the nitty-gritty of calibrating your monitor and setting up color profiles so that Photoshop can be your color interpreter.

What Is a Color Space and Why Is It So Important?

Every scanner, digital camera, software program, monitor, and printer — every device or program that you use to create, manipulate, or output images — renders color in a different way. Each device works within its own *color space,* the portion of the color spectrum that it can reproduce.

For instance, a computer monitor uses red, green, and blue light to create color; a color inkjet printer uses cyan, yellow, magenta, and black inks to create color; and a digital camera records the color it sees using daylight (which has a yellowish cast) or a flash (which has a bluish cast). How can any of these devices ever manage to create some kind of color match without some help? They can't. That's where color management goes to work.

Calibrating Your Monitor

The first step in setting up a color management system is to calibrate your monitor. For Windows users, Photoshop defines the color space on your monitor with the Adobe Gamma utility program. For Mac users, you need to use OS X's built-in Display Calibrator Assistant.

Before you calibrate your monitor, you need to turn it on, and if you're using a CRT monitor, let it warm up for at least 30 minutes. Also, make sure that your room lighting is set at a constant level and that your monitor is set at an angle that works for you. If you are working with an LCD monitor, different viewing angles can make colors change, so be sure that your monitor is angled for optimal viewing.

For Windows users

Follow these steps to calibrate your monitor:

1. **Choose Start⇨Control Panel.**

    The Windows XP control panel opens displaying various system utilities.

2. **Double-click Adobe Gamma to open the utility.**

    The Adobe Gamma dialog box opens, displaying the *composite gamma,* which is the combination of red, green, and blue light that makes up the visible colors of what you're seeing (see Figure 4-1).

    To calibrate your monitor more accurately, you turn this off to set the red, green, and blue ranges for your monitor separately.

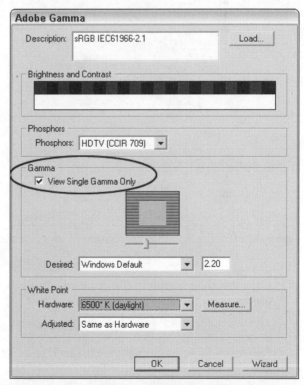

• **Figure 4-1: Make sure to remove the check mark from the View Single Gamma Only check box.**

3. **In the Gamma area, click the View Single Gamma Only check box to remove the check mark and deselect this option.**

The Adobe Gamma dialog box changes to display the individual monitor colors of red, green, and blue, as shown in Figure 4-2.

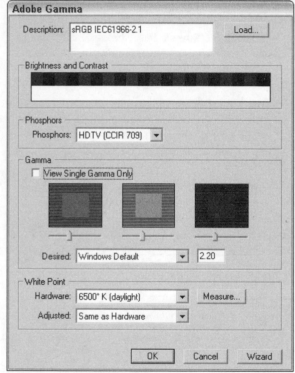

• **Figure 4-2: Use the individual color channels to accurately calibrate your monitor.**

4. **Click the Load button to find your monitor model.**

The Open Monitor Profile dialog box opens and displays a list of monitor models and color profiles followed by an .icm file extension (Figure 4-3). For instance, I'm using a ViewSonic PF790 monitor. To identify my monitor to the Adobe Gamma utility, I selected PF790.icm from the list.

If you can't find your monitor model in the Open Monitor Profile dialog box, click Cancel to return

to the Adobe Gamma dialog box, and use the default monitor profile provided by the utility. Skip Step 5 and continue with Step 6.

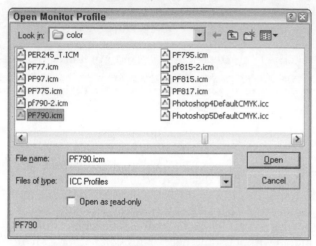

• **Figure 4-3: The Open Monitor Profile dialog box provides color space information for many monitor models.**

5. **Select your monitor model and click Open.**

The Open Monitor Profile dialog box closes and the monitor color space is loaded into the Adobe Gamma utility.

6. **Use the Phosphors drop-down list to select your monitor type.**

If your monitor is not listed (a good basic setting for monitors is Trinitron), then choose Custom and enter the Red, Green, and Blue phosphors settings for your monitor. To find these settings, consult the manual that came with your monitor.

If you selected a monitor model in Step 4, the utility automatically enters the Phosphors settings.

7. **In the Gamma area, use the slider bars under the red, green, and blue areas to adjust each color.**

For each color, make the inner square match the outer color as closely as possible.

8. **Click OK.**

The Save As dialog box opens with the Color folder selected (this is where all the other color profiles are saved on your computer).

9. **Enter a name for your custom profile in the File Name text box, and then click Save.**

Your custom profile is saved and the Adobe Gamma dialog box closes. Every time you use Photoshop, these settings transfer to Photoshop so that the program knows how to set your monitor's color space.

For Mac users

To calibrate your monitor with Mac OS X, follow these steps:

1. **Choose System Preferences⇨Displays.**

The Displays pane of the System Preferences dialog box opens showing the Display and Color tabs, as shown in Figure 4-4.

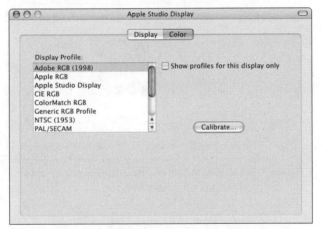

• **Figure 4-4: Use the Color tab in the Displays pane to access monitor calibration.**

2. **Select the Color tab and click the Calibrate button.**

The Display Calibrator Assistant opens, as shown in Figure 4-5. The Display Calibrator uses Apple's system-wide color management system called ColorSync.

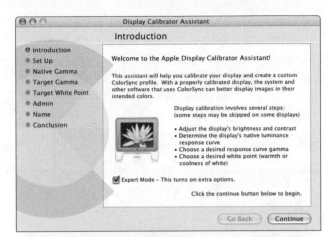

• **Figure 4-5: The Display Calibrator Assistant helps guide you through calibrating your monitor.**

3. **Select the Expert Mode check box.**

Expert mode gives you more control over how your monitor is calibrated.

4. **Click Continue.**

The next Display Calibrator Assistant pane enables you to set the neutral tones of the display, as shown in Figure 4-6.

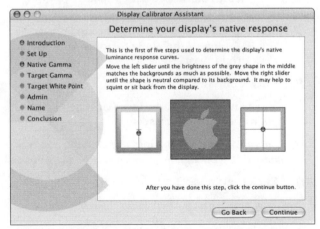

• **Figure 4-6: Use the sliders to make the apple match the background.**

5. **Move the blue dot sliders in the squares to the left and right of the apple to adjust neutral tones.**

Move the sliders until the apple matches the background as closely as possible. (It may help to squint!)

6. **Click Continue.**

The next panel of the Display Calibrator Assistant sets the brightness values, as shown in Figure 4-7.

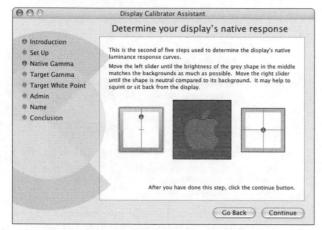

• **Figure 4-7:** Use the sliders to make the apple's brightness match the striped background.

7. **Move the blue dot sliders in the squares to the right and left of the apple to adjust your monitor's brightness.**

8. **Click Continue.**

Shown in Figure 4-8, the next panel helps you set your monitor's luminescence.

9. **Move the blue dot sliders to make the apple match the background as closely as possible.**

10. **Click Continue.**

This next panel is used to set the lower end of your monitor's color range, as shown in Figure 4-9.

11. **Move the blue dot sliders to make the dark gray apple blend into the striped background.**

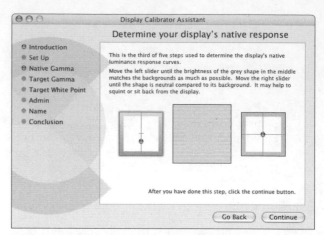

• **Figure 4-8:** Move the sliders to make the gray apple match the background.

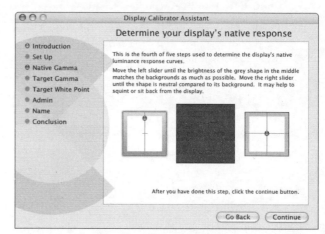

• **Figure 4-9:** Use the sliders to make the dark gray apple match the background.

12. **Click Continue.**

13. **Move the sliders to make the black apple blend into the background.**

When the apple is blended in correctly, the background appears almost black.

14. **Click Continue.**

The next panel of the Display Calibrator Assistant sets the contrast of your monitor's display (see Figure 4-10).

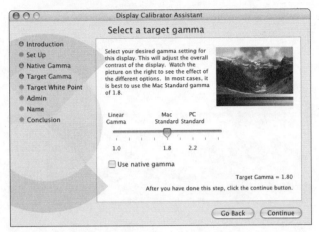

• **Figure 4-10:** Use the slider to set your monitor's contrast.

15. **Use the slider to set the contrast setting you want to use.**

Two basic options are noted on the slider:

▶ **1.8 Mac Standard:** The standard setting for the Mac OS.

▶ **2.2 PC Standard:** Choose this setting if you are creating images for display on PCs or televisions.

16. **Click Continue.**

Figure 4-11 shows the next panel of the Display Calibrator Assistant, which sets the color cast of your monitor's display.

17. **Move the slider to select a white point that is appropriate for the type of work you do.**

The slider bar sets the color cast or *white point* of your monitor. You can move the slider from left to right through various light qualities: from warm yellow lighting (which is good for graphics art work) through a cooler setting that is similar to daylight (good for Web graphics) to cool blue lighting (which is similar to television display).

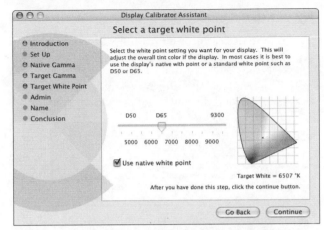

• **Figure 4-11:** Move the slider to select the tint of your monitor's display.

18. **Click Continue.**

If you are logged into the computer as an administrator, the next panel, shown in Figure 4-12, lets you set whether other users have access to the calibration settings.

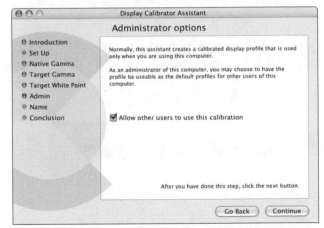

• **Figure 4-12:** If you have administrator privileges, you can give other users access to this calibration.

19. **Select the Allow Other Users to Use This Calibration check box to give access, if you want.**

20. Click Continue.

21. Name the calibration profile that you just set.

22. Click Continue.

The Display Calibrator Assistant saves all the settings and displays your selections in a final panel (see Figure 4-13).

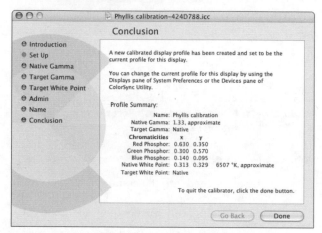

• **Figure 4-13:** The final panel displays the settings you selected.

23. Choose System Preferences➪Displays, and then click the Color tab.

You should see that the calibration profile you just created is selected.

Setting a Working Space

After you calibrate your monitor and identify it, you'll use Photoshop to select a color space — also called a *working space* — depending upon the type of work you do. Just follow these steps:

1. In Photoshop, choose Edit (Photoshop on the Mac)➪Color Settings.

The Color Settings dialog box opens, as shown in Figure 4-14, displaying a huge array of choices. Don't be put off by all the options; the Color

Settings dialog box comes with several predefined settings that you can select from the Settings drop-down list.

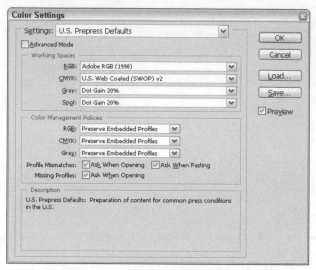

• **Figure 4-14:** You can select the color management settings with the Color Settings dialog box.

2. Use the Settings drop-down list to select a working space based on the type of work you do.

Some options you can choose from include:

▶ **Color Management Off** turns Photoshop's color management system off entirely.

▶ **ColorSync Workflow** (only available on the Mac) uses the Mac's built-in ColorSync system to manage color.

▶ **U.S. Prepress Defaults** manages color using typical printing conditions in the U.S.

▶ **Web Graphics Defaults** manages color for images created for the Web.

Other options include European and Japanese Prepress settings, which use color settings based on typical printing conditions for those regions.

I use U.S. Prepress Defaults because it sets the RGB working space to Adobe RGB (1998), which gives the widest range of possible colors. Also, it allows you to accurately view high-end 24-bit images.

 To find out more about a particular option in the Color Settings dialog box, pass your mouse over that option. An explanation of the feature appears in the Description area at the bottom of the dialog box.

3. **Click OK to close the dialog box and save your color management settings.**

Setting Color Space Conversions

Another part of Photoshop's color management system is to set how images embedded with a color profile are handled when they don't match your color settings. This comes up when you open an image that uses color settings different from yours.

To set your color management policy, follow these steps:

1. **Choose Edit (Photoshop on the Mac)↪Color Settings.**

2. **Use the CMYK, RGB, and Gray drop-down lists in the Color Management Policies area to set how images should be handled.**

   As shown in Figure 4-15, you have three options to choose from for each:

   ▶ **Off:** Turns color management off when an image is imported or opened.

   ▶ **Preserve Embedded Profiles:** Uses the color setting saved with the image. It does not convert the image to current Photoshop settings. (Photoshop can have any number of images with different color settings open at the same time.)

   ▶ **Convert to Working RGB:** Converts the image to the current color settings.

3. **Select the Profile Mismatches: Ask When Opening and Missing Profiles: Ask When Opening check boxes.**

   Each of these options sets Photoshop to ask how to proceed with color conversion when an image that doesn't match your color settings is opened or imported.

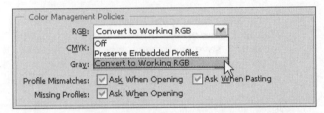

• **Figure 4-15: Set how imported or opened images are handled in the Color Management Policies area.**

4. **Click OK to close the dialog box and save your color management policy settings.**

Converting to Another Color Space

If you open or import an image into Photoshop that uses different color profile settings (depending upon your color management policy settings), Photoshop automatically converts the image to the current color settings, asks whether you want to convert the image, or doesn't do anything. (To find out how to set your color management policy, turn to the preceding section, "Setting Color Space Conversions.")

If Photoshop is set to ask how to proceed with the conversion, the Embedded Profile Mismatch dialog box shown in Figure 4-16 opens, offering three choices:

- ✔ **Use the Embedded Profile (Instead of the Working Space):** This option tells Photoshop to open the image using the color profile setting saved with the image.

- ✔ **Convert Document's Colors to the Working Space:** This option converts the image to the current color space settings.

- ✔ **Discard the Embedded Profile (Don't Color Manage):** This option throws away the color profile setting saved with the image and opens the image without any color translation in the current color space.

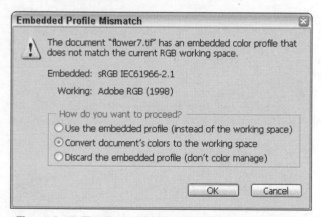

• **Figure 4-16: The Embedded Profile Mismatch dialog box lets you choose how you want color space conversion handled.**

Technique 5

Making Image Editing Easier

The other day my little 2-year-old son was using a magnifying glass to look at an ant. There he was, nose almost to the ground, first looking at the ant without the magnifying glass, and then popping the magnifying glass in front of his eyes to view the ant close up. With Photoshop you can get out your virtual magnifying glass and take a close look at your images. When you're working on an image, seeing the details is really important. Being able to edit down at the pixel level can make all the difference (especially when working on small Web graphics).

You can change the magnification (or *view size*) of an image to see it at actual size, pixel by pixel, or any magnification in between. View sizes are expressed in percentages, so 100% shows the image at its actual size; 200% doubles the size of the image on-screen, magnifying it; and 50% halves the size on-screen, shrinking the image.

This technique covers the ins and outs of zooming. You might think you know everything you need to know about magnifying images in Photoshop, but a few tips here may surprise you and come in handy.

Using the Navigator Palette

The Navigator palette, shown in Figure 5-1, is one of the palettes I use all the time. With this palette you can zoom in and out and quickly move around the image window to see hidden areas. If you don't see this palette on-screen (by default it is docked with the Info palette), choose Window➪Navigator.

View box

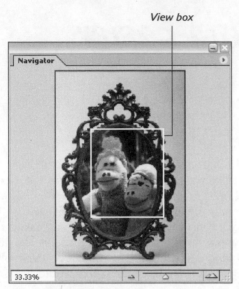

33.33%

• **Figure 5-1: The Navigator palette is your key to quick zooming.**

You can zoom in and out using the Navigator palette in four different ways:

✔ Type a magnification percentage in the Magnification box (in the lower-left corner), and then press Enter/Return.

✔ Click the Zoom In button to increase the magnification, viewing more and more pixel detail every time you click the button.

✔ Drag the Zoom slider to change the magnification. If you drag to the left, the image zooms out; if you drag to the right, the image zooms in.

✔ Click the Zoom Out button to decrease the magnification and view more of the image.

Just so you know, here are a few more tidbits about the Navigator palette that can help you edit images:

✔ You can drag the View box inside the image thumbnail in order to view another part of the image in the image window.

✔ By default, the View box is cyan (Windows) or red (Mac). You can change the color of the View box (this is particularly helpful if the image is light, making the View box hard to see). To change the color of the View box, choose Palette Options from the Navigator palette menu. Use the Color drop-down list in the Palette Options dialog box to select a color. (You can also select a color by clicking the color you want to use in the image window.)

✔ Hold down the Ctrl/⌘ key and drag a new View box in the image thumbnail of the Navigator palette. This is a quick way to change the magnification and move to a different area of the image.

✔ If you have screen real estate available, you can drag the Size box to make the Navigator palette bigger. As the palette gets larger, the image thumbnail also gets bigger. This makes navigating much easier.

Other Zooming Techniques

You should know a few other ways to zoom in and out. These shortcuts can help you work more efficiently:

✔ Press Ctrl+plus (+)/⌘+plus (+) to zoom in.

✔ Press Ctrl+minus (-)/⌘+minus (-) to zoom out.

✔ Type an exact magnification percentage or ratio in the Magnification box at the lower-left corner of the image window (see Figure 5-2), and then press Enter/Return. 100% magnification is the actual pixel size of the image. The same magnification using a ratio is 1:1; 200% magnification is expressed as the ratio 2:1; 50% magnification is expressed as 1:2, and so on.

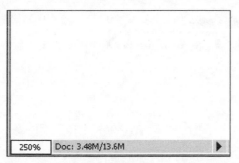

• **Figure 5-2: Zoom in or out by typing a percentage or ratio in the Magnification box, and then pressing Return/Enter.**

✔ Zoom in or out with the Zoom tool by clicking the image window (be sure to select either the Zoom In or Zoom Out button on the Options bar), or by dragging a marquee to change the magnification.

✔ If you hold down the Ctrl/⌘ key and the spacebar at the same time, the mouse cursor temporarily changes to the Zoom In tool. After you finish zooming, release the keys to return to the previous tool.

✔ If you hold down the Alt/Option key and the spacebar at the same time, the mouse cursor temporarily changes to the Zoom Out tool. After you're done changing the view size, release the keys to return to the previous tool.

Viewing an Image in Two Windows

One technique I use constantly when editing an image is looking at the image in two windows. The first window I use to zoom way in so that I can see pixels — this is the image window in which I do the actual image editing. The other window is set to 100% magnification (or whatever fits on-screen); I use this window to see how my edits are working.

You don't have to paint at a higher magnification, and then zoom out to see how it looks, zoom in to paint more, zoom out to check it again. Just open two windows and preview your edits as you make them.

To open a second image window, choose Window⇨ Arrange⇨New Window. As shown in Figure 5-3, I've set one window so that I can see the entire image. The second window is magnified. Every time I make a stroke with a brush or edit the image, the edit appears simultaneously in *both* windows. Paired with the Navigator palette, I can move around, zoom, and edit to my heart's content, seeing exactly what I'm doing all the while.

• **Figure 5-3: Opening a second image window makes image editing and manipulation much easier.**

Technique 6

Creating Your Own Tool Presets

Photoshop comes with many features that help you save time and work more efficiently. One of these great features is tool presets.

A *tool preset* is a tool setting that Photoshop remembers. This tool setting includes any settings selected on the Options bar, the Brushes palette (for painting or retouching tools), and the Character palette (for type tools). After you save a tool preset, you can access those tool settings at any time by clicking the name of the preset in the Tool Presets palette or Tool Presets picker. Also, tool presets are saved with Photoshop, not just a specific image file. So, you can use the same tool presets with any number of image files.

You can define many types of presets in Photoshop besides tool-specific presets — including presets for brushes, gradients, contours, swatches, styles, patterns, and custom shapes. You can access these presets in the palette or picker for each type of preset.

This technique deals exclusively with creating presets for tools. Brushes can also be saved as presets and, yes, brushes are tools. But, I don't cover brushes here. Because brushes are so very special and important to your work in Photoshop, I devote an entire technique to creating custom brushes and brush presets. So, if you want to create brush presets, flip through the book to Technique 23.

Working with the Tool Presets Palette and the Tool Presets Picker

The Tool Presets palette and the Tool Presets picker are like smart storage bins for tool presets. The palette and the picker store exactly the same tool presets; they are just different ways to access the tool presets. As shown in Figure 6-1, by default, the Tool Presets palette resides in the Palette Well at the right side of the Options bar; the Tool Presets picker lives at the left side of the Options bar.

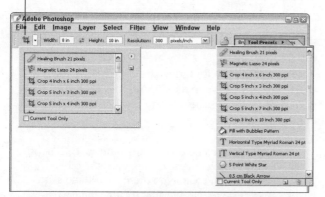

• **Figure 6-1:** By default, the Tool Presets picker and Tool Presets palette are both on the Options bar.

Because the Tool Presets palette is, well, a palette, you can pull it out of the Palette Well into the program area if you want complete access to it, or you can close it if you don't need it. (For more about moving, grouping, and docking palettes, take a look at Technique 2.) If you don't see the Tool Presets palette anywhere in the Photoshop program area, choose Window➪Tool Presets.

Both the Tool Presets picker and the Tool Presets palette work in exactly the same way. All you need to do to select a tool preset is to open the Tool Presets picker or the palette, and then click the tool preset you want to use. The tool is automatically selected from the Toolbox with the saved attributes selected.

By default, all the tool presets that are loaded into the Tool Presets palette and picker are displayed. If you want to see tool presets only for the currently selected tool, then you must select the Current Tool Only option in either the picker or the palette. (When you turn this option on in one, it is automatically selected in the other.)

Loading a Tool Preset Library

You may not know it, but Photoshop ships with four tool preset libraries that are not automatically loaded

into Photoshop. These libraries include presets for the Art History Brush, Brush tool, Horizontal Type tool, and the Crop and Rectangular Marquee tools.

To load a tool preset library, follow these steps:

1. Select one of the tool preset libraries from the bottom of the Tool Presets palette menu, as shown in Figure 6-2.

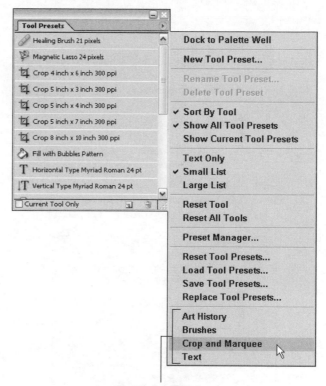

Tool Preset libraries

• **Figure 6-2:** Select one of the tool preset libraries from the bottom of the Tool Presets palette menu.

An Adobe Photoshop dialog box appears, as shown in Figure 6-3.

2. Click OK, Cancel, or Append.

▶ **Click OK** to replace the tool presets currently listed in the Tool Presets palette with the tool presets in the library you selected.

▶ **Click Cancel** to back out of the entire loading operation.

▶ **Click Append** to add the tool preset library you selected to the tool presets currently listed in the Tool Presets dialog box.

• **Figure 6-3:** Use this dialog box to set how you want the selected tool preset library loaded into the Tool Presets palette.

 If you decide you don't want to use a tool presets library that you loaded, you can unload it by choosing Reset Tool Presets from the Tool Presets palette menu, and then clicking OK.

Figure 6-4 shows the Crop and Marquee preset library loaded into the Tool Presets palette.

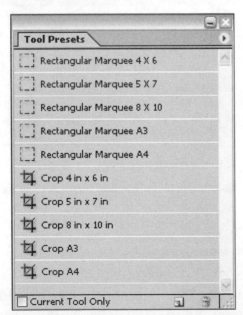

• **Figure 6-4:** The Tool Presets palette is loaded with Crop tool and Rectangular Marquee tool presets.

Creating Your Own Tool Presets

Imagine that you're working on a text intensive Photoshop project with four other artists. And, coming up with the type styles needed for the project is your job. This job includes the type's font, size, and other attributes, such as alignment, color, and horizontal or vertical scale — any feature that you can set for one of the Type tools.

 After you come up with the type specifications, how do you deliver the specs to the other artists? You could type them all out and send them via e-mail, but that means that each artist has to enter multiple attributes into Photoshop as they need text — not a pretty picture when you think about time spent and the errors that could creep in. Instead, you can create a tool preset for each type spec, save the presets with descriptive names, and then e-mail them to your co-conspirators. The other artists load the tool presets into their versions of Photoshop, and that's it. Everyone has the same specs and can use them with a click of the mouse.

Besides creating a new tool preset from scratch, you can also create a tool preset based on an existing tool preset.

To create a new tool preset from scratch, follow these steps:

1. Select the tool from the Toolbox for which you want to create the preset.

2. Choose the settings you want to save with the tool preset.

Depending upon the tool you select, you can use the Options bar, Brushes palette, or Character palette to choose the tool's settings.

3. Select New Tool Preset from the Tool Presets palette menu.

The New Tool Preset dialog box appears, as shown in Figure 6-5.

• **Figure 6-5: Enter a descriptive name in the New Tool Preset dialog box.**

4. **Type a name for the tool preset.**

Depending upon the tool you're creating the preset for, a special check box may also be included in the New Tool Preset dialog box:

▶ **Brush, Pencil, or Shape tool:** Select Include Color to tell Photoshop to remember the currently selected Foreground and Background color.

▶ **Gradient tool:** Select Include Gradient to save the currently selected gradient.

▶ **Pattern Stamp tool:** Select Include Pattern to save the currently selected pattern.

5. **Click OK.**

The new tool preset appears at the bottom of the Tool Presets palette.

Follow these steps to create a new tool preset based on an existing tool preset:

1. In the Tool Presets palette, select the existing tool preset that you want to use as the basis for the new tool preset.

2. Modify the tool preset settings by using the Options bar, Brushes palette, or Character palette.

3. Select New Tool Preset from the Tool Presets palette menu.

The New Tool Preset dialog box appears (refer to Figure 6-5).

4. Type a name for the tool preset.

5. Click OK.

The new tool preset appears at the bottom of the Tool Presets palette.

Creating identical Type tool presets

Creating new tool presets based on existing tool presets works especially well for the Type tools.

For instance, suppose you want to create two Type tool presets that have the same formatting attributes (font, size, horizontal spacing), but one preset uses the Horizontal Type tool and the other uses the Horizontal Type Mask tool. Here's how to create two different presets:

1. **Create the original tool preset by using the Horizontal Type tool.**

2. **Select the tool preset in the Tool Presets palette.**

   When you select the tool preset, all of the type attributes load into the Options bar and Character palette.

3. **Select the Horizontal Type Mask tool from the Toolbox.**

   Even though you select a different Type tool, the type attributes remain set in the Options bar and Character palette.

4. **Choose New Tool Preset from the Tool Presets palette menu.**

5. **Type a name for the tool preset in the New Tool Preset dialog box.**

6. **Click OK.**

Storing and Deleting Tool Presets

When you finish with a project, cleaning up and doing a little bit of housekeeping is always a good idea. The Tool Presets palette and picker can get so filled up with presets that finding the new presets you create is hard.

You have two options: You can save a project's presets (think of it as archiving the presets in case you need them at some later date) and then delete them from the Tool Presets palette; or delete the tool presets without saving them. If you decide to delete the tool presets without saving them, be sure you won't need them in the future because once they're gone, they're gone.

Saving tool presets

1. **Choose Preset Manager from the Tool Presets palette menu or choose Edit➪Preset Manager.**

    The Preset Manager opens, as shown in Figure 6-6. You can use the Preset Manager to create, load, save, and delete presets.

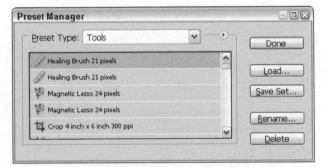

• **Figure 6-6: The Preset Manager organizes all kinds of presets including tool presets.**

2. **Select Tools from the Preset Type drop-down list or press Ctrl+8/⌘+8 to display the tool presets.**

    The list box in the Preset Manager displays all the tool presets currently loaded into the Tool Presets palette.

3. **Working down the list box, Shift+click and/or Ctrl/⌘+click to select the tool presets you want to save.**

    You can select as many or as few presets as you like.

4. **Click Save Set.**

    The Save dialog box opens with the Tools folder selected, as shown in Figure 6-7. The tool presets are stored by default in the Tools folder.

5. **Enter a name for the tool presets in the File Name text box.**

• **Figure 6-7: Enter a name for the tool presets in the File Name text box.**

6. **Click Save.**

    The tool presets are saved for later use. You can now safely delete them from the Tool Presets palette and picker.

7. **Click Done to close the Preset Manager.**

Deleting tool presets

You can delete tool presets by using either the Tool Presets palette or Preset Manager.

To delete tool presets using the Tool Presets palette, simply drag the tool presets you want to discard to the trashcan at the bottom of the palette.

 You can also restore the tool presets loaded by default into the Tool Presets palette and picker by choosing Reset Tool Presets from the palette or picker menu, and then clicking OK. This discards any tool presets that are not part of the default set.

To delete tool presets by using the Preset Manager, follow these steps:

1. **Choose Preset Manager from the Tool Presets palette menu or choose Edit⇨Preset Manager.**

   The Preset Manager opens (refer to Figure 6-6).

2. **Select Tools from the Preset Type drop-down list or press Ctrl+8/⌘+8 to display the tool presets.**

   The Preset Manager displays all the tool presets currently loaded into the Tool Presets palette.

3. **Working down the list box, Shift+click and/or Ctrl/⌘+click to select the tool presets you want to delete.**

   You can select as many or as few presets as you like.

4. **Click Delete.**

5. **Click Done to close the Preset Manager.**

Technique 7

Moving Back in Time: Getting Rid of Mistakes

Sometimes you make little mistakes, sometimes you make big ones. This technique covers what you can do to help yourself out *before* you make a big mistake (or think you may be headed down the path towards a whopper) — a course of action that can save you both time and aggravation in the long run.

What can you do when you make a big mistake? If you've been working on an image for days or even a few hours, deleting the entire file is certainly out of the question. Thankfully, Photoshop comes with several powerful tools and commands that you can use to prepare a safety net for yourself.

Testing Techniques Using Duplicates

If you want to try out a technique that you're not sure about — for instance, you want to apply a filter to the red color channel, adjust the curves of the blue channel, and then flatten all the layers and apply another filter to the entire image — don't mess around with your image file; create a duplicate image and run tests on the duplicate. After you try your test, if you like the effect you can then save the duplicate and continue to work on it, keeping the original image file as a backup. Or, if you hate the effect you create, you can delete the duplicate and no harm done.

Creating a duplicate is simple:

1. **With the image file selected in the program window, choose Image⇨Duplicate.**

   The Duplicate Image dialog box opens, as shown in Figure 7-1.

2. **Enter a name for the duplicate in the As text box.**

   If your image contains layers and you want the duplicate image to retain those layers, *do not* put a check mark in the Duplicate Merged Layers Only check box. If you want the layers flattened in the duplicate image, put a check mark in the check box.

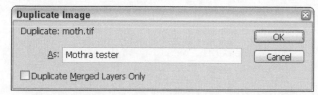

Duplicate Image

Duplicate: moth.tif

As: Mothra tester

☐ Duplicate Merged Layers Only

OK Cancel

• **Figure 7-1:** Type a name for the duplicate image in the text box.

3. **Click OK.**

The duplicate image appears on-screen.

 This duplicate image is not saved until you save it by choosing File⇨Save.

Using Revert and Undo

Revert and Undo are two simple little commands that can help you out of a bind.

Everyone, of course, knows about unassuming little Undo. Undo appears in almost every program there is (frankly, I can't think of a program that doesn't include Undo).

You have to remember that Undo only moves you back one step. If you apply a filter and then add a Type layer, Undo removes the Type layer but not the filter. (To go back more than one step, use the all-powerful History palette as described later in "Stepping Back with the History Palette.")

But, Undo does work well for the quick one-step fix. Choose Edit⇨Undo or press Ctrl/⌘+Z to do the undo.

Revert is another simple command, but it can pack a wallop. When you use revert by choosing File⇨ Revert or pressing F12, Photoshop restores the image file to its last saved version. Depending upon how much you save a file as you work on it, this command can take you back one step or twenty steps. Unfortunately, unless you keep mental track of when you last saved the image, you might not know what state the image will be in when you use Revert.

 Using the History palette gives you an advantage over using Revert. With the History palette, you can revert to the original image regardless of whether you saved along the way. Revert reloads the last saved version, which may include some undesireable changes.

If you use Revert and then realize it was a mistake, don't worry! You can use Undo to remove the Revert or use the History palette to move back because Revert is recorded in the History palette.

Creating Backups

Another ally in the war against major catastrophe is the backup. Using the Save As command, you can save a copy of a file. Save As does more than create identical copies; you can also use it to save a copy in another color mode (for instance, create a copy in CMYK color mode and keep the original in RGB color mode) and another file format.

Here's how to create a backup:

1. **Choose File⇨Save As or press Ctrl+Shift+S/ ⌘+Shift+S.**

The Save As dialog box appears, as shown in Figure 7-2.

2. **Type a new name or modify the existing file name in the File Name text box (Windows) or Save As text box (Mac).**

3. **Select a folder where you want to save the backup.**

4. **If you want, choose a different file format for the backup using the Save As drop-down list (Windows) or the Format pop-up menu (Mac).**

 If your image file contains layers and you choose a file format that does not support layers, the Layers check box is grayed out and the backup copy is automatically flattened.

• **Figure 7-2: The Windows XP Save As dialog box (top) and the Mac OS Save As dialog box.**

5. **In the Save and Color areas, select any options that you need.**

If you select the As a Copy option, the image copy remains closed and the original remains open. If you want to include a color profile with the backup, select the Embed Color Profile option (Mac) or Color: ICC Profile option (Windows). (To find out how to create a color profile, turn to Technique 4.)

6. **Click Save.**

If you click Save and you haven't changed the name of the backup copy from the original, the Adobe Photoshop dialog box shown in Figure 7-3 appears.

• **Figure 7-3: Photoshop warns you that you are going to save the copy over the original file.**

Click OK to save over the original file or click Cancel to return to the Save As dialog box where you can change the backup copy's filename.

Stepping Back with the History Palette

The History palette is Photoshop's amazingly powerful undo tool. With the History palette you can undo up to 99 previous *states*. Each state is something that you do that modifies the image, such as using a command or stroking in the image window with a brush.

The History palette records all your modifications and keeps a running list of states. As you perform each edit, Photoshop names the state and labels it with a corresponding icon depending upon the tool or command used.

You can use the History palette to move back any number of edits if you decide that you made a mistake. In addition, the History palette works with the History Brush and Art History Brush, which you can use to selectively restore areas to a prior state. (To find out more about using the History Brush and Art History Brush, turn to Technique 25.)

By default, the History palette is grouped with the Actions palette at the right side of the Photoshop program window. If you don't see it, choose Window⇨ History to display the palette, shown in Figure 7-4.

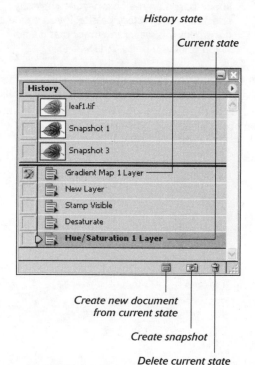

History state

Current state

Create new document from current state

Create snapshot

Delete current state

• **Figure 7-4: The History palette records each action you make, allowing you to return to any given point in time.**

Reverting to a previous state

When you discover that you've done something to an image that you don't like or didn't intend, use the History palette to step back in time as far as you need to go.

You can use the History palette in several different ways to revert to a previous state:

- ✔ Click a previous state on the History palette.

- ✔ Drag the slider on the left side of the palette up to the desired state.

- ✔ Choose Step Backward from the History palette menu to move back one history state. Keep selecting this command to move back as many states as you want.

- ✔ Press Ctrl+Alt+Z/⌘+Option+Z to move back one history state. Keep pressing this key combination to move back as many states as you need.

Taking snapshots

A *snapshot* is a special copy of a history state with an important difference. Unlike a history state, which can be deleted (because you reached the maximum number of history states or the palette is cleared), a snapshot remains in the History palette until the image file is closed. When a file is closed, the snapshots are automatically deleted.

You can take a snapshot at any time you need. Creating a snapshot before performing a long series of edits or running an action is always a good idea.

You can select two automatic snapshot settings in the History Options dialog box (see Figure 7-5). To open the dialog box, choose History Options from the History palette menu.

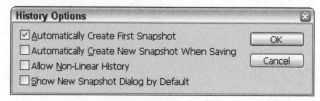

• **Figure 7-5: Use the History Options dialog box to select snapshot settings.**

Here are the two settings:

- If Automatically Create First Snapshot is selected, Photoshop automatically takes a snapshot each time an image file is opened. This setting is handy. In case you come to some point of no return (for instance, suppose you clear the History palette by mistake so there's no way to undo anything), at least you have a snapshot of the image when it's first opened.

- If Automatically Create New Snapshot When Saving is selected, Photoshop automatically makes a snapshot every time you save an image. For me, this setting just doesn't work out. I hit Ctrl+S/⌘+S almost unconsciously, so I'd probably end up with 500 snapshots in the course of a morning's work. Snapshots take up memory, so I leave this option unselected.

It's time to get down to brass tacks, now. Taking a snapshot is quite easy; just click the Create Snapshot button at the bottom of the History palette. The new snapshot appears at the top of the History palette with a default name (something imaginative such as "Snapshot 1"). You can rename the snapshot by clicking the snapshot's name, typing a new name, and then pressing Enter/Return.

Another button on the History palette is very handy: Create New Document from Current State. Click this button to create a duplicate image based on the history state currently selected in the History palette. If you create a document this way, remember that it's not saved until you press Ctrl+S/⌘+S.

If you find that you need to revert to the state that you captured when you took the snapshot, click the snapshot in the History palette. The image instantly returns to that history state.

Technique 8

Creating Actions

Save Time By

- Creating action sets
- Recording and playing actions
- Getting rid of actions you don't need
- Loading action set libraries

What happens when you want to repeat certain actions over and over again? For instance, suppose you need to convert 50 images from RGB to grayscale? Well, you could open every image and then choose Image⇨Mode⇨Grayscale 50 times, but that would take a long time and be very tedious. Instead, you can record a mini-program, known in Photoshop as an *action,* and play it, simultaneously applying the action to the entire folder of 50 images. In a few seconds, an action can perform the repetitive task that would take an hour.

Also, while actions are great for performing repetitive tasks, you can use actions to automate *any* process you can come up with in Photoshop. Suppose you create a cool effect that changes a regular old black letter B into a stunning B that has the appearance of translucent liquid blue gel. You can record the steps that create this effect, and then play them back, instantly transforming any letters you want.

An action can consist of anything from a keyboard shortcut to a complex series of commands that trigger other actions. You can create actions in Photoshop or ImageReady. The Actions palette (see Figure 8-1) is used to record, play, edit, save, delete, and load other actions. And, to make using actions easier, you can assign keyboard shortcuts to them.

As shown in Figure 8-1, Photoshop comes with several actions already loaded into the Actions palette. Some of these actions include Sepia Toning (which re-colors a layer to look like it is sepia toned), Water Reflection (which adds a wavy-looking reflection to type), and Vignette (which creates a frame around a selection).

This technique takes you through the process of recording and playing actions, as well as grouping the actions together into *action sets*. You also find out how to load the extra action sets that ship with Photoshop and where to find action sets available for download on the Web.

Commands within the action

An Action set

An Action

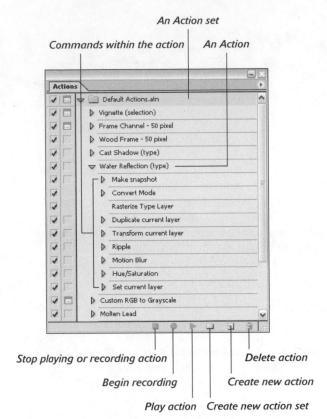

Stop playing or recording action

Begin recording

Play action

Delete action

Create new action

Create new action set

• **Figure 8-1:** Use the Actions palette to create actions, mini-programs that can save you lots of time and increase productivity.

Viewing Actions and Their Commands

You can view actions in the Actions palette in two ways: Button mode and Command mode. Each mode gives different access to actions and the commands contained within an action. Button mode is the simplest, displaying each action as a button, while Command mode displays all the commands within an action.

Button mode

Button mode hides all the commands within an action and also hides the record/playback buttons located at the bottom of the Actions palette when the menu is viewed in Command mode. Button mode displays each action as a button, as shown in Figure 8-2.

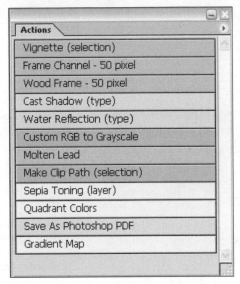

• **Figure 8-2:** When the Actions palette displays in Button mode, just click a button to play an action.

To play the action, just click the button. To view the Actions palette in Button mode, open the Actions palette menu and choose Button mode.

Command mode

While giving access to an action set so that you can select and play it, Command mode also lets you view and manipulate the commands within an action, and gives access to the record/playback buttons at the bottom of the Actions palette.

By default, the Actions palette displays in Command mode. If your Actions palette is displayed in Button mode and you want to switch to Command mode, make sure Button mode is unselected on the Actions palette menu. Figure 8-3 shows the Actions palette displayed in Command mode.

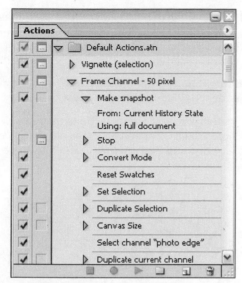

• **Figure 8-3: Command mode gives access to all the commands within an action.**

To work with the commands in an action, you need to view them. To do so, click the tiny right-pointing arrow next to an action. The action expands, showing the commands contained within the action in a nested fashion.

Using Command mode, you can set how much of an action plays back. If a command is within an action that you don't want to use, remove the check mark from the left-most column next to the command. Also, if you don't want to play an action from the beginning but want to start with a command within the action, highlight the command within the action, and then click Play. The action plays from the selected command to its end.

Creating an Action Set

Notice in Figure 8-3 that actions are grouped together in the Actions palette. This group is called an *action set*. Action sets make organizing actions easy so that you can quickly find the action you want to play.

To create an action set, follow these steps:

1. **If the Actions palette is not displayed in Command mode, open the Actions palette menu and deselect Button mode.**

2. **Click the Create New Set button at the bottom of the Actions palette.**

   The New Set dialog box appears.

3. **Enter the name for the action set.**

4. **Click OK.**

   The new set appears in the Actions palette.

 You can move action sets up or down the list in the Actions palette the same way you can restack layers in the Layers palette. Just drag the action set up or down in the Actions palette to its new position.

Recording an Action

When you create an action, the commands you select are recorded. When you finish creating the action, the commands appear in the Actions palette indented under the action's name.

1. **Open an image or create a new image.**

   You use this image to select the steps you want recorded. If you're not sure about all the steps you want to record, you can always create a duplicate of the image by choosing Image⇨Duplicate, and then practice on the duplicate image.

2. **If the Actions palette is not displayed in Command mode, open the Actions palette menu and deselect Button mode.**

3. **Click the Create New Action button at the bottom of the Actions palette.**

   In the New Action dialog box, shown in Figure 8-4, enter a name for the action and assign a keyboard shortcut for the action, if you want to. You can also select a color for the action so that it appears in your chosen color in the Actions palette.

• **Figure 8-4:** Use the New Action dialog box to name the action and assign a keyboard shortcut and color for the action.

4. Click Record to close the New Action dialog box and start recording.

5. Select the commands that you want to record, applying them as you normally would.

> If you enter values in text boxes, they are recorded. If you cancel out of a dialog box, the canceled item is not recorded. You cannot use several tools when recording an action. Check out the sidebar "What can I record?" to find out which ones they are.

6. When you finish applying commands, click the Stop button on the Actions palette or press the Esc key.

> The recording stops and your custom action appears in the Actions palette. If you look at your action, all the commands that you recorded are listed under the action's name.

Playing an Action

After recording an action, you can then play it back on an individual image file or a folder containing many image files.

Playing an action on one image

1. Open the image on which you want to play the action.

2. If the Actions palette is displayed in Command mode, select the action you want to play, and then click the Play button at the bottom of the Actions palette.

If the Actions palette is displayed in Button mode, click the action you want to play.

Try this with some of the actions that come with Photoshop. Figure 8-5 shows two actions, Water Reflection and Cast Shadow, applied to some type.

• **Figure 8-5:** You can use the actions that come with Photoshop to enhance your images.

What can I record?

You can use many tools and palettes when recording an action and a few that you cannot.

These items can be used when recording an action:

- ✔ Tools: All selection tools, Crop, Eyedropper, Gradient, Magic Eraser, Move, Notes, Paint Bucket, all shape tools, Slice, all type tools.

- ✔ Palettes: Actions, Channels, Color, History, Layers, Paths, Styles, Swatches.

These items cannot be used when recording an action:

- ✔ Tools: Blur, Brush, Burn, Clone Stamp, Dodge, Pattern Stamp, Pencil, Sharpen, Sponge.

- ✔ Commands found on the View and Window menus.

Before playing an action on an image file, create a snapshot to save the way the image looks (also called a *state*). If you don't like the effect the action has on the image, you can then use the snapshot to revert to the earlier state. To find out more about snapshots and how to create them, turn to Technique 7.

Playing an action on a folder of images

1. Move all the files to which you want to apply the action to the same folder.

2. Choose File⇨Automate⇨Batch or in the File Browser choose Automate⇨Batch.

The Batch dialog box, shown in Figure 8-6, opens. Use this dialog box to select the folder where the images are stored and the action you want to play.

3. Select the action you want to play from the Action drop-down list in the Play area.

4. Select Folder from the Source drop-down list.

5. Click the Choose button to select the folder where the images are located.

6. In the Destination drop-down list, select the destination for the files after the action is played.

Use the Destination drop-down list to select None, Save and Close, or Folder:

- ▶ **None** leaves the images open in Photoshop after the action is played.

- ▶ **Save and Close** saves the images and then closes them, leaving them in their original folder.

- ▶ **Folder** saves the images after the action is played in a new folder. If you select Folder, click Choose to select the folder where you want the images stored.

7. Click OK to play the action and apply it to the images in the selected folder.

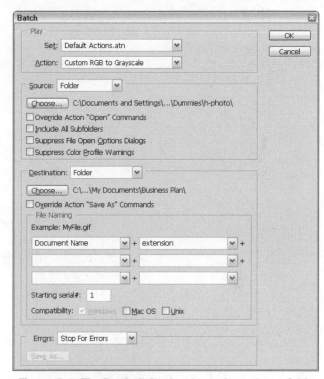

• **Figure 8-6:** The Batch dialog box is used to select a folder and an action.

Deleting an Action

After you finish using an action, you can quickly delete it by dragging the action to the trashcan icon at the bottom of the Actions palette. Actions can take up a lot of memory, so do some housekeeping from time-to-time and remove unnecessary action items.

Loading Action Sets

When Photoshop is installed, only one default action set is loaded into the Actions palette. (It's listed as `Default Actions.atn` at the top of the Actions palette.) Seven more libraries of action sets ship with Photoshop.

These action sets include actions that create frames, special image and text effects, and textures. To load an action set into the Actions palette, open the Actions palette menu, and then choose the action set from the bottom of the menu, as shown in Figure 8-7.

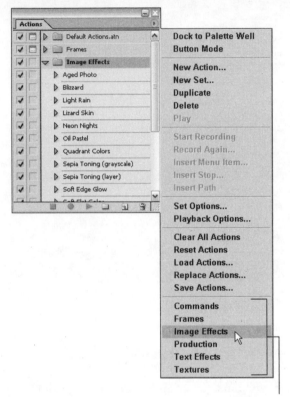

Action sets

• **Figure 8-7: Select an action set from the bottom of the Actions palette menu.**

Figure 8-8 shows some of the great actions that you can load into the actions palette.

Original image

Image Effects action set:
Fluorescent Chalk

Frames action set:
Brushed Aluminum Frame

• **Figure 8-8: Check out the great actions that ship with Photoshop.**

Downloading actions from the Web

Many Photoshop artists have come up with actions of their own that are available for download from the Web. For some great resources, check out Adobe Studio Exchange at share.studio.adobe.com, Team Photoshop at www.teamphotoshop.com, and Action Addiction at www.actionaddiction.com. To find other sites offering actions, just type **Photoshop actions** into your favorite Web search engine.

Technique 9

Automating Photoshop Functions

Save Time By

- Letting Photoshop rename a folder of files
- Automating actions
- Using droplets

This technique focuses on ways that you can modify batches of files while letting Photoshop do (most of) the work for you. The big time sink for you is setting up the automation. After you have the automation in place, though, Photoshop can do the work in a matter of seconds.

So, what can you automate? Using the tools included in Photoshop, you can

- Rename batches of files, saving the renamed files in the same folder as the original files or a new folder.

- Modify any number of images using actions that you record, and then save the modified image files in the original folder or a new folder.

- Create mini-programs called *droplets* that bring recorded actions to the Windows or Mac desktop. From there, you drop selected files or a folder of files on the droplet in order to play the action.

None of these features is very difficult to use. Working your way through the various dialog boxes may take some figuring out the first time, but when you're familiar with the way each of these features works, setting up automated processes in the future is really a snap.

Programming Photoshop using scripts

For those of you who are interested in programming, Photoshop can be customized using short programs or *scripts* written in AppleScript, JavaScript, or Visual Basic. In Photoshop 7, scripting was included as an optional plug-in that needed to be installed. With Photoshop CS, scripting is integrated into the program, so any system running Photoshop CS supports scripting by default.

If you decide to write scripts for the Mac exclusively, you need to use AppleScript and a script editor. Both of these come with Mac OS X and can be found in the Applications folder. To find out more about AppleScript, check out www.apple.com/applescript.

Windows users interested in writing scripts exclusively for Windows machines can use Visual Basic or the Windows Scripting Host. To download Windows Scripting Host, go to www.msdn.microsoft.com/scripting.

Photoshop users who decide to create scripts for both the Windows and Mac platforms can use JavaScript. In fact, Photoshop includes a built-in cross-platform framework for playing JavaScripts.

Four scripts are installed by default in Photoshop; access them by choosing File➪Scripts. Photoshop also ships with scripting manuals and many sample scripts written in the three scripting languages. You can find these manuals and scripts in the Scripting Guide folder of your Photoshop CS installation.

Renaming a Bunch of Files

The Batch Rename command lets you rename any number of files in one operation. You can rename a few selected files, or rename an entire folder of files. When renaming the files, you have the option of leaving the files in their original folder or moving them to a new folder.

You can select up to six filenaming options when setting how the files will be renamed. They include:

- Three Document Name options that set whether the file is renamed using upper- or lowercase characters or a combination.

- Three Serial Number options that add a one, two, or three digit serial number to the filename.

- Two Serial Letter options that add either an upper- or lowercase letter to the filename.

- Seven date options that let you add the month/ day/year in various permutations to the filename.

To use the Batch Rename command, you have to use the File Browser. If you aren't familiar with the File Browser, take a look at Technique 1 for a quick refresher.

Here's how to automate renaming files:

1. **Open the File Browser by clicking the Toggle File Browser button on the Options bar or choosing File➪Browse.**

2. **Using the Folders palette, move to the folder containing the files you want to rename.**

When you select the folder, the image files display as thumbnails in the Preview pane.

3. **Select the image files you want to rename.**

You can select individual files by clicking them in the Preview pane or select an entire folder of image files by selecting the folder in the Folders palette.

4. **Choose Automate➪Batch Rename.**

The Batch Rename dialog box, shown in Figure 9-1, opens.

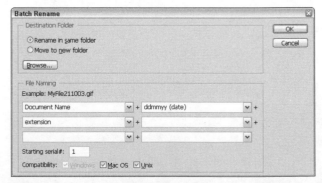

• **Figure 9-1: You can select where the renamed files are stored with the Batch Rename dialog box.**

5. **In the Destination Folder area, select where the renamed files are stored.**

Select **Rename in Same Folder** to leave the files in their current folder.

Select **Move to New Folder** to move the files to a different location. If you select this option, click the Browse button and use the Browse For Folder dialog box, shown in Figure 9-2, to locate the folder where the renamed files will be stored.

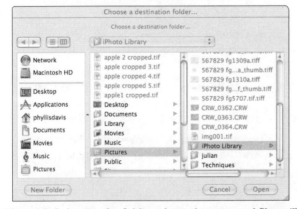

• **Figure 9-2: Locate the folder where the renamed files will be stored using the Browse For Folder dialog box (Windows, top) or using the Choose a Destination Folder dialog box (Mac, bottom).**

6. **In the File Naming area, select the options that you want to use to rename the image files.**

Using the drop-down lists shown in Figure 9-3, select up to six options.

If you select one of the Serial Letter/Number options, enter the first number or letter in the

Starting Serial # text box (Photoshop automatically counts up from there).

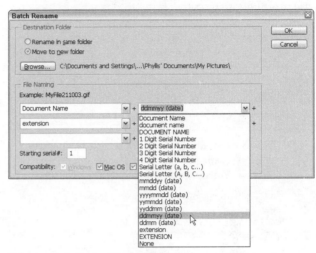

• **Figure 9-3: In the File Naming area, select up to six naming options.**

7. **Put check marks in all Compatibility check boxes.**

This step ensures that the renamed files work on any computer.

 You cannot undo the file renaming after it is completed, so make sure all your settings are right before you click OK.

8. **Click OK.**

Photoshop goes to work, and in the blink of an eye, all the selected files are renamed.

Automating Image Modifications

The Batch command modifies entire selected images using actions that you create. Actions are mini-programs that perform specific steps that you record. Actions can automate almost any Photoshop technique, such as applying filters, creating new layers, deleting channels — you name it. To find out how to create actions, turn to Technique 8.

The Batch command, like its cousin the Batch Rename command, gives you the option of leaving the modified image files in the folder where they currently reside or moving them to a new folder. If you choose to move the files to a new folder, you also have the option of renaming the files using the exact same options that the Batch Rename command offers, including selecting up to six filenaming variables, such as adding the date, a serial number, or serial letter.

1. **In the Photoshop program window, choose File⇨Automate⇨Batch or in the File Browser choose Automate⇨Batch.**

The Batch dialog box opens, as shown in Figure 9-4.

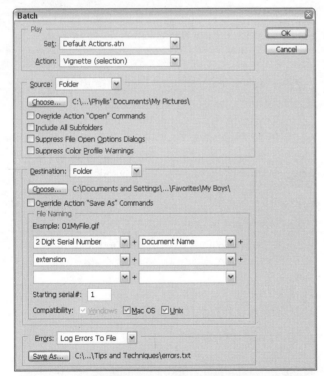

• **Figure 9-4: Select an action, folder of files to modify, and a folder destination for the modified files in the Batch dialog box.**

2. **In the Play area, use the Set drop-down list to select the action set containing the action you want to play.**

3. **In the Play area, select the action you want to play using the Action drop-down list.**

4. **Use the Source drop-down list to select the location of image files on which you want to play the action.**

You can choose from

▶ **Folder:** Select this option to designate a folder of image files. If you choose this setting, click Choose and use the Browse For Folder dialog box (Windows) or Choose a Batch Folder dialog box (Mac) to locate the folder containing the files.

▶ **Import:** Select this option to import image files from a PDF document or peripheral device, such as a digital camera or scanner. If you select this option, use the From drop-down list to select from where the image files will be imported.

▶ **Opened Files:** Select this option to play the action on the image files currently open in Photoshop.

▶ **File Browser:** Select this option to play the action on image files selected in the File Browser.

5. **Use the Destination drop-down list to select how the modified image files are saved and/or stored.**

You can select from

▶ **None:** Select this option to leave the modified image files open in Photoshop. If you select this option, skip to Step 8.

▶ **Save and Close:** Select this option to save the modified files and close them, leaving them in their original folder. If you select this option, skip to Step 8.

▶ **Folder:** Select this option to save the files and move them to a new folder. If you select this option, click Choose and use the Browse For Folder dialog box (Windows) or Choose a Destination Folder dialog box (Mac) to locate the folder where you want to store the files. Also, when you select the Folder option, you can also rename the files.

6. **In the File Naming area, select the options that you want to use to rename the image files.**

Using the drop-down lists, select up to six options (refer to Figure 9-3).

If you select one of the Serial Number options, enter the first number in the Starting Serial # text box (Photoshop automatically counts up from there).

7. **Put check marks in the Compatibility check boxes.**

This step ensures the renamed files work on any computer.

8. **Decide how you want errors handled by choosing an option from the Errors drop-down list.**

Sometimes errors occur when actions are played on image files. For instance, the action specifies a specific image size minimum and the image is not large enough.

▶ Select **Stop for Errors** from the Errors drop-down list to halt the Batch command. A dialog box displaying the error appears and the batch operation is aborted; you need to set up the entire batch process again.

▶ Select **Log Errors to File** to send error reports to a text file. The batch processing continues even if an error occurs. If you choose this option, click the Save As button to set a folder location and name for the error log text file.

9. **When you're sure all the settings are correct, click OK.**

Photoshop goes to work processing the image files using the action and settings you selected.

Working with Droplets

A *droplet* is an action that is encapsulated into an executable program. You can put droplets directly on your desktop or save them in a convenient folder. If you drag an image file or a folder full of files over a droplet, the droplet executes, playing the action on the files. (If Photoshop isn't open when the droplet is activated, the droplet automatically opens Photoshop.)

Because a droplet is a standalone program, you can pass it to other Photoshop users and use it on other computers, even cross-platform.

 If you create a droplet on a Windows computer, it can be used by a Mac computer and vice versa. All you need to do is convert it to the right platform. To make a Mac-made droplet usable with Windows, add an .exe extension after the droplet's name. To make a Windows-made droplet work on the Mac, locate the Photoshop CS application icon, and then drag the droplet over it.

Creating a droplet

The first thing you need to do before creating a droplet is to record the action that you will use when creating the droplet. If you need a refresher on recording actions, turn to Technique 8. After you record the action, follow these steps to create a droplet:

1. **Choose File⇨Automate⇨Create Droplet.**

The Create Droplet dialog box opens, as shown in Figure 9-5. You use this dialog box to name the droplet, set the location where the droplet is saved, and set how files are handled when they are modified by the droplet.

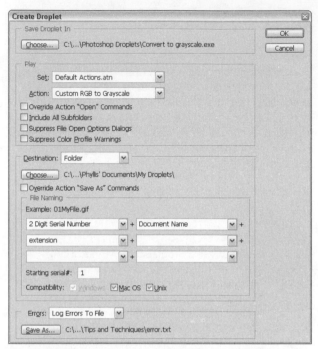

• **Figure 9-5: The Create Droplet dialog box specifies which action is encapsulated in the droplet.**

2. **Click the Choose button in the Save Droplet In area.**

   Select a folder where the droplet will be stored in the Save dialog box that opens and type a name for the droplet in the File Name (Windows)/Save As (Mac) text box. Then click Save.

 The sample droplets that come with Photoshop are stored in the Photoshop CS\Samples\ Droplets\Photoshop Droplets folder of your Photoshop installation.

3. **In the Play area, use the Set drop-down list to select the action set containing the action you want to use.**

4. **Select an action using the Action drop-down list.**

5. **Use the Destination drop-down list to select how the modified image files are saved and/or stored.**

You can select from

▶ **None:** Select this option to leave the modified image files open in Photoshop. If you select this option, skip to Step 8.

▶ **Save and Close:** Select this option to save the modified files and close them, leaving them in their original folder. If you select this option, skip to Step 8.

▶ **Folder:** Select this option to save the files and move them to a new folder. If you select this option, click Choose and use the Browse For Folder dialog box (Windows) or Choose a Destination Folder dialog box (Mac) to locate the folder where you want to store the files. Also, when you select Folder, you can also rename the files.

6. **In the File Naming area, select the options that you want to use to rename the image files.**

   Using the drop-down lists, select up to six options (refer to Figure 9-3).

   If you select one of the Serial Number options, enter the first number in the Starting Serial # text box (Photoshop automatically counts up from there).

7. **Put check marks in the Compatibility check boxes.**

   This step ensures that the renamed files work on any computer.

8. **Decide how you want errors handled by choosing an option from the Errors drop-down list.**

   Sometimes errors occur when actions are played on image files. For instance, the action specifies a specific image size minimum and the image is not large enough.

   ▶ Select **Stop for Errors** from the Errors drop-down list to halt the Batch command. A dialog box displaying the error appears and the batch operation is aborted; you need to set up the entire batch process again.

▶ Select **Log Errors to File** to send error reports to a text file. The batch processing continues even if an error occurs. If you choose this option, click the Save As button to set a folder location and name for the error log text file.

9. **When you're sure all the settings are correct, click OK.**

Photoshop creates the droplet and stores it in the folder you selected in Step 2. Figure 9-6 shows several droplets on the Windows XP desktop.

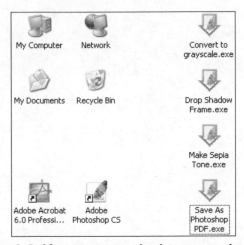

• **Figure 9-6: After you create a droplet, you can place it on your desktop for easy access.**

Using a droplet

After you create a droplet, using it to modify batches of files is simple. From your desktop, locate the folder containing the droplet (if you haven't placed it on the desktop) and set that window aside. Next, locate and select the files or folder of files that you want to modify. Drag the selected files or folder on top of the droplet. This action triggers the droplet and it goes to work, modifying the files and saving them in a new folder if you specified that when creating the droplet.

Creating droplets in ImageReady

When working on Web graphics in Photoshop's sister program, ImageReady, you can create actions using commands just like in Photoshop. But, you can also create droplets that are used to help you quickly *optimize* Web graphics, compressing them as much as possible for quick downloading.

Turn to Technique 57 to find out more about optimizing Web graphics and creating droplets using ImageReady.

Part II

Getting Images Into and Out of Photoshop

The 5th Wave   By Rich Tennant

"...and I'd also like to thank Doug Gretzel here for all his work in helping us develop our interactive, multimedia stapling division."

Technique 10

Importing Images Using a Scanner

Better quality and good prices are making peripheral devices, such as digital cameras and scanners, almost as common a household appliance as toasters and blenders. (Actually I have two digital cameras, two scanners, and only one toaster — go figure!)

Only a few years ago scanners weren't so commonplace and you had to go to a service bureau. These days, scanning images such as photographs is an everyday occurrence. This technique takes you through the world of importing images using a scanner. You find out everything you need to know about image resolution so that you can create scans that work for your project — be it a Web page, a printed item such as a brochure, or a high-end scan for offset printing.

Then, you create a scan using the simple steps that I include in this technique. Scanning causes more headaches for people and I've heard so many complaints about scans not working right that I want to help as much as I can. Because so many different types of scanners exist, I try to make this technique as generic as possible. You may find, however, a few differences between my descriptions and what you experience with your device.

You probably don't want to hear it, but of course, the first thing you really need to do is read the documentation that came with your scanner. It may be a bit on the dry side, but knowing how your scanner works is the first step on the way to getting great results with it.

What's in a Pixel?

Creating excellent scans that work for your projects is all about resolution. And, resolution boils down to pixels.

Here's a quick pixel refresher. *Pixels* are the tiny colored dots that, put together in an orderly grid, make up a Photoshop image. The display on your computer monitor is also made up of pixels. The number of screen pixels on your monitor depends on the display setting you're using. For instance, a typical setting is 1024 x 768, meaning 1,024 pixels run across the screen and 768 pixels run down the screen. Multiply them together and you get . . . well, you use a calculator. These screen pixels are so tiny that you may not be able to see them even if you flatten your nose to the screen.

To get a look at image pixels more closely, open an image in Photoshop and magnify it to 200%. (For a refresher on zooming and magnifying images, turn to Technique 5.) At 200% magnification, image pixels are magnified to four times their previous size. One image pixel now measures two screen pixels wide and two screen pixels high and 2 x 2 = 4. Next, magnify the image to 400%. That single image pixel is now magnified to sixteen times its original size and measures four screen pixels wide and four screen pixels high (4 x 4 = 16). Take a look at Figure 10-1 to see how different magnifications affect the appearance of image pixels on-screen.

Magnifying an image in Photoshop has nothing to do with the size at which an image prints — it only affects how the image looks on-screen. To view an image at its approximate print size, choose View⇨Actual Pixels.

The quality of the way an image looks on-screen and on a printed page depends upon the *resolution* of the graphic.

Images scanned for the Web need to be a resolution different from images scanned for the printed page. A typical PC monitor resolution is 96 pixels per inch (on a Mac, it's 72 ppi); this low resolution creates small file sizes and images that work well for the Web. If I print an image set at 96 ppi, it looks very pixilated, as shown in Figure 10-2. The higher the resolution, the finer and sharper a printed page looks. A typical printed image is set at 300 ppi. Many home and office printers offer resolutions upwards of 720 ppi or even 1200 ppi.

When you scan an image, you can use the scanner's software to set the resolution of the scan. Know what you are using the scanned images for — the Web or print — and set the resolution accordingly.

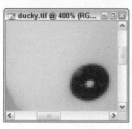

• **Figure 10-1:** Increasing the magnification makes an image appear larger on-screen but doesn't affect the printed image.

• **Figure 10-2:** Check out the pixels: 96 ppi (top), 150 ppi (left), and 300 ppi (right).

Scanning Images: Windows Users

Depending upon your scanner, you may have two import standards to choose from when scanning an image on a Windows computer. One standard is available on all scanners: TWAIN, a cross-platform interface that ensures that the software you install on your computer works correctly and consistently when you use a peripheral device, such as a scanner. The other standard, WIA, is a more recent development from Microsoft and is installed with many newer scanners. The WIA standard ensures that the software installed on your computer uses the same dialog boxes and interfaces that you typically see in Windows XP. So, when you import images into Photoshop using a scanner, you may see both of these options on the Import menu.

Which one should you use? Either standard gets you to the scanning software installed on your computer. The WIA interface inserts a few more dialog boxes that allow you to select where to save scanned images and gives you a little more control over color management. Try both and see which one you prefer. For me, I tend to use the WIA interface because of the color management options. (To find out more about color management and setting up a color management system on your computer, turn to Technique 4.)

To scan and import an image using Windows, follow these steps:

1. **Make sure your scanner is on and launch Photoshop CS.**

2. **Choose File⇨Import to view the submenu shown in Figure 10-3.**

3. **Choose WIA Support from the submenu.**

   A WIA Support wizard opens. You can select a peripheral device (see Figure 10-4). (Of course, you can go with the TWAIN option if you want. For this example, I use the WIA Support wizard.)

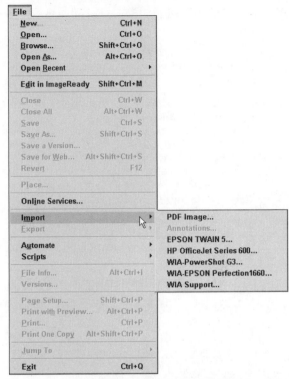

• **Figure 10-3: The Import menu displays installed scanners and lets you choose between the TWAIN and WIA standards.**

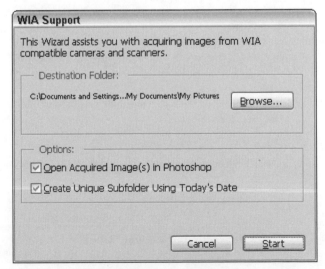

• **Figure 10-4: The WIA Support wizard makes importing images using a scanner easy.**

4. **In the Destination Folder area, click the Browse button.**

Use the Browse For Folder dialog box to select the folder where you want the scanned images stored.

5. **In the Options area, select the Open Acquired Image(s) in Photoshop option.**

You can also select the Create Unique Subfolder Using Today's Date option, if you want. This option automatically creates a folder within the destination folder you specified in Step 4, and places the scanned images in this sub-folder.

6. **Click Start to continue.**

The Select Device dialog box opens, as shown in Figure 10-5.

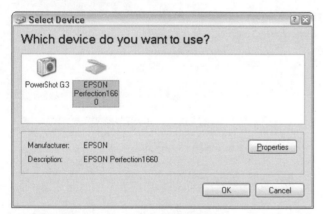

• **Figure 10-5:** In the Select Device dialog box, choose the device you want to use.

7. **Choose the device you want to use in the Select Device dialog box.**

8. **Click the Properties button.**

The Properties dialog box for your scanner opens.

Figure 10-6 shows the Properties dialog box for the scanner I'm using, an Epson Perfection 1660.

9. **Click the Color Management tab.**

The Color Management panel gives you access to the color profile associated with the scanner

(see Figure 10-7). When you installed your scanner software, chances are the software automatically installed a color profile. This color profile tells Photoshop what color space the scanner is working in and helps Photoshop adjust an image's colors as it is imported into Photoshop. If the color correction works as it should, the colors in the scanned image closely match the colors in the original photograph.

If a color profile is selected, skip to Step 12.

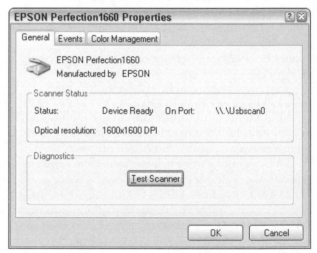

• **Figure 10-6:** Check out the properties for your scanner to see if a color profile is loaded.

10. **If you need to, click Add to load a color profile for your scanner.**

In the Add Profile Association dialog box that then appears, use the list box to select the color profile for your scanner. If you're not sure which profile is the right one for your scanner, check the documentation that came with your scanner.

 You don't need to select a color profile every time you use your scanner. You just need to set this up the first time. In the future, you can Skip Steps 7 through 12.

11. **When you find the color profile for the scanner, select it, and then click Add.**

The Add Profile Association dialog box closes, returning you to your scanner's Properties dialog box.

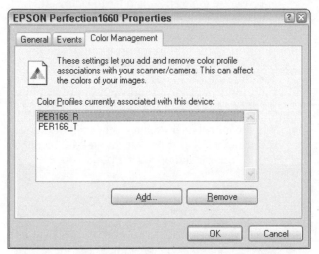

• **Figure 10-7:** If you need to, find your scanner's color profile on the Color Management tab in the Properties dialog box.

12. Click OK to return to the Select Device dialog box.

13. Click OK.

Your scanner's software takes over, opening an appropriate dialog box, similar to the one shown in Figure 10-8. Refer to your scanner's sofware manual for settings.

14. Set the resolution of your scan.

As shown in Figure 10-8, the dialog box that I use to choose settings contains a Resolution drop-down list. I can use this drop-down list to select the resolution I need, 96 ppi for Web graphics, 300 ppi for a typical printed page, 720 ppi or 1200 ppi for a fine photographic print. No doubt the dialog box you're using is different, but look around. Somewhere a text box or drop-down list is labeled Resolution.

15. Click Scan.

The scanner's dialog box closes and the scan begins. The scanned image imports and opens in Photoshop, as shown in Figure 10-9.

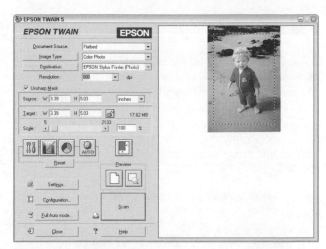

• **Figure 10-8:** Select output settings using your scanner's software.

 If you scan two or more photos at once, you can use Photoshop's new Crop and Straighten Photos command to separate them and open them in individual image windows.

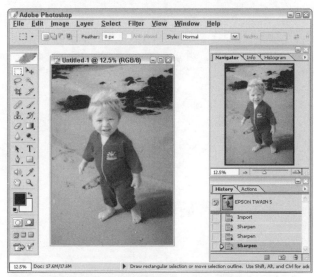

• **Figure 10-9:** The scanned image imports and opens in Photoshop.

Turn to the "Using Crop and Straighten Photos" section, later in this technique, to find out how to use the Crop and Straighten Photos command.

Scanning Images: Mac Users

Scanning images on a Mac is pretty straightforward. Peripheral devices, such as scanners, use the TWAIN compliant software to acquire images and import them into Photoshop. TWAIN is a cross-platform standard that ensures that the software you install on your computer works correctly and consistently. To find out more about the TWAIN standard, you can visit www.twain.org.

To scan and import an image on a Mac, follow these steps:

1. **Make sure your scanner is on and launch Photoshop CS.**

2. **Choose File⇨Import to view the submenu shown in Figure 10-10.**

• **Figure 10-10: The Import submenu shows the TWAIN compliant devices installed on your computer.**

3. **Choose your scanner from the Import submenu.**

Your scanner's software takes over, opening the appropriate dialog box, similar to Figure 10-11.

4. **Follow the steps outlined by your scanner's software to import the image.**

Don't forget to set the resolution of your scan. Select 96 ppi for Web graphics, 300 ppi for a typical printed page, or 720 ppi or 1200 ppi for a fine photographic print.

When your scanner finishes acquiring the image, the scanner's dialog box closes and the scanned image imports and opens in Photoshop.

Try scanning objects, too!

Try scanning objects and other items not normally used for a scan. This can come in handy when trying to design three-dimensional objects in Photoshop. For instance, if you're working on a project that includes cubes or spheres, you can scan some blocks or balls to use as a pattern to trace (see the following figure).

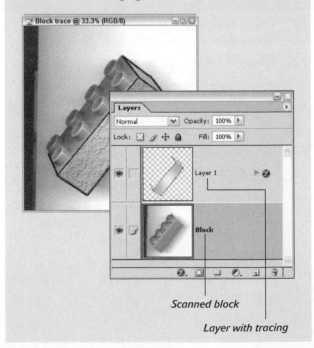

Scanned block

Layer with tracing

Using Crop and Straighten Photos

If you scan more than one photo at a time, you can use a new Photoshop CS command, Crop and Straighten Photos, to separate the photos, crop them to their edges, and then place them into their own image windows. Most times Crop and Straighten Photos works like a charm; but once in a while, it doesn't divide two photos correctly (probably because the photos are too close together and the command can't detect the edges of the photos). Overall, though, this command works pretty well and can be quite a time saver.

Here's how to use this command:

1. **Scan several photos at once and import them into Photoshop.**

   When the photos are imported into Photoshop, they appear as one giant image (see Figure 10-12).

2. **Choose File➪Automate➪Crop and Straighten Photos.**

   The command goes to work, separating and cropping the photos. When it's finished, all the photos are in their own image windows (see Figure 10-13).

 Some of the photos may need to be rotated. Choose Image➪Rotate Canvas and choose the correct rotation.

 Even though the separated photos are in their own image windows, they are not saved until you press Ctrl+S/⌘+S.

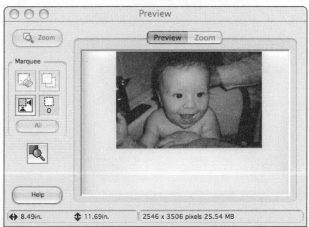

• **Figure 10-11:** Use your scanner's software to select settings and scan the image.

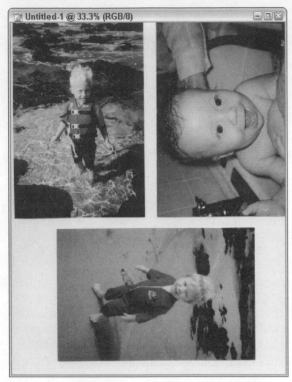

• **Figure 10-12:** When scanning several images into Photoshop, they appear in one image window.

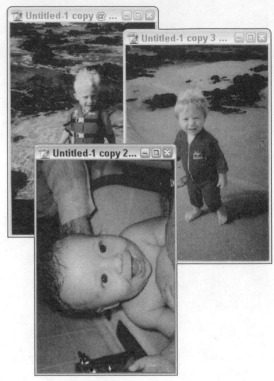

• **Figure 10-13:** After the images separate and crop, they appear in their own image windows.

Technique 11

Getting Professional Results with the Camera Raw Format

This technique dives into the world of photography exploring the truly sensational Camera Raw capabilities built into Photoshop. Introduced as a plug-in with Photoshop 7, the newly integrated Photoshop CS Camera Raw format lets you open and professionally *process* your digital negatives, which lets you set the tone, color, and brightness of your photos without losing important image data. Also, you get better resolution.

What you find in this technique is a discussion about Camera Raw, what it is, and how it works in Photoshop. You use the extensive Camera Raw interface built in to Photoshop to process your own digital photos, and then save these new originals in specific file formats depending upon your needs.

Getting to Know Camera Raw

It's best to work with the Camera Raw features just like you would with a traditional camera print. Traditional cameras use film that must be sent to a photo lab for processing. Negatives are made from the film for each picture. The photo lab creates prints by shining light through the negatives onto light-sensitive photographic paper. The photographs may differ in color, tone, and brightness depending upon how long the photographic paper is exposed to light. But throughout the entire process, the negative does not change. The prints are only affected by the amount of light passing through the negative.

Most digital cameras for consumers produce JPEG or TIF images. The JPEG format uses *lossy* compression. This means that the compression process that saves a JPEG photo can lose some of the data that makes up the image, especially if you resave the image many times. Also, when an image is saved in a format such as JPEG, the picture information is interpreted by the format, which automatically sets colors, tone, brightness, and other parameters for the photo. In other words, you can never get back to the naked image — the unaltered image that the camera captured.

Camera Raw format does not lose vital image information, nor does it format the digital negative by altering color, tone, or any other aspect of the photo. Instead Camera Raw format saves the image data as the camera captures it without further processing. This raw image is saved on your hard drive. When you open a Camera Raw photo in Photoshop, a copy of the image is opened, not the original. You use Photoshop's built-in Camera Raw interface to process the copied photo by adjusting exposure, tone, color, and other settings, creating your own original. The digital negative is never touched.

Digital photography has come a long way in the past few years. Digital cameras have become more common and cameras with high-end features are becoming more affordable. You can set many of these cameras to save photos in either JPEG or Camera Raw format. Camera manufacturers that make cameras with the Camera Raw features include Canon, Fujifilm, Leaf, Minolta, Nikon, and Olympus. To find out whether your camera can use Photoshop's Camera Raw features, go to www.adobe.com/products/photoshop/cameraraw.html for a complete list of the cameras supported by Photoshop CS's Camera Raw interface.

Using the Camera Raw Interface

When you're ready to open a Camera Raw image, double-click the image in the File Browser or choose File⇨Open and use the Open dialog box. The Camera Raw file format extension is .crw.

Whichever way you decide to open the image, the image automatically opens in the Camera Raw dialog box, as shown in Figure 11-1.

Photo processing settings

Histogram

Set resolution and color space here

Zoom box

• **Figure 11-1: The Camera Raw dialog box is used to process digital negatives.**

Opening images directly from the camera in Windows XP

Depending upon your camera, you may be able to open photos directly from your camera without downloading them first. With your camera connected to your computer, choose File⇨Open. Use the Look In drop-down list to find My Computer and select it. Your camera should be included in the list of drives and folders. Double-click the camera icon to see the images currently saved in the camera.

The Camera Raw dialog box has a lot of options to select from, but you don't need to reset them every time you open a raw image. The dialog box has what is called *sticky settings* — it saves the settings that you used last and opens with those settings selected. After tweaking settings for your camera, you can save the settings and apply them to other raw images.

The rest of this section walks you through the many features and settings available in the Camera Raw dialog box. You can use as many or as few of these settings as you need to get the results you want. If you need a specific setting, just skip to the topic that covers it.

Looking at the features

Before you do anything, take a look around the dialog box. Notice that the camera type, filename, and camera settings such as F-stop, exposure time, and lens diameter are listed in the Title bar of the dialog box (see Figure 11-2).

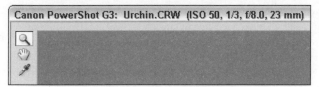

• **Figure 11-2: The Title bar lists camera information as well as the image's filename.**

Do yourself a favor and rename your digital photos

Have you noticed how inscrutable digital photo filenames are? Take CRW267_0359.CRW for instance. You would never know that this picture is of seashells.

Every time you take a camera load of pictures and download them, do yourself the favor of renaming them while you still know what they are. Put them in a folder with the day's date or a quick descriptive word, whatever. You'll thank yourself two weeks later when you're looking for that great surf photo you took. For a look at renaming files in batches, turn to Technique 9.

The image itself is viewed in a large Preview pane. The Preview pane is dynamic, so every time you make a setting change, the preview updates to let you see what you've done.

Also, notice that three tools are at the upper left as shown in Figure 11-2: the Zoom, Hand, and Eyedropper tools. As you may have guessed, the Zoom tool is for magnifying the image and the Hand tool is for moving the image around in the Preview pane. The Eyedropper tool (actually called the White Balance tool in this dialog box) is for setting the options that compensate for various lighting conditions. I discuss its use later in the section "Setting adjustment options."

The lower-left area of the dialog box contains four drop-down lists that you can use to set color space, resolution, and size. I discuss these drop-down lists in the section "Setting resolution and color space."

Below the OK and Cancel buttons at the upper-right area of the dialog box are two radio buttons: Basic and Advanced. When you select the Basic radio button, only the Adjust and Detail tabs show in the Settings area. If you select the Advanced radio button, you have access to two more tabbed panels of settings, Lens and Calibrate.

Underneath the Basic and Advanced radio buttons is a histogram, shown in Figure 11-3. This histogram shows a combined RGB histogram in white and separate red, green, and blue histograms (one for each color channel). The histogram shows the range of color values in the image.

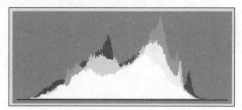

• **Figure 11-3: The Histogram determines the range for each color channel.**

Setting resolution and color space

At the bottom left of the Camera Raw dialog box are four drop-down lists (see Figure 11-4). You can set resolution, image size, bit-depth, and the color space. (*Bit-depth* is the amount of color information in a pixel.) Here's a description of each option and possible settings.

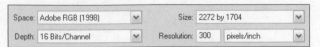

• **Figure 11-4: These drop-down lists are used to set the photo's resolution and color space.**

Color space

The Space drop-down list sets the color space. The *color space* is the range of the color spectrum (also called *gamut*) in which a device, such as a monitor or digital camera, works. (For more about color spaces and color management systems, take a look at Technique 4.)

You can choose from four options in the Space drop-down list:

✔ **Adobe RGB (1998):** This color space offers the widest range of colors. Adobe RGB is a good choice for high-quality digital photographs. I usually select this color space.

✔ **ColorMatch RGB:** Many publishers and commercial printers use this color space. If you are creating photos for offset printing, check with your printer to see whether this color space is the one to use.

✔ **ProPhoto RGB:** Kodak created this color space for its high-end professional digital cameras. ProPhoto RGB offers a wider range of colors than the other color spaces, but should only be used with Kodak cameras.

✔ **sRGB IEC61966-1:** Also called sRGB for short (for *standard RGB*), this color space offers a smaller range of colors and is a good choice for Web graphics.

Depth

The Depth drop-down list offers two bit-depth options: 8 Bits/Channel and 16 Bits/Channel. The *bit-depth* is the amount of color information in a pixel, per channel. The more bit-depth that an image has, the more colors are available. So, the higher the bit-depth, the more accurate the color representation is on-screen and the printed page.

Some typical bit-depth values are 1-bit, 8-bit, and 16-bit. For example, a 1-bit pixel has two possible color values, black and white. An 8-bit pixel has 256 possible color values, and a 16-bit pixel has 65,536 possible color values.

Because Photoshop CS now has the ability to work with 16-bit color images (Photoshop 7 does not), it's up to you to choose the bit-depth you want to use. The only word of caution is that when you select a greater bit-depth, invariably file size goes up.

Size

The Size drop-down list gives you some image size options in pixels. The image size selected by default in the drop-down list is the size at which your camera captured the image. You can scale up or down depending upon your needs.

 Scaling up can have some consequences. Because a larger image needs more pixels, Photoshop adds those pixels to the image, coloring them by selecting color from surrounding pixels. The resulting image can look fuzzy, not clear and sharp like the original.

Resolution

The Resolution text box and drop-down list let you set how many pixels per inch (ppi) (or pixels per centimeter) your image has. A higher resolution makes for a crisper-looking printed page. Typically, a better digital camera captures Camera Raw images at 240 ppi or greater. (By comparison, the same camera saves the image at 180 ppi when the image is saved as a JPEG.) A good setting for Web graphics and images is 96 ppi.

Setting adjustment options

The Adjust tab panel at the right of the dialog box lets you set the White Balance, Exposure, Shadows, Brightness, Contrast, and Saturation by using slider bars (see Figure 11-5).

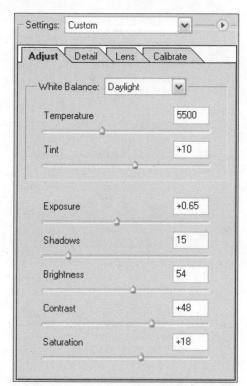

• **Figure 11-5: The Adjust tab panel lets you adjust the lighting quality and tonal values.**

White Balance

White Balance describes the lighting conditions in a photograph and how the eye perceives them.

The White Balance area contains two slider bars: Temperature and Tint. Temperature (actually expressed in Kelvin) attempts to reproduce light's actual color. At lower Temperature settings, a photo appears more cyan; at higher Temperature settings, a photo appears more yellow. The Tint slider bar adjusts the light quality. Lower Tint settings are bluish, while higher Tint settings are redder.

Another feature is the White Balance drop-down list with preset lighting configurations that attempt to re-create different types of light, such as daylight, fluorescent lighting, and flash. Figure 11-6 shows the available options on the White Balance drop-down list.

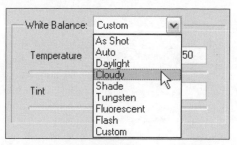

• **Figure 11-6: The White Balance drop-down list and sliders set lighting quality.**

Exposure and shadows

The Exposure slider controls highlights, while the Shadows slider controls the shadows (of course!).

When the Exposure slider is dragged left, fewer highlights appear in the photo. Drag the Exposure slider to the right and more highlights appear.

To decrease the amount of shadows, drag the Shadow slider to the left. Drag to the right to increase shadows.

 Hold down the Alt/Option key while using either of these slider bars to see a threshold view of the image. This threshold view is handy for finding the lightest and darkest areas of an image, and determining whether any shadows or highlights are getting lost (or *clipped*).

Brightness, contrast, and saturation

The Brightness, Contrast, and Saturation sliders are pretty self-explanatory; they do what they say. If you need more brightness, contrast, or saturation correction after opening the image in Photoshop, you can use the commands on the Image➪Adjustments menu.

Adding detail

The Detail tab panel offers three slider bars: Sharpness, Luminance Smoothing, and Color Noise Reduction, as shown in Figure 11-7.

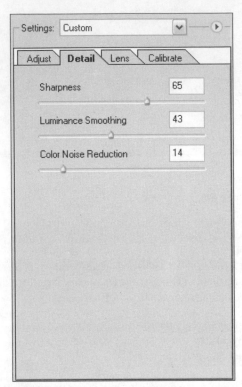

• **Figure 11-7: The Detail tab panel adjusts your photos' sharpness and reduces noise.**

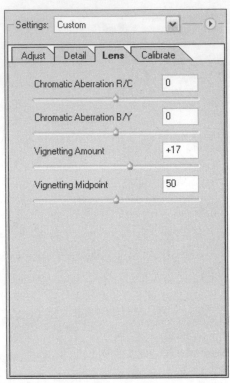

• **Figure 11-8: The Lens tab panel helps you correct color and shadow problems created by the camera lens.**

The Sharpness settings in the Camera Raw interface work pretty well. Usually, I do 10% of the sharpening here and the rest in Photoshop using the powerful Unsharp Mask. (Take a look at Technique 37 for tips on using the Unsharp Mask.)

The Luminance Smoothing and the Color Noise Reduction controls remove noise from your photos. When you use these sliders, the Camera Raw interface tries to keep as much sharpness on the edges as possible, but if you go too far, the photo can become a bit fuzzy. Use these settings with a light touch.

Adjusting lens irregularities

You can view the Lens tab panel (shown in Figure 11-8) only if you first select the Advanced radio button. The Lens tab panel is used to correct lens conditions that create problems with color focus.

Fixing chromatic aberrations

The Chromatic Aberration R/C slider (R/C stands for *Red/Cyan*) and Chromatic Aberration B/Y slider (B/Y stands for *Blue/Yellow*) corrects color problems at the edges of a digital photograph. Sometimes the colors at the edges of a photograph don't line up, causing what is called *fringing*. This fringing can create a colored halo effect that is very subtle. To see whether your photo has fringing, you need to zoom in on one of the edges of your photo at the highest magnification, 400%. Slide the Chromatic Aberration sliders back and forth to test how this fringing looks. Return the sliders to a position where you don't see any color halos.

Removing shadowed vignettes

Both the Vignetting Amount and Vignetting Midpoint sliders correct another lens defect where the corners of the photograph are darker than the center (see Figure 11-9).

• **Figure 11-9:** Shadowy vignettes at a photo's edges (top) is a problem created by the lens that Photoshop can correct (bottom).

The Vignetting Amount slider corrects the brightness at the corners of the photo. Moving the slider to the left darkens the corners, while moving the slider to the right brightens the corners.

The Vignetting Midpoint slider adjusts how the brightness moves from the center of the photo to the edges. When you move this slider to the left, the photo appears brighter in the center and darker at the edges. As you move the slider right, the brightness spreads to the photo's edges.

Calibrating color and tone

You can see the Calibrate tab panel only if the Advanced radio button is selected. This tab panel, shown in Figure 11-10, sets color and tone by adjusting the color cast in shadowed areas and using the red, green, and blue channels.

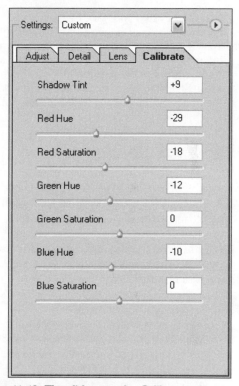

• **Figure 11-10:** The sliders on the Calibrate tab pane adjust color and tone.

Adjusting the color tone of shadows

The Shadow Tint slider works with the White Balance value set on the Adjust tab panel. After a white balance is set, a tinted colorcast can still remain in the shadowed portions of a photo. Move the slider left to increase the greenish cast of shadows; move the slider right to make the shadows redder. If you hold down the Alt/Option key while moving the slider, a threshold view of the shadows in the image indicates whether some shadowed areas are getting lost.

Calibrating the color channels

The Red Hue/Saturation, Green Hue/Saturation, and Blue Hue/Saturation sliders adjust the actual colors in the image. Use these sliders to adjust skin tones or any other image colors until they appear right to your eye.

 Don't forget that you have the power of Photoshop at your fingertips after opening the image. You don't need to do all your adjustments using the Camera Raw interface. If a color cast doesn't look right after you open the image in Photoshop, use the commands on the Image⇨Adjustments menu to help out.

Saving Your Settings

After you adjust the settings to your satisfaction, you can save them for future use. To save your settings, follow these steps:

1. **Click the arrow at the right side of the Camera Raw dialog box and choose Save Settings, as shown in Figure 11-11.**

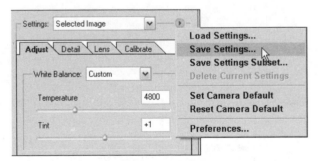

• **Figure 11-11: Click the tiny arrow button to open the dialog box menu.**

The Save Raw Conversion Settings dialog box opens, as shown in Figure 11-12.

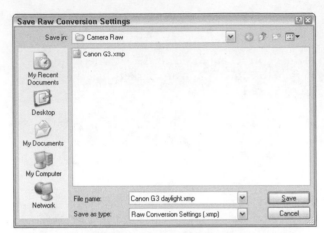

• **Figure 11-12: Save your custom settings using the Save Raw Conversion Settings dialog box.**

2. **Enter a name for your settings in the File Name text box (Windows) or Save As (Mac) text box.**

If you have more than one digital camera, you can use the model number or brand of the camera for a name. That way, you know which camera setting to select in the future.

3. **Click Save.**

The new setting is automatically selected in the Settings drop-down list.

 If you want to use saved settings for other photographs, you can select them from the Settings drop-down list in the Camera Raw dialog box or choose Automate⇨Apply Camera Raw Settings in the File Browser.

For details on applying settings using the File Browser, turn to "Applying Camera Raw Settings to Several Images."

Saving the Imported Camera Raw Image

When you finish adjusting the photograph using the Camera Raw interface, click OK in the Camera Raw dialog box to open the image in Photoshop. A copy of the original camera raw file opens. (Remember that one benefit of using Camera Raw is that the digital negative never gets touched.) This file is not saved until you press Ctrl+S/⌘+S or choose File⇨Save.

Depending upon your use for the photograph, you can save the image in several file formats, including Photoshop's native PSD, TIF, JPEG, or as a Photoshop PDF.

Applying Camera Raw Settings to Several Images

Dealing with that huge Camera Raw dialog box every time you want to open a Camera Raw file is a bit much, especially if you save your adjustment settings. Thankfully, the File Browser makes applying your saved Camera Raw settings to one or more images at a time easy. Here's how:

1. Open the File Browser and move to the folder where the Camera Raw photos are stored.

2. Select the Camera Raw photos to which you want to apply your saved settings.

You can select one or more photos.

3. Choose Automate⇨Apply Camera Raw Settings.

The Apply Camera Raw Settings dialog box opens with the Basic radio button selected, as shown in Figure 11-13.

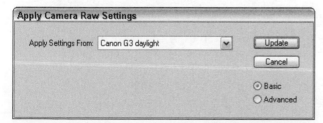

• **Figure 11-13: The Basic radio button is selected when the Apply Camera Raw Settings dialog box opens.**

4. Use the Apply Settings From drop-down list to select the custom settings that you want to use.

If the setting you select works to your satisfaction, skip to Step 6. If you need to make some adjustments before applying the Camera Raw settings, continue with Step 5.

5. Click the Advanced radio button to see more settings (see Figure 11-14).

When you select the Advanced radio button, the dialog box expands, giving you access to all the Camera Raw settings.

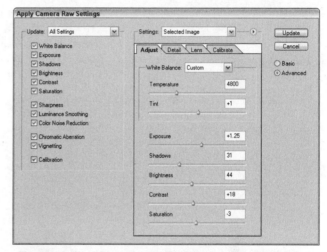

• **Figure 11-14: After selecting the Advanced radio button, all the Camera Raw settings are available.**

6. Select the settings you want to include and adjust any sliders necessary.

Use the check boxes at the left side of the dialog box to include or exclude any settings.

7. Click Update.

The Camera Raw settings are applied to the photos you selected in the File Browser.

Technique 12

Using Tablets and Pressure-Sensitive Devices

Save Time By

✔ Choosing a tablet

✔ Configuring stylus settings

✔ Practicing with your tablet

Whether you're a Photoshop professional or hobbyist, you may find yourself wishing, at times, for a better or easier input device than a mouse. Some folks that I've spoken with consider drawing with a mouse like trying to draw with a chunk of wood or a bar of soap. A drawing tablet and pen (also called a *stylus*) can be an answer for those artists who want a more reality-based drawing experience. (See Figure 12-1.) Using a tablet and stylus feels much closer to sketching with a traditional pencil or pen than using a mouse on a mouse pad does.

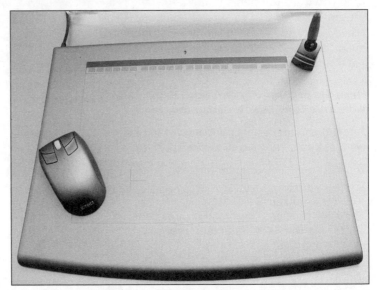

• Figure 12-1: A drawing tablet and stylus can easily double your output and increase the overall speed and quality of your Photoshop work.

A drawing tablet and stylus can be used anytime that you need to perform some type of painting or stroking. This includes using any of the brush tools, Dodge and Burn tools, Eraser tools, Pen tools, Stamp tools, Healing Brush and Patch tools, and selection tools. (Did I miss anything?) As you can see, virtually every tool can be used when drawing or editing with a stylus.

Another feature of a tablet and stylus is the pressure sensitivity that enables you to draw more realistically. With different strokes, you can create lines that are thicker or thinner, more opaque or translucent, depending on the amount of pressure that you use as you drag the stylus across the tablet.

But, before you go off and buy a tablet, take one out for a test drive. Find a friend who has a tablet, bring some coffee and muffins, and doodle for an hour. Or go to your local computer store and check out the tablet display. Don't expect great results right from the start when drawing with a stylus. The feel is different from a traditional pencil on paper. Although the stylus feels more like a traditional pen or pencil, the tablet doesn't feel like paper. Artists who are used to working with traditional media will need to get used to this. You need to practice and practice, and then practice some more to find out how you like to work with a tablet, what brush settings you like, how hard you like to press, and many other factors.

 If you're used to drawing with pencil and paper and find the tablet surface too smooth and slippery, tape a piece of your regular drawing paper to the tablet and use the stylus to draw on top of that. The grain and roughness of the paper can make you feel right at home and give you more control.

 After I purchased my first tablet, hooked it up to my computer, and got used to working with it, I couldn't believe how fast I could work! My output per hour doubled at the least. Also, after intense sessions that would last for hours, my hand wasn't stiff or sore. If you get the chance, try out a tablet. You really might like it.

When buying a tablet, one big question is which one? Several tablet manufacturers exist, including AIPTEK, GTCO CalComp Inc., Summagraphic, and Wacom. Most of these include Windows and Mac drivers, but some only include Windows drivers (sorry Mac users). The best known of these companies is Wacom. Wacom's tablets are generally considered the best artistic input devices because of

their added levels of sensitivity (1024 compared to other manufacturers' 512) and their *tilt* capabilities. (When you're drawing with a Wacom stylus, the width of the stroke can vary depending on the angle or tilt at which you hold the pen.) Also, all Wacom tablets are Windows and Mac compatible. However, pick a tablet based on your needs and your pocketbook. Super-sensitivity may not be something you need, and a $130 tablet is a lot less expensive than one that sells for $549.

Another question that comes up when considering tablets is which size should you buy? Tablets come in a range of sizes including 4 x 5, 6 x 8, 9 x 12, and 12 x 18 inches. Consider the type of work that you do, how big your strokes tend to be when drawing, and the size of your monitor. If you have a small monitor and buy a large tablet, you'll be all over the monitor in no time; or if you have a large monitor and buy a small tablet, you may find that you use up the tablet area before you've touched half the available monitor area. I have a 21-inch monitor and use a 9-x-12-inch tablet. They work together really well. Most of the time, I don't use the entire tablet area, but when I get painting, my strokes can get quite large and I don't run out of room on the bigger tablet.

Saving the pain!

When you're editing and working on images in Photoshop, hours can go by like nothing. (You may at some point think, "Wait a minute! I'm sure I looked at the clock only a few minutes ago, but the clock says it's been two hours!") Cricks in the neck and aching arms are standard territory for many graphic artists. Some people use a stylus instead of a mouse because of arm fatigue or carpal tunnel syndrome. Instead of having to move the cursor by dragging a mouse around, you can just point and tap. This avoids the excessive wrist and arm mousing motions that can lead to pain.

Configuring a Tablet

After you buy a tablet and get started with it, you need to configure its settings. Selecting settings isn't a one-time thing, however. As you work with the tablet and stylus, you get used to the feel and possibly will need to modify settings.

Some settings that need to be configured include how fast you tap the pen to set up a double-tap (which works just like the double-click on a mouse), pressure-sensitivity, and *mapping* (the amount of tablet area that is used to cover the monitor area). Typically, you can find the applet that's used to configure the tablet on the Start⇨All Programs menu (Windows) or Applications/Wacom (Mac). Figure 12-2 shows a Wacom Tablet configuration screen.

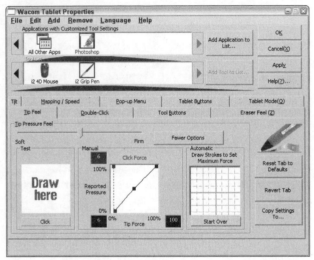

• **Figure 12-2:** This is the Windows configuration dialog box for the Wacom Intuos 2 tablet.

The following two sections show you how to configure double-taps and pen pressure. Depending on the type of tablet and stylus that you own, you probably need to set up some other features. If you need help setting up these features, take a look at the documentation that came with the tablet, or choose Help in the tablet's configuration dialog box.

Setting double-tap speed

To access stylus features in the configuration dialog box, you need to tap the stylus on the tablet to let the configuration program know that the stylus is active. When you do, several tab panels that are used to set up stylus features appear in the configuration dialog box shown in Figure 12-3.

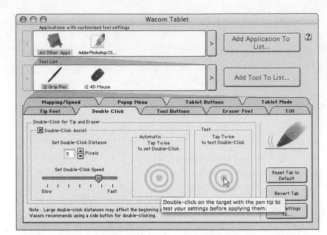

• **Figure 12-3:** Tap your tablet to access tab panels for stylus features.

Here's how to set up your double-tap:

1. **Click the Double Click tab to access that panel.**

2. **In the Automatic area, double-tap the bull's eye.**

   The tablet configuration program automatically adjusts the Set Double-Click Speed slider to how fast you tap.

3. **In the Test area, double-tap the bull's eye to confirm that the double-tap speed is set correctly.**

   If your confirmation double-tap matches the set speed, you get a thumbs-up. (See Figure 12-4.)

4. **Click OK to close the configuration dialog box and save your settings.**

Setting pen pressure

Pen pressure settings should be adjusted as you get used to using the tablet. When you first start using a tablet, you may find yourself pressing harder than you normally would with pencil and paper. Then, as you grow more comfortable using the tablet, your maximum pressure evens out to what's comfortable for your hand. Here's how:

1. **Click the Tip Feel tab to view that tab panel. (See Figure 12-5.)**

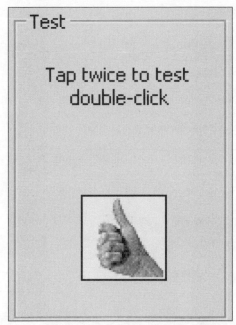

• **Figure 12-4:** When your tap matches the setting, a thumbs-up gives confirmation.

2. In the Automatic area, press as hard as you can while doodling in the grid area. (See Figure 12-6.)

The tablet's configuration program automatically sets the weight of your stroke in the Manual area text boxes shown in Figure 12-7.

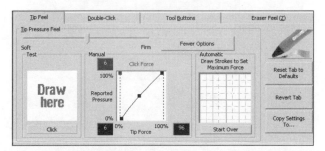

• **Figure 12-5:** The Tip Feel tab is used to configure the pen's pressure sensitivity.

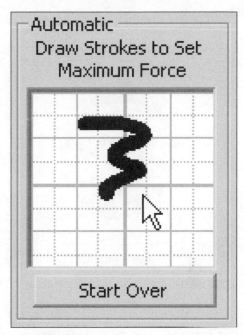

• **Figure 12-6:** Stroke on the grid to adjust your maximum stroke.

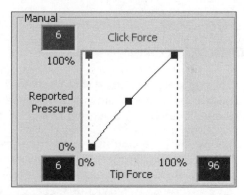

• **Figure 12-7:** Your stroke pressure is automatically recorded in the Manual area grid and Tip Force text boxes.

3. Doodle in the Test area to see if the pressure sensitivity is set to your liking. (See Figure 12-8.)

If you need to reset the amount of pressure that you use, start again at Step 2.

4. Click OK to close the configuration dialog box and save your settings.

• **Figure 12-8: Doodle in the Test area to make sure that the pressure sensitivity setting is right.**

Getting Started with Your Tablet

So how do you start practicing with a tablet? When you consider how many brushes and brush settings are available, it can be a bit overwhelming.

Simple is best. Select a medium-size brush — say about 20 pixels in diameter, with a hardness setting of 100 percent. Stick to black and white for now. Create a new white canvas by choosing File➪New, and then doodle! Draw circles and rectangles, and get a feel for how the stylus moves on the tablet surface.

After you get comfortable using a simple brush, start experimenting with the brush combinations in the Brushes palette. Many settings use pressure sensitivity and pen tilt to shape brush strokes. I discuss creating brushes and selecting pressure-sensitive brush settings in detail in Technique 23.

nik multimedia penPalette

nik multimedia offers some great filters and plug-ins that extend the capabilities of Photoshop. penPalette is an excellent program that lets you set up filter effects such as color, tone, and noise by using custom dialog boxes (shown in the following figure). *Then,* using your tablet and stylus, you can brush the effects on in the areas where you want them. Check out penPalette at `www.nikmultimedia.com`.

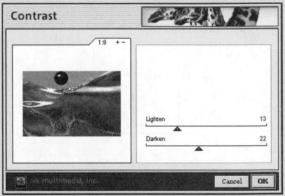

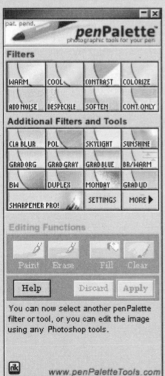

Technique 13

Printing to a Desktop Printer

Save Time By

✔ Solving resolution issues

✔ Selecting the right printer

✔ Setting printing options

Have printer, will print, right? Well, maybe. When everything is working correctly, printing is easy and you get the results that you want. When something is out of whack — for instance, your image resolution is low so you end up with pixilated output or the color you see on the monitor does not match the printed page — things can get a little out of hand.

This technique covers the easy aspects of printing and the not-so-easy aspects, like the gnarly glitches that lead to headaches and hair pulling. First, you find out how image resolution relates to the printed page. Next, you discover how to set a default printer and set printer-specific options. Then, you take a look at paper options and other printing options available to you in Photoshop. The end of this technique covers the three commands that you can use to print your images. By the way, if you're preparing artwork for a commercial printer, turn to Technique 14, where you can find much of the information that you need to make your offset printing project a success.

Resolving Resolution: Getting the Apples and Oranges to Line Up

Sometimes when Photoshop users print an image that they've been working on, they're upset that the printed image doesn't look like the image on the monitor. The printed image looks jaggy or *pixilated*. When comparing an on-screen image to the image on the printed page, it's like comparing apples and oranges: The screen image is composed of square *pixels* and the printed image is composed of tiny round dots, and (here's the important part) both devices deliver high-quality images at *different* resolutions.

Pixels are the tiny squares that make up Photoshop images. Pixels are very small and when viewed from a distance, the colors in these tiny pixels combine to make up the image you see. Image resolution on the screen is discussed by using the term *pixels per inch* or *ppi*. Typical Web graphics are saved at 72 or 96 ppi. (A Mac monitor's normal ppi is 72 and a PC monitor's maximum ppi is 96.) All the images that you create in Photoshop look great at 100% magnification on the monitor at 96 ppi.

Printed images, on the other hand, are created with tiny round dots of ink or toner. Image resolution for the printed page is discussed in *dots per inch* or *dpi*. A square inch removed from an image printed at 96 dpi contains 96 tiny dots across and 96 tiny dots down, making 9,216 dots in that one-inch area. A square inch removed from an image printed at 300 dpi contains 300 dots across and 300 dots down, for a total of 90,000 dots per square inch. As you can imagine, having more dots packed into an inch of printed area makes for a smoother-looking image. A typical LaserJet prints good-quality images at 300 dpi. Many home printers even go as high as 720 dpi. Commercial imagesetters can print images at 1200 dpi, 2400 dpi, and up.

Take a look at Figure 13-1. I saved the same image at three different resolutions. Check out how the different resolutions look on the printed page.

So, where does this leave you when you want to make great prints? First off, look at the documentation that came with your printer and find out what the maximum resolution output is for the printer. Next, choose Image➪Image Size to open the Image Size dialog box shown in Figure 13-2.

Take a look at the Resolution text box in the Document Size area. What does it say — 72 ppi, 96 ppi, 150 ppi, or 300 ppi? If you're at the upper end (250 ppi or 300 ppi) your image will, most likely, print well and look pretty good. If your image is at the lower end, say 100 ppi, you're going to have problems with dots and jaggies. You need to spend a little time experimenting with printing your image at different resolutions to see what kind of results you can get with your printer. (Also, some printers need special paper to create quality images. If you're printing on standard office paper, chances are that you're not going to get very good results.)

• **Figure 13-1:** The same image saved at 72 ppi (top), 150 ppi (middle), and 300 ppi (bottom).

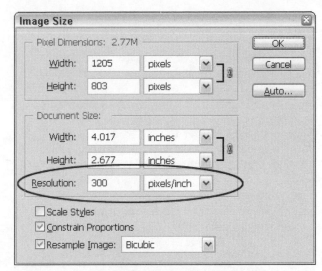

• **Figure 13-2: Use the Image Size dialog box to find out the resolution of your image.**

If you need to change the resolution of your image to make it look better in print, you can do it in one of two ways — by using the Image Size dialog box shown in Figure 13-2 or by using Photoshop's Print Preview feature. The Image Size dialog box gives you more control over the exact resolution, whereas the Print Preview dialog box lets Photoshop come up with the resolution based on the scaling size that you select.

To set a new resolution by using the Image Size dialog box:

1. **With the image open in Photoshop, choose Image⇨Image Size to open the Image Size dialog box shown in Figure 13-2.**

2. **Enter a value in the Resolution text box in either pixels per inch or pixels per centimeter.**

 Here's another way to let Photoshop help you out. In the Image Size dialog box, click Auto to open the Auto Resolution dialog box shown in Figure 13-3. Enter a line screen setting of 133 lines per inch (or 52 lines per centimeter), and then select a Quality radio button to define the output quality that you want. Click OK to close the Auto Resolution dialog box and return to the Image Size dialog box. Based on your selections in the Auto Resolution dialog

box, Photoshop calculates the resolution that it thinks will work best and enters it in the Resolution text box. Try printing with this resolution and see if the results work for you.

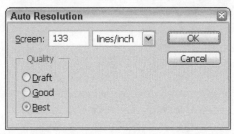

• **Figure 13-3: Use the Auto Resolution dialog box to let Photoshop calculate a resolution for you.**

3. **Optional: Uncheck the Resample Image check box.**

If you turn off this option, Photoshop doesn't add or subtract pixels (depending on whether you are increasing or decreasing the resolution). Photoshop leaves the pixels intact and changes only how many pixels print per inch. (Test this and see if it works for your printer.)

4. **Click OK.**

The Image Size dialog box closes and Photoshop adjusts the resolution of your image. Now you're ready to make a test print and see if the image prints to your satisfaction.

 If you find that the resolution you set doesn't work, you can always return to the original resolution by using the History palette to select a history state before the resolution change. To find out more about the History palette, turn to Technique 7.

To let Photoshop set the resolution by using Print with Preview:

1. **With the image open in Photoshop, choose File⇨Print with Preview.**

In the Print dialog box that opens (see Figure 13-4), use the Scaled Print Size area of the dialog box to set the size of the image on the printed page.

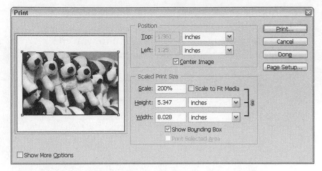

• **Figure 13-4:** Use the Scaled Print Size area to let Photoshop figure out the resolution.

2. **Enter a percentage in the Scale text box, select the Scale to Fit Media check box, or enter actual printed dimensions in the Height and Width text boxes.**

Percentages in the Scale text box work just like percentages when zooming in and out in Photoshop. 100% scale prints the image at actual size, 200% scale prints the image at twice its actual size, and 50% scale prints the image at half its actual size.

 By changing the scale of the image in the Print Preview dialog box, you're only changing the size of the printed image, not the size of the actual image.

 Scaling the printed image greater than 100% lowers image resolution, and scaling the image below 100% increases resolution.

3. **Click Print to continue with the printing process.**

Selecting a Printer

The first step on the path to printing nirvana is to pick the printer that you're going to use. The process is a little different for Windows and Mac users, though it all boils down to selecting a currently installed printer as your default printer.

Or, if the printer that you want to use is not installed, you can install the *printer drivers* that you need.

What you're doing when you install a printer on your computer is actually installing printer drivers, the software that tells Windows or Mac OS, the printer, and Photoshop how to translate your images from the computer to the printed page. Normally, you want to select a printer that's directly hooked up to your computer or available via a network. However, if you're preparing artwork for commercial printing and the printing company has asked that you select a high-end printer such as an imagesetter, you can install printer drivers even if that printer isn't connected to your computer.

To select a default printer in Windows XP, use the following steps:

1. **Choose Start➪Printers and Faxes to open the Printers and Faxes dialog box shown in Figure 13-5.**

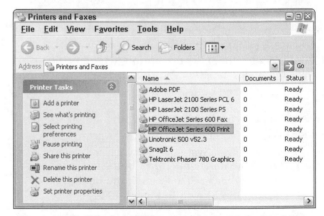

• **Figure 13-5:** Windows XP users can set a default printer with the Printers and Faxes dialog box.

2. **Right-click the printer that you want to use as your default printer and select Set as Default Printer from the context-sensitive menu, as shown in Figure 13-6.**

If you want to install a new printer, click Add a Printer in the Printer Tasks area at the left of the Printers and Faxes dialog box, and then follow the Add Printer Wizard directions.

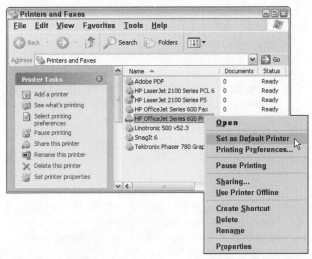

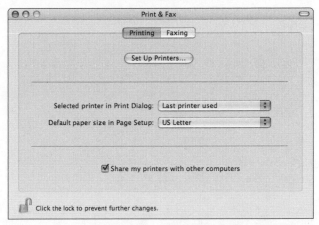

• **Figure 13-7: The Print & Fax dialog box lets you install printers and select a default printer.**

• **Figure 13-8: Use the Printer List to designate a default printer.**

• **Figure 13-6: Right-click the printer that you want to use as the default and choose Set as Default Printer.**

 If you want to change printers when working in Photoshop, choose File⇨Page Setup and select the printer that you want to use from the Printers drop-down list in the Page Setup dialog box. To find out more about the Page Setup dialog box, take a look at the following section, "Setting Paper Size."

To set a default printer in Mac OS X, do the following:

1. **On the Apple menu, choose System Preferences or click the System Preferences icon in the Dock.**

2. **In the System Preferences dialog box, click Print & Fax to open the Print & Fax dialog box shown in Figure 13-7.**

3. **Click the Set Up Printers button to open the Printer List shown in Figure 13-8.**

4. **Select the printer that you want to use as the default printer, and then click Make Default.**

If you want to install a new printer, click Add and use the dialog box pane that slides down to select printer specifications.

Setting Paper Size

The Page Setup dialog box is used to select the page orientation and the paper size that you're going to print on.

In Photoshop, choose File⇨Page Setup to open the Page Setup dialog box. Figure 13-9 shows the settings available for a Lexmark C912 color laser printer in both the Mac OS X and Windows XP Page Setup dialog boxes.

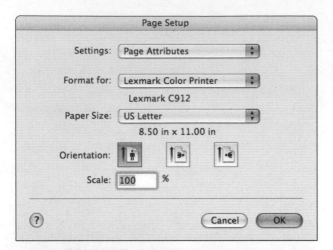

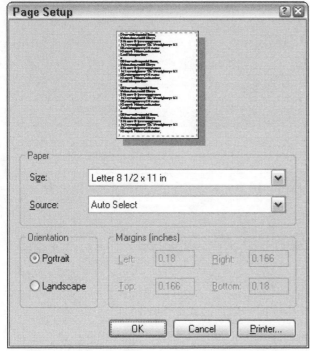

• **Figure 13-9:** Use the Page Setup dialog box to set paper size and orientation.

The Page Setup dialog box changes depending on the type of printer that you have installed, but the following options are always available:

- ✔ **Paper Size:** Use this drop-down list to select from a list of standard paper sizes. Select the paper size that you need for your project.

- ✔ **Source (Windows XP only):** This drop-down list is used to select whether you want to manually feed the paper into the printer or select another paper cartridge (if your printer has more than one).

- ✔ **Orientation:** Select either radio button to set whether the image prints upright on the page (*portrait* orientation) or prints sideways (*landscape* orientation).

- ✔ **Scale (Mac OS X only):** You can enter a percentage in the scale text box to change the size of the printed image. Although this feature does work, it depends on the printer to do the scaling, not Photoshop. So if you want to change the printed size of your image, you're better off using the Scaled Print Size area in the Print dialog box accessed by choosing File➪Print with Preview, as discussed in "Resolving Resolution: Getting the Apples and Oranges to Line Up," earlier in this technique.

> In Windows XP, if you want to select a new printer or set printer-specific options, click Printer. To select a new printer in Mac OS X, use the Format For drop-down list.

Setting Printing Options

To make your project as perfect as possible, you can select a few other printing options by using the Print with Preview command.

Open the Print dialog box by choosing File⇨ Print with Preview (see Figure 13-10), and take a look at the options. Be sure to select Show More Options and then select Output from the drop-down list to see all the settings that the dialog box has to offer.

✔ Use the **Position** area at the top of the dialog box to set exactly where your image will print on the page. You can select the Center Image option, or type exact measurements into the Top and Left text boxes.

✔ If you use one of the Marquee Tools to select an area of the image before you open the Print dialog box, you can print just that selected area by selecting the **Print Selected Area** check box (grayed out in Figure 13-10).

✔ Click **Page Setup** to access the Page Setup dialog box described in "Setting Paper Size," earlier in this technique. Use this dialog box to set paper size and orientation, select a different printer, and set printer properties.

✔ Click **Background** to open the Color Picker and select a background color that fills in all the unused white areas of the printed page.

✔ Add a black border to the image by clicking **Border** and entering a value in millimeters, inches, or points.

✔ Add printer's marks by selecting any of the following check boxes: **Calibration Bars, Registration Marks, Corner Crop Marks,** or **Center Crop Marks.**

✔ Select the **Description** check box to add a printed description underneath the image on the printed page. You can enter the text that's used for the description in the File Info dialog box, which you can open by choosing File⇨File Info. Type the text in the dialog box's Description text box.

✔ Print image file information above the image by selecting the **Labels** check box. This option can come in handy if you print many images and want to remember which image filename goes with which printed image.

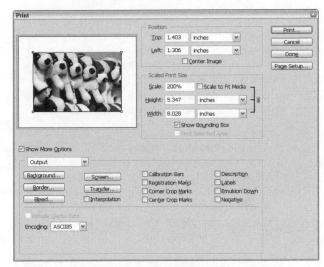

• **Figure 13-10: Special printing options can make your printed project perfect.**

When you finish selecting the printing options that you need, click Done to save the settings and close the Print dialog box, or click Print to print the image.

Let It Rip: Printing Those Pages

After you do all the legwork — you set image resolution, selected a printer, set paper size and orientation, and selected all the printing options you need — you're ready to print. This all may seem like a ton of work (actually, it is!) but, after you select the settings that you need, you don't have to select them again. Photoshop remembers your settings for you. So, from here on out, you can just flat out print your images or perform a few minor tweaks if you have a special image. (For instance, you might need to change the scale of the printed image.)

Photoshop, being the versatile and deep program that it is, offers not one but three commands that you can use to print your image. They're listed here, from the simplest bare bones command to the one that offers the most options:

- ✔ Choose File➪Print One Copy or press Alt+Ctrl+ Shift+P/Option+⌘+Shift+P to print (you guessed it) one copy of your image without having to click Print in any dialog boxes. This option automatically uses the printer and paper options that you selected by using the Page Setup and Print with Preview commands earlier in this technique.

- ✔ Choose File➪Print or press Ctrl+P/⌘+P to open the simple Print dialog box shown in Figure 13-11. You can use this dialog box to have one last chance at selecting a printer and setting printer-specific options. In addition, you can choose whether the entire image or just a selected area of the image prints and how many copies are printed. Click OK to print.

- ✔ Choose File➪Print with Preview to open the Print dialog box that contains all the possible printing options in Photoshop. (Refer to Figure 13-10.) After you select the options that you need, click Print. The Print dialog box opens (see Figure 13-11), giving you a last chance to select printer settings. Click OK to print.

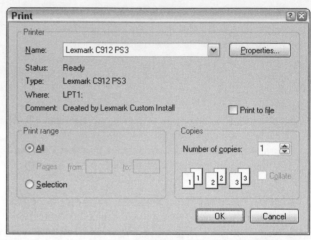

• **Figure 13-11:** This Print dialog box is used to set printer options and how many copies are printed.

Technique 14

Getting Files Ready for Offset Printing

Save Time By

- Selecting prepress settings
- Soft proofing your project
- Checking for out-of-gamut colors
- Adding spot color channels

Photoshop includes many high-end features that let users create professional-quality separations for high-quality offset printing. Typically, you create your Photoshop projects in RGB (red, green, blue) color mode; this is based on the colored light projected by your monitor. Commercial printing presses use a different color mode, CMYK (cyan, magenta, yellow, black), based on the inks used by the presses. Converting RGB images to CMYK mode and getting the printed results to match your monitor can be a time-consuming and sometimes frustrating process.

Using the tools included with Photoshop, you can cut down on the frustration by selecting CMYK prepress settings provided by your commercial printer, and *soft proofing* your project files — previewing a fairly accurate approximation of the printed image on-screen. In addition, you can check the colors in your image to make sure they are all printable. *Out-of-gamut* (non-printable) colors can then be corrected before your project goes out the door.

This technique walks you through the world of offset printing and preparing files for high-end output. You find out how to select color settings based on printing press settings, convert the image to CMYK mode, soft proof your project, and add printer's marks. From there, you find out what spot colors are and how you can use them to give your projects real visual punch.

Although some folks might find this all a bit daunting, don't worry! I explain everything as simply as possible, and if you follow the step-by-step directions, you shouldn't have trouble — even if you've never worked with a commercial printer before.

How Offset Printing Works

When you prepare a project, such as a brochure, poster, book, and so on, for commercial printing, you need to work with a commercial printer and possibly a service bureau.

Traditionally, a service bureau uses your prepared Photoshop files to either print the image with a high-resolution printer, giving you camera-ready output, or (more likely) images the files onto film. If you get camera-ready output, the commercial printer uses a camera or scanner to capture the output and create film.

However, because many graphic artists have the ability to save files on transportable large storage media, such as writable CD-ROMs, Zip drives, and removable storage media, the artists skip the service bureau entirely, cutting out the intermediate step of film or camera-ready output. Instead, they go directly to the commercial printer with their files. Many commercial printers work with Photoshop, so files saved in the native Photoshop PSD format are usually acceptable. However, some printers may prefer to use encapsulated PostScript (EPS) files.

The commercial printer takes any of these media — camera-ready output, film, or computer files — and uses them to make *printing plates*. Printing plates are usually made out of acid-etched metal. If your project uses more than one color, one plate is created for each color. The plates are put on large rollers on a printing press by the press operator, a *pressman*. The pressman uses registration marks to make sure that all the plates are exactly aligned so that the colors line up. He or she then runs the press. As the rollers rotate, the plates are dipped in ink. The inked plate is then rolled across paper, transferring the ink to the paper.

After the ink dries, the paper is trimmed and folded as necessary, using *crop marks* as guides. The *print job* is then stapled or bound, depending upon the number of pages. The completed print job is packed into boxes and shipped to you.

Talk to the commercial printer or service bureau first!

Many commercial printers and service bureaus use Photoshop, so they may ask for regular Photoshop PSD files. To ensure that your files work for the printer or service bureau, talk to them first. They'll tell you what printer to specify, which printer's marks to select, and any other specialized output settings that should be used. If this is too much for you to deal with, many printers and service bureaus will even take your completed Photoshop files and perform any conversions or add the necessary output settings for you.

Working with CMYK

Computer monitors display color by blending red, green, and blue light; this is called RGB color mode. You typically use RGB mode when working on projects in Photoshop. Printing presses create color by blending cyan, magenta, yellow, and black inks; this color mode is called CMYK. Because RGB mode and CMYK mode create color in such different ways — one uses lights in three colors, and the other uses inks in four colors — it's very hard to convert colors exactly from RGB to CMYK and get the results that you want. However, Photoshop's color management system helps with the conversion by letting you select standard printing setups, and proofing the settings by printing a color proof and matching it to the proof on-screen.

Here's a checklist that you need to follow when working on a project that will end up as CMYK separations, ready for offset printing:

1. **Make sure that your monitor is correctly calibrated. (See Technique 4.)**

2. **Convert your RGB image to CMYK color mode.**

3. **Call your commercial printer and get the custom CMYK settings for the printing press and paper type you're using.**

   Different types of paper absorb ink in different ways, so the amount of ink used needs to be adjusted depending on the paper.

4. Enter the custom CMYK settings into Photoshop by using the Color Settings dialog box and choosing Edit⮕Color Settings/Photoshop⮕ Color Settings.

5. Use the custom CMYK settings to soft proof your art, previewing how the image will look when printed as I describe in "Setting up soft proofing."

6. Look at your image with Photoshop's Out-of-Gamut feature, adjusting any colors that aren't printable.

7. Use the Unsharp Mask to resharpen the image.

Take a look at Technique 37 for more information about the Unsharp Mask feature.

8. Soft proof again to be sure that the image looks just the way you want it.

9. Print a CMYK proof by using a high-end color PostScript printer, and then use a *spectro-colorimeter* (a machine that measures color values) to determine the exact colors in your image.

Commercial printers usually help you with this step. If any of the colors are off, readjust the Photoshop image, and then print and analyze another proof. (Using adjustment layers is a great way to make color corrections. Check out Technique 22 to find out more about adjustment layers.)

10. Using the Print Preview dialog box, set up the various printer's marks that you need.

The printer's marks include registration marks, crop marks, and a calibration bar (used for checking the colors). Check with your commercial printer to see which printer's marks they recommend using.

11. If your commercial printer doesn't accept Photoshop PSD files, create CMYK separations for your image saved in EPS format.

Phew! Some list, huh? The next six sections take you through these steps, showing you how to convert your image from RGB to CMYK, enter custom CMYK

printing press settings, set up soft proofing, check for unprintable colors, add the printer's marks that you need, and then create CMYK separations. I know it sounds like a lot, but take it step by step and you discover that this isn't so hard after all.

Entering and saving custom CMYK printer settings

Choosing custom CMYK settings gives you more control over the amount of ink coverage that a printing press uses when printing your project. You can get these custom settings from your commercial printer. Many times, the default settings that come with Photoshop (such as the U.S. Prepress Defaults) are good enough and the printer specifies them. Here's how to set up custom CMYK settings:

1. Choose Edit⮕Color Settings/Photoshop⮕ Color Settings.

The Color Settings dialog box opens, as shown in Figure 14-1, ready for you to select the prepress settings that you need.

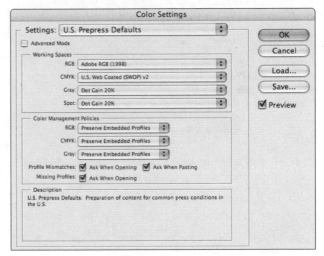

• **Figure 14–1:** The Color Settings dialog box is used to enter custom CMYK prepress settings.

2. In the Working Spaces area, use the CMYK drop-down list to select the prepress settings that you need. (See Figure 14-2.)

If you aren't in the United States, select prepress settings based on your geographic location.

If one of the predefined prepress settings works for you, you do not need to create a custom CMYK setting, so skip to Step 9.

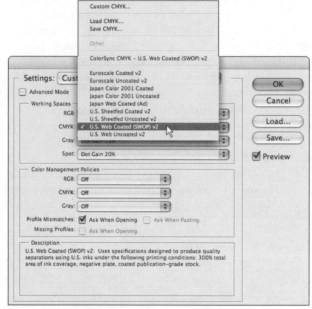

• **Figure 14-2:** Select one of the prepress settings that matches the press and paper type that you're using.

3. If you need to select custom settings, choose Custom from the CMYK drop-down list.

The Custom CMYK dialog box opens, as shown in Figure 14-3, giving you access to ink settings.

4. Type a name for the custom CMYK settings in the Name text box.

5. Select an ink type from the Ink Colors drop-down list, and use the Dot Gain text box to enter the correct percentage.

This information should be supplied by your commercial printer.

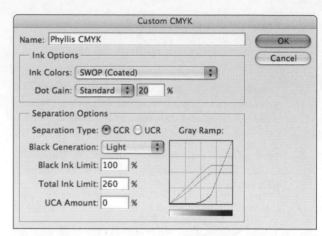

• **Figure 14-3:** Use the Custom CMYK dialog box to select the amount of ink coverage.

6. In the Separation Options area, use the radio buttons and text boxes to select the proper settings.

The commercial printer should also provide these settings. In the Separation Options area, you can set the following:

▶ **Separation Type:** Your options are GCR (Gray Component Replacement) or UCR (Undercolor Replacement). This setting tells Photoshop what type of printing press is being used.

▶ **Black Generation:** This option sets how much black is used when your RGB image is converted into CMYK. This prevents the CMYK inks from becoming muddy when they're mixed together.

▶ **Black Ink Limit, Total Ink Limit,** and **UCA Amount:** Enter a percentage in each of these text boxes to set the amount of ink that's used on each printing plate.

7. Click OK to close the Custom CMYK dialog box and return to the Color Settings dialog box.

8. Click Save, enter a name for the color settings in the Save dialog box that appears, and then click Save. (See Figure 14-4.)

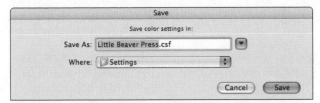

• **Figure 14-4:** Saving your custom CMYK color settings.

The Save dialog box closes and your custom-named CMYK settings appear selected in the CMYK drop-down list in the Working Spaces area of the Color Settings dialog box.

9. **Click OK to close the Color Settings dialog box.**

Great job! You're on your way to using Photoshop to proof and create CMYK separations. The next step is to convert your image to CMYK color mode.

Checking for unprintable colors

Out-of-gamut (non-printable) colors are a problem when printing a project at a commercial press because they can lead to unexpected results.

When you convert an image from RGB mode to CMYK mode, any out-of-gamut RGB colors are forced into the printable CMYK color range. This can lead to unwanted color shifts.

So, before you convert to CMYK and soft proof your project, check for unprintable colors. Here's how:

1. **Choose View➪Proof Setup➪Working CMYK.**

2. **Choose View➪Gamut Warning.**

The non-printable colors in the image are covered with an opaque gray mask, as shown in Figure 14-5.

 By default, out-of-gamut colors are shown using a medium gray mask. You can change the color and opacity of this mask by choosing Edit (Photoshop on a Mac)➪Preferences➪Transparency & Gamut, and then changing the settings in the Gamut Warning area of the Preferences dialog box.

• **Figure 14-5:** An opaque gray mask covers the out-of-gamut colors.

3. **Choose Select➪Color Range.**

This opens the Color Range dialog box shown in Figure 14-6.

4. **Use the Select drop-down list to select Out of Gamut, and then click OK.**

All out-of-gamut areas in the image are selected, as shown in Figure 14-7. This protects the areas that contain printable colors and contains your work to the non-printable areas.

5. **Select the Sponge tool from the Toolbox.**

6. **Select Desaturate from the Mode drop-down list on the Options bar.**

7. **Use the Flow slider bar to select a percentage.**

Flow sets how quickly pixels are desaturated. A higher percentage desaturates an area faster than a lower percentage.

8. **Use the Brush picker to select the diameter of the sponge.**

9. **Stroke across the selected, out-of-gamut areas.**

When the color in an out-of-gamut area moves into printable colors, the gray mask disappears. Be careful when using the Sponge tool though: Too much desaturation can make colors dull.

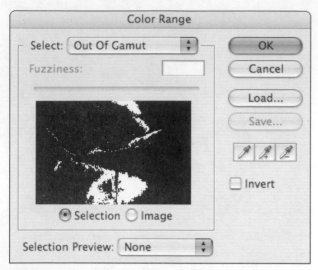

• **Figure 14-6:** Use the Color Range dialog box to select the out-of-gamut areas.

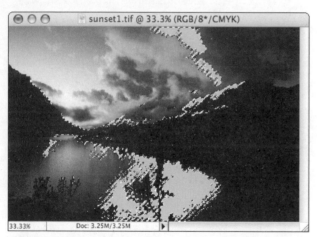

• **Figure 14-7:** By selecting the out-of-gamut areas, the printable colors are protected from editing.

 Really zoom in on the areas that you're desaturating so that you can see exactly when pixel colors move from out-of-gamut to printable.

Converting to CMYK color mode

This next step is a breeze. All that you need to do is choose Image➪Mode➪CMYK Color. When you convert to CMYK mode, notice that CMYK appears in the title bar of your image next to the filename.

As the conversion occurs, you may also notice that the colors in the image become a bit dull-looking. This is because of the color shift that occurs when Photoshop converts the image from one color space to another. You can correct this shift by adjusting the tone using levels and curves. For more information about color correction, turn to Technique 30.

 Be sure to select your custom CMYK settings by using the Color Settings dialog box (as I describe earlier in "Entering and saving custom CMYK printer settings") before you convert your image from RGB to CMYK. If you perform the color mode conversion before selecting the custom settings, none of the custom settings will be applied to your image, making the image inconsistent with the color settings. Such inconsistencies can mess up soft proofing and color reproduction later in the printing process.

Setting up soft proofing

Soft proofing lets you see a pretty accurate preview of your image by using the default prepress settings or custom CMYK settings that you selected and saved in the earlier section, "Entering and saving custom CMYK printer settings." To ensure that the image colors that you see while soft proofing are correct, you need to calibrate your monitor first. For directions on calibrating your monitor, turn to Technique 4.

Here's how to set up soft proofing:

1. **Choose View➪Proof Setup➪Custom.**

The Proof Setup dialog box opens, as shown in Figure 14-8. This dialog box is used to select a custom CMYK color setting and how color is converted when your image moves from one color space (your monitor and Photoshop program) to another color space (the printing press).

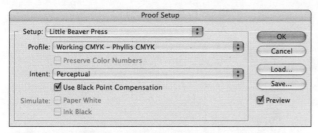

• **Figure 14-8:** The Proof Setup dialog box is used to select soft proofing options.

2. **Make sure that the Profile drop-down list has the right prepress settings selected.**

The default prepress or custom CMYK settings that you created in "Entering and saving custom CMYK settings" should already be selected. If the settings are not selected, use the drop-down list to find and select them.

3. **Use the Intent drop-down list to select a color-conversion setting.**

Your commercial printer should provide the setting. You have four options to choose from:

► **Perceptual:** Converts color values in a way that produces little color shift. Good for photographs and other continuous-tone images.

► **Saturation:** Converts color values with the intent of preserving vivid colors. This option can produce a noticeable color shift. Good for sharp-edged images, such as charts and graphs.

► **Relative Colorimetric:** The default setting, this option converts color based on the monitor's whitepoint setting. This option can produce a noticeable color shift.

► **Absolute Colorimetric:** Converts color based on the printable color range (gamut), and attempts to convert colors that are out-of-gamut into printable colors. This can produce color shifts in non-continuous areas of the image, making for some unintended results.

4. **Click Save, enter a name for the proof setup in the Save dialog box, and then click Save. (See Figure 14-9.)**

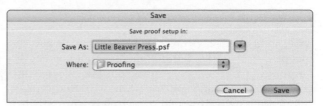

• **Figure 14-9:** Use the Save dialog box to enter a name for your custom soft proof settings.

5. **Click OK to close the Proof Setup dialog box.**

 The soft proof settings that you saved are now available at the bottom of the View➪ Proof Setup menu.

6. **Choose Proof➪View Colors or press Ctrl+Y/⌘+Y to turn on soft proofing.**

When soft proofing is turned on, notice that the selected proof setting name appears in the title bar of the image window, as shown in Figure 14-10.

• **Figure 14-10:** The selected soft proof setting appears in the image's title bar.

 If your project contains several images that you want to soft proof by using the same custom proof settings, you need to turn on soft proofing and select the settings for each image.

Adding printer's marks

Depending on your project, you may need to use various printer's marks. For instance, if your project — suppose it's a brochure — uses four ink colors (this would be called a *4-color* or *4-c* job), you would need to include registration marks so that the pressman could exactly align the printing plates on the press. A calibration bar would be needed to measure colors exactly. The edges of the brochure and any folds would need to be indicated with crop marks. Figure 14-11 shows some typical printer's marks.

• **Figure 14-11: Printer's marks tell the pressman and other workers at the printing company how to align, calibrate, trim, and fold your project.**

Using the Print dialog box, you can quickly add printer's marks to any image. Here's how:

1. **Choose File⇨Print with Preview or press Alt+Ctrl+P/Option+⌘+P.**

   The Print dialog box opens, as shown in Figure 14-12, and displays the image in the Preview Pane.

2. **Select the Show More Options check box.**

   As shown in Figure 14-13, the Print dialog box expands to display more available settings.

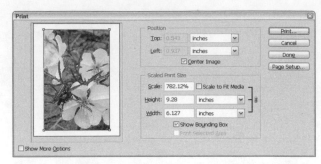

• **Figure 14-12: Use the Print dialog box to set up printer's marks.**

• **Figure 14-13: Click Show More Options to see added options in the Print dialog box.**

3. **Use the drop-down list below the Show More Options check box to select Output.**

4. **Use the various check boxes to select the printer's marks that you need.**

   You can select from calibration bars, registration marks, corner and/or center crop marks, description, and labels.

   As you select the various printer's marks, they appear around the image in the Preview pane.

5. **When you're finished selecting printer's marks, click Done.**

Saving your image as an EPS file

Depending on the commercial printer that you're using, you may not need to save your image as an EPS file. Many printers will take it from here and accept a Photoshop PSD file. But, if your printer doesn't have access to Photoshop and needs your image in EPS file format, this section tells you all you need to know.

When saving your image in EPS format, you actually want to save a copy of the image. This protects your original image file, in case you need to edit the image in the future.

Check with your commercial printer for the settings that you need to use when saving your image files in EPS format.

1. **With your CMYK image open, choose File⇨ Save As.**

The Save As dialog box opens, as shown in Figure 14-14.

2. **Type a name for the image in the File Name (Windows) or Save As (Mac) text box.**

• **Figure 14-14:** Use the Save As dialog box to save a copy of your image in EPS file format.

3. **Use the Format drop-down list to select Photoshop EPS (*.EPS).**

4. **Select the As a Copy check box.**

5. **Select the Use Proof Setup and Embed Color profile check boxes.**

This ensures that your image is saved with the custom CMYK settings that you created in the section "Entering and saving custom CMYK printer settings," earlier in this chapter.

6. **Click Save.**

The EPS Options dialog box opens, as shown in Figure 14-15.

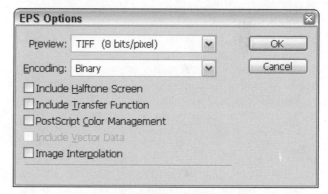

• **Figure 14-15:** The EPS Options dialog box is used to set how the file is saved.

7. **Select an option from the Preview drop-down list.**

If you choose a 1 bit/pixel option, the file is saved with a black and white preview. The 8 bits/pixel option saves the file with a color preview.

8. **Use the Encoding drop-down list to select how the image file data is saved.**

Binary is a good default option to select because it doesn't lose any image data. Some printers, however, cannot use binary encoded data. If this is the case, select ASCII85. Ask your commercial printer which option is the best one to use.

9. **Click OK.**

Photoshop saves your image in EPS format.

Working with Spot Colors

Spot colors, also called custom colors, are used to exactly match a particular color — for instance a lapis blue corporate logo or a book title in silver metallic letters for a book cover. No way could you exactly match that lapis blue with a mixture of CMYK inks, *and* you certainly couldn't create metallics from those inks. (By the way, CMYK inks are also referred to as *process color.* You may hear your commercial printer refer to them this way.)

That's when you need to turn to custom colors created by companies such as Pantone, TRUMATCH, TOYO, and DIC. These custom colors are used in addition to (or instead of) the standard CMYK inks. Spot colors are selected by using a printed swatch book that you can buy at the better art supply stores or directly from the ink manufacturer. When you select a spot color in Photoshop, the color that you see is only an approximation. Spot colors must be selected from printed swatch books.

Each spot color needs its own plate on the printing press. (If you plan to include a varnish for your project, the varnish is also considered a spot color and needs a separate plate.) Spot color information is saved in Photoshop in its own channel. When you want to export the spot color channels, you need to save the image file in Photoshop DCS 2.0 or Photoshop PDF format.

Adding a spot color to your image

Selections are used to create spot color channels. A spot color channel can contain any shape or type that you can create in Photoshop. This example uses type to create a spot color channel. Here's how:

1. **Open the image to which you want to add the spot color channel.**

2. **Make sure white is selected as the Foreground color.**

    Using white for the type creation makes it easier to see how the spot color affects the type later.

3. **Select the Horizontal Type Tool and add type to the image.**

    When you add type to an image, the type is automatically placed on a type layer, as shown in Figure 14-16. You can add any special effects, such as drop shadows, glows, or bevels, to the type by using Layer Styles. (Take a look at Technique 20 to find out more about Layer Styles.)

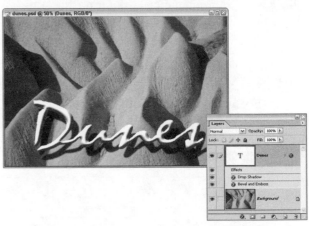

• **Figure 14–16: Type is automatically placed on its own type layer.**

4. **When the type is shaped to your satisfaction, Ctrl+click/⌘+click the type layer in the Layers palette.**

    This creates a selection around the type.

5. **In the Channels palette, choose New Spot Channel from the palette menu, as shown in Figure 14-17.**

    Use the New Spot Channel dialog box shown in Figure 14-18 to select a spot color.

6. **In the Ink Characteristics area, click the square next to Color.**

    The Color Picker opens, showing CMYK process color combinations.

7. **Click Custom in the Color Picker.**

    The Color Picker changes to show custom spot colors. (See Figure 14-19.)

• **Figure 14-17:** Choose New Spot Channel from the Channels palette menu.

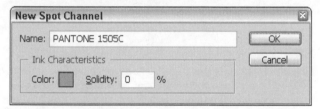

• **Figure 14-18:** The New Spot Channel dialog box is used to select a spot color.

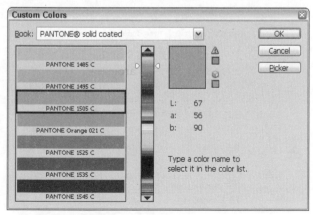

• **Figure 14-19:** Use the Color Picker to select an ink manufacturer and ink type.

8. Use the Book drop-down list to select the color-matching system that you're using.

9. Click a spot color in the Swatch area at the left of the Color Picker.

10. **Click OK to close the Color Picker and return to the New Spot Channel dialog box.**

The name of the spot color that you selected, such as Pantone 2727C, appears in the Name text box.

11. **Enter a percentage in the Solidity text box.**

Your commercial printer should be able to give you this information. This setting is used only to simulate on-screen how the printed spot color will look. It doesn't affect how the spot color is actually printed. A setting of 100 percent makes the ink completely opaque, covering up any ink below it. Typically, if I don't have any information from the printer, I leave this setting at 0 percent. That way, I can see the selected color and any shading or bevels added to the type.

12. **Click OK.**

The spot color channel appears in the Channels palette named after the spot color that you selected in Step 9. (See Figure 14-20.)

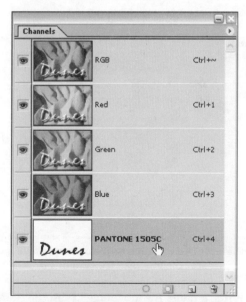

• **Figure 14-20:** The spot color channel appears in the Channels palette.

Saving spot color separations

You may not need to save your spot color as separations. Many commercial printers can handle Photoshop's PSD files and are happy to accept them. But, if you find that you need to save spot color as separations, here's how:

1. **Press Ctrl+S/⌘+S to save your image.**

2. **Choose File➪Save As.**

The Save As dialog box opens, as shown in Figure 14-21.

• **Figure 14-21:** Use the Save As dialog box to save a copy of the image in DCS 2.0 or PDF format.

3. **Enter a name for the image in the File Name (Windows) or Save As (Mac) text box.**

4. **Use the Format drop-down list to choose either Photoshop DCS 2.0 or Photoshop PDF.**

5. **Select the Spot Colors check box.**

6. **Click Save.**

The Save As dialog box closes and the DCS 2.0 Format or PDF Options dialog box opens. (See Figure 14-22.)

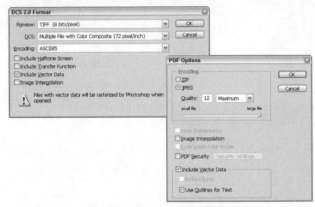

• **Figure 14-22:** Use the DCS 2.0 Format dialog box to set how the image and spot color channels are saved.

7. **Choose the settings based on the dialog box that you're using:**

If you're using the PDF Options dialog box: Set the JPEG Encoding to Maximum.

If you're using the DCS 2.0 dialog box: Use the Preview drop-down list to choose TIFF 8 Bits/Pixel; use the DCS drop-down list to select Multiple File with Color Composite. (Check with your commercial printer about this setting.) Select Binary from the Encoding drop-down list.

8. **Click OK.**

The image and spot color channels are saved in either DCS 2.0 or PDF format.

Part III

Using Layers to Save Time, Protect Your Work, and Create Cool Images

The 5th Wave   By Rich Tennant

"So far he's called up a cobra, 2 pythons, and a bunch of skinks, but still not the file we're looking for."

Technique 15

Working with and Organizing Layers

Layers are one of Photoshop's fundamental building blocks. You simply can't work in Photoshop without using at least a layer or two (or sometimes 60). If you aren't using the full power of layers, you should. If you use layers all the time, how do you keep them organized?

If you're asking, "What are layers?" here's a brief rundown. (If layers are as familiar as the back of your hand, skip this paragraph and the next one, too.) Imagine that you have three pieces of clear window glass and three colored markers, say orange, black, and red. In your mind, take the orange marker and scribble on the first piece of glass. Next, take the black marker and scribble on the second piece of glass. Then, take the red marker and scribble on the third piece of glass. You now have three pieces of glass with a different colored scribble on each one. Take the three pieces of glass and place them one on top of the other with the orange scribble on the bottom, the black scribble in the middle, and the red scribbled glass on top. As you look through the glass you see three different scribbles. If you want to erase some of the red scribble, you can do so because the red scribbled glass is on top. But, notice that if you want to change the orange scribble, you have to reshuffle the deck of glass to get to it because it's on the bottom. Also, any change that you make to a scribble on one piece of glass affects only that piece of glass. The other scribbles are separate and don't change.

Each layer is like one piece of clear glass. The different colored scribbles are your drawings, brush strokes, type, or whatever on each layer. You can *activate* layers individually and edit the contents of a layer without affecting any of the other layers. Layers are great for trying out something (you can always toss a layer in the trash) or separating different parts of an image. (For instance, you can group all your type layers into one *layer set.*) Layers are listed in the Layers palette in a *stacking order* — the layer at the top of the list is in front of the layer stack, and the layer at the bottom of the list is at the back. (For a more detailed explanation of layers and how they work, take a look at *Photoshop CS For Dummies* by Deke McClelland and yours truly, published by Wiley.)

Figure 15-1 shows a drawing of a hip cat surfing a wave. The Layers palette shows that the drawing is made up of three layers: Surf Cat, Surf Board, and Wave. Figure 15-2 shows each layer separately. When these three layers are viewed at the same time, you see the entire *composite* image. Notice how the layers are stacked in the Layers palette. The Wave layer is on the bottom, so it is in the back of the image. The Surf Board is next up in the stacking order, so it appears on top of the Wave layer. And, finally, the Surf Cat is at the top of the list, so it's on top of the surfboard. If I moved the Surf Board layer to the top of the stacking order, the surfboard would hide the cat's feet in the picture.

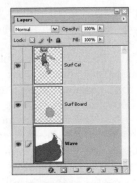

• **Figure 15-1: Notice how the separate layers are stacked in the Layers palette and the order in which they appear in the image.**

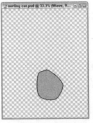

• **Figure 15-2: The checkerboard areas of the separate layers indicate transparency.**

Granted, the surf cat example has only three layers. But, what happens when you start working with more layers? Anytime that I have more than ten layers, I find that it gets confusing unless I group and color code the layers. This technique shows you the ins and outs of working with layers, changing stacking order, color coding layers, and grouping layers into layer sets.

Getting to Know Layers

This section is a mini-refresher on layer basics. Using the Layers palette, you can rename and hide layers, change their stacking order, flip them horizontally or vertically, and even copy a layer from one image to another. You probably know how to do most of these things already, but you may glean a few tidbits here:

- ✔ **Open the Layers palette:** Press F7 on the keyboard or choose Window⇨Layers.

- ✔ **Select a layer:** Click the layer in the Layers palette. Remember that a layer needs to be selected in order for you to edit it.

- ✔ **Rename a layer:** Double-click the layer's name, type a new name in the text box, and then press Enter/Return.

- ✔ **Change the stacking order:** Drag a layer up or down the list in the Layers palette to a new position.

- ✔ **Hide or show a layer:** Click the eye icon to the left of the layer in the Layers palette.

- ✔ **Convert the Background to a regular layer:** Double-click the Background in the Layers palette, type a name in the New Layer text box, and then click OK. Or, select the Background in the Layers palette, and then choose Layer⇨ New⇨Layer From Background.

- ✔ **Convert a regular layer to the Background:** Select a layer in the Layers palette, and then choose Layer⇨New⇨Background From Layer.

- ✔ **Flip a layer vertically or horizontally:** Select the layer in the Layer palette, and then choose Edit⇨Transform⇨Flip Vertical or Flip Horizontal.

- ✔ **Copy a layer from one image to another:** Open both images in Photoshop, select the layer that you want to copy in the Layers palette, and then drag the layer to the image window where you want it copied. The layer automatically adds itself to the Layers palette for that image.

Color Coding Layers

Color coding layers is a pretty quick and effective way to separate one type of layer from another. Suppose that you have ten layers that contain

brushed shadows and eight layers that contain furniture pieces in a darkened room. Knowing which layer is a shadow and which layer contains a sofa could take a few minutes to figure out. But, if you color code all the shadow layers blue, they're easy to pick out.

To color code a layer:

1. **Select the layer that you want to color code in the Layers palette.**

2. **Right-click/Control+click and choose Layer Properties from the context-sensitive menu or choose Layer Properties from the palette menu.**

The Layer Properties dialog box shown in Figure 15-3 appears.

• **Figure 15-3: Use the Color drop-down list in the Layer Properties dialog box to color code the selected layer.**

3. **Use the Color drop-down list to select the color that you want to use.**

4. **Click OK.**

The layer in the Layers palette changes to that color.

Four Ways to Lock Layers

Using the locking buttons at the top of the Layers palette, you can lock a portion of a layer's pixels, lock the layer's position, or lock everything down — pixels *and* position. Figure 15-4 shows the four buttons.

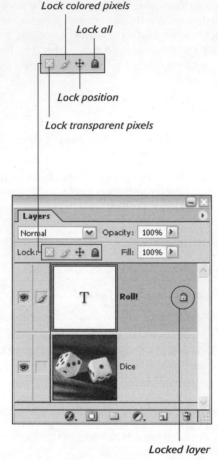

Lock colored pixels

Lock all

Lock position

Lock transparent pixels

Locked layer

• **Figure 15-4: By using the Lock buttons at the top of the Layers palette, you can protect your work.**

Locking layers is great for protecting your work if you don't want to edit a part of a layer or move it by accident. Here's what each button does:

✔ To **lock all transparent pixels** on a layer so that they can't be changed, click the leftmost button. With this lock in place, you can edit only colored pixels.

✔ To **lock all colored pixels** on a layer so that they can't be edited, click the button second from the left. Only transparent pixels are available for editing.

✔ To **lock the layer in position**, click the button second from the right.

✔ To **lock layer position and all pixels** (colored or transparent), click the rightmost button.

When you use any of the Lock buttons, a tiny padlock appears to the right of the layer's name.

Of course, you can use any of these buttons in a temporary fashion: If you decide that you want to unlock a portion of a layer, just click the appropriate button again.

Creating Layer Sets

Layer sets are great for organizing layers into groups. After you've divided layers into layer sets, you can view just the name of the layer set in the Layers palette or click the tiny arrow to show all the layers contained within the layer set.

Here's how to create a layer set:

1. Choose Layer⇨New⇨Layer Set or Alt+click/ Option+click the Create New Set button at the bottom of the Layers palette. (See Figure 15-5.)

If you click the Create New Set button without holding down Alt/Option, Photoshop creates a layer set with a default name and no color coding.

2. Use the New Layer Set dialog box shown in Figure 15-6 to select the layer set's properties.

▶ Type a name for the layer set into the **Name** text box. By default, Photoshop automatically enters the name Set followed by a number. You can use any descriptive name that works for you.

▶ Use the **Color** drop-down list to color code the layer set.

▶ Use the **Mode** drop-down list to select a blending mode. The default setting is Pass Through mode. With this blending mode selected, any blending mode or adjustment layers applied to a layer within the layer set affect the rest of the layers below it (even if the layers are not in the layer set). Any other setting using the Mode drop-down list restricts blending mode or adjustment layer effects to the layers within the layer set.

3. **Click OK.**

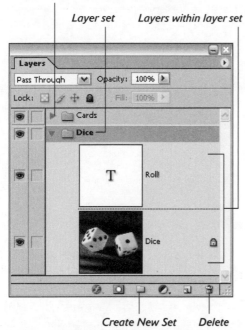

Click to view/hide layers within a set

Layer set   *Layers within layer set*

Create New Set   *Delete*

• **Figure 15-5:** Alt+click/Option+click the **Create New Set** button to access layer set properties.

• **Figure 15-6:** Use the **New Layer Set** dialog box to name and color code the layer set.

 Layer sets can be repositioned in the stacking order just like layers. Just drag the layer set up or down the list to a new position in the Layers palette.

Layer Set Techniques

After you create a layer set, you want to add layers to it. Also, as your project goes along, you may find that you need to change color coding, remove layers from the set, or even copy the entire layer set. The following is a list of techniques that you can use to manage your layer set:

✔ **Add a layer to a layer set:** Drag the layer over the layer set's name.

✔ **Remove a layer from a layer set:** Drag the layer outside the layer set.

✔ **Rename a layer set:** Double-click the layer set's name, type a new name in the text box, and then press Enter/Return.

✔ **Color code an existing layer set:** Select the layer set and then choose Layer Set Properties from the Layers palette menu. Use the Color drop-down list to select a color.

✔ **Copy an entire layer set:** (This includes the layers contained within the layer set.) Drag the layer set over the Create New Layer button at the bottom of the Layers palette.

✔ **Nest an existing layer set:** (This includes the layers contained within the layer set inside a new layer set.) Drag the layer set over the Create New Set button at the bottom of the Layers palette.

✔ **Delete a layer set:** Select the layer set and then click the trashcan icon at the bottom of the Layers palette. The dialog box shown in Figure 15-7 appears. You can choose to delete the layer set and all the layers contained in the layer set, or delete only the layer set and leave the layers intact. (To delete a layer set and all the layers contained in the layer set and bypass the dialog box shown in Figure 15-7, drag the layer set on top of the trashcan icon.)

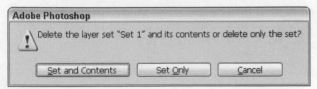

• **Figure 15-7: Use the dialog box to select how you want to delete a layer set.**

You can nest a layer set within another layer set. In fact, you can nest down to five layer sets deep!

Technique 16

Getting to Know Layer Comps

Save Time By

- ✔ Creating layer comps
- ✔ Sifting through layer comps
- ✔ Updating layer comps

When working for clients, I often create several versions of a layout or image to show them. The clients can then choose the version that they like best. In the past, this meant saving several separate image files in Photoshop, one for each version. But, with Photoshop CS and layer comps, all this has changed.

Layer comps are used to create virtual snapshots of every Layer palette setting including position, stacking order, opacity, blending mode, and applied layer styles. And unlike history snapshots, which are deleted when an image is closed, layer comps are saved with the image and are available every time the image is reopened. So instead of showing my clients several image files, I can open just one image file and cycle through the layer comps. Figure 16-1 shows the same image file viewed with two different layer comps. Notice that the type layer's appearance and position changes depending on which layer comp is selected.

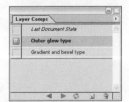
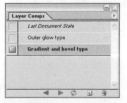

• **Figure 16-1: The same image is viewed with two different layer comps.**

This technique shows you everything you need to know about layer comps: creating and updating them, cycling through layer comps, deleting them, you name it. Give layer comps a try and experiment with them. I think you'll find that they can be a useful tool for client presentations and everyday work. If you want to try out a blending mode, different layer position, or layer effect, use layer comps to save the original and the tester, and then cycle back and forth between the two to see which you like best.

 You can also think of layer comps as layer version control. Before you change something about a layer's attributes, you can save the original settings with a layer comp.

Creating Layer Comps

To work with layer comps, you need to use the Layer Comps palette shown in Figure 16-2. By default, the Layer Comps palette is docked in the Palette Well on the Options bar. If you don't see the Layer Comps palette, choose Window⇨Layer Comps to view it.

Creating a layer comp is pretty straightforward. Here's how:

1. **Position layers and set layer opacity, blending mode, and other layer attributes the way that you want them by using the Layers palette.**

2. **Click the Create New Layer Comp button at the bottom of the Layer Comps palette.**

3. **Use the New Layer Comp dialog box that opens, as shown in Figure 16-3, to set layer comp options.**

Using the dialog box you can

▶ Type a descriptive **name** for the layer comp in the Name text box.

▶ Select which **layer attributes** are saved: Visibility, Position, and Appearance.

▶ Type a **description** of the layer placement or changes in the Comment text box.

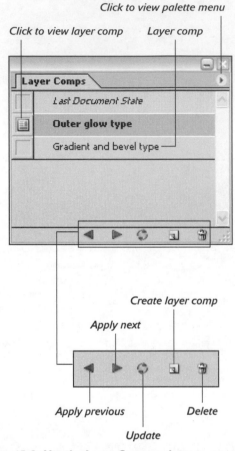

• **Figure 16-2:** Use the Layer Comps palette to create and manage layer comps.

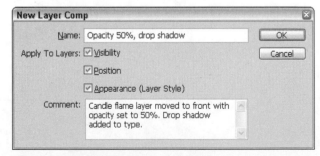

• **Figure 16-3:** Use the New Layer Comp dialog box to select layer comp options.

4. **Click OK.**

The new layer comp appears selected in the Layer Comps palette.

 Don't worry about your file size when saving layer comps with an image — layer comps take up only about 1K.

Cycling through Layer Comps

After creating the layer comps that you need, you want to view the layer comps to compare the different layer settings.

You can cycle through layer comps in two ways: Select them one-by-one in the Layer comps palette or use the arrow buttons to move backward or forward through the layer comps. Here's how:

✔ **View layer comps individually:** Click in the column to the left of the layer comp. The tiny layer comp icon appears in the column and the layer comp is selected.

✔ **Cycle forward through the layer comps:** Click the Apply Next button at the bottom of the Layer Comps palette.

✔ **Cycle backward through the layer comps:** Click the Apply Previous button at the bottom of the Layer Comps palette.

Managing Layer Comps

An image constantly changes as you work on it. This means that layer comps need to be updated from time to time to keep track of the changes. You also may find that you need to change layer comp options, restore your image to the last layer state, or delete a layer comp entirely. Here's how:

✔ **Update** a layer comp to the current layer settings by selecting it in the Layer Comps palette, and then clicking the Update button at the bottom of the Layer Comps palette.

✔ **Change layer comp options** by double-clicking the layer comp, and then using the Layer Comp Options dialog box that appears. This dialog box looks exactly the same as the one shown in Figure 16-3; only its name is different.

✔ **Restore** your image to the last applied layer state by clicking the column to the left of Last Document State at the top of the Layer Comps palette.

✔ **Delete** a layer comp by selecting it and then clicking the trashcan icon at the bottom of the Layer Comps palette. You can also drag the layer comp over the trashcan icon.

Validating a Layer Comp

Layer comps are snapshots of all the layers and their attributes. If one layer (or more) is merged into another layer, deleted, or converted into a Background layer, a tiny warning icon appears in the Layer Comps palette next to the layer comps that are affected, as shown in Figure 16-4.

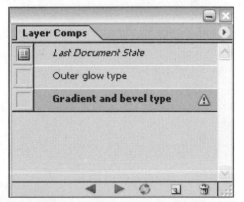

• **Figure 16-4: The tiny warning icon tells you that a layer comp is out of date.**

You can do a few things in this situation:

✔ Ignore the warning icon altogether. If you do this, you might lose some layers that are important to you.

✔ Use the History palette to activate a history state before any layer deletion, merging, or conversion. (For more about the History palette, turn to Technique 25.)

✔ Right-click/Control+click the warning icon to view a menu that lets you choose Clear Layer Comp Warning or Clear All Layer Comp Warnings.

✔ Click the Update button at the bottom of the Layer Comps palette to make the layer comp current.

✔ Delete the layer comp with the problem.

Technique 17

Enhancing Images with Blending Modes

Save Time By

- Applying luminosity
- Fading filter effects
- Creating grainy shadows

This technique zeroes in on another powerful Photoshop feature — blending modes. What is a blending mode? I thought you'd never ask. Suppose that you're using two layers and you select a blending mode for the upper layer. The blending mode defines the way pixels on the upper, active layer affect the appearance of the pixels on the layer immediately below it. Some blending modes affect lighter pixels, some affect darker pixels, and some affect neutral tones. When you think about blending modes, remember this: Blending modes are all about how the color being applied interacts with existing color.

This may all seem a bit mysterious, and if you are a "show me" person like I am, you want to see what blending modes can really do. Because Photoshop has 25 blending modes, I can't show them all in a few short pages. However, I take you through which tools and dialog boxes make blending modes available, and how blending modes affect changes to pixels when they're applied. Then, I focus on a few blending modes and show you how to use them. My one directive throughout this technique is don't hesitate to experiment! A blending mode that you think *can't possibly* work may give you some really cool results.

A Blending Mode Rundown

Before you can use blending modes, you need to know where to find them. One place is the Layers palette. Figure 17-1 shows the open Blending Mode drop-down list. As shown in Figure 17-1, the blending modes are divided into six different sections on the drop-down list according to the type of pixels they affect.

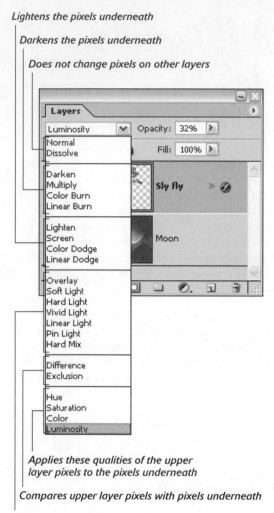

Lightens the pixels underneath

Darkens the pixels underneath

Does not change pixels on other layers

*Applies these qualities of the upper
layer pixels to the pixels underneath*

Compares upper layer pixels with pixels underneath

Changes the contrast of the pixels underneath

• **Figure 17-1:** Whenever you encounter the Blending
Mode drop-down list, you see that it's
organized into six categories. Here the
drop-down list is shown in the Layers
palette.

The other places that you can access blending modes
are certain dialog boxes and the Options bar when
a brush or painting tool is selected. The blending

modes are available on the Options bar when the
following tools are selected: Art History, Blur, Brush,
Bucket, Color Replacement, Gradient, Healing Brush,
History Brush, Pencil, Sharpen, and Smudge. The
blending modes are also available in the following
dialog boxes: Apply Image, Calculations, Fade, Fill,
and Layer Styles.

The first two modes, **Normal** and **Dissolve**, don't
change pixels on the layers underneath. Normal
mode combined with 100% Opacity displays every
pixel in the active layer no matter what colors are
present on layers underneath. Dissolve mode works
best on semi-transparent areas such as drop shadows or fade outs, changing them into a random spray
of pixels. Take a look at the section "Creating a Grainy
Shadow," later in this chapter, to see Dissolve mode
in action.

The next four modes, **Darken**, **Multiply**, **Color Burn**,
and **Linear Burn**, use darker pixels to create results.
White pixels are neutral, so they don't affect the pixels underneath, but instead become clear.

Next on the blending mode drop-down list are the
opposites of the four darkening blending modes
above: **Lighten**, **Screen**, **Color Dodge**, and **Linear
Dodge**. These blending modes use lighter pixels to
create results. Black pixels are neutral, so they don't
affect the pixels underneath, but instead become
clear.

The fourth group down on the blending mode drop-
down list includes six blending modes: **Overlay**, **Soft
Light**, **Hard Light**, **Vivid Light**, **Linear Light**, and **Pin
Light**. These blending modes change the contrast of
underlying pixels. 50% gray pixels are neutral, so
they don't affect the pixels underneath, but instead
become clear. Pixels that are darker than 50% gray
darken the underlying pixels; pixels that are lighter
than 50% gray lighten the underlying pixels. Turn to
the section "Fading a Filter," later in this chapter, to
see what Vivid Light mode can do.

The next blending mode group, **Difference** and **Exclusion**, uses comparison to create results. White areas on the active layer invert underlying pixels. Black areas on the active layer don't affect the pixels underneath.

The final group of blending modes, **Hue**, **Saturation**, **Color**, and **Luminosity**, apply that quality of the active layer to the pixels underneath. Look at the following section, "Applying a Blending Mode," to see how the Luminosity mode blends pixels.

The Behind and Clear blending modes

When you use the Brush, Bucket, Gradient, History Brush, or Pencil tools, two blending modes are available on the Options bar Blending Mode drop-down list that are not offered in the Layers palette: Behind and Clear. (Clear is only available with the Brush, Bucket, and Pencil tools.)

Behind mode protects colored pixels on a layer just as if you had clicked the Lock Image Pixels button on the Layers palette. Only transparent (non-colored) pixels are affected by the blending mode.

Clear mode works like an eraser, removing color from pixels and making them transparent. This lets the layer below show through completely.

Applying a Blending Mode

The directions that follow show how to apply a blending mode by using the Layers palette. If you've never used blending modes before, open two images and give this a try. Also, this example uses the Luminosity blending mode. Don't limit yourself to this particular blending mode; cycle through them all and see how they affect your images.

1. Open two images in Photoshop.

For this example, I use an image of the moon and a bug that I dubbed Sly Fly, as shown in Figure 17-2. My ultimate goal with these two images is to blend the fly onto the moon to make it look like there's a bugly in the moon (instead of a man in the moon).

• **Figure 17-2: For this example, I'm combining these two images.**

2. Make sure that both images are contained on regular layers, not the Background layer.

If you need to convert a Background layer to a regular layer, choose Layer⇨New⇨Layer from Background. In the New Layer dialog box, enter a name for the layer in the Name text box, and then click OK.

3. Drag one image layer from the Layers palette onto the other image window.

This copies the layer containing one image to the other image window.

For this example, because I want the fly positioned on top of the moon, I drag the layer containing the fly onto the Moon image window. The fly layer was automatically added to the Layers palette, as shown in Figure 17-3.

If you look at the two layers in Figure 17-3, you notice that the fly is too big to fit in the moon area and that the fly is completely opaque. It doesn't blend into the moon layer at all.

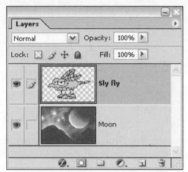

• **Figure 17-3:** I dragged the layer containing the fly to the Moon image window.

The first thing that I need to do is use the Transformation commands to scale and rotate the bug so that it fits into the moon area, as shown in Figure 17-4. (I discuss transformations in detail in Technique 18.) Next, I use a blending mode to blend the fly's pixels with those of the moon.

4. **In the Layers palette, use the Blending Mode drop-down list to select a mode.**

For this example, I chose Luminosity, which colors and shades the fly exactly like the moon behind it.

5. **Adjust the layer's opacity, if necessary.**

The final touch for my bugly in the moon is to put the opacity down to 30%, letting more of the moon's texture and lighting show through. (See Figure 17-5.)

• **Figure 17-4:** After the fly is scaled and rotated, it fits into the moon area.

• **Figure 17-5:** Lowering the opacity of the Sly Fly layer makes the moon's texture and lighting visible.

Fading a Filter

This blending mode example uses the Fade dialog box to apply a blending mode. First, a filter is applied to a copy of the image. Then, the Fade dialog box is used to set the layer's opacity and blending mode.

1. **Open an image in Photoshop.**

The image in this example is a picture of a window contained on one layer, as shown in Figure 17-6.

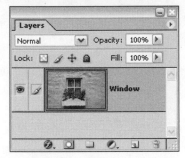

• **Figure 17-6:** The window image is contained on one layer.

2. **Duplicate the layer that the image is on by dragging the layer to the Create New Layer button at the bottom of the Layers palette.**

A copy of the layer appears in the Layers palette above the original layer.

3. **Apply a filter to the copied layer.**

For this example, the Graphic Pen filter is applied to the copied layer.

4. **Choose Edit⇨Fade.**

The Fade dialog box shown in Figure 17-7 opens.

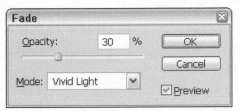

• **Figure 17-7:** Use the Fade dialog box to select a blending mode.

5. **Set the layer's Opacity and choose a blending mode from the Mode drop-down list.**

In this example, Opacity is set to 30% and Vivid Light mode is selected.

6. **Click OK.**

The faded layer's pixels blend with the original image pixels to create interesting texture and lighting, as shown in Figure 17-8.

• **Figure 17-8:** The Vivid Light blending mode adds more contrast to the image.

Creating a Grainy Shadow

This blending mode example uses Dissolve mode to make a drop shadow appear grainy. You use the Layer Style dialog box to apply the shadow and blending mode. (To find out more about layer styles, turn to Technique 20.)

1. Open a new image window and use the Horizontal Type tool to create some type.

2. In the Layers palette, make sure that the Type layer is selected.

3. Click the Add Layer Style button at the bottom of the palette and choose Drop Shadow from the menu.

The Layer Styles dialog box opens with Drop Shadow selected. Use the Drop Shadow area at the center of the dialog box (see Figure 17-9) to set the size and opacity of the shadow and select a blending mode.

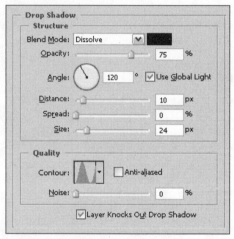

• **Figure 17-9:** Use the Drop Shadow area to create your drop shadow.

4. Use the Blend Mode drop-down list to select Dissolve mode and move the Opacity slider to the desired opacity.

For this example, Opacity is set at 75%. In addition, Distance is set to 10 pixels and Size is set to 24 pixels.

5. Click OK.

The grainy drop shadow appears behind the type. Figure 17-10 shows two versions of the drop shadow. One uses Normal mode (top) and the other uses Dissolve mode (bottom).

• **Figure 17-10:** Dissolve mode changes the shadow into a spray of pixels.

Technique **18**

Transforming Images, Layers, and Selections

Transformation is one of those fun, tangible Photoshop toys. You can flip, rotate, skew, and add perspective to anything in Photoshop. Transformation always makes me feel like a magician. I wiggle my fingers, there's nothing up my sleeves, and click! The model is suddenly standing on her head. Click: Her head is facing the other direction. Click: She's as big as Mount Rushmore. *Fun.*

This technique shows you how to use the transformation commands to flip, spin, and gain a little perspective. First, you take a look at transforming entire images. Then, you move on to transforming layers and selections. If you've worked with transformations before, some of this material may be old hat. But keep your eye out for a myriad of interesting tricks and tips — it could be a transforming experience.

Doing the Big Flip

With Photoshop, you can rotate, horizontally flip, or vertically flip an entire image. The commands that perform such transformations are in the Image⇨Rotate Canvas menu shown in Figure 18-1. Most of the commands shown in Figure 18-1 are pretty self-explanatory, but I quickly run down the Image⇨Rotate Canvas menu:

- ✔ Rotate an image to stand it on its head by choosing **180°**.

- ✔ Choose **90° CW** or **90° CCW** to rotate the image one quarter turn clockwise or counterclockwise, respectively.

- ✔ Rotate an image a specific number of degrees clockwise or counterclockwise by choosing **Arbitrary**.

- ✔ Flip the image so that left becomes right and right becomes left by choosing **Flip Canvas Horizontal**.

- ✔ Choose **Flip Canvas Vertical** to flip the image upside down.

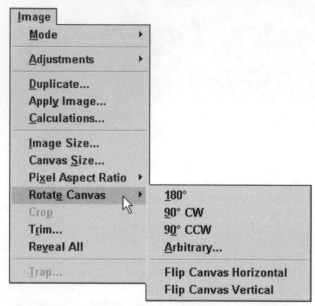

• **Figure 18-1:** Use the Rotate Canvas menu to transform entire images.

 If you want to skew, distort, or add perspective to an entire image, you have to perform the transformations by linking all the layers together and then performing a layer transformation. For details on how to link layers together, take a look at the "Linking layers" sidebar in this technique.

Prestidigitation with Transformation

When you want to transform a layer or selection, use the commands on the Edit⇨Transform menu, as shown in Figure 18-2.

A brave young boy from the audience has volunteered to demonstrate the Edit⇨Transform menu commands. This lad is shown in Figure 18-3.

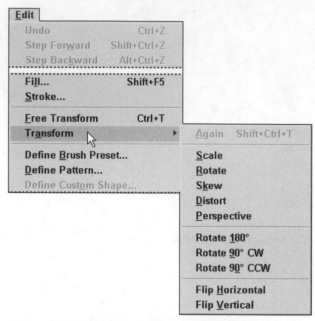

• **Figure 18-2:** Use the commands on the Edit⇨Transform menu to transform layers and selections.

• **Figure 18-3:** This brave lad is ready to be transformed.

To get you started, I give full directions for scaling an image. After that, I tell you how to perform the other transformations by using a quick list.

To scale an image, use the following steps:

1. **Use the Layers palette to select a layer or use any of the selection tools to select an area to be transformed.**

2. **Choose Edit⇨Transform⇨Scale.**

    A bounding box with small square handles appears around the layer or selection, as shown in Figure 18-4.

• **Figure 18-4: The brave lad is enclosed within a bounding box.**

3. **Position the mouse pointer over one of the square handles, click the mouse button, and drag.**

    Drag a corner handle to change both the horizontal and vertical scale. Drag the handle on the left or right side of the bounding box to change the

vertical scale. Drag a top or bottom handle to change the horizontal scale. Figure 18-5 shows our brave volunteer being scaled horizontally.

 If you need to quickly scale a layer or selection proportionally, just hold down the Shift key while dragging a corner handle.

• **Figure 18-5: Drag a handle or part of the bounding box to scale the layer or selection.**

4. **When you're finished scaling, release the mouse and press Enter/Return to accept the change or press Esc to cancel the scaling.**

    You can also click the Commit check mark button on the Options bar to accept changes or click the Cancel button on the Options bar.

 While using any of the transformation commands on the Edit menu, you can access another type of transformation by right-clicking/Control+clicking inside the bounding box and selecting another transformation command.

You can't transform the Background layer. If you want to transform part or all of the Background layer, you have to convert the Background to a regular layer first. To do this, select the Background in the Layers palette and then choose Layer➪New➪Layer from Background.

If the layer's locked, you can't transform it!

None of the commands on the Edit➪Transform menu are available to you if the layer that you're trying to transform is locked. If the transformation commands are grayed out after you select a layer, check to see whether a tiny padlock appears to the right of the layer's name in the Layers palette. Chances are that the Lock: Position button or the Lock: All button at the top of the Layers palette is selected.

For the rest of the Edit➪Transform commands, I list them by command and then tell you how to move the bounding box handles to perform the transformation. Use the earlier directions on scaling an image and substitute each of the following bullet points for Steps 2 and 3:

- To **rotate** a layer or selection, choose Edit➪ Transform➪Rotate. The bounding box with square handles appears. (Refer to Figure 18-4.) Position the mouse over one of the handles and drag clockwise or counterclockwise.

- To **skew** a layer or selection, choose Edit➪ Transform➪Skew. Slide the left or right sides of the bounding box to skew vertically, as shown in Figure 18-6. Slide the top or bottom sides of the bounding box to skew horizontally. Hold down Alt/Option and drag to skew around the center point (located on the boy's nose).

- To **distort** a layer or selection, choose Edit➪ Transform➪Distort. Drag a handle or bounding line in any direction to simultaneously skew, scale, and add perspective to the layer or selection. (See Figure 18-7.)

- To add **perspective** to a layer or selection, choose Edit➪Transform➪Perspective. Drag any handle or bounding line in any direction.

• **Figure 18-6:** Slide the bounding box right or left to skew the layer or selection vertically.

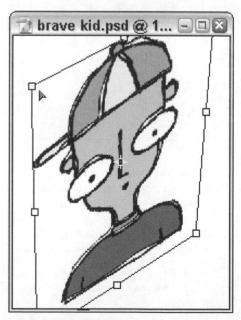

• **Figure 18-7:** Drag in any direction to distort the layer or selection.

You can move the center point (located on the boy's nose in Figure 18-6) to change the fixed point that the transformation moves around. Moving the center point is like anchoring a corner or side to a door hinge and letting the image swing around that hinge.

Linking layers

If you want to transform two or more layers at the same time, you need to link them by using the Layers palette. Here's how: In the Layers palette, select one of the layers that you want to link. Click the column to the left of another layer that you want to link to the selected layer. A tiny chain link appears in the column (shown in the following figure), showing that the layers are linked. Continue clicking in the column to the left of each layer that you want to link.

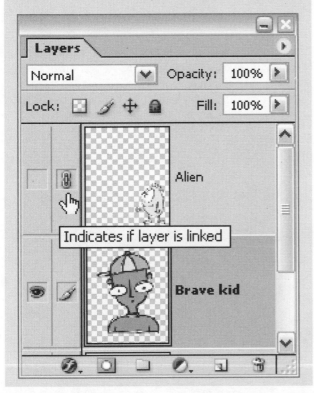

Going Wild with Free Transform

The Free Transform command does everything that is available on the Edit⇨Transform menu. Using this one command, you can scale, rotate, skew, distort, or add perspective to any layer or selection. The Free Transform command is used in conjunction with key-strokes to access each particular transformation. Here's how:

1. **Use the Layers palette to select a layer or use any of the selection tools to select an area to be transformed.**

2. **Choose Edit⇨Free Transform or press Ctrl+T/ ⌘+T.**

   A bounding box with square handles appears around the layer or selection. (Refer to Figure 18-4.)

3. **Perform the transformations that you want.**

   ▶ Drag one of the handles to **scale** the layer or selection. Hold down the Shift key while dragging a corner handle to scale proportionately. Alt/Option+drag to scale around the center point.

   ▶ To **rotate** the layer or selection, position the mouse pointer outside the bounding box, and then drag clockwise or counterclockwise. Shift+drag to rotate the layer or selection in 15-degree increments.

   ▶ **Skew** the layer or selection by Ctrl/⌘+dragging a side handle. Ctrl+Alt+drag/Ctrl+Option+ drag to skew around the center point.

   ▶ Ctrl+drag/Option+drag a corner handle to **distort** the layer or selection.

   ▶ To add **perspective** to a layer or selection, Ctrl+Alt+drag/⌘+Option+drag one of the handles. This changes the perspective along one axis. To change the perspective along two axes at the same time, Ctrl+Alt+Shift+drag/ ⌘+Option+Shift+drag.

If you want to undo the last transformation and remain within free transform mode, press Ctrl/⌘+Z.

4. **Press Enter/Return to accept the final transformation or Esc to cancel.**

You can also click the Commit check mark button on the Options bar to accept the transformation, or click the Cancel button on the Options bar.

 You can move the image in the image window when performing a transformation by dragging within the bounding box.

The Move tool, alias the Free Transform tool

Here's an oft-forgotten use for the Move tool: transformations! Believe it or not, you can set the Move tool to work exactly like the Free Transform command.

Here's how: Select the Move tool, and then select the Show Bounding Box check box on the Options bar. A transformation bounding box with handles appears around the layer or selection. To perform transformations, use the same keystrokes+dragging that you would for the Free Transform command.

Technique 19

Going Transparent with Opacity and Fill

Save Time By

↳ Lowering Opacity and Fill

↳ Blending layers together

Have you ever seen an advertisement where a ghost appears to hover in the background behind an unsuspecting person? Or, how about an animated Web graphic that appears to fade in and fade out? Both of these effects can be created in Photoshop by using opacity settings to make the image or type semi-transparent. This technique focuses on the Opacity and Fill settings found on the Layers palette. I show you how to change these settings to blend layers together, making them semi-transparent or even transparent.

You can also set the opacity of the colors that you apply to layers, including brush strokes (Technique 23), patterns (Technique 29), fills (Technique 21), and layer styles (Technique 20). For more details about setting opacity for each of these features, take a look at the techniques I've listed here. To find out how to make an animated Web graphic that fades in and out, take a look at Technique 60.

Words can be opaque

When talking with other Photoshop artists about transparency, you might find some discrepancies between meanings. First, everyone agrees that transparent is the opposite of opaque. But semi-opaque and semi-transparent can be used to describe the same effect (sort of the glass is half full or half empty depending how you look at things). Then there's translucent. Translucent is a toughie because part of the word, *lucent,* indicates light, so you would imagine that the layer or image appears lit or has some kind of light source behind it. However, some folks use translucent to mean transparent and others use it to mean semi-transparent. I guess pictures can be worth a thousand words after all.

Using Opacity and Fill

You may have noticed two little text boxes at the top of the Layers palette labeled Opacity and Fill, as shown in Figure 19-1.

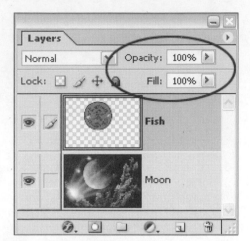

Opacity: 100%, Fill: 100%

• **Figure 19-1: The Opacity and Fill text boxes set layer opacity in different ways.**

The Opacity and Fill text boxes both affect a layer's opacity, but in different ways. The Opacity setting affects the entire layer. Every pixel on the layer is altered when the Opacity setting is changed. The Fill setting changes the opacity of the entire layer except areas where layer styles are applied. Take a look at Figure 19-2 to see what I mean.

Opacity: 40%, Fill: 100%

In Figure 19-2, I used layer styles to add a drop shadow and bevel to a quilt piece (top). Then, I lowered Opacity to 40% and left the Fill at 100% (middle). Notice how both the quilt piece and layer styles are semi-transparent. Next, I raised the Opacity back to 100% and lowered the Fill to 40% (bottom). As you can see, the quilt piece becomes semi-transparent, but the layer styles remain unchanged.

 You can adjust layer styles opacity settings in the Layer Styles dialog box.

Depending on the effect that you want to create, you can use the Opacity setting to blend layers together in different ways. The Fill setting can be used to fade the layer contents, emphasizing the effect of the layer styles. You can even set the Fill to 0% and make the layer transparent, leaving only the layer styles effect. (See Figure 19-3.)

Opacity: 100%, Fill: 40%

• **Figure 19-2: With layer styles applied to the quilt pieces, the Fill slider doesn't change the opacity of the layer effects (bottom).**

• **Figure 19-3:** With Fill set to 0%, the layer disappears entirely, leaving only the layer styles.

If you want to play around with the Opacity and Fill sliders, apply a layer style such as a drop shadow or bevel to two different layers. Then, lower the Opacity of one layer, and lower the Fill setting for the other layer. The results quickly become apparent. (Turn to Technique 20 for directions on applying layer styles.)

 If you want to create a gradual fade-in/fade-out effect on a single layer, you must use a layer mask. Turn to Technique 50 for details.

Blending Layers Together

To blend two (or more) layers together, you should use the Opacity slider on the upper layer. This makes the top layer semi-transparent so that the layer

underneath becomes visible. You can create some interesting effects with this technique. Here's how:

1. **In the Layers palette, make sure that the two layers that you want to blend to are directly next to one another, as shown in Figure 19-4.**

• **Figure 19-4:** Use the Layer's palette to place the layers next to one another.

2. **Select the uppermost of the two layers.**

3. **Click the arrow button next to the Opacity text box and use the slider that appears to adjust the layer's opacity, as shown in Figure 19-5.**

 If you're using the Move tool, you can quickly change the active layer's opacity by typing the percentage on the keyboard.

 You can't change the opacity of the Background layer or a layer that's locked. If you want to change the opacity of the Background, you have to convert it to a regular layer first. To do this, choose Layer⇨New⇨Layer from Background.

• **Figure 19-5: Use the slider to set the layer's opacity.**

Technique 20

Creating Great Effects with Layer Styles

Layer styles are really fabulous. With a few clicks of the mouse, you can add drop shadows, bevels, textures, patterns, strokes, and more to any layer, type layer, or vector shape on a shape layer. Layer styles work hand-in-hand with the Styles palette. When you come up with a layer style effect that you like, you can save the effect on the Styles palette as a preset for later use.

This technique is an introduction to using layer styles. First, you find out how to apply bevels and emboss layers to add three-dimensional qualities and depth. Then, you work with inner and outer glows to add shine to your layers and apply a colored overlay. From there, you see how to save layer styles that you create and then apply them with the Styles palette.

As you can see, I get you started. I show you how to use the Layer Styles dialog box to access these great effects, but you take it from there. You can create hundreds of effect combinations, including several layer style options not demonstrated here — drop shadows and contours; texture, pattern, and gradient overlays; satin effects and strokes. (I discuss drop shadows in Technique 44.) Use your imagination to come up with your own amazing effects!

Getting to Know Layer Styles

The Layer Style dialog box shown in Figure 20-1 is the place to go for special layer effects. As shown in Figure 20-1, the layer style effects are listed with check boxes on the left side of the dialog box. When a box is checked, that layer style is applied to the active layer. To view the settings for a layer style, click the effect's name in the left column. The settings for a selected layer style appear in the center of the dialog box. Most of the layer effects include several settings that you can change.

Effect applied when checked

Selected effect

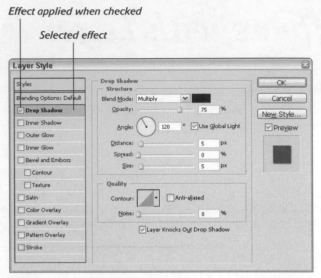

• **Figure 20-1:** The Layer Style dialog box is special effects central.

You have two ways to access the Layer Style dialog box:

1. **Use the Layers palette to select a layer.**

2. **Click the Add Layer Style button at the bottom of the palette, as shown in Figure 20-2.**

3. **Select the effect that you want to apply from the menu.**

Here's the second way:

1. **Use the Layers palette to select a layer.**

2. **Choose Layer⇨Layer Style and select the effect that you want to apply from the menu.**

In both cases, the Layer Style dialog box opens with that effect selected. You can then select the settings you need for that effect and add any other effects that you would like to apply as well.

 Layer styles can't be applied to the Background layer, a locked layer, or a layer set.

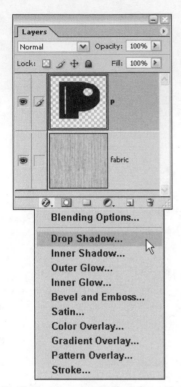

• **Figure 20-2:** Choose a special effect from the menu.

Adding Bevels and Embossing

Bevels and embossing add depth to a layer by using highlights and shadows to give it a chiseled, three-dimensional look. Using the Bevel and Emboss panel of the Layer Style dialog box shown in Figure 20-3, you can create five different effects with the Style drop-down list.

The five different bevel and emboss effects are Outer Bevel, Inner Bevel, Emboss, Pillow Emboss, and Stroke Emboss. An example of each type is shown in Figure 20-4. (At the bottom of Figure 20-4 is an extra example of a Stroke Emboss that includes a Pattern Overlay. Hey, I had the room and I wanted to show a variation!)

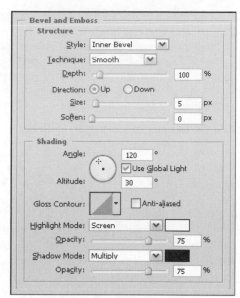

• **Figure 20-3:** In the Bevel and Emboss panel, use the Style drop-down list to select a bevel and emboss type.

As shown in Figure 20-3, you get to choose from a ton of settings when applying a bevel and/or emboss to a layer. Notice how the settings are divided into two sections: a Structure area and a Shading area. The following directions run through all the options. Use whatever settings you need to achieve the look that you're after and, by all means, experiment!

1. **Select a layer in the Layers palette.**

2. **Click the Add Layer Style button at the bottom of the Layers palette, and then choose Bevel and Emboss from the menu.**

The Layer Style dialog box opens with the Bevel and Emboss effect selected. (Refer to Figure 20-3.)

3. **Select settings in the Structure area to shape the bevel and emboss.**

▶ Use the **Style** drop-down list to select a Bevel and Emboss effect. You can choose from Outer Bevel, Inner Bevel, Emboss, Pillow Emboss, and Stroke Emboss. Refer to Figure 20-4 to find the type of effect you're looking for.

▶ Select a look for the effect by using the **Technique** drop-down list. You can choose from Smooth, Chisel Hard, and Chisel Soft.

▶ Select a **Direction** radio button to set whether the bevel and emboss appears to go up or down.

▶ Use the **Size** slider to set how large the bevel and emboss is.

▶ Drag the **Soften** slider to smooth any rough edges.

Outer Bevel *Inner Bevel*

Emboss *Pillow Emboss*

Stroke Emboss *Stroke Emboss with Pattern Overlay*

• **Figure 20-4:** The five types of bevel and emboss.

4. **In the Shading area, select settings to set the angle, shadows, and highlights. (See Figure 20-5.)**

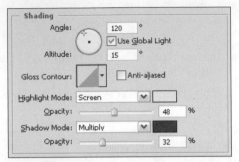

• **Figure 20-5: Use the Shading area to set how the shadows and highlights look.**

▶ Set the direction of the light source by entering a degree in the **Angle** text box or by dragging the tiny crosshair around the circle.

▶ Use the **Altitude** text box to enter a number in degrees for the height of the light source. Zero degrees shines light straight across the layer from the left. Ninety degrees shines light straight down onto the layer.

▶ Click the **Gloss Contour Picker** to select the shape of the highlights and shadow, as shown in Figure 20-6.

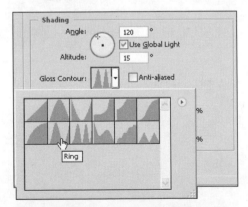

• **Figure 20-6: Use the Gloss Contour Picker to select highlight and shadow shape.**

▶ Select blending modes by using the **Highlight Mode** and **Shadow Mode** drop-down lists. To select a different highlight or shadow color, click the color square to the right of the drop-down list. Set shadow and highlight opacity with the sliders. (To find out more about Blending Modes, turn to Technique 17.)

5. **Click OK to close the Layer Style dialog box.**

Applying Inner and Outer Glows

When you want to make a layer element stand out or look like it's lit from within, try applying an inner glow or an outer glow. Glow effects work best with a lot of contrast because the glow is typically a lighter color, such as yellow or pink. So if you try to apply a glow to a layer where the background color is white, you probably won't be able to see the glow until you change the background to a darker color (or until you change the glow to a darker color). Figure 20-7 shows both types of glows.

• **Figure 20-7: Inner and outer glow layer styles.**

The setting options for the two glows are the same in the Layer Style dialog box. As shown in Figure 20-8, the settings for the inner or outer glow are divided into three areas: Structure, Elements, and Quality.

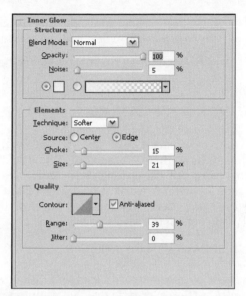

• **Figure 20-8:** The settings are divided into three areas.

Open an image or create some type and give these glows a try:

1. **Select a layer in the Layers palette.**

2. **Click the Add Layer Style button at the bottom of the Layers palette, and then choose Inner Glow or Outer Glow from the menu.**

   The Layer Style dialog box opens with the Inner Glow or Outer Glow effect selected. (Refer to Figure 20-8.)

3. **In the Structure area, select the color and opacity for the glow effect.**

   ▶ Use the radio buttons to select whether the glow is a **solid color** or a **gradient**. By default, solid light yellow is selected. To change the solid color, click the color square to open the Color Picker. To select a gradient, click the arrow to the right of the gradient swatch to open the Gradient Picker.

   ▶ Set the opacity of the glow by using the **Opacity** slider.

   ▶ To make the glow look grainy, use the **Noise** slider.

   ▶ Use the **Blend Mode** drop-down list to select a blending mode. (Blending modes are discussed in Technique 17.)

4. **In the Elements area, set whether the glow originates from the center or edge, and set the glow's size.**

   ▶ Use the **Technique** drop-down list to select whether the glow is Softer or Precise. Precise can create some jagged edges.

   ▶ Set the **Source** of the glow by selecting either the Center or Edge radio button.

   ▶ Use the **Choke** and **Size** sliders to set how large the glow is.

5. **In the Quality area, select the options that determine the shape of the glow.**

   ▶ Click the arrow to the right of the **Contour** sample to open the Contour Picker. Contour sets the shape of the glow.

   ▶ Use the **Range** slider to set the size of the glow contour.

   ▶ If you selected a gradient to color the glow, use the **Jitter** slider to make the glow grainy.

6. **Click OK to close the Layer Style dialog box.**

Blending a Color Overlay

Applying a color overlay to a layer can dramatically change the color of the layer depending on the blending mode that you select. If you select the Normal blending mode, the solid color is applied to the layer. However, select any other blending mode and the color overlay blends with the layer's current colors to create something entirely different. Figure 20-9 shows a type layer before and after a color overlay is applied. (For more about blending modes, turn to Technique 17.)

• **Figure 20-9:** Color overlays can change a layer's color radically.

Here's how to apply a color overlay:

1. Select a layer in the Layers palette.

2. Click the Add Layer Style button at the bottom of the Layers palette, and then choose Color Overlay from the menu.

The Layer Style dialog box opens with the Color Overlay effect selected. (See Figure 20-10.)

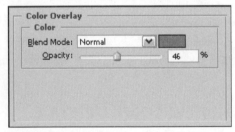

• **Figure 20-10:** The Color Overlay settings are pretty straightforward.

3. Click the color square to the right of the Blend Mode drop-down list to select a color with the Color Picker.

4. Use the Blend Mode drop-down list to select a blending mode.

Experiment with the blending modes to see what kind of interesting effects you can create.

5. Use the Opacity slider to set whether the color overlay is solid (100%) or semi-transparent.

6. Click OK to close the Layer Style dialog box.

Saving Layer Styles

After you create a great layer style, you probably want to save it so that you can apply it to other layers. This can really come in handy — and save you some time — if you're working on a project and need to use the same effect over and over. Layer styles are saved as presets in the Styles palette.

Here's how to save a layer style:

1. Open the Layer Style dialog box by double-clicking the layer style that you want to save in the Layers palette.

2. Click the New Style button.

The New Style dialog box opens, as shown in Figure 20-11.

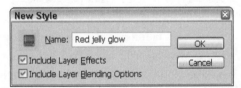

• **Figure 20-11:** Use the New Style dialog box to save a layer style as a preset.

3. Enter a name for the new preset in the Name text box.

4. Select both the Include Layer Effects check box and the Include Layer Blending Options check box.

This saves the layer effect and blending mode settings.

5. Click OK to close the New Style dialog box.

6. Click OK to close the Layer Style dialog box.

Check out your new layer style preset in the Styles palette. (See Figure 20-12.)

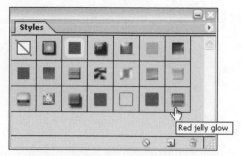

• **Figure 20-12:** The new layer style preset appears at the end of the list in the Styles palette.

 Presets are saved with Photoshop, not just with an image file, so the layer style presets that you create are always available for later use.

Applying Layer Style Presets

You can apply a layer style to a layer in several ways. The first way that comes to mind is applying a layer style preset to a layer by using the Styles palette. To apply a layer style preset, just select a layer in the Layers palette, and then click the preset in the Styles palette.

You can also apply a layer style that you've created (but not saved as a preset) by copying it to another layer in the same image file or by copying it to an entirely different image.

To copy a layer style to a different layer in the same image or a different image, use the following steps:

1. **In the Layers palette, right-click/Control+click the layer style that you want to copy and choose Copy Layer Style from the contextual menu.**

   If you want to copy a layer style effect that's made up of several layer styles, such as a drop shadow, bevel, and color overlay, right-click/Control+click the word Effects in the Layers palette and choose Copy Layer Style from the contextual menu. (See Figure 20-13.)

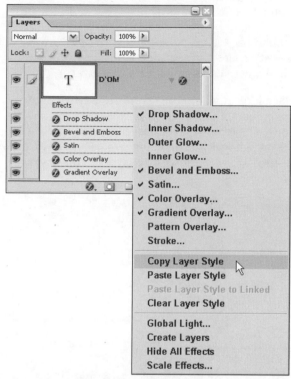

• **Figure 20-13:** Right-click/Control+click the layer style that you want to copy.

2. **Select the layer that you want to copy the layer style to in the Layers palette.**

   If you're copying the layer style to another image, select the image to make it active, and then select the layer that you want to copy it to.

3. **Right-click/Control+click the selected layer and choose Paste Layer Style from the contextual menu.**

Taking Layer Styles Apart

Layer styles can be really informative. If you ever create a style and then say, "How does it do that?" you can take the layer style apart to see what makes it tick.

To check out the anatomy of a layer style, select the layer containing the style in the Layers palette, and then choose Layer⇨Layer Style⇨Create Layers. Each layer style effect is separated onto its own layer (some layer styles may create two layers).

Take a look at where the layers are located in the Layers palette and check out their order. Figure 20-14 shows a heart with several layer styles applied: a drop shadow, a bevel, and an inner glow. Figure 20-15 shows the effects broken down into layers in the Layers palette.

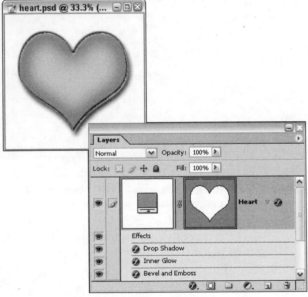

• **Figure 20-14:** The layer styles applied to this vector shape can be separated into layers.

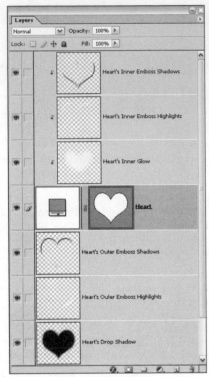

• **Figure 20-15:** When the layer style is separated into individual layers, you can really get a good idea how each effect works.

Painting on a Photo

Color Plate 24-1

Thanks to Photoshop's capabilities, Technique 24 uses a photograph as if it were wet paint.

The first step in painting on a photograph is to prepare the "canvas." I started with the original photograph (top) and added a layer filled with speckles created with the Noise filter. Then, using the Layer's palette, I set the speckled layer to Soft Light blending mode. When painting, these speckles give the brush strokes texture. The final prep step is to add an empty layer that would be used for the actual painting.

Next, I selected the Smudge tool and used the Brush Preset picker to select a brush tip. After checking Use All Layers on the Options bar, I started stroking with the Smudge tool in the image window (middle). For this painting, I used the 100 Rough Round Bristle preset in the default brush set, varying the brush's diameter as I worked.

When I was finished painting, I added a layer created using the Emboss filter that added texture to the strokes and set it to Overlay blending mode. Then I created another layer and added a canvas texture using the Texturizer filter (bottom). Finally, I set the canvas layer to Soft Light blending mode and lowered the Opacity to 30%.

Original Photograph

Painting with the Smudge tool

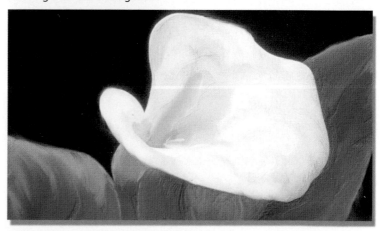

Texture layer and Canvas layer added

Match Color

Original image

Color palette

Match color being applied

Neutralize checked

Color Plate 26-1

Using the Match Color command in Technique 26, you can apply the color and tone from one image and apply it to another. This command is especially terrific when trying to match skin tones.

In this example, I started with a rather dark image of a woman's face (top). I liked the photo, but her face was so shadowed, it was hard to see her features.

After selecting the photograph I planned to borrow the tone and color from (middle left), I chose the Match Color command and applied the colors to the photograph of the woman. The tonal change was dramatic, but a little too red (middle right). After selecting the Neutralize option, the skin tones and overall color evened out (bottom).

Gradient Mapping

Color Plate 27-1

Gradient maps can be used to recolor images as shown in Technique 27. Depending upon the gradient you select and how you apply it, the recoloring can go from subtle to wild.

In this series of images, I applied the listed gradient directly to the vultures in the left column. This certainly did change the bird from its original colors, but the results were rather startling.

The images in the right column use the same gradients that were applied to their mates in the left column, but instead of applying the gradient map to the image, I applied it to a copied layer. Then I adjusted the blending mode for the copied layer, blending the recolored layer with the original. I set the top right image to Luminosity blending mode, the middle right image to Hue blending mode, and the lower right image to Color blending mode.

Blue, yellow, blue

Luminosity blending mode

Violet, green, orange

Hue blending mode

Copper

Color blending mode

Adjusting Levels

Original image

Red channel adjustment

Green channel adjustment

After blue channel adjustment

Color Plate 30-1

Technique 30 shows you how to adjust the tone and color of an image using Levels.

The color cast of this great photograph of Mount Banner (top) is a little dark, the snow isn't as white as it should be, and the sky could be more blue.

I could have adjusted the tone and color by using Auto Levels, which tends to work well generally, but because this photo is so special, I really wanted to adjust the colors by hand.

After opening the Levels dialog box, I started by choosing the Red channel and adjusting the highlights and midtones using the histogram (middle left). Next, I chose the Green channel and adjusted its highlights and midtones as well (middle right). Finally, I selected the Blue channel and adjusted the midtones and highlights to create a lovely blue sky (bottom).

Photo Filter Effects

Color Plate 33-1

Real-world photo filters are used by photographers to correct lighting conditions, enhance specific colors, and create special effects. As shown in Technique 33, the photo filters included with Photoshop can be used to enhance tone or completely recolor an image.

The mountain photograph shown at the top seemed perfect for a bit of experimentation with photo filters.

After selecting the Photo Filter command, I tested the preset photo filters available in the dialog box. Three of these filters really struck my fancy: The Warming Filter (85) (middle left) adds warm, reddish hues; the Violet filter changed the image to a misty morning sunrise (middle right); the Deep Yellow filter gave the mountains the look of a warm sunny afternoon (bottom).

Original image

Warming FIlter (85)

Violet

Deep Yellow

Colorizing a Photograph

Original image

Art History Brush

Hue/Saturation

Gradient Map

Channel Mixer

Deep red photo filter

Color Plate 35-1

Colorizing photographs in Photoshop is really interesting because there are so many ways to go about it. Technique 35 shows you several methods for colorizing black and white photos.

For this example, I started with a color photograph of flowers (top left), converted it to Grayscale mode, and then reconverted it to RGB mode. Next, I set the tiny Art History Brush source icon in the Layers palette to the history state before the Grayscale conversion. Then, I started experimenting.

First, I just used the Art History Brush, set in Normal blending mode, to bring back the color in a few flowers (top right).

The next version went back to square one, where I started with the grayscale image. After applying the Hue/Saturation command with the Colorize option selected, the image took on a lovely sepia tone (middle left). Then, I used the Art History Brush, set to Soft Light blending mode, to gently bring back some of the color in the flowers.

In my third experiment, I recolored a layer copy of the original grayscale image using the Yellow, pink, green gradient (middle right). Then, I set the copied layer to blend with the original using the Difference blending mode. The result is a startling wheat and brown mix with deep blue flowers.

Finally, two other recoloring methods came to mind. I used the Channel Mixer to give the original RGB converted grayscale image an overall blue cast (bottom left). Also, I tried a deep red photo filter to recolor the image (bottom right).

Creating Duotones

Color Plate 35-2

As discussed in Technique 35, duotones use specified ink colors to print images. An image that uses one color to print is a monotone. When two inks are used, the print is a duotone. With three inks, it's a tritone, and four inks make it a quadtone.

I started with a grayscale image of stone arches. The first monotone I created used blue as the ink (top left). Then I added black as the second ink, creating a duotone (top right). Notice how the addition of black adds depth and shading.

I created the next monotone I created with brown (middle left). Then, I added orange to create a duotone (middle right). From there, I progressed to a tritone when I added violet to the ink mix (bottom left). Finally, I added green to create a quadtone (bottom right). It's really interesting to see how the colors mix and what the results are.

Monotone: blue

Duotone: blue, black

Monotone: brown

Duotone: brown, orange

Tritone: brown, orange, violet

Quadtone: brown, orange, violet, green

Unsharp Mask Filter

Original image

Amount 50%, Radius 1

Amount 100%, Radius 3

Amount 350%, Radius 5

Red channel only

Green channel only

Blue channel only

Blue channel, Ink Outlines

Color Plate 37-1

The Unsharp Mask filter is one of the all-time great filters. Technique 37 shows you how to use it to nudge a little sharpness into an image, or how to use it to increase the sharpness until the effect is right over the edge.

I started with an image of two masks that was pretty good, though a bit blurry around the edges (top left). I then applied the Unsharp Mask filter to three duplicate images using increasing settings each time (top right, upper middle left and right).

In the next three images, I applied the Unsharp Mask filter to only one channel in each image. Notice how the edges are enhanced with the specific color (lower middle left and right, and lower left).

For the final image (lower right), I also applied the Ink Outlines filter to the blue channel.

Painting a Watercolor

Color Plate 38-1

Photoshop includes so many great filters. I love using them because they give so much in the way of results with very little effort. But, while many of the filters work well, you can enhance their effects, and make them look really special with just a little work.

The Watercolor filter is a great example of a filter that works well; it gives you a nice image with the appearance of a watercolor painting. But, with a few tweaks, as shown in Technique 38, the watercolor can really come alive.

I started with a Maine coastal photograph (top); I then applied the Watercolor filter to the image (middle left).

Then, I copied the filtered layer and applied the Underpainting filter, set the layer's opacity to 60%, and selected the Soft Light blending mode (middle right).

Finally, I copied the filtered layer one more time and applied the Note Paper filter and set the blending mode to Soft Light (bottom). I think the result was worth the extra effort. There's more detail and more texture.

Original image © Harold Davis.

Original image

Watercolor filter

Underpainting filter

Note Paper filter

Making a Silkscreen

Original image

Equalize and High Pass

Threshold filter

Median filter

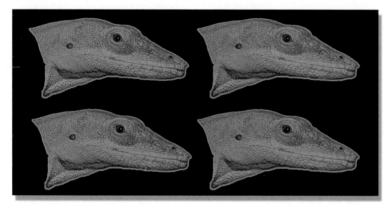

Threshold

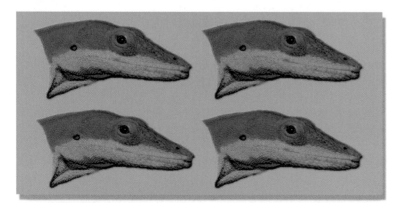

Red, green channels

Color Plate 40-1

I have always enjoyed Andy Warhol's photo silkscreens. So, I thought it would be great if I could duplicate the effect using Photoshop. Technique 40 explores one way to do this.

I started with a friendly looking green lizard (top left), and applied the Equalize and High Pass filters to the Blue and Green channels (top right). Next, I applied the Threshold filter to the Red channel (upper middle left), then switched to the Blue channel and applied the Median filter (upper middle right). Finally, I applied the Threshold filter to the Blue channel and added a black background (lower middle).

As an experiment, I ran through the steps again, but instead started with the Red and Green channels for the first steps, then switched to the Blue channel for the final steps. The results — with a green background — are unique to say the least (bottom).

Creating Sketches

Color Plate 41-1

Some of the filters on the Filter⇨Sketch menu imitate different drawing methods. When used alone, these filters work well, but they're nothing to write home about.

I wanted to improve upon the results, so instead of applying the sketch filters to the original image in Technique 41, I applied the filters to a copied layer, and then adjusted the blending mode.

I started with a photograph of a rowboat pulled up on the shore of a lake (top).

For my first sketch, I applied the Chalk & Charcoal filter to the copied layer and set the blending mode to Lighten (middle left).

For the second sketch, I started fresh with the image and applied the Graphic Pen filter to the copied layer, and then set the blending mode to Hard Light (middle right).

The last sketch I created applied the Charcoal filter to the copied layer using navy blue as the Foreground color (resulting in a blue sketch). Then, I set the blending mode to Soft Light.

Three different filters applied using three different blending modes give very different results.

Original image

Chalk & Charcoal

Graphic Pen

Charcoal

Metal Type

COPPER

Original black type

COPPER

Bas Relief filter

COPPER

Drop Shadow, Inner Shadow

COPPER

Color Overlay

COPPER

Curves

COPPER

Chrome filter

Color Plate 46-1

I have always liked type, so creating special effect type is a great treat.

This color plate shows the steps I took in Technique 46 to evolve plain black type into metallic copper type.

I started with black type set in the Copperplate font, and then applied the Bas Relief filter to give the type a beveled edge and added light.

Then, I headed into the Layer Style dialog box and applied Drop and Inner Shadows, and a copper colored Overlay.

Next, I used curves to adjust the tone and contrast of the type. Finally, I added a new layer with gray type shaped just like the original black type, and applied the Chrome filter using the Overlay blending mode.

Lava Type

My kids love volcanoes, so I started wondering if I could create type that looked like lava was melting it.

In Technique 47, I started with black type set in the Impact font, rasterized the type, and then used the Liquify filter to make the type look like it was melting.

Next, I added a new layer and used the Freeform Pen tool to create a path that looked like dripping lava and filled it with bright red. Then, I applied an Outer Glow and Bevel & Emboss to the red lava to give it texture.

Finally, I went back to the liquified type and added an outer glow to make it look red-hot.

Type after Liquify filter is applied

Lava layer added

Outer Glow, Bevel & Emboss applied to Lava layer

Outer Glow applied to liquified type layer

Jelly Type

Color Overlay

Drop Shadow, Inner Shadow

Outer Glow, Inner Glow

Bevel & Emboss, Satin

Chrome layer added, Soft Light blending mode

Color Plate 48-1

This jelly type in Technique 48 is *the* layer style blowout. It's amazing that almost all the effects that change the type from flat black to the appearance of three-dimensional jelly are created using layer styles.

I started with black type set in Brush455 BT and jumped right into the Layer Styles dialog box and added a bright red Color Overlay. Next, I added Drop and Inner Shadows, which started to pull the type up off the page.

Then, I added Outer and Inner Glows to add more saturation to the type and shadows. Next, the Bevel & Emboss layer style gave the type a puffy molded quality, and the Satin effect added a mottled color.

Finally, I really got the jelly type bouncing off the page when I added a new layer with gray type shaped just like the original type, applied the Chrome filter, and set the blending mode to Soft Light.

Layer Masks

Color Plate 49-1

Layer masks are such a versatile Photoshop feature. As Technique 49 shows, being able to make a portion of a layer invisible or partially transparent is crucial to many effects.

For this image, I started with a view of a planet in some other galaxy (top). I wanted to add a photograph of a morning glory (middle left) on top of the moon, and add the goats (middle right) to the alien landscape.

I placed the Morning Glory layer above the alien planet layer and added a layer mask shaped like the moon. That way, only the portion of the morning glory covering the moon would show. Then, I set the blending mode to Lighten and the Opacity to 95%.

The goats were a much more tricky masking task. I created a layer mask that blocked out all the shrubs and vegetation around them, then positioned them behind some rocks on the planet's surface. I left the layer Opacity at 100% and set the blending mode to Luminosity. This made the goats' color change to blend in with the alien landscape (middle right).

Finally, I created a new layer and added shadows for the goats. This shadow layer I set to 40% Opacity and Soft Light blending mode (bottom).

Original planetscape

Morning Glory layer

Goat layer

Original image © Harold Davis.

Goats' shadows added

Channel Mixing

Original image

Red and green channels swapped

Red and blue channels swapped

Blue and green channels swapped

Color Plate 54-1

Technique 54 shows you how to use the Channel Mixer to recolor images without affecting the detail. The Channel Mixer works by changing how the channels mix together. It adjusts the output of each channel by adjusting how light or dark the channel is.

Swapping the color channels creates different color blends, which results in image recoloring.

I started with a photograph of a white peacock (top). Then, I used the Channel Mixer to swap the contents of the Red channel with the Green channel and vice versa. The result was a violet peacock (second from top).

Then, I went back to the original image and swapped the contents of the Red channel with the Blue channel and vice versa. This resulted in a golden peacock (third from top).

For the final change of plumage, I returned once more to the original image and swapped the contents of the Blue and Green channels. This created a peacock with cyan feathers (bottom).

Technique 21

Recoloring with Fill Layers

Save Time By

- Applying a fill layer
- Cheating using Hue/Saturation

One day, you're working on an advertising project for a client who just *has* to include a particular photograph in the ad. The client says that the photo is really great except that the shirt the model is wearing is the wrong color or the background clashes with the furniture or the flowers should be yellow, not pink! All you have to do is say, "No problem," get to your computer, and then use Photoshop to recolor the area with a fill layer.

Fill layers are used to recolor a layer or selection by using another layer instead of applying the correction to the actual image and altering the image pixels forever. This layer-based recoloring leads to an amazing amount of flexibility. You can always change the color without changing the image itself. Also, because the area being recolored is defined with a layer mask, you can adjust the layer mask anytime that you need to include or exclude an area. (If you find that you need to alter the layer mask after you create a fill layer, turn to Technique 49 for a complete discussion on working with layer masks.)

This technique takes you through recoloring an image with a fill layer. It may sound a bit scary or difficult, but it's not! Using fill layers is really easy. After you try them out, you discover just how flexible they are.

Applying a Fill Layer

A fill layer can be applied to an entire layer or a selection on a layer. If you're going to apply the fill layer to a selected area, really take the time to make a good selection with the various selection tools. Be careful about the edge of the selection. If the edge is *high-contrast,* meaning that there's an abrupt color change from the selected to unselected area (for instance, dark blue to light tan), you might want to feather the selection by one or two pixels. To feather a selection, choose Select➪Feather. (For a complete rundown of the selection tools and selecting, take a look at the selections chapter in *Photoshop CS For Dummies* by Deke McClelland and yours truly, published by Wiley.)

The other thing that you should be aware of when using fill layers is blending modes. Blending modes affect the way the fill layer's color blends with the layer underneath. If the new color that you're using in the fill layer is similar in saturation to the old color, the Hue, Soft Light, or Color blending modes may work best. If the new color is significantly darker, experiment with the Multiply blending mode. Try the Screen blending mode if the new color is quite a bit lighter. Work with the blending modes until you achieve the color that you're looking for. (For a complete discussion about blending modes, turn to Technique 17.)

Here's how to apply a fill layer:

1. **In the Layers palette, select the layer to which you want to apply the fill layer.**

However, if you want to recolor only a portion of a layer, select the area on the layer. For this example, I selected the white blouse worn by the woman in Figure 21-1. Using a fill layer, I'm changing the blouse color to medium blue.

• **Figure 21-1: I selected the white blouse with the Magnetic Lasso and Lasso tools.**

2. **Click the Create New Fill or Adjustment Layer button at the bottom of the Layers palette and choose Solid Color from the menu, as shown in Figure 21-2.**

When applying a fill layer to an image, you can also use a gradient or pattern. If you want to do so, select either Gradient or Pattern from the menu.

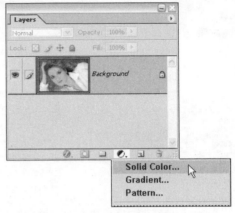

• **Figure 21-2: Choose Solid Color from the Create New Fill or Adjustment Layer menu.**

3. **Use the Color Picker to select a color.**

If you want to use the Color Picker to select a specific spot or process color, click Custom, use the Book drop-down list to select a color swatch book, such as PANTONE Solid Coated, and then select the specific color. (See Figure 21-3.)

As you select the color, notice that it appears in the image window, though it may not blend in well. (Don't worry — you can fix that with a blending mode.)

4. **When you're finished selecting a color, click OK to close the Color Picker.**

The fill layer appears in the Layers window and the new color appears in the image window, as shown in Figure 21-4.

5. **In the Layers palette, use the Blend drop-down list to select a blending mode.**

After you select the right blending mode, the fill layer's pixels blend with the underlying layer. For this example, I used the Multiply mode to blend the pixels. The result is shown in Figure 21-5.

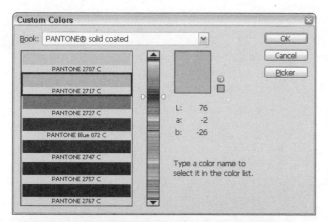

• Figure 21-3: You can use the Color Picker to select a custom color.

• Figure 21-5: The right blending mode makes the fill layers pixels blend with the image pixels.

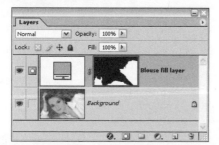

• Figure 21-4: The new color appears in the image window, though it may not blend well, yet.

Recoloring the Sneaky Way

Another way to recolor an image is to use the Hue/Saturation command. This doesn't allow the exact color matching that using a fill layer does, but it's a fast way to change the color of a layer or selected area. It's not quite cheating, but it is a quick trick.

You can apply the Hue/Saturation command to the actual layer pixels by choosing Image⇨Adjustments⇨ Hue/Saturation, or by applying the command by using an adjustment layer (which I recommend). Using an adjustment layer is similar to a fill layer in that it does not alter the image pixels forever. (Take a look at Technique 22 for a complete discussion about adjustment layers and what they can do.)

Whichever way you decide to make the adjustment (to the actual pixels or by using an adjustment layer), here's how to shift the color in an image:

1. **In the Layers palette, select the layer that you want to recolor.**

    If you want to recolor only a portion of a layer, select an area on the layer.

2. Choose Image⇨Adjustments⇨Hue/Saturation to apply the change to actual image pixels, or click the Create New Fill or Adjustment Layer button at the bottom of the Layers palette and choose Hue/Saturation from the menu.

The Hue/Saturation dialog box shown in Figure 21-6 opens.

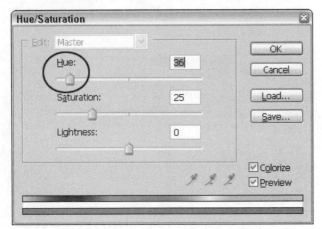

• **Figure 21-6:** Use the Hue/Saturation dialog box to shift the color in the image.

3. Select the Colorize check box.

4. Use the Hue slider to recolor the layer or selection.

Notice that as you move the Hue slider, the new color appears in the color bar at the bottom of the Hue/Saturation dialog box.

5. Click OK when the image is the right color.

Using the Hue/Saturation command, I changed the blue blouse from Figure 21-5 to light tan, as shown in Figure 21-7.

Figure 21-7: Using Hue/Saturation, I shifted the blouse color from blue to tan.

Working with Adjustment Layers

Save Time By

✔ Applying adjustment layers

✔ Adjusting the adjustments

Using Photoshop CS, you can change the color and tone of an image for correction purposes (a photograph might be underexposed) or to create a special effect. Typically, you turn to the Image⇨ Adjustments menu to find the command that makes the change you want: Levels, Hue/Saturation, or Color Balance just to name a few (actually, Photoshop has more than a dozen adjustment commands; I discuss many in detail in Part V).

But, while the adjustment commands accessed on the Image menu work just fine, they affect only the active layer and they permanently change the layer's pixels. What happens if you have a complex image containing eight layers and you want to correct six of them at once? Well, you can merge the layers together, but that ruins any further individual layer editing. So that solution is certainly out of the question. You could also apply the adjustment commands to each layer one at a time, but that is tedious, time consuming, and also permanently changes the layers' pixels — definitely out of the question. As you're starting to pull your hair out, you exclaim, "But, Photoshop has everything so there must be an answer!"

Indeed there is and it's a great one, too. The answer is to use adjustment layers.

Adjustment layers use the same commands found on the Image⇨ Adjustments menu, but they work as layer-based corrections. This gives you an amazing amount of flexibility. Here are a few of the pluses inherent in adjustment layers:

✔ Layer-based corrections are not permanent unlike the commands on the Image⇨Adjustment menu. They blend only with the pixels on the layers below; they don't permanently change pixels. If you decide you need to change the adjustment later, you can. If you decide you don't want to use the adjustment layer, you can either hide it by clicking the eye icon on the Layers palette or delete it altogether.

✔ The number of layers affected by the adjustment layer depends upon where the adjustment layer is located in the stacking order in the Layers palette. Every layer under an adjustment layer is modified. Any layers above the adjustment layer are not modified. You can move the adjustment layer up and down the stacking order to affect more or fewer layers.

✔ Because these corrections are layer-based, you also have the option of selecting a blending mode and opacity. While you can use Edit⇨Fade to employ a blending mode and opacity when using the commands on the Image⇨Adjustments menu, the Fade command is available only immediately after using the adjustment command. Conversely, the Blend drop-down list and Opacity slider are always available to the adjustment layer in the Layers palette.

Quite a list, huh? I almost never use the commands on the Image⇨Adjustments menu; instead, I usually opt for an adjustment layer. This technique shows you how to add the power of adjustment layers to your projects. Open an image and give them a try. After you discover the full potential of adjustment layers, I guarantee you won't turn back.

Applying Adjustment Layers

Using adjustment layers is quite easy. Here's how:

1. **Select the layer you want the adjustment layer to appear above.**

You can also use the selection tools to select a specific area that you want to correct.

For this example, I'm using an underexposed photograph of bottles (see Figure 22-1), and I use the Levels command to correct it.

glass.psd @ 33.3% (Levels 1, Layer Mask/8)

• **Figure 22-1:** This photograph is way underexposed.

2. **Click the New Fill or Adjustment Layer button at the bottom of the Layers palette, and choose an adjustment command from the menu (see Figure 22-2).**

The top three commands on the menu are for creating a fill layer. If you need to recolor an image, turn to Technique 21 to find out how to apply a fill layer.

Depending on the adjustment command you select, the dialog box for that command appears, as shown in Figure 22-3.

3. **Use the dialog box to make the adjustments, and then click OK.**

The adjustment layer appears in the Layers palette and the image is corrected (see Figure 22-4).

Adjustment commands

Fill commands

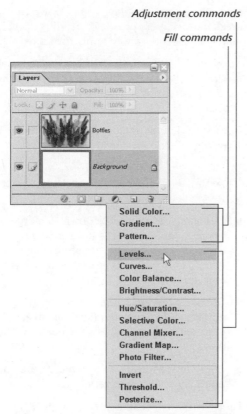

Adjustment layer

• **Figure 22-2:** Choose an adjustment command from the New Fill or Adjustment Layer menu.

• **Figure 22-4:** The Levels adjustment layer corrects the photograph's underexposure.

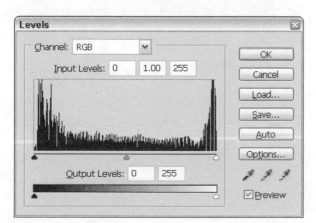

• **Figure 22-3:** For this example, I used the Levels command.

Adjusting the Adjustments

After you have an adjustment layer in place, you can alter the applied command depending upon your needs. Here's a kitchen sink list of what you can do with an adjustment layer:

✔ Change the adjustment layer's blending mode or opacity using the Blend drop-down list or Opacity slider in the Layers palette.

✔ Change the amount of correction by changing the command's settings. To change the selected settings for an adjustment layer, double-click the layer's thumbnail to open the command's dialog box.

✔ Target the adjustment layer corrections to a specific area by altering the layer mask attached to the adjustment layer. (For details on working with layer masks, turn to Technique 49.) For instance, in Figure 22-5, I altered the layer mask attached to the Levels adjustment layer (shown in Figure 22-4), making the Levels correction appear only on the right side of the image.

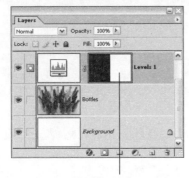

Modified layer mask

• **Figure 22-5: Altering the attached layer mask targets the adjustment layer's correction.**

✔ Move the adjustment layer up or down the layer stack in the Layers palette depending upon how many layers you want to apply the adjustment to.

✔ Copy an adjustment layer within the same document by dragging the adjustment layer in the Layers palette down over the Create New Layer button.

✔ Copy an adjustment layer to another image by dragging the adjustment layer from the Layers palette onto the other image window.

✔ Make the effects of the adjustment layer permanent by selecting it and then either:

▶ Choosing Layer⇨Merge Down to merge the adjustment layer to the layer below it. This command applies the adjustment layer's effects *only* to the layer with which it is merged.

▶ Choosing Layer⇨Merge Visible to merge the adjustment layer with all visible layers (the ones with the eye icons showing in the Layers palette).

▶ Choosing Layer⇨Flatten to merge the adjustment layer with all layers.

✔ Hide the effects of an adjustment layer by clicking the eye icon to the left of the adjustment layer in the Layers palette.

✔ Delete an adjustment layer by dragging it to the trashcan icon at the bottom of the Layers palette.

Part IV

Painting and Coloring to Enhance Your Images

The 5th Wave   By Rich Tennant

"You might want to adjust the value of your 'Nudge' function."

Technique 23

Everything You Ever Needed to Know about Creating Brushes

Brushes, brushes everywhere! So many to use and so little time! Photoshop is your ultimate source for virtual brushes. Any kind of brush that you can imagine you can design and save in Photoshop. With so many options, you can create literally *millions* of brushes.

Brushes set the size and shape of the mouse cursor. When you select a brush, you're in effect selecting a *brush tip*. The shape of the brush tip could be anything — round with a soft edge like a magic marker, or square with a chalky texture like a pastel, for instance. (Also, don't confuse brushes with the Brush tool, which some Photoshop artists also refer to as "the brush.")

Many tools in Photoshop use brushes to define the size and shape of the tool. Any tool that you use to stroke an image uses brush settings. When working with these tools, besides selecting brush size and shape, you also need to select other settings for the tool by using the Options bar; possible settings include opacity, blending modes, and flow. Check out the sidebar "Which tools use brushes?" for a complete list of tools.

This technique takes you into the wonderful and sometimes wacky world of Photoshop brushes. Here, you find out where to locate brushes, how to select them, and how to create your own custom brushes. If you use a tablet with a pressure-sensitive stylus, I show you what settings work with pressure and tilt. (For instance, you could set a brush to splatter paint farther from the mouse cursor depending on how hard you're pressing.) From there, you discover how to save the brushes that you create as presets and in brush libraries. Finally, you take a quick look at brushes available on the Web and how to load them for your use in Photoshop.

Which tools use brushes?

Many tools in Photoshop use brushes to define the size and shape of the tool. These tools are Art History Brush, Background Eraser, Blur, Brush, Burn, Clone Stamp, Color Replacement, Dodge, Eraser, History Brush, Pattern Stamp, Pencil, Sharpen, Smudge, and Sponge.

Looking for Brushes in All the Right Places

You can go to two places in Photoshop to find brushes: the Brush Preset picker and the Brushes palette.

The Brush Preset picker, located on the Options bar and shown in Figure 23-1, lets you select from brush presets and also lets you change brush size and hardness.

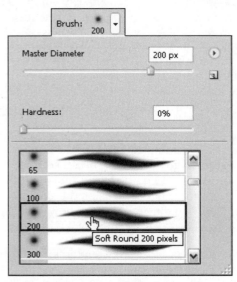

• **Figure 23-1:** The Brush Preset picker is used to select brush presets and change brush size and hardness.

The Brushes palette is where to go to select brushes, change any kind of brush settings, and create custom brushes. By default, the Brushes palette is docked in the Palette Well. If you want, you can drag it by the palette tab out into the Photoshop workspace, as shown in Figure 23-2. If you don't see the Brushes palette, choose Window➪Brushes or press F5.

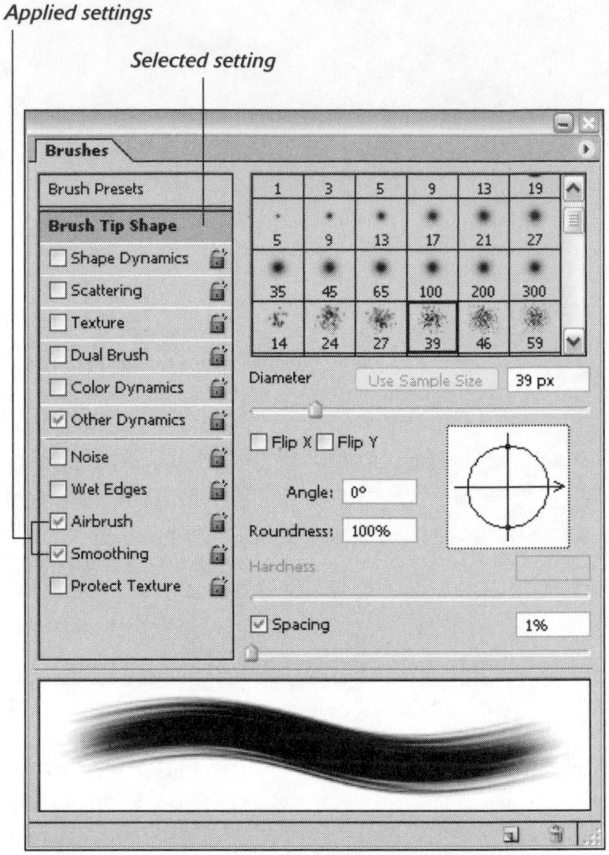

• **Figure 23-2:** The Brushes palette is the central station for brush selection and creation.

As shown in Figure 23-2, the Brushes palette is divided into three areas. On the left in the rectangular box are the brush settings. A check mark next to a brush setting indicates that that setting is applied to the currently selected brush. Options that you can select for each brush setting are located at the right side of the palette. These options change depending on which brush setting is selected. At the bottom of the palette is a brush preview area. When you select a brush or create a new brush, a preview of the stroke appears in this area.

Creating Brushes

When you first start creating your own custom brushes, keep it simple. Because so many options are available in the Brushes palette, starting out can be a bit overwhelming. If you start simply, you discover which brush setting affects a particular aspect of the brush appearance. Otherwise, you may add so many options that you don't know which setting does what.

Because Photoshop never does anything by halves, you can actually create brushes in two ways:

- ✔ Select an existing brush in the Brushes palette, and then modify its appearance with the various brush settings.

- ✔ Create a brush by selecting pixels in the image window and then using this selection to create a new brush. The selected pixels could be anything from a colorful speckled area to an actual image, like a duck or shoe.

Using the Brushes palette

The first thing that you should do when creating a custom brush with the Brushes palette is select Brush Presets in the brush settings area, and then choose a brush tip from the list as shown in Figure 23-3.

The next step is to change the settings of the brush that you selected to meet your needs by using any of the brush settings available in the Brushes palette.

In this section, I run through each available brush setting. You can select and set as many or as few brush settings as you want. For those of you using a tablet and pressure-sensitive stylus, I highlight these settings in each section. When you're finished creating your custom brush, turn to the section "Saving Presets and Libraries," later in this technique, to save your brush.

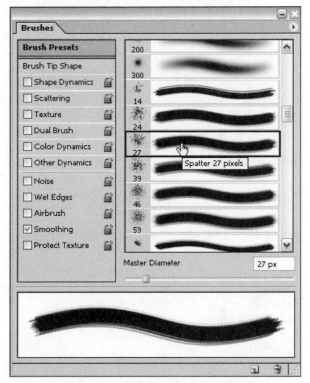

• **Figure 23-3:** Select a brush preset in the Brushes palette.

 You may have noticed the tiny padlocks next to each brush setting in the Brushes palettes. (See Figure 23-4.) When a padlock is selected, it locks those particular brush settings, freezing them so that they can't be changed by mistake.

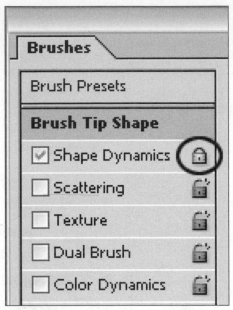

• **Figure 23-4:** Click the tiny padlock to freeze brush settings.

Brush Tip Shape

Use the Brush Tip Shape settings to select the brush's diameter, angle, hardness, and spacing, as shown in Figure 23-5. Figure 23-6 shows the effects of these settings.

Make the most of the following Brush Tip Shape settings:

✔ Change brush width by moving the **Diameter** slider. Moving the slider to the left makes the brush tip smaller, and moving the slider to the right makes it bigger.

✔ The brush that you selected might be directional: for instance, a leaf leaning to the right. Select the **Flip X** check box to flip the brush tip horizontally (this would make the leaf lean to the left), and select the **Flip Y** check box to flip the brush tip vertically (this would flip the leaf upside down).

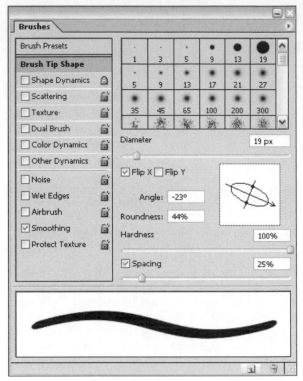

• **Figure 23-5:** The Brush Tip Shape settings are used to set brush diameter and spacing.

✔ Adjust **Roundness** to make the brush tip shape elliptical. A setting of 100% is round. The lower the percentage, the shorter and fatter the brush tip becomes.

✔ If your Roundness setting is less than 100%, you can enter a percentage in the **Angle** text box to slant the brush tip. You can also change the brush Angle by dragging the arrowhead in the circle to the right of Angle and Roundness.

✔ Soften the edges of the brush tip by adjusting the **Hardness** setting. The lower the setting, the softer the brush.

✔ Use the **Spacing** setting to determine how often a drop of paint falls from your brush tip. When you stroke with a brush tip that's set to a lower percentage, a solid line is created. Higher percentages spread out the paint drops, making dotted lines.

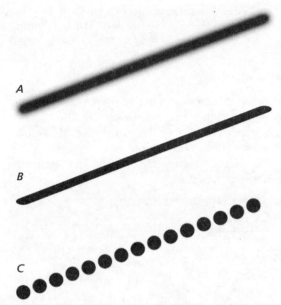

• **Figure 23-6:** A: 0% Hardness, 100% Roundness, 25% Spacing. B: 100% Hardness, 50% Roundness, 25% Spacing. C: 100% Hardness, 100% Roundness, 125% Spacing.

Shape Dynamics

Shape Dynamics are used to vary the width, angle, and roundness during a brush stroke. In the Brushes palette, click the name Shape Dynamics (*not* the check box) to view the settings shown in Figure 23-7.

Notice how the Shape Dynamics settings are divided into three areas: Size Jitter, Angle Jitter, and Roundness Jitter. *Jitter* refers to how randomly these settings are applied during a brush stroke. For instance, 0% Size Jitter doesn't change the size of the brush during a stroke, but 100% Size Jitter allows random size changes during a stroke.

Each setting also includes a Control drop-down list. Control sets how the random effect is manipulated. All of these effects have the following Control settings:

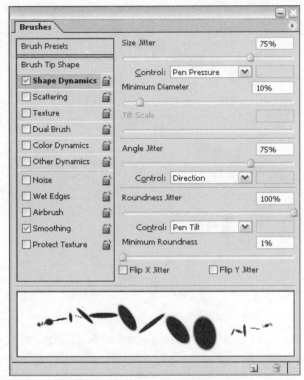

• **Figure 23-7:** Shape Dynamics are used to vary the width and shape of a brush stroke.

✔ **Fade:** This option sets how a stroke fades out from the start of the stroke to the end of the stroke.

✔ **Pen Pressure**, **Pen Tilt**, and **Stylus Wheel:** These three options are for use with a pressure-sensitive tablet and pen.

Take a look at Figure 23-8 to see the Shape Dynamics settings in action. The stroke labeled A is the base stroke. Stroke B adds the Size Jitter option, stroke C adds the Angle Jitter option to stroke B, and stroke D adds Roundness Jitter to stroke C.

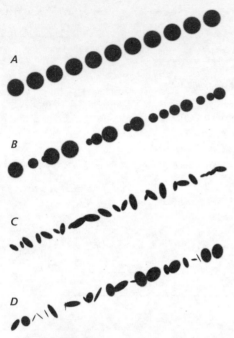

• **Figure 23-8: A: 90% Hardness, 120% Spacing, 0% Size Jitter. B: 75% Size Jitter, 10% Minimum Diameter. C: 75% Angle Jitter. D: 100% Roundness Jitter, 1% Minimum Roundness.**

Here's the scoop on the Jitter bug:

✔ Use the **Size Jitter** slider to set how randomly the brush tip size changes during a stroke. A setting of 0% allows for no change, and a 100% setting allows for the maximum amount of random change.

✔ If your brush tip is set to less than 100% roundness on the Brush Tip Shape panel, you can use the **Angle Jitter** slider to set how randomly the angle of the brush tip changes during a stroke. The higher the setting, the more angle changes occur.

✔ Use the **Roundness Jitter** slider to set how much the roundness of the brush tip changes during a stroke. A higher setting makes for more variation.

Scattering

Scattering sets how a brush mark is placed during a stroke. The higher the Scatter setting, the more marks spread away from the stroke's path. Figure 23-9 shows the Scattering options available in the Brushes palette. Figure 23-10 shows the Scattering brush effect in action.

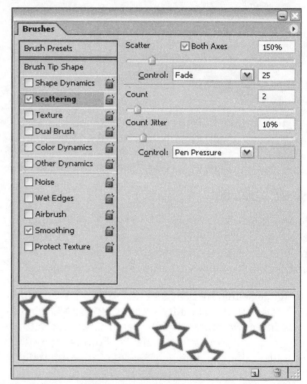

• **Figure 23-9: Use the Scattering brush settings to splatter the paint around the brush stroke.**

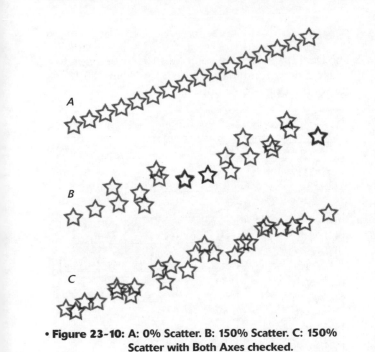

• **Figure 23-10:** A: 0% Scatter. B: 150% Scatter. C: 150% Scatter with Both Axes checked.

The following list is your guide to Scattering nirvana:

- Move the **Scatter** slider to set how widely brush marks are placed around the path of a stroke. The higher the setting, the farther the brush marks are from the stroke.

- Use the **Count** option to set how many brush marks occur as a stroke is made (based on the Spacing setting selected on the Brush Tip Shape panel). The **Count Jitter** setting randomizes the Count option setting.

- Both the Scatter and Count settings include a **Control** drop-down list. Control sets how the effect is manipulated. The Control settings are:

   ▶ **Fade:** This option sets how a stroke fades out from the start of the stroke to the end of the stroke.

   ▶ **Pen Pressure**, **Pen Tilt**, and **Stylus Wheel:** These three options are for use with a pressure sensitive tablet and pen.

Texture

The Texture brush settings can be used in two ways: to create the effect of painting on a textured surface such as burlap or rice paper, or to add a special textured effect that makes your brush strokes stand out. Figure 23-11 shows the Texture settings in the Brushes dialog box. Figure 23-12 shows a few textured strokes.

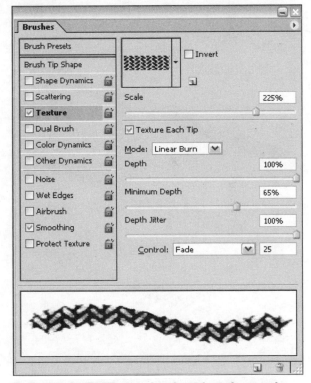

• **Figure 23-11:** The Texture brush settings changes the surface quality of your strokes.

Add some texture to your world with the following options:

- ✔ Click the **Pattern Picker** to select a pattern for the texture.

- ✔ Use the **Scale** slider to set how large the pattern is. The higher the percentage, the larger the pattern.

- ✔ Choose blending mode from the **Mode** drop-down list to set how the stroke colors blend with the colors already present in the image. (For more about blending modes, turn to Technique 17.)

- ✔ Select the **Texture Each Tip** check box to set how the selected blending mode mixes the brush colors throughout the stroke.

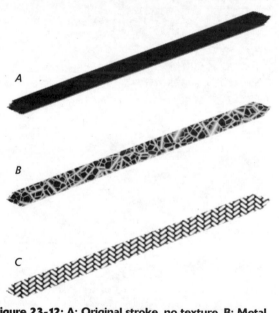

• **Figure 23-12:** A: Original stroke, no texture. B: Metal Landscape pattern applied. C: Herringbone 2 pattern applied.

Dual Brush

The Dual Brush setting combines two brush tips to create a new, combination brush tip. Figure 23-13 shows the Dual Brush options.

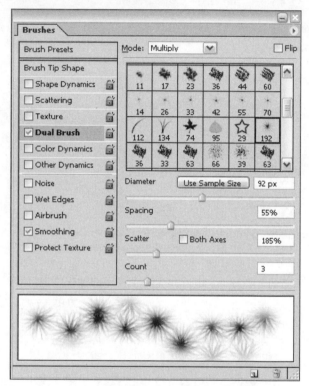

• **Figure 23-13:** By using the Dual Brush settings, you can stroke with two brush tips at the same time.

Use the following steps to create a combination brush tip:

1. **Use the brush tip picker at the right of the Brushes palette to select a second brush tip, as shown in Figure 23-13.**

2. **Select a blending mode from the Mode drop-down list.**

   This sets how the two brush tips blend together.

3. Move the Diameter slider to set the width of the second brush tip.

4. Move the Spacing slider to set how far apart each second brush tip dab is when you stroke with the combination brush.

5. Use the Scatter slider to set how far the second brush tip's mark spreads within the area of the first brush tip.

6. Move the Count slider to set how many of the second brush's marks are made based on the Spacing setting for the first brush.

Take a look at Figure 23-14 to see two examples of combination brush tips.

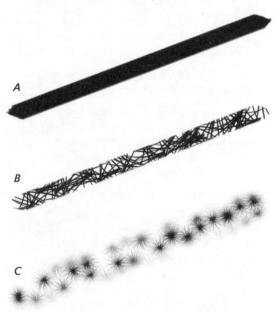

• **Figure 23-14:** A: First brush selected. B: Grass brush added to A, 0% Scatter. C: Fuzzball brush added to A, 150% Scatter.

Color Dynamics

Color Dynamics are really fabulous: They set how the color of the brush tip changes as you stroke with it. So instead of creating a stroke that's just bright red, for instance, that stroke could change from bright red to pink to burgundy, or even further through the color spectrum to include an entire rainbow of colors. Figure 23-15 shows the Color Dynamics options in the Brushes palette.

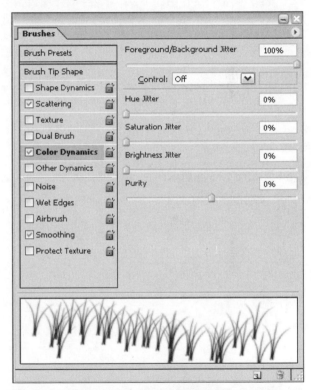

• **Figure 23-15:** Use the Color Dynamics settings to change your strokes from mono-color to multicolor.

Before selecting Color Dynamics settings, you need to select the Foreground and Background colors that you want to use as the basis for the color change as you stroke. So, click the Foreground and Background color squares in the Toolbox and use the Color Picker to select colors.

For dynamic color, set the following options:

- Move the **Foreground/Background Jitter** slider to set how much variation exists between the Foreground and Background colors. The **Control** drop-down list is used to set how the effect is manipulated.

- Use the **Hue Jitter**, **Saturation Jitter**, and **Brightness Jitter** sliders to set how far the color can vary from the Foreground and Background colors. Lower settings keep the colors within the Foreground and Background color's tonal range. Higher settings move the colors farther from the original tonal range.

- Move the **Purity** slider to change the saturation of the color. A higher setting adds more saturation.

Figure 23-16 shows two brush strokes. The first stroke, A, uses just one color (the Foreground color). The second stroke, B, has Color Dynamics settings applied with two colors (the Foreground and Background colors).

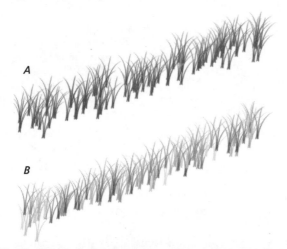

• **Figure 23-16: A: Original stroke without Color Dynamics applied. B: Stroke with 100% Foreground/ Background Jitter applied.**

Other Dynamics

Use the Other Dynamics settings to select Opacity Jitter and Flow Jitter. Opacity Jitter sets how much the opacity changes during a stroke. Flow Jitter sets how the amount of paint applied during a stroke changes. Both of these settings are based on the Opacity and Flow settings selected in the Options bar for the tool that you're using.

Noise, Wet Edges, Airbrush, Smoothing, Protect Texture

The rest of the brush settings in the Brushes palette add special effects or limitations to your strokes.

- **Noise** adds a grainy quality to strokes. This setting works best with brush tips that have softer edges (that is, they have a lower Hardness setting).

- Select **Wet Edges** to give the brush stroke a watercolor appearance.

- The **Airbrush** option works just like the Airbrush button on the Options bar. With this option selected, the paint pumps from the brush tip, letting it build up. This works especially well if you hold the mouse in one position.

- **Smoothing** evens out the rough spots of your strokes.

- Select **Protect Texture** if you're painting textured lines and you want the lines to match. With this option selected, Photoshop restricts brush stroke textures, keeping them consistent from one brushstroke to the next.

Using an image

You can also create brush tips by using any selected pixels in the image window. This could be a spray of dots that might imitate a real-life stipple brush or an image such as a duck. Here's how:

1. **Choose File➪New to create a new Photoshop image with a white background.**

Alternatively, open the image that you want to use for a new brush tip and skip to Step 5.

2. **Select the Brush tool from the Toolbox and select a brush tip from the Brushes palette.**

You can use any of the brush settings described in the section "Using the Brushes palette," earlier in this chapter, to customize the brush tip.

3. **Click once with the mouse in the image window.**

A single brush dab appears in the image window, as shown in Figure 23-17.

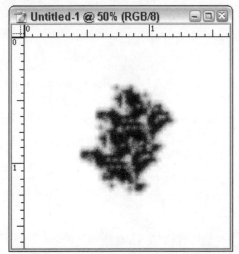

• **Figure 23-17:** A single click of the mouse creates a dab that can be used to create a brush tip.

4. **Apply any filters or commands to the brush dab to create the brush tip texture that you're looking for.**

Figure 23-18 shows the same dab from 23-17 after the Poster Edges and Water Color filters have been applied.

5. **Use the Rectangular Marquee tool to select the area of the image window that you want to use for the new brush tip.**

6. **Choose Edit➪Define Brush Preset or choose New Brush Preset from the Brush Preset picker's menu.**

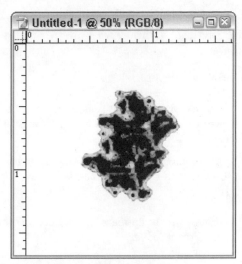

• **Figure 23-18:** The modified brush dab.

7. **Enter a name for the brush in the Brush Name dialog box shown in Figure 23-19, and then click OK.**

The new tip shape appears at the bottom of the Brush Preset picker list. If you want to permanently save the brush tip, see the following section.

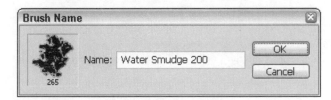

• **Figure 23-19:** Enter a name for your custom brush.

Saving Presets and Libraries

After you create a brush, you no doubt want to save it for future use. Brushes that you create with the Brush palette are added to the bottom of the palette list. But, if you reset the brushes in the palette or load a different set of brushes in, you lose the brush.

Thankfully, you can easily save a brush as a preset and also save it in a library with other brushes that you create.

Here's how to save a brush as a preset:

1. **Open the Brush Preset picker or open the Brush palette menu and choose New Brush Preset.**

2. **Type a name in the Brush Name dialog box (shown earlier in Figure 23-19).**

3. **Click OK.**

    Your new preset appears at the bottom of the Brush Preset picker.

To save one or more brushes in a brush library, use the following steps:

1. **Choose Edit⇨Preset Manager.**

2. **Choose Brushes from the Preset Type drop-down list.**

    The Preset Manager displays all the brush presets, as shown in Figure 23-20.

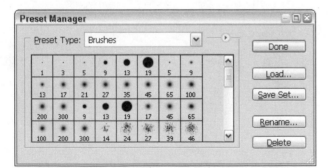

• **Figure 23-20:** Use the Preset Manager to save brush libraries.

3. **Ctrl/⌘+click to select the brushes that you want to include in the library.**

4. **Click Save.**

5. **In the Save dialog box, enter a name for the brush library in the File Name (Windows) or Save As (Mac) text box.**

6. **Click Save to close the Save dialog box and return to the Preset Manager.**

7. **Click Done to close the Preset Manager.**

Your new brush library won't be available on the Brushes palette or Brush Preset picker menu until Photoshop is shut down and relaunched.

Saving brushes as tool presets

You can also save a custom brush as a tool preset. Saving brushes as tool presets can come in handy if you are using a particular brush or set of brushes over and over again.

To save a brush as a tool preset:

1. **Open the Tool Preset picker located at the left end of the options bar.**

2. **Choose New Tool Preset from the picker's menu.**

3. **Type a name for the brush tool preset in the New Tool Preset dialog box.**

    If you want to include the color of the brush with the tool preset, enable the Include Color check box.

4. **Click OK.**

    The New Tool Preset dialog box closes and your brush tool preset appears in the Tool Preset picker.

To find out more about tool presets, take a look at Technique 6.

Loading Brush Libraries

Several brush libraries ship with Photoshop but aren't automatically loaded into the Brushes palette or Brush Preset picker. Some of these brush libraries include calligraphic, square, and special effects brushes. Load a new brush library and give it a try. Having a few new brushes is a great way to expand your Photoshop painting and editing repertoire. Here's how:

1. **Open the Brushes palette menu or the Brush Preset picker menu and select a brush library from the bottom portion of the menu. (See Figure 23-21.)**

   If you don't see the brush library that you want to choose, continue with Step 2. If you do find the brush library that you want, skip to Step 5.

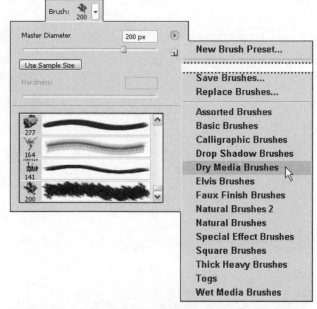

• **Figure 23-21:** Choose a brush library from the menu.

2. **If you don't see the brush library you want to use, choose Load Brushes from the palette menu.**

3. **Select a brush library by using the Load dialog box.**

   If you don't see the library that you want to load in the default Photoshop brush folder, use the Load dialog box to move to the folder location where the brush library is located.

4. **Click Load.**

5. **Use the dialog box that appears, as shown in Figure 23-22, to determine how the brushes are loaded.**

▶ Click **OK** to replace the brushes currently loaded in the Brushes palette and Brush Preset picker with the selected brush library.

▶ Click **Append** to add the brush library to the end of the brush list in the Brush Preset picker and Brushes palette.

▶ Click **Cancel** to discontinue the entire operation.

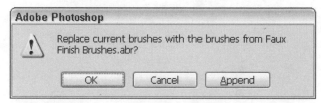

• **Figure 23-22:** Use this dialog box to select how the brush library is loaded into the Brushes palette.

Downloading brushes from the Web

Many Photoshop artists have created great brushes and brush libraries that are available for download on the Web. Two of my favorites are shown here. In the following figure is a sample of Togs brushes by Sage Winyard. Togs brushes and many other brush libraries designed by Sage are available at www.photoshop.brushes.btinternet.co.uk/Photoshopbrushes.html.

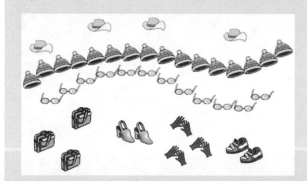

The next figure shows a sample of Elvis brushes by Sacha Raby. They're available at www.photoshop-stuff.com/Photoshop-Downloads/Photoshop-Brushes.html.

(continued)

If you want to search for more great brushes, just type **Photoshop brushes** into your favorite search engine and check out the results.

Creating a Painting by Using an Image

Save Time By

✔ Preparing the canvas

✔ Selecting brushes and painting

✔ Adding canvas texture

As you can imagine, almost as many ways of painting in Photoshop exist as Photoshop artists exist to paint with them. Three of the most commonly used painting methods range from simple at first glance (but really rather difficult to use) to slightly roundabout (and really easy to use):

✔ **Starting from scratch:** Start with a blank image window (a *canvas*) and use the painting tools to stroke on color, outlines, and textures. Although this method is the simplest to set up, it can actually be the hardest because you're starting entirely from scratch.

✔ **Tracing an image:** Use *tracing paper* over an image or photo. The tracing paper is a new, empty layer positioned above an image. You trace the image and then select colors and use the paint tools to fill in the colors. Although this method isn't as hard as starting from scratch, it does include selecting colors by using either the image or the Color Picker, selecting brushes, and sketching.

✔ **Painting over an image:** Use the colors in a photo or image as if they were wet paint. You stroke with various brushes to create the outlines and textures while simultaneously sampling the colors from the image. Although this method seems a little bit roundabout, it's actually remarkably easy because you're using the colors and textures already available in the image.

This technique explores the third method. You prep the canvas by first opening the image that you're going to use and then adding two layers. The first layer will be filled with a simple noise pattern. This speckled noise layer is used to mix with the "paint" from the image to help show brush strokes and add texture. The second layer is empty and you can use it to actually paint on.

After you're finished painting, you add two more layers. The first one gives your paint strokes the appearance of more texture, making the strokes appear to stand out from the canvas. The second layer is filled with a canvas pattern to make the painting look like it was actually painted on canvas.

This all may sound rather complicated, but in practice it's simple to do! Just follow the steps. You can see the results in color if you check out Color Plate 24-1.

Think of this technique as a mini painting lesson at your local art studio. Don your smock, grab your palette, easel, and brushes, and get ready to paint by using an existing image. And don't forget to have fun!

Preparing the Canvas

As any painter knows, before you start painting you need to prepare your canvas. In this case, the canvas is an image opened in Photoshop with two extra layers added. Here's how:

1. **Open the image that you want to use for your painting.**

   For this example, I use a photograph of a calla lily, which is shown in Figure 24-1.

• **Figure 24-1:** For this example, this photograph is the basis for a painting.

2. **Choose File⇨Save As to save the image with another filename.**

   That way, your original image has not been altered and is always available.

3. **Click the Create New Layer button at the bottom of the Layer palette.**

   A new empty layer appears above the image. You can rename the layer to something meaningful, if you want. For this example, I renamed the layer Noise Speckle.

4. **Select white as the Foreground color.**

   A fast way to do this is to press D, and then press X.

5. **Select the Bucket tool from the Toolbox and click in the image window.**

   The layer is filled with solid white, obscuring the image below.

6. **With the white layer still selected in the Layers palette, choose Filter⇨Noise⇨Add Noise.**

7. **Use the Add Noise dialog box to select noise settings.**

   Set the Amount to 20%, select the Gaussian radio button under Distribution, and select the Monochromatic check box, as shown in Figure 24-2.

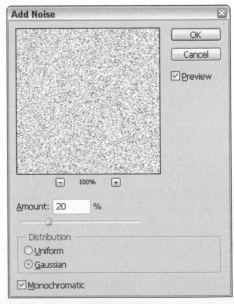

• **Figure 24-2:** Use the Add Noise dialog box to create a speckled appearance.

8. **Click OK to close the Add Noise dialog box and apply the filter to the white layer.**

The layer is now speckled.

9. **With the white speckled layer selected in the Layers palette, use the Blending Mode drop-down list in the Layers palette to select Soft Light.**

Soft Light mode blends the white speckled layer with the image layer below, giving a grainy appearance. As you paint, this white speckled layer helps to show your strokes and add texture.

10. **Click the Create New Layer button at the bottom of the Layers palette.**

A new empty layer appears above the speckled layer. You're going to paint on this layer. You can rename it, if you want. For this example, I've renamed the layer Painting, as shown in Figure 24-3. You now have three layers and your canvas is prepared. Get ready to paint!

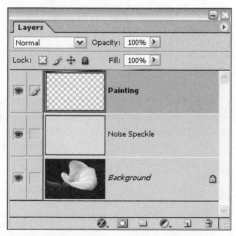

• **Figure 24-3:** You're going to paint on the upper, empty layer.

Ready, Get Set, Smudge!

Huh? You thought that you were painting didn't you? Well, you are. Two types of tools in the Toolbox use brushes to define their shape. These tools are the ones that you use when creating a Photoshop painting. The painting tools (the Brush and Pencil tools) apply a selected color to an image. The editing tools (the Blur, Sharpen, Smudge, Dodge, Burn, and Sponge tools) modify existing colors in an image. All these tools are used in the same way: You stroke them across the image window to apply or modify color just like you would a real-life brush on canvas.

For this technique, the Smudge tool is used to sample the colors from the bottom image layer as you set it up in the previous section. The sampled color is actually stroked onto the empty layer above the image layer and noise layer shown in Figure 24-3. (If you haven't prepared your image for painting, go back to "Preparing the Canvas" and follow the steps.) Time to get started!

1. **Select the Smudge tool from the Toolbox.**

2. **Select the settings that you need on the Options bar.**

▶ Use the **Mode** drop-down list to select Normal.

▶ Move the **Strength** slider 100%.

▶ Enable the **Use All Layers** check box.

▶ Make sure that the **Finger Painting** check box is unchecked.

3. **Use the Brushes palette to select a brush tip.**

You can use brushes from any of the brush libraries. (To find out how to load brush libraries and create custom brushes, turn to Technique 23.) If this is your first time painting in Photoshop, select a large, textured brush. One of my favorites is 100 Rough Round Bristle found in the default brush set. This brush gives big textured strokes.

4. **With the empty painting layer selected, start stroking the canvas.**

Keep your strokes small and follow the lines of the image with your strokes, as shown in Figure 24-4. For instance, if you're trying to paint a leaf, stroke in the direction of the leaf's veins. Pull any darker shaded areas up into lighter areas for contrast. You can always switch brushes if you need a smaller brush or one with a differently shaped tip. Also, a tablet and stylus can really come into their own. If you have a tablet, use it. You'll be surprised at the good results.

If your strokes don't look right, or if you feel that you made a mistake, don't worry! You can always undo the previous stroke by pressing Ctrl/⌘+Z or by using the History palette to move back a few history states. If after a while you're *really* unsatisfied with your painting, you can always select the entire layer, and then choose Edit⇨Clear to start fresh with an empty layer.

• **Figure 24-4:** As you stroke with the Smudge tool, the color from the image layer is painted onto the empty painting layer.

5. **Continue painting with the Smudge tool until you're satisfied.**

If you're working on a small area, you can zoom in to see it more clearly. Also, if you're working close up, open a second image window as described in Technique 5 to view your painting at actual size as you stroke the magnified image.

Use the Brush tool to add highlights to any areas that need special outlining or emphasis. Use the Eyedropper tool to select a highlighting color from the image and select a hard, small brush to perform the highlighting. You can stroke this highlighting onto the same layer that you've been painting on with the Smudge tool, or you can create a new layer above the painting layer just for highlights. I recommend this extra highlighting layer because you can always correct or add any highlights later without affecting the painting layer.

Finishing Your Painting

After you finish working with the Smudge tool, you can finish your painting by adding two layers on top of the painting layer. The first layer gives your brush strokes the appearance of more texture in an interesting and — to my mind — rather clever way. The second layer adds a canvas texture to give the impression that the image was actually painted on canvas. Here's how:

1. **In the Layers palette, select the painting layer.**

2. **Choose Layer⇨New⇨Layer Via Copy.**

This copies the selected layer. The new copied layer appears in the Layers palette above the original. Rename this copied layer if you want. For this example, I've renamed the layer Texture.

3. **With the copied layer selected in the Layers palette, choose Filter⇨Stylize⇨Emboss.**

4. **Use the Emboss dialog box to select settings, as shown in Figure 24-5.**

> ▶ Set the **Angle** to follow the direction of the lighting in your image. For the calla lily photograph that I'm using, the light is coming from the upper-left corner, so a setting of 135 degrees works well.

> ▶ Set the **Height** to 5 pixels.

> ▶ Set the **Amount** to 125%. (Higher settings add more texture.)

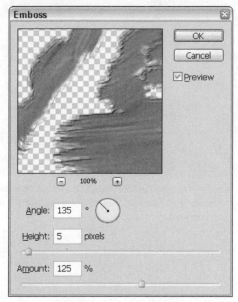

• **Figure 24-5:** Select the Emboss settings to add more texture to the brush strokes.

5. **Click OK to close the Emboss dialog box.**

6. **In the Layers palette, select Overlay from the Blending Mode drop-down list.**

This blends the embossed paint strokes with the painting layer below. You can also use Soft Light blending mode for a softer appearance.

7. **With the embossed layer still selected, click the Create New Layer button at the bottom of the Layers palette.**

A new, empty layer appears at the top of the layer stack. You can rename this layer, if you want. For this example, I've renamed the layer Canvas.

8. **Select white as the Foreground color.**

A fast way to do this is to press D, and then press X.

9. **Select the Bucket tool from the Toolbox and click in the image window.**

The new layer is filled with solid white, obscuring the painting below. You should now have five layers, as shown in Figure 24-6.

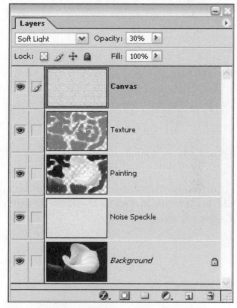

• **Figure 24-6:** After adding the two new layers, you should have five layers in your painting.

10. **Choose Filter⇨Texture⇨Texturizer.**

11. **Use the Texturizer dialog box to select the settings shown in Figure 24-7.**

> ▶ At the right side of the dialog box, use the **Texture** drop-down list to select Canvas.

> ▶ Set the **Scaling** to 200%.

▶ Set the **Relief** to 15.

▶ Use the **Light** drop-down list to select the direction from which the light comes in your image. For my example, because the light is coming from the upper left in the original calla lily photograph, I selected the Top Left option.

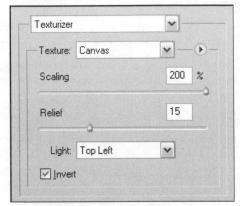

• **Figure 24-7:** Select the settings that create a canvas texture.

12. Click OK to close the Texturizer dialog box and apply the canvas texture to the white layer.

13. With the canvas layer selected in the Layers palette, use the Blending Mode drop-down list to select Soft Light.

This blends the canvas layer with the rest of the painting.

14. **Use the Opacity slider to lower the opacity until you can see only a hint of the canvas texture.**

Adjust the slider until you're happy with the results. For my calla lily painting, a setting of 30% works pretty well, as shown in Figure 24-8. Color Plate 24-1 shows the calla lily painting in full color. Sit back and enjoy your painting!

• **Figure 24-8:** After you add the embossed paint strokes and the canvas texture, the painting looks pretty good.

Technique 25

Painting Back in Time

Only with a time machine or with Photoshop can you paint backward through history. Thanks to the powerful History palette, you can select a previous *history state* and use either the History Brush or Art History Brush to stroke away the image's current state and reveal the past history state.

This technique uses a simple example to show you how you can paint backward in time. First, I give you a quick look at the History palette just to show you what's available there and how to use it. Then, you apply a filter to an image and use the History Brush to remove the effects of the filter. Using the History Brush is interesting and easy.

Getting to Know the History Palette

The History palette records every command and operation that you use in Photoshop. This includes brush strokes, Foreground and Background color changes, blending mode changes, and anything that you do that affects the image window. Figure 25-1 shows the History palette with a selected history state. By default, the History palette is grouped with the Actions palette at the right side of the program window. If you don't see the History palette, choose Window⇨History.

You can do many things with the History palette. I don't list all of them here, but the following list gives you an idea of the power and scope of this great palette:

- Move back to a previous history state by selecting it in the History palette. When you click the previous history state, the image in the image window reverts to that previous state. You can set how many history states the History palette records by choosing Edit⇨ Preferences⇨General (Windows) or Photoshop⇨Preferences⇨General (Mac), and then entering a number from 1–100 in the History States text box.

- Create a new document based on the currently selected history state by clicking the Create New Document from Current State button at the bottom of the History palette.

✔ Create a snapshot of an image before performing a complicated editing procedure by clicking the Create New Snapshot button at the bottom of the History palette. This snapshot saves the entire state of the image, including layers, blending modes, active selections — you name it. If you make a mistake or want to revert to the state saved by the snapshot for any reason, simply click the snapshot at the top of the History palette. Turn to Technique 7 to find out more about creating and using snapshots.

✔ Select a previous history state as the *source* for the History Brush and Art History Brush by clicking in the left column next to the desired history state. When a history state is set as the source, any painting that you do with the History Brush or Art History Brush restores those areas to the selected history state.

The fourth bullet point is the focus of this technique.

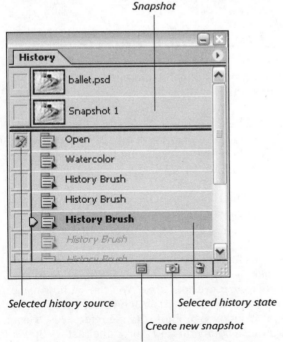

Snapshot

Selected history source

Create new snapshot

Selected history state

Create new document from current state

• **Figure 25-1: The History palette records everything that affects the image window.**

Painting with History

The example that I use here is very simple. It shows you how to use the History Brush by selecting a previous history state as a source. Here are the basic steps that I've taken to accomplish this:

1. **Apply a filter to an image.**

2. **Select the history state before the filter command as the source for the History Brush.**

3. **Use the History Brush to return portions of the image to its original appearance before the filter was applied.**

Even though the example is simple, the principle always works the same: No matter how many history states are recorded in the History palette, you can use any history state as a source for the History brush. Just follow these steps:

1. **Open an image that you want to use as the basis for painting with the History Brush.**

   For this example, I'm using the ballerina photograph shown in Figure 25-2.

• **Figure 25-2: Select an image to use as the basis for a painting.**

2. **Choose File➪Save As and save the image with another filename.**

That way, your original image is not altered and is always available.

3. **Make any tonal adjustments that you think necessary to improve the color and balance of the image.**

For the ballerina photograph, I increased the saturation and adjusted the highlights by using Levels.

4. **Apply a filter to the image.**

For this example, I applied the Watercolor filter to the ballerina photograph, as shown in Figure 25-3.

• **Figure 25-3: The ballerina photograph looks quite different after the Watercolor filter is applied.**

5. **With the current history state selected in the History palette, click in the left column next to the previous history state, as shown in Figure 25-4.**

Be sure that you don't select the previous history state.

6. **Select the History Brush from the Toolbox.**

7. **Use the Brushes palette to select a brush tip shape.**

For the ballerina example, I selected a small round brush of medium hardness. (To find out more about the Brushes palette, turn to Technique 23.)

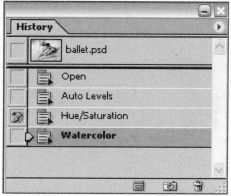

• **Figure 25-4: Click the left column to select the previous history state as the source for the History Brush.**

8. **Use the Options bar to select History Brush settings.**

▶ Use the **Mode** drop-down list to select the Normal blending mode.

▶ Set **Opacity** and **Flow** to 100%.

Experiment with different settings to see what kind of results you get.

9. **Stroke in the image window with the History Brush.**

As you stroke, notice that the previous history state is revealed. For the ballerina example, I'm just stroking over the ballerina's face and arms to return them to the state before the Watercolor filter was applied, as shown in Figure 25-5.

• **Figure 25-5:** After stroking the ballerina's face and arms with the History Brush, the skin tones are returned to the previous history state.

Technique 26

The Big Color Swap Meet

Suppose you're designing a family Web site and you have five photographs of your children that you want to put on one Web page. The pictures were taken at different times and in different lighting conditions, so unfortunately the tone of each photograph is different — one has a bluish cast, one looks yellow, another is reddish, well, you get the picture (pun intended). Because the photographs are all going on one Web page, they should be as uniform as possible in color range and tone. But, how are you going to do it?

Photoshop has the answer: the Match Color command. By using the Match Color command, you can select the color and tone from the photograph that you like best and apply it to the other photos, adjusting their colors and tones to match. You can also use the Match Color command to apply the colors from one layer to another within the same image or from one selection to another within the same image or different images.

The Match Color command is especially good for matching skin tones. So, if you have three photographs of the same model, but the color cast of her face is slightly different in each photograph, you can use the Match Color command to even out the skin tones between the three photographs.

In this technique, you find out how to use the Match Color command to enhance your images by evening out tone and color. You also discover how to save and load Match Color settings for later use. Color Plate 26-1 shows you the results of the images used in this technique.

 The Match Color command works only on images set in RGB color mode.

Swapping Colors

For this example, I'm selecting an area of one image as the color source and applying this color source to a target image. The color source is going to be the selected area in Figure 26-1, the lighter portion of the man's face. The color cast in his face is rather red. This photograph is saved as `Man.psd`.

• **Figure 26-1:** The selected area of the man's face is going to be used as the color source.

The target image that will receive the colors from the selected source area is going to be the rather dark photograph of a woman shown in Figure 26-2. The woman's face is obscured by shadow and the color cast of the entire photograph is rather bluish. This photograph is saved as `Woman.psd`.

• **Figure 26-2:** This dark photograph is going to change dramatically when the color source is applied to it.

Okay, here's how the Match Color command works:

1. **Open the image(s) that you want to use to match colors.**

   If you want to select portions of an image or layer for use as the source color or as target areas, use the selection tools to select those areas.

   For this example, I'm using two images: `Man.psd` and `Woman.psd`, shown in Figures 26-1 and 26-2.

2. **Make sure that the target image is selected and in front or the target layer is selected in the Layers palette.**

3. **Choose Image⇨Adjustments⇨Match Color.**

   The Match Color dialog box shown in Figure 26-3 opens. Notice the upper area of the dialog box, labeled Destination Image. This area is used for target settings. The bottom area, labeled Image Statistics, is used to select source settings.

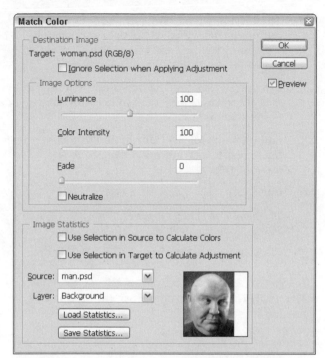

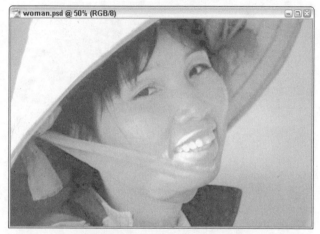

• **Figure 26-3:** The Match Color dialog box is divided into two areas: Target settings are on the top, and source settings are on the bottom.

 When the Match Color command is selected, the mouse pointer automatically changes to the Eyedropper tool if you need to sample colors from an image.

4. **In the Image Statistics area, select the color source by using the various drop-down lists and check boxes.**

▶ Use the **Source** drop-down list to select an image as the color source.

▶ Use the **Layer** drop-down list to select a layer as the color source.

▶ If you selected an area in a different image as the color source, enable the **Use Selection in Source to Calculate Colors** check box.

▶ If you selected an area within the target image as the color source, enable the **Use Selection in Target to Calculate Adjustment** check box.

Because I'm using a selection in the `Man.psd` image as the source image, I selected the image by using the Source drop-down list and selected the Use Selection in Source to Calculate Colors check box. After I've selected the source, the colors in my target image, `Woman.psd`, change dramatically. (See Figure 26-4.) However, the color cast is way too red and overly bright. I fix these problems in the next step.

• **Figure 26-4:** When the colors from the selected source area are applied to the photograph of the woman, the colors change dramatically.

5. **In the Destination Image area, use the sliders and check box to modify the color adjustment.**

▶ Drag the **Luminance** slider to the left to make the target image darker. Drag it to the right to make the image brighter.

▶ Drag the **Color Intensity** slider left to decrease the saturation of the target image. Drag it right to increase the saturation.

▶ Drag the **Fade** slider to fade the amount of the color adjustment.

▶ Select the **Neutralize** check box to bring the color cast to a more neutral tonal range area. This reduces excessive color casts.

For my example, I selected the Neutralize check box to reduce the reddish cast of the target image. Then, because the image looked a little washed out, I lowered the Luminance slightly (to 84) and adjusted the Fade to 20. Figure 26-5 shows the finished target photograph. Quite a difference from its original color and tone as it originally appears in Figure 26-2.

• **Figure 26-5:** After the color and tone in this image are adjusted, the photograph looks quite different.

6. **When you're finished adjusting the target image settings, click OK to close the Match Color dialog box.**

Saving and Loading Match Color Settings

If you want to apply the same color adjustment settings to several photographs, the best thing that you can do is save the Match Color settings and then load them when you need them later. Here's how:

1. **After you finish adjusting the target image settings as described in the previous section, "Swapping Colors," click Save Statistics at the bottom of the Match Color dialog box.**

2. **Use the Save dialog box that opens to move to the folder where you want to keep the Match Color information.**

3. **Enter a name for the information in the Name text box (Windows) or the Save As text box (Mac).**

4. **Click Save.**

   The Save dialog box closes and you return to the Match Color dialog box.

5. **Click OK to close the Match Color dialog box.**

After you've saved Match Color settings, you can easily apply them to any image or photograph by following these steps:

1. **Open the image to which you want to apply the Match Color settings.**

2. **Choose Image⇨Adjustments⇨Match Color.**

3. **At the bottom of the Match Color dialog box, click Load Statistics.**

4. **Use the Load dialog box to locate the folder where the Match Color information is stored and select the file.**

5. **Click Load to load the color information, close the Load dialog box, and return to the Match Color dialog box.**

   The saved Match Color settings are applied to the image that you opened in Step 1.

6. **Use the Destination Image area in the Match Color dialog box to modify the color adjustment.**

   Take a look at the previous section, "Swapping Colors," for more information about these settings.

7. **Click OK to close the Match Color dialog box.**

27

Technique

Recoloring with Gradients

Save Time By
- Applying a gradient map
- Using blending modes

In Photoshop, a *gradient* is a smooth transition from one color to another, or from a color to transparency. For instance, gradients can contain one color that fades to transparency, two colors such as black and white where the transition area between the black and white are various shades of gray, or many colors that blend from one color to the next.

One way that you can change the color of an image in Photoshop is by using *gradient maps*. Gradient maps recolor an image by looking at the image as if it were set in grayscale mode, finding the lightest and darkest pixels in the image, and then assigning colors (or *mapping* them) to the pixels based on the lights and darks.

This technique focuses on recoloring images by using gradient maps. First, you adjust image color by applying a gradient map directly to an image. You can check out the results and see if they're something that you think you could use. Then, you take a look at applying gradient maps to layers and using blending modes to blend image pixels. You might be surprised at the sometimes subtle, oft times wacky results that can happen. Check out Color Plate 27-1 to see the different colorful results.

Applying a Gradient Map

You can apply a gradient map to a colored image to recolor it with new color tones and hues. Or, you can apply a gradient map to a grayscale image to colorize it. This can result in an image that looks something like a duotone or tritone depending on the number of colors in the gradient that you use. (To find out how to create actual duotones, turn to Technique 35.)

 You don't have to recolor an entire layer or image. You can always select a portion of a layer for recoloring and apply a gradient map to the selected area only.

To recolor an image by using a gradient map:

1. **Open the image that you want to recolor.**

2. **Choose Image⇨Adjustments⇨Gradient Map.**

The Gradient Map dialog box opens, as shown in Figure 27-1.

• **Figure 27-1:** In the Gradient Map dialog box, the gradients are selected with the Gradient picker.

3. **Use the Gradient picker to select a gradient.**

4. **Select the Dither check box if you want to add some noise to smooth the gradient's colors.**

5. **Select the Reverse check box if you want to change the direction of the gradient.**

6. **Click OK.**

The Gradient Map dialog box closes and the image is recolored, as shown in Figure 27-2.

 Several gradient libraries ship with Photoshop that aren't automatically installed in the Gradient picker. To load a gradient library while using the Gradient Map dialog box, click the tiny arrow at the upper right of the Gradient Picker and choose a gradient library from the bottom of the menu, as shown in Figure 27-3.

Although the Gradient Map command does quickly recolor an image, the color change shown in Figure 27-2 is rather crude and doesn't really resemble the original's shading of lights and darks.

• **Figure 27-2:** My pal the vulture dressed in his original feathers (left) and recolored with a Copper gradient (right).

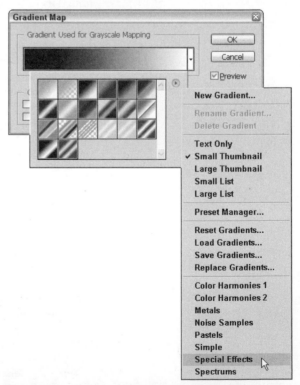

• **Figure 27-3:** Select a gradient library to load from the bottom of the Gradient picker menu.

Recoloring an Image Using Layers and Blending Modes

Another way to recolor an image with gradient mapping is to use layers and blending modes. What you do is create a copy of the layer containing the image that you want to recolor, apply a gradient map to the copied layer, and then use a blending mode to blend the copied layer's pixels with the original layer. Find an image and give this a try:

*Copper gradient,
Color blending mode*

1. **Open the image that you want to recolor.**

   I'm using my feathered vulture friend again. (He was last seen lurking in Figure 27-2.)

2. **In the Layers palette, select the layer containing the image that you want to recolor.**

3. **Choose Layer⇨New⇨Layer via Copy.**

   A copy of the original layer appears in the Layers palette.

4. **Select the copied layer in the Layers palette.**

5. **Choose Image⇨Adjustments⇨Gradient Map.**

6. **In the Gradient Map dialog box that appears (refer to Figure 27-1), use the Gradient picker to select a gradient.**

7. **Click OK to close the Gradient Map dialog box and apply the gradient to the copied layer.**

*Transparent Pastels gradient,
Lighten blending mode*

8. **In the Layers palette, use the Blending Mode drop-down list to select a blending mode.**

   For a first try, I suggest using Color mode. This blends the colors in the copied layer with the colors in the original layer. Experiment with the blending modes to see what kind of results you get. Some can be quite subtle, but others are downright bizarre. Check out the vulture's recoloring in Figure 27-4. (He doesn't look too happy about it!)

You can also apply a gradient map as an adjustment layer. To find out more about adjustment layers and how to use them, take a look at Technique 22.

*Sunrise gradient, Reverse
checked, Hue blending mode*

• **Figure 27-4: The vulture is recolored by using various
gradients and blending modes.**

To enhance the contrast between the colors added by the gradient mapped layer, insert a Posterize adjustment layer between the original layer and the copied layer. You can do this by selecting the original layer and then clicking the Create New Fill or Adjustment Layer button at the bottom of the Layers palette. Select Posterize from the menu and then set the number of levels to 4 or 5. (Turn to Technique 22 for more about adjustment layers.)

Technique 28

Creating Custom Patterns

Save Time By

✔ Using textures

✔ Using the Pattern Maker filter

Patterns are fantastic! You can use them to create backgrounds, add texture, fill layers, even stamp and paint. You have many ways to create patterns. You can use filters to create textures that can be saved as patterns, use the Pattern Maker filter to create a pattern by using an image, or scan textured or marbled papers for use as patterns.

This technique explores how to create patterns by using various filters, including the Pattern Maker filter. You also find out how to save and load pattern libraries. (Did you know that Photoshop ships with several pattern libraries that aren't automatically loaded into the Pattern picker?) After creating some great patterns here, turn to Technique 29 to find out how you can use them!

Downloading patterns from the Web

Many great sites offer patterns for download from the Web. Some of the pattern sets are free, and some cost a few bucks. To get you started, here are two sites that offer free downloads: Adobe Studio Exchange at http://share.studio.adobe. com and Free Photoshop at www.freephotoshop.com/html/downloadables. html. To find more sites offering patterns for download, type **Photoshop patterns** into your favorite search engine.

Creating Patterns by Using Textures and Scans

You can create patterns by using any kind of textures. If you have access to a scanner, you can scan cloth, paper, wood, or anything that has a nice texture. If the color of the scan doesn't suit you, you can always change it in Photoshop before turning the scan into a pattern. Filters are also great for creating textures even if you are just using a solid white layer as the basis for the texture. (You can, of course, use any colors that you want.) If you want to scan some paper or cloth to create a texture but need help with performing the scan, turn to Technique 10.

If you want to create a pattern tile for use as a background for a Web page, use the Tile Maker filter in ImageReady, Photoshop's sister program. For details on how, turn to Technique 61.

Creating a texture

For this example, I show you how to create a brick texture and turn it into a pattern. You can, of course, substitute any texture for the brick texture. Here's how to create the texture:

1. **Choose File⇨New to create a new document.**

   The New dialog box appears.

2. **Select the settings for the new document.**

   Set the Width and Height to something rather large (say 3 x 3 inches). Set the resolution to 300 ppi, the Color mode to RGB, and the Background Contents to white.

3. **Click OK to close the New dialog box.**

   The new document appears in the program window.

4. **Click the Foreground color square in the Toolbox to open the Color Picker.**

5. **Select a dark red color in the Color Picker.**

6. **Select the Paint Bucket tool in the Toolbox.**

7. **Click in the image window to fill the entire area with the dark red.**

8. **Choose Filter⇨Texture⇨Texturizer.**

   The Texturizer dialog box shown in Figure 28-1 opens.

9. **At the right side of the Texturizer dialog box, use the Texture drop-down list to select Brick.**

10. **Set the Scaling to 200% and the Relief to 15.**

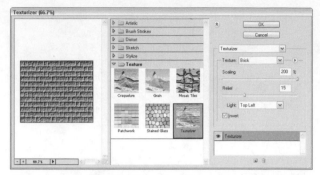

• **Figure 28-1:** Use the Texturizer filter to create a texture for a pattern.

11. **Click OK to close the Texturizer dialog box and apply the brick texture to the red image window.**

    Now you have something that looks like a brick wall. (See Figure 28-2.) This is the texture that you use to create a pattern.

You can find other filters to create great patterns on the Filter⇨Noise⇨Add Noise menu, and under any of the filters on the Filter⇨Texture menu.

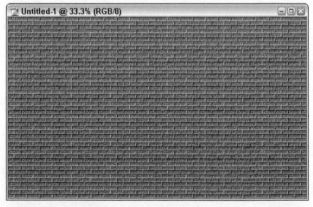

• **Figure 28-2:** The image window now looks like a brick wall.

Defining a pattern

After you have a texture, you can turn it into a pattern. Keep in mind that you can use these directions to turn *anything* in the image window into a pattern. For instance, suppose that you have a duck image open. You could select the duck and turn it into a pattern.

1. **Use the Rectangular Marquee tool to select a portion of the image window.**

The area that you select can be any size. Pattern size isn't limited in Photoshop. However, for a standard size pattern, stick to a small area such as 200 x 200 pixels.

2. **Choose Edit⊅Define Pattern.**

3. **In the Pattern Name dialog box, enter a name for the pattern in the Name text box, as shown in Figure 28-3.**

• **Figure 28-3: Type a name for the pattern in the Pattern Name dialog box.**

4. **Click OK.**

Your new pattern appears at the end of the list in the Pattern picker. (You can check this out by selecting the Pattern Stamp tool in the Toolbox and opening the Pattern picker on the Options bar.) Figure 28-4 shows the brick texture made in the previous section applied as a pattern to some type.

• **Figure 28-4: The brick pattern applied to type by using layer styles.**

Working with the Pattern Maker Filter

The Pattern Maker filter uses the image in the image window as the basis for a pattern. As you use the Pattern Maker, you can decide whether you want to use all or only a portion of the image. Also, as you use the filter, you can generate previews of patterns and quickly save any that you like in the Pattern picker.

1. **Open the image that you want to use as the basis for a pattern.**

For this example, I'm using the photograph of fabric shown in Figure 28-5.

• **Figure 28-5: I'm using this fabric to create some patterns.**

2. Choose Filter⇨Pattern Maker.

The Pattern Maker dialog box opens, as shown in Figure 28-6. Notice that the controls are on the right side, divided into three areas: Tile Generation, Preview, and Tile History.

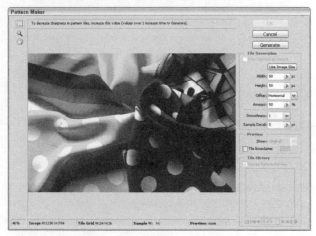

• **Figure 28-6:** In the Pattern Maker dialog box, the controls are on the right side.

3. Select the Rectangular Marquee tool at the upper-left corner of the dialog box.

4. In the Preview pane, drag to select the area of the image that you want to turn into a pattern.

5. In the Tile Generation area, enter a Width and Height for the tiles in pixels.

If you want to use the size of the image as the tile size, click Use Image Size.

6. Choose an Offset setting from the drop-down list and use the Amount slider to set how much the pattern tiles are offset.

None leaves the pattern tiles lined up in a grid. **Horizontal** shifts every other row horizontally as specified by the Amount setting. For instance, a Horizontal shift with a 50% Amount setting moves every other row to the right the width of half a tile. **Vertical** shifts every other column vertically down the specified Amount setting.

7. If you want to see where the tiles' edges are in the pattern, enable the Tile Boundaries check box in the Preview area.

This option shows the tile boundaries only while you're working in the Pattern Maker dialog box. The boundaries don't show when you save the pattern.

8. Click Generate.

Pattern Maker goes to work creating the first tile preview, as shown in Figure 28-7. If you don't like the pattern, click Generate again to see another rendering.

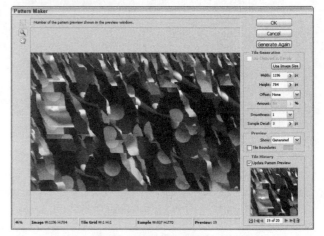

• **Figure 28-7:** The rendered pattern appears in the Preview pane.

9. To save a pattern rendering that you like, click the tiny Save Preset Pattern at the lower left of the Tile History area. (The button looks like a floppy disk.)

10. When you finish generating and saving patterns, either click OK to fill the image window with the pattern currently in the Preview pane, or click Cancel to close the Pattern Maker dialog box without applying the pattern to the image window.

Saving Pattern Libraries

When you create patterns that you like, you can save them in a library. That way, if you reload the Pattern picker with other pattern libraries, you don't lose the patterns that you've made. Here's how:

1. **Choose Edit⇨Preset Manager.**

The Preset Manager dialog box opens.

2. **Press Ctrl+5 or use the Preset Type drop-down list to select Patterns.**

3. **In the pattern sample area, Ctrl/⌘+click to select the patterns that you want to save.**

4. **Click Save Set.**

5. **In the Save dialog box, enter a name for the pattern set in the File Name text box (Windows) or Save As text box (Mac).**

6. **Click OK to close the Save dialog box and return to the Preset Manager.**

7. **Click Done to close the Preset Manager.**

 If you save a set of patterns, you can always e-mail the set to friends or colleagues so that they can also use your custom patterns.

Loading Pattern Libraries

Several pattern libraries ship with Photoshop that aren't automatically loaded into the Pattern picker. These include Nature, Rock, and Texture pattern sets, which can be quite useful.

You can load patterns into the Pattern picker by using either the Pattern picker's menu or the Preset Manager.

Here's how to load patterns with the Preset Manager:

1. **Choose Edit⇨Preset Manager.**

The Preset Manager dialog box opens.

2. **Press Ctrl+5 or use the Preset Type drop-down list to select Patterns.**

3. **Open the Preset Manager menu and choose a pattern library from the bottom of the menu, as shown in Figure 28-8.**

If you don't see the pattern library that you want to load listed on the menu, close the menu. Then click Load, select the pattern library in the Load dialog box, and click Load.

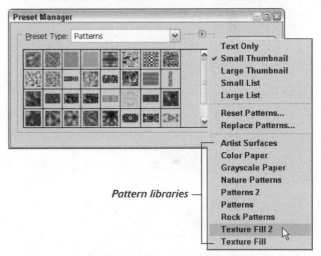

Pattern libraries

• **Figure 28-8:** Choose a pattern library from the bottom of the Preset Manager menu.

4. **In the dialog box that appears (see Figure 28-9), click OK or Append.**

If you click **OK,** the patterns that are currently loaded in the Pattern picker are cleared and the new library is loaded.

If you click **Append,** the new pattern library is added to the patterns that are currently loaded in the Pattern picker.

5. **Click Done to close the Preset Manager.**

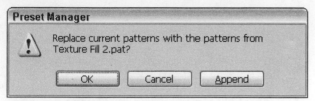

• **Figure 28-9: Click OK or Append to load the patterns into the Pattern picker.**

To load patterns using the Pattern Picker, follow these steps:

1. **With one of the tools that use patterns selected in the Toolbox, open the Pattern picker on the Options bar.**

Some of the tools that use patterns include the Bucket, Healing Brush, and Pattern Stamp tools.

2. **Open the Pattern picker's menu and choose a new pattern library from the bottom of the menu.**

If you don't see the pattern library that you want to load listed on the menu, close the menu. Then, click Load Patterns, select the pattern library in the Load dialog box, and click Load.

3. **In the dialog box that appears (refer to Figure 28-9), click OK or Append.**

If you click **OK,** the patterns that are currently loaded in the Pattern picker are cleared and the new library is loaded.

If you click **Append,** the new pattern library is added to the patterns that are currently loaded in the Pattern picker.

Technique

29

Filling and Painting with Patterns

Save Time By

- ✔ Filling layers
- ✔ Jazzing up type
- ✔ Painting pictures

Photoshop is a great tool for generating and applying patterns. You can apply patterns to layers or selections with the Healing Brush, Pattern Stamp, and Paint Bucket tools, and the Fill and Layer Styles commands.

This technique shows you how to apply patterns to your projects in various ways. You find out how to use the Fill command to apply a pattern to a layer or selection. Next, you take a look at applying patterns to type as a special effect by using Layer Styles. Finally, you use the Pattern Stamp tool to paint with a pattern. If you don't have the pattern that you need for a project, take a look at Technique 28 for directions on creating patterns and downloading them from the Web.

 If you want to create pattern tiles for use as a background for a Web page, turn to Technique 61 for directions.

Filling with Patterns

You have three ways to fill areas or selections with patterns in Photoshop:

- ✔ Using the Paint Bucket tool is really straightforward. Select an area or layer that you want to fill, select a pattern by using the Pattern picker on the Options bar, and also set a blending mode and opacity, if you want. Then, click within the selection. Done deal.

- ✔ The Fill command also lets you fill a layer or selection with a pattern. While selecting a pattern by using the Fill dialog box, you can also select an opacity and blending mode. I don't recommend setting a blending mode or opacity by using the Fill command because after you apply the command, that's it. You can't change it. Instead, use the Layers palette to set blending modes and opacity; you can change either setting later.

✔ Creating a fill layer is an infinitely flexible way to apply a pattern. A fill layer is used to apply a pattern to a layer or selection by using another layer instead of applying the pattern to the actual image, altering the image pixels forever. Because the fill layer is a separate layer, you can set blending mode and opacity at any time. Also, you can change the selected pattern and if you decide that you don't like the effect, delete the fill layer altogether. I discuss fill layers in detail in Technique 21; if you want to apply a pattern by using a fill layer, turn to the directions there.

Here's how to fill a layer or selection with the Fill command:

1. **Use the Layers palette to select the layer to which you want to apply the pattern.**

If you want to apply the pattern to an area on the selected layer, use the selection tools to create the selection.

2. **Choose Edit➪Fill or press Shift+F5.**

3. **Select a pattern with the Pattern picker in the Fill dialog box, as shown in Figure 29-1.**

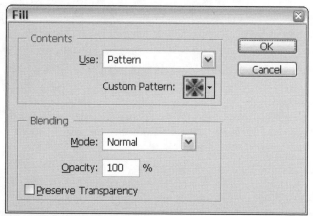

• **Figure 29-1: Select a pattern in the Fill dialog box.**

4. **In the Blending area, use the Mode drop-down list to select a blending mode and use the Opacity slider to set the pattern's transparency, if you want.**

5. **Select the Preserve Transparency check box if portions of the selected area or layer are transparent and you don't want the pattern to fill those areas.**

6. **Click OK.**

The pattern fills the selected area or layer.

Applying Patterns to Type

You can apply patterns to type in several ways. One way, which is rather roundabout and not very flexible, is to rasterize the type layer, and then use the Paint Bucket tool to fill each character with a pattern. Although this method does work, it has a few serious minuses: After rasterizing a type layer, you can no longer edit the type with the Type tools. Also, if you want to add drop shadows, bevels, or any other special effects, you have to jump through a few hoops.

The easiest and most versatile way to apply a pattern to type is to use layer styles. Using layer styles, you can fill the type with a pattern and add any other effects that you need at the same time. (To find out more about working with layer styles, turn to Technique 20.)

Here's how to apply a pattern to type by using layer styles:

1. **Create the type that you need by using the Type tool.**

2. **With the type layer selected in the Layers palette, click the Add Layer Styles button at the bottom of the palette and choose Pattern Overlay from the menu, as shown in Figure 29-2.**

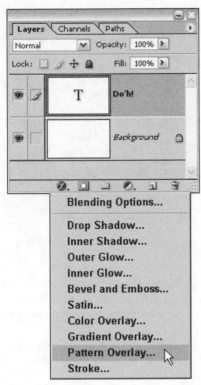

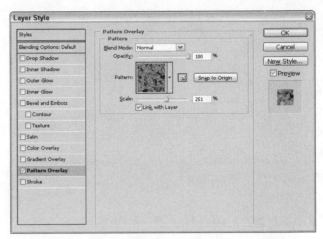

• **Figure 29-2:** Choose Pattern Overlay from the Add Layer Styles menu.

• **Figure 29-3:** The Layer Styles dialog box opens with Pattern Overlay selected.

The Layer Styles dialog box opens with the Pattern Overlay style selected, as shown in Figure 29-3.

3. **In the Pattern area, use the Pattern picker to select a pattern.**

 Several pattern libraries that ship with Photoshop aren't loaded into the Pattern picker. You can load them into the picker by opening the Pattern picker's menu and selecting a pattern library from the bottom of the menu.

4. **Use the Scale slider to size the pattern.**

5. **Set the pattern's transparency by using the Opacity slider.**

6. **To blend the pattern's pixels with the type's pixel color, use the Blend Mode drop-down list and choose a blending mode.**

(To find out more about blending modes and how they affect pixels, turn to Technique 17.)

7. **Use the Layer Styles dialog box to add any other special effects that you want, such as a bevel or drop shadow.**

8. **Click OK.**

The pattern (and any other special effects that you chose) is applied to the type, as shown in Figure 29-4.

 Even after you apply layer styles to a type layer, you can still edit the text with the Text tools.

• **Figure 29-4:** A flower pattern and drop shadow applied to type.

Painting with Patterns

Did you ever think that you could paint with patterns? Well, you can! Here's a very interesting technique to turn an image, scan, or photograph into a pattern, and then use the pattern to paint.

1. **Open the image that you want to use for the painting.**

For this example, I'm using a heart paperweight and some fabric that I scanned, as shown in Figure 29-5.

2. **Choose Select⇨Select All or press Ctrl/⌘+A.**

A selection marquee appears around the entire image.

3. **Choose Edit⇨Define Pattern.**

The Define Pattern dialog box opens.

4. **Enter a name for the pattern, and then click OK.**

5. **Click the Create New Layer button at the bottom of the Layer palette.**

A new empty layer appears above the image. You can rename the layer to something meaningful, if you want. For this example, I renamed the layer Noise Speckle.

• **Figure 29-5:** For this painting example, I'm using a scan of some fabric and a heart paperweight.

6. **Select white as the Foreground color.**

A fast way to do this is to press D, and then press X.

7. **Select the Bucket tool from the Toolbox and click in the image window.**

The layer is filled with solid white, obscuring the image below.

8. **With the white layer still selected in the Layers palette, choose Filter⇨Noise⇨Add Noise.**

The Add Noise dialog box opens, as shown in Figure 29-6.

9. **Select the noise settings.**

Set the **Amount** to 20%; under Distribution, select **Gaussian**; and select the **Monochromatic** check box.

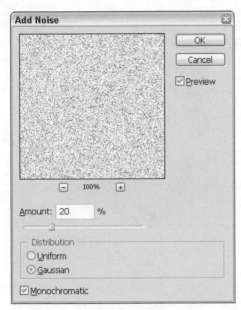

• **Figure 29-6:** Use the Add Noise dialog box to create a speckled appearance.

10. Click OK to close the Add Noise dialog box and apply the filter to the white layer.

The layer is now speckled.

11. With the white speckled layer selected in the Layers palette, use the Blending Mode drop-down list in the Layers palette to select Soft Light.

Soft Light mode blends the white speckled layer with the image layer below, giving a grainy appearance. When you paint, this white speckled layer helps show your strokes and add texture.

12. Click the Create New Layer button at the bottom of the Layers palette.

A new empty layer appears above the speckled layer. This is the layer you're going to paint on. You can rename it, if you want. For this example, I've renamed the layer Pattern Painting, as shown in Figure 29-7. You now have three layers and your canvas is prepared. Get ready to paint!

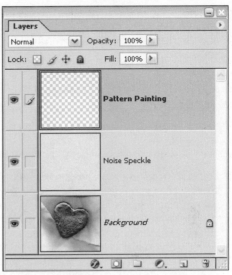

• **Figure 29-7:** You should now have three layers: the image layer, noise layer, and painting layer.

13. Select the Pattern Stamp tool from the Toolbox.

14. On the Options bar, choose Mode: Normal, Opacity: 100%, and Flow: 100%.

15. Select the pattern of your image that you created in Step 4 by using the Pattern picker.

16. Select the Aligned check box.

17. If you want to give your painting an impressionist feel, select the Impressionist check box.

As I painted this example, I selected Impressionist for the large washed areas, and deselected Impressionist when I needed to paint in some detail.

18. Select a brush tip by using the Brush Preset picker on the Options bar or the Brushes palette.

For my example, I loaded the Wet Media brush library into the Brush Preset picker, and used Oil Medium Brush Wet Edges and Oil Heavy Flow Small Tip. (To find out more about brushes and how to load brush libraries, take a look at Technique 23.)

As you paint, you can increase the size of the brush tip by pressing] (right square bracket) and decrease the tip size by pressing [(left square bracket).

19. **Stroke with the Pattern Stamp tool to create your painting.**

Figure 29-8 shows my example, which I painted with the Pattern Stamp tool.

 If you want to add more texture to your strokes after you finish painting, select the painting layer in the Layers palette, and then choose Layer⇨New⇨Layer Via Copy. Next, choose Filter⇨Sketch⇨Conté Crayon. In the Conté Crayon dialog box, set Forground Level to 12, Background Level to 6, and the Texture to Canvas. Click OK to apply the filter to the copied layer, and then use the Blending Mode drop-down list in the Layers palette to select Color Burn.

• **Figure 29-8: The completed pattern painting.**

Part V

Restoring and Retouching Images for Quick, Beautiful Results

The 5th Wave   By Rich Tennant

"My God! I've gained 9 pixels!"

Technique 30

Enhancing Tone and Color

Save Time By

- Applying quick Auto fixes
- Adjusting levels
- Performing precise corrections with curves

Not every photograph is perfect. Some are underexposed, others are overexposed, while some are a tad too red or blue. Whatever you see as the problem with a photograph can be quickly and expertly fixed in Photoshop. Depending upon how much of a "hands on" person you are, you can adjust the tonal corrections yourself or let Photoshop do the work.

This technique covers several ways that you can enhance the tone and color by adjusting the light and dark values in your photographs. Using various commands on the Image➪Adjustments menu, you can automatically correct color or tone, or make more precise corrections using Levels or Curves. These corrections can be applied to an entire image, an individual layer, or a selected area of a layer; you can even apply corrections as an adjustment layer for more flexibility. (Turn to Technique 22 to find out more details about adjustment layers and how they work.)

So pull out your favorite digital photographs and give them a brighter, clearer appearance using some of the commands described here!

Going to the Automat

Three commands are on the Image➪Adjustments menu that do all the work for you: Auto Levels, Auto Contrast, and Auto Color. While they may not give the more perfect results that you could get if you hand adjusted levels or curves, they are quick and work pretty well most of the time.

The Auto Levels command enhances contrast in an image by *clipping* (throwing away) a portion of the darkest shadows and brightest highlights and redistributing the lights and darks throughout the image on a channel-by-channel basis. (Take a look at Technique 52 if you want to find out more about channels.) To apply the Auto Levels command to an image, choose Image➪Adjustments➪Auto Levels.

Auto Contrast, like Auto Levels, enhances contrast in an image by clipping a portion of the shadows and highlights in an image and redistributing the lights and darks. Where it differs from the Auto Levels command is that Auto Contrast does not work on a channel-by-channel basis but instead uses the *composite* (combined) channel made up of all the channels in the image. To apply the Auto Contrast command to an image, choose Image➪Adjustments➪Auto Contrast.

The Auto Color command adjusts contrast and color by searching the image and assigning 50% gray as the neutral midtone color, and then redistributing the highlights and shadows out from that midpoint. To apply the Auto Color command to an image, choose Image➪Adjustments➪Auto Color.

 If the tone or color of the image still isn't quite right after using one of the Auto commands, complete the correction using the Levels dialog box, as described in "Setting Levels to Adjust Tone and Color."

You can also apply the three Auto commands as adjustment layers, though you do need to go through a few hoops to get there. An adjustment layer uses the same commands found on the Image➪Adjustments menu, but they work as layer-based corrections, giving you an amazing amount of flexibility. Layer-based corrections are not permanent and you can modify them at any time. Turn to Technique 22 to find out more about adjustment layers.

To apply the Auto Levels, Auto Contrast, or Auto Color command as an adjustment layer:

1. In the Layers palette, select the layer you want the adjustment layer to appear *above*.

2. Click the Create New Fill or Adjustment Layer button at the bottom of the Layers palette and choose Levels from the menu.

The Levels dialog box opens.

3. Click Options.

The Auto Color Correction Options dialog box, shown in Figure 30-1, opens.

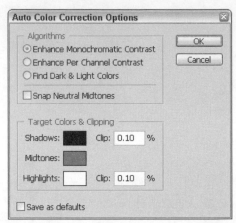

• **Figure 30-1: The Auto Color Correction Options dialog box is used to automatically enhance photos.**

4. Use the Algorithms area to select an automatic color correction.

▶ Choose **Enhance Monochromatic Contrast** to apply the Auto Contrast command.

▶ Choose **Enhance Per Channel Contrast** to apply the Auto Levels command.

▶ Choose **Find Dark & Light Colors** and select **Snap Neutral Midtones** to apply the Auto Color command.

5. Click OK to close the Auto Color Correction Options dialog box.

6. Click OK to close the Levels dialog box and apply the automatic correction as an adjustment layer.

Setting Levels to Adjust Tone and Color

Levels are used to correct the tone and color balance in an image by adjusting shadows, midtones, and highlights. You can apply levels to an entire image, an entire layer, or a selected area on a layer.

You can also apply a level as an adjustment layer. Open an image and choose Image➪Adjustments➪ Levels or press Ctrl/⌘+L to view the Levels dialog box, shown in Figure 30-2. (To apply levels as an adjustment layer, click the Create New Fill or Adjustment Layer button at the bottom of the Layers palette and choose Levels from the menu. The dialog box shown in Figure 30-2 appears on-screen.)

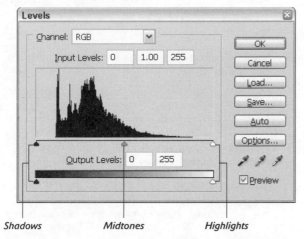

Shadows   Midtones   Highlights

• **Figure 30-2:** Use the sliders in the Levels dialog box to adjust highlights, midtones, and shadows.

Notice how the Levels dialog box is set up. At the top is a Channel drop-down list that lets you select an individual channel or the composite channel for correction. Below that is the *histogram,* which shows a graphical representation of how the lights and darks in the image are distributed. When you adjust levels, you use the Histogram palette as a guide. Take a look at the sidebar "How do you read a histogram?" for details on how the histogram works.

Directly below the histogram are the really important sliders in this dialog box: Input Shadow, Midtone, and Highlight. Here's how they work:

✔ Move the **Shadow** slider to the right to increase the dark tones in the image, making all the pixels darker. As the Shadow slider moves right, so does the Midtone slider.

✔ Slide the **Midtone** slider to the left to make the midtones lighter. Move the slider to the right to make the midtones darker.

✔ Move the **Highlight** slider to the left to increase the highlights, making all the pixels lighter. As the Highlight slider moves left, so does the Midtone slider.

Below the input sliders are the output Shadows and Highlights sliders at the bottom of the Levels dialog box. Use these sliders (very judiciously) when you finish color correcting the image and just want to heighten the overall intensity of the shadows and highlights.

 You can always reset the settings in the Levels dialog box and start over by pressing Alt/ Option and then clicking Reset.

Take a look at Color Plate 30-1 to see the amazing changes levels can make.

Curves Are Levels on Steroids

After you adjust the overall tonal range of a photograph by using the Auto commands and the Levels dialog box, you can use curves to adjust particular portions of the tonal range without affecting other parts of the range.

As the section title states, curves are levels on steroids. Instead of adjusting just three tonal areas — shadows, midtones, and highlights — as you do with levels, you can adjust up to 14 areas along the entire tonal range.

You can apply curves to an entire image, layer, selection, or as an adjustment layer. Open an image and try using curves to adjust the tones in your image. While the Curves dialog box looks a bit scary at first, as you become familiar with it, you may find yourself using it frequently for precise adjustments.

How do you read a histogram?

As you probably know, the tonal ranges in levels are divided into three parts: shadows, highlights, and midtones. The histogram shows a graphical representation of where these tonal ranges are concentrated in an image.

Take a look at the three images shown in the following figure. Superimposed on each image is the image's histogram. Notice how the tonal range for the top photo, which is underexposed, is concentrated on the left side of the histogram in the shadows area. The tonal range of the middle photo, which is overexposed, is concentrated at the right side of the histogram in the highlights area. And, the bottom photo, which is properly exposed, shows a pretty even distribution along the length of the histogram.

Open the Histogram palette by choosing Window⇨ Histogram. As you adjust the levels in an image, look at the Histogram palette to see how the lights and darks are balanced. As you move the Shadow, Midtone, and Highlight sliders, notice how the lights and darks redistribute in the palette, helping you to create a more tonally balanced image.

To adjust the tones in your images with curves:

1. Choose Image⇨Adjustments⇨Curves or Press Ctrl/⌘+M to directly correct a layer or selection.

Or if you want to apply curves as an adjustment layer, click the Create New Fill or Adjustment Layer button at the bottom of the Layers dialog box and choose Curves from the menu.

The Curves dialog box opens, as shown in Figure 30-3.

2. Select a channel using the Channel drop-down list, if you want.

The default selection is the composite channel that represents a blending of all the channels in the image.

3. Position the mouse over the graph area and click the plotted line to create a point.

You can create up to 14 points on the plotted line. By the way, the plotted line is also called the *curve*, hence the name for this type of adjustment.

 You can change the graph from a 4 x 4 grid to a 10 x 10 grid by Alt/Option+clicking the graph.

4. Drag the point to adjust the tone and color.

You can delete a point by Ctrl/⌘+clicking it.

5. Continue adding points and adjusting the curve until you get the results you need.

Keep an eye on the Histogram palette to see how your corrections are going. To find out how to read the Histogram palette, take a look at the sidebar, "How do you read a histogram?" earlier in this technique.

6. Click OK to close the Curves dialog box and apply the adjustments to your image.

 If you want to start over while working in the Curves dialog box, press Alt/Option and click Reset.

Tonal range   Midtones   Highlights

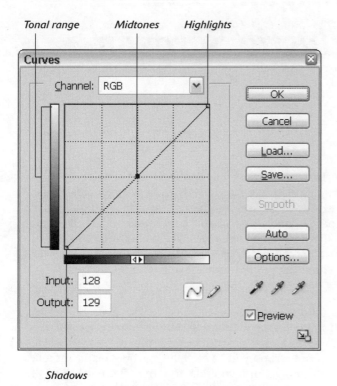

Shadows

• **Figure 30-3:** **Adjust isolated areas of the tonal range using curves.**

Be Your Own Plastic Surgeon

Technique 31

Save Time By

- Quickly cleaning up wrinkles and blemishes
- Performing a speedy nose job

No one has perfect skin. No one has a perfect body. Not even the perfect looking models in magazine ads. Take a really close look at almost any ad showing a serious amount of skin — whether a face, leg, or other body part — and you probably can detect some telltale sign of image doctoring. Perhaps an edge looks slightly mushy or the skin tone or texture doesn't quite match. In the ads, image manipulation can be pretty obvious where the photographs have been quickly (and cheaply) doctored.

Because our skin and bodies are less than perfect (whatever perfect is!), having Photoshop to help fix the wrinkles and tighten tummies is a good thing. Photoshop comes with some really super tools that let you professionally retouch any photograph you have. Some of this plastic surgery can be quite time consuming, but if you take the time, there won't be any telltale signs in your photos to give your retouching away.

This technique zeroes in on fixing physical irregularities. First, you find out how to brush away the years as you remove wrinkles, blemishes, and brown spots. Then, you go to medical school and learn how to smooth noses. So, pull out your best (or worst!) photographs and start retouching!

Ridding Your Photos of Wrinkles and Blemishes

The tools you use most when performing plastic surgery include the Clone Stamp and Healing Brush tools. Both of these tools copy areas using cloning, but the Healing Brush tool is the Clone Stamp tool's smarter cousin. While the Clone Stamp tool copies the hue and brightness of an area, the Healing Brush tool also copies the texture of an area, which is particularly important when dealing with skin. Copying skin texture helps the cloned areas blend in more seamlessly.

Another handy Photoshop feature is the Dust & Scratches filter. Use this filter when you want to even out skin texture. If the subjects in your photograph have some irregularities or pitting on their cheeks or chin, this filter can quickly smooth things out.

My likely candidate for wrinkle and blemish removal is the woman shown in Figure 31-1. As you can see, she has a few wrinkles around the eyes, some slight blemishes on her nose, and some skin texture problems that look like old pitting scars from acne. With Photoshop, the Clone Stamp tool, Healing Brush, and the Dust & Scratches filter, I can erase a few years in a few minutes.

• **Figure 31-1: Even though she doesn't know it, this woman is going to have her wrinkles and blemishes removed and her skin texture smoothed out.**

The real trick when retouching a photograph is to use a different layer for each type of retouching activity, such as removing blemishes, removing wrinkles, and defining eyes. That way, you never touch the original photograph and if you go a little too far with the retouching or don't like something you do, you can always start over.

Instead of creating one long list of steps covering blemish and wrinkle removal, and skin smoothing, I've divided the directions into the three sets so that you can find what you need more easily.

To remove blemishes, follow these steps:

1. **Open the photograph you want to retouch.**

   If you need to scan the photograph and import it into Photoshop, take a look at Technique 10. The photograph I'm using in this example is shown in Figure 31-1.

2. **Select the layer containing the photograph if it isn't already active.**

3. **Click the Create New Layer button at the bottom of the Layers palette.**

   A new, empty layer appears above the photograph. This is the layer you are going to use to remove blemishes, so rename the layer something appropriate such as Blemish Removal.

4. **Select the Clone Stamp tool from the Toolbox.**

5. **Use the Options bar to select the Clone Stamp tool settings.**

   Select Normal blending mode using the Mode drop-down list, set Opacity to 75%, uncheck Aligned, and check Use All Layers.

6. **Select a small, soft brush using the Brush Preset picker.**

   For this example, I used a 5 pixel diameter brush with a 0% Hardness setting.

7. **Hold down the Alt/Option key and select a clone source near the blemish.**

8. **Stroke over the blemish to remove it.**

As shown in Figure 31-2, the Clone Stamp tool removed the dark spots and blemishes from her cheek, chin, and nose.

• **Figure 31-2:** The Clone Stamp tool works really well for removing spots and blemishes.

Follow these steps to remove wrinkles:

1. **Open the photograph you want to retouch.**

If you need to scan the photograph and import it into Photoshop, take a look at Technique 10. The photograph I'm using in this example is shown in Figure 31-2.

2. **Select the layer containing the photograph if it isn't already active.**

3. **Click the Create New Layer button at the bottom of the Layers palette.**

A new, empty layer appears above the photograph. This is the layer that you use to remove blemishes, so rename the layer something appropriate such as Wrinkle Removal.

4. **Select the Healing Brush tool from the Toolbox.**

5. **Use the Options bar to select the Healing Brush settings.**

Select the Replace blending mode using the Mode drop-down list, set Source to Sampled, uncheck Aligned, and check Use All Layers.

If you don't want some layers in the image included in the wrinkle removal, click the eye icon to the left of each layer in the Layers palette to hide them.

6. **Select a small, soft brush using the Brush Preset picker.**

For this example, I used a 9 pixel diameter brush with a 10% Hardness setting.

7. **Hold down the Alt/Option key and select a clone source near the wrinkles.**

8. **Use small strokes to remove the wrinkles.**

Be careful not to overdo it. You want to remove some wrinkles but not all the character in the person's face. Also, because you want to match skin tone and texture as much as possible, resample the clone source frequently (see Step 7).

Figure 31-3 shows the example photograph minus a few of the wrinkles originally shown in Figure 31-2.

• **Figure 31-3:** The Healing Brush makes wrinkle removal pretty easy.

• **Figure 31-4:** The Dust & Scratches filter is great for smoothing skin texture.

To smooth out skin texture, follow these steps:

1. **Open the photograph you want to retouch.**

   If you need to scan the photograph and import it into Photoshop, take a look at Technique 10. The photograph I'm using in this example is shown in Figure 31-3.

2. **Select the layer containing the photograph if it isn't already active.**

3. **Choose Filter⇨Noise⇨Dust & Scratches.**

   This filter is very powerful, so small changes in the Radius setting can make for big results. For my example, I slightly smoothed the woman's skin by using a Radius setting of 2 and a Threshold setting of 1. That's all it took to smooth the skin areas along her cheeks and chin, as shown in Figure 31-4.

Getting a Nose Job

Not everyone can be a plastic surgeon, but with Photoshop you don't need to go to medical school in order to perform a few nips and tucks.

The following steps describe how to make a nose smaller, but you could use these steps for many body parts. All you have to do is select the area you want to change and then use one of the transformation commands, such as Distort, Skew, or Perspective, to reshape the selected area. After that, any mismatched shadows or areas can be deftly corrected using the Healing Brush.

To slim down a nose, follow these steps:

1. **Open the photograph you want to use.**

2. **Use the Lasso tool to loosely select around the nose area, as shown in Figure 31-5.**

• **Figure 31-5:** Select a wide area around the nose.

3. **Choose Layer⇨New⇨Layer via Copy or press Ctrl/⌘+J.**

   A copy of the nose area appears on a new layer above the original image, as shown in Figure 31-6. Rename the layer, if you want. For this example, I renamed my copied layer Nose Job.

4. **With the copied nose layer selected, choose Edit⇨Transform⇨Distort.**

   A bounding box with handles appears around the copied nose layer, as shown in Figure 31-7.

5. **Drag the upper corner handles toward each other to make the top of the nose slimmer.**

   Don't drag the handles too far or the nose ends up looking out of place.

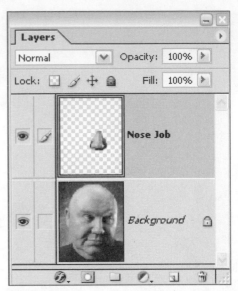

• **Figure 31-6:** A copy of the nose area appears on a new layer.

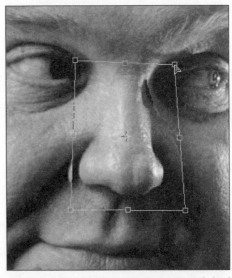

• **Figure 31-7:** A bounding box appears around the layer you're going to modify.

6. **Drag the lower corner handles to reshape the lower portion of the nose.**

As you drag, be aware of the surrounding face area. Try to line up shadows and skin texture as best as you can.

7. **Click the Commit Transform button on the Options bar or press Enter/Return to apply the changes to the copied nose layer.**

After the nose is reshaped, mismatched shadows and extra bits of nose may show from the layer underneath, as shown in Figure 31-8.

• **Figure 31-8:** After altering the shape of the copied nose, a few creases and shadows may need fixing.

8. **Select the Healing Brush from the Toolbox.**

9. **Use the Options bar to select Healing Brush settings.**

Select Replace blending mode using the Mode drop-down list, set Source to Sampled, uncheck Aligned, and check Use All Layers.

10. **Select a small, soft brush using the Brush Preset picker.**

For this example, I used a 5 pixel diameter brush with a 10% Hardness setting.

11. **Hold down the Alt/Option key and select a clone source near an area that needs fixing, such as a shadow.**

12. **Use small strokes to remove the wrinkles.**

As shown in Figure 31-9, the man in the photograph isn't so sure about his new nose. (I also removed the blemish on his chin and a few wrinkles.)

• **Figure 31-9:** Performing a virtual nose job is really painless.

Technique 32

Getting Rid of Red Eye

Save Time By

✔ Getting to know the Color Replacement tool

✔ Using the Color Replacement tool

How many times have you taken a wonderful photograph, only to see a red glow coming from the eyes of your subject? No, the person or animal in the photograph doesn't have any demonic traits; the red eyes are caused by light from a flash bouncing off the back of the subject's eye. (Actually, animals tend to get "yellow-eye" or "green-eye" because of the shape of their eyes, but all those flashing eyes are still referred to as "red eye.")

Understanding the Color Replacement Tool

Correcting red eye in Photoshop is really easy when you use the Color Replacement tool. This technique shows you how to correct red eye in your photographs. You find out what settings to use and what kind of brush works best. If you want to correct a real-world photograph, follow the directions in Technique 10 on how to import images into Photoshop using a scanner.

Here's how this tool works. First, you use the Eyedropper tool to sample the color you want to replace in the Toolbox's Background color square. Then, you choose the color you're using as the replacement in the Foreground color square. After that, you select various settings on the Options bar, select a brush, and stroke on the new color while the old sampled color is automatically replaced.

 If you removed red eye using various methods in previous versions of Photoshop, you know how time consuming this process can be. The new Color Replacement tool in Photoshop CS removes red eye so quickly you'll be amazed!

Brushing Away the Red

To demonstrate how the Color Replacement tool eliminates red eye, I'm using a snapshot of my little son, Nicholas, shown in Figure 32-1. Even in a grayscale image, the red eye is pretty obvious.

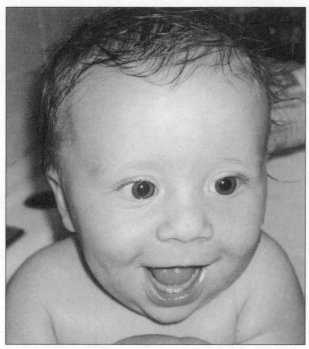

• **Figure 32-1:** My little guy's eyes are distinctly luminous.

Open an image and give these steps a try:

1. Select the Background color square in the Toolbox if it isn't already active.

2. Select the Zoom tool from the Toolbox.

3. Zoom in on an eye containing the red eye.

   In Figure 32-2, I've zoomed in on the left eye.

4. Select the Eyedropper tool.

5. On the Options bar, choose the 3 by 3 Average setting from the Sample drop-down list.

   Unless you want to replace a single color, the 3 by 3 Average or 5 by 5 Average settings work best for this purpose.

6. Sample the red color you want to replace.

7. Click the Foreground color square in the Toolbox to open the Color Picker, as shown in Figure 32-3.

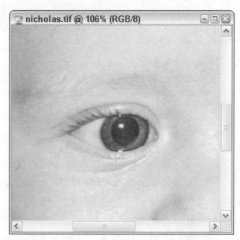

• **Figure 32-2:** Zoom in so that you can see what you're doing.

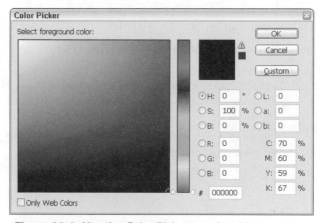

• **Figure 32-3:** Use the Color Picker to select black as the replacement color.

8. Select black as the replacement color using the Color Picker or Swatches palette.

9. Click OK to close the Color Picker.

10. Select the Color Replacement tool from the Toolbox.

11. Use the Options bar to select the tool's settings.

▶ Choose **Color** using the Mode drop-down list.

▶ Choose **Background Swatch** from the Sampling drop-down list. This setting uses the Background color that you selected using the Eyedropper tool in Step 6.

▶ Use the Limits drop-down list to select **Contiguous**. This setting paints the replacement color only to neighboring pixels.

▶ Set the **Tolerance** to 10%. This setting limits the range of colors that are replaced.

▶ Check **Antialiased**. This option blends the edges of the painted pupil with the iris.

12. Open the Brush Preset picker and select a small, slightly soft brush.

For this example, I'm using a brush set at a 5 pixel diameter and 90% Hardness.

13. Stroke on the pupil to replace the red eye.

Don't worry if you slip a little and the mouse cursor slides out to the iris area. Because the Tolerance setting is so low, the iris color isn't replaced.

Figure 32-4 shows the finished results. My son's eyes look just the way they should.

• **Figure 32-4:** The Color Replacement tool takes the red out in no time.

Technique 33

Adding Professional Photo Filter Effects

Save Time By

- ✔ Using the Photo Filter command
- ✔ Making photos look like sepia prints

Professional photographers use filters — thin lenses that fit over a camera or enlarger lens — to correct lighting conditions, enhance specific colors, and create special effects such as fog, vignettes, and cross stars. (Have you ever wondered how cameramen created those wonderful soft vignette shots of actresses in old black and white movies from the 1940s? The photographer actually smeared Vaseline around the outside edge of the lens to diffuse the light on the edges of the image but keep the center sharp, creating a portrait with a "halo" effect. Stretching a black stocking over the camera lens sometimes created soft focus effects.)

You can apply photographic-style filters in Photoshop using the Photo Filter command. The Photoshop photo filters recolor photographs by enhancing warm or cool colors, or by completely retinting the photograph to a specific hue such as yellow, magenta, brown, or blue.

In this technique, you find out how to apply Photoshop's photo filters to recolor your photographs. Also, you discover how to make your photographs look like old-time sepia-toned photos. So, find an interesting photograph and experiment with photo filters!

Take a look at Color Plate 33-1 to see the results of recoloring a photograph using the Photo Filter command.

Recoloring with Photo Filters

You can apply photo filters directly to a layer or as an adjustment layer. If you apply a photo filter directly to a layer, the layer's pixels are permanently altered. But, if you apply the photo filter as an adjustment layer, you can always change the photo filter being used, modify its effect by lowering opacity or changing blending modes, or completely remove the photo filter without changing any image pixels. (Turn to Technique 22 to find out more about adjustment layers.)

For me, the choice is clear; I use an adjustment layer to apply a photo filter. It's infinitely more flexible. But, in the spirit of completeness, I'm including directions for applying a photo filter either way.

Here's how:

1. **Open the image to which you want to apply the photo filter.**

For this example, I'm using the photograph shown in Figure 33-1.

• **Figure 33-1:** I'm adjusting the tone of this photograph using photo filters.

2. **In the Layers palette, select the layer you want to apply the photo filter effect to.**

3. **Click the Create New Fill or Adjustment Layer button at the bottom of the Layers palette and choose Photo Filter from the menu (shown in Figure 33-2).**

If you want to apply the photo filter command directly to a layer, choose Image➪Adjustments➪ Photo Filter.

• **Figure 33-2:** Choose Photo Filter from the menu.

The Photo Filter dialog box opens as shown in Figure 33-3.

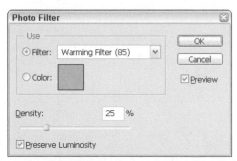

• **Figure 33-3:** Use the Photo Filter dialog box to apply different color tones to your photograph.

4. **In the Use area, choose a preset photo filter from the Filter drop-down list or click the color square and select a color using the Color Picker.**

Preset photo filter effects range from Warming Filter and Cooling Filter to Underwater.

5. Move the Density slider to adjust how much the filter affects the photograph.

The higher the setting, the more the photo filter affects the image.

6. Click OK to apply the photo filter to the photograph.

Even though Figure 33-4 is grayscale, you can see the difference that a Magenta photo filter makes.

• **Figure 33-4: Photo filters change the color tone of a photograph.**

Creating Old-Time Sepia Photos

You can create a sepia-toned photograph in Photoshop in several ways:

✔ Apply a sepia-toned photo filter.

✔ Use the Hue/Saturation command to colorize the photo.

✔ Use an action that ships with Photoshop that automatically creates a sepia-toned look for you.

Which works best? Well, which method you use depends upon the qualities of the photograph you're using and the look you're after. Open a photograph and try these different methods.

If you want to apply a sepia photo filter, follow the directions for applying a photo filter in "Recoloring with Photo Filters." In Step 4, choose Sepia from the Filter drop-down list. When you apply a sepia-toned photo filter, the results are a brighter brownish-yellow cast, but retain the original colors in the photograph.

The Hue/Saturation command produces a monotone brownish-red sepia look. Here's how:

1. In the Layers palette, select the layer you want to look like a sepia-tone.

2. Click the Create New Fill or Adjustment Layer button at the bottom of the Layers palette and choose Hue/Saturation from the menu.

If you want to apply the photo filter command directly to a layer, choose Image➪Adjustments➪Hue/Saturation.

The Hue/Saturation dialog box opens, as shown in Figure 33-5.

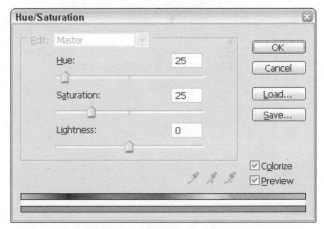

• **Figure 33-5: Use the Hue/Saturation dialog box to adjust the photograph's tone.**

3. Put a check in the Colorize check box.

4. Set the Hue to 25 and the Saturation to 25.

These settings give you a nice-looking sepia color. If you need to, adjust the sliders until you get the look you want.

5. Click OK to close the Hue/Saturation dialog box and apply the color adjustment to the photograph.

To apply a sepia-tone using an action that ships with Photoshop:

1. In the Layers palette, select the layer you want to look like a sepia-tone.

2. Open the Actions palette by choosing Window⟿ Actions.

3. Open the Default Actions set in the Actions palette, as shown in Figure 33-6.

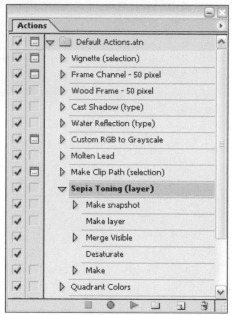

• **Figure 33-6:** Click the tiny arrow next to the Default Actions set to view the actions in that set.

4. Select Sepia Toning (Layer).

5. Click Play at the bottom of the Actions palette.

The action goes to work and recolors your photograph, producing a good-looking sepia-toned photograph.

Figure 33-7 shows the original photograph on the top and an aged sepia-toned version on the bottom. I applied a Grain filter set to Speckle to create the old-fashioned outlined look. To access the Grain filter, choose Filter⟿Texture⟿Grain.

• **Figure 33-7:** The original photograph (top) and the sepia-toned aged photograph (bottom).

 You can also use the Photo Corner action found in the Frames Action set to add an interesting photo album border.

Turn to Technique 8 to find out more about actions and loading action sets.

Creating Grayscale Images: Your Choices and the Results

Technique 34

Fine black and white photographs can be truly wonderful. If you've ever seen some of the great Ansel Adams photographs of Yosemite Valley, you know what I mean. While few of us walk around with black and white film in our cameras these days (actually, I can't remember when I last used film), you can convert color images into good-looking black and white images in Photoshop.

Black and white images in Photoshop are called *grayscale*. Because these images are made up of 256 levels of gray, from black (0) to white (255), calling them grayscale makes a certain amount of sense.

You need to know, however, that the easiest road to grayscale is not necessarily the best way to create a fine-looking grayscale image. You can use several methods to convert a color image to grayscale in Photoshop:

✔ **Converting a color image by switching from a color mode, such as RGB or CMYK, to Grayscale color mode.** This method is indeed the easiest of the three. However, the results sometimes aren't optimal. Many times the finer details of the image's darker areas lose definition and can become muddy.

✔ **Selecting one of the grayscale channels that make up a color image.** This method can work quite well because you retain fine details.

✔ **Using the Color blending mode and a solid black fill layer.** This method usually creates a great grayscale image.

Which method you decide to use depends upon your image and the amount of time you have to test results. Comparing the figures in this technique to see the difference between grayscale conversions may help you decide which method to use.

If you're interested in adding a bit of color to your grayscale images, take a look at Technique 35. There I give you directions on how to colorize grayscale images to accent and emphasize important features in your photographs.

Converting Color Modes

By far the easiest way to convert an image to grayscale is to change color modes. To do so, choose Image⇨Mode⇨Grayscale. With the Grayscale mode conversion, Photoshop throws away the color information in the image and converts the brightness of the pixels in the image to 256 levels of gray.

The resulting grayscale image is pretty good, but the finer areas can become a bit fuzzy and the overall cast can be a bit dark. Figure 34-1 shows a lovely photograph of Arches National Park converted from RGB mode to grayscale.

• **Figure 34-1:** Converting a color image to grayscale using color modes works pretty well, but the overall cast can be a bit dark.

 When you convert an image with more than one layer to grayscale color mode, Photoshop asks whether you want to merge the layers. If you want to keep the layers separate, select Don't Merge.

Selecting a Channel

Another way to convert an image to grayscale is to select one of the channels that make up the image. Each color image has three or four color channels (depending upon if the image is set in RGB or CMYK mode). Each one of these channels contains specific color information. For instance, an image set in RGB mode has red, green, and blue channels. Channels are themselves grayscale images. (If you're interested in finding out more about channels, take a look at Technique 52.)

Take a look at the Channels palette shown in Figure 34-2. The Arches National Park photo that I'm using for these examples is set in RGB color mode, so you see three individual color channels. (At the top of the Channels palette is the composite channel that shows the three channels combined.)

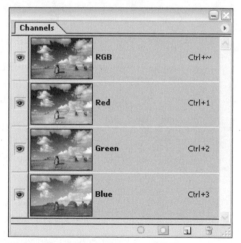

• **Figure 34-2:** You can select a channel for use as a grayscale image.

To select an individual channel for use as a grayscale image, click each channel in the Channels palette to view it in the image window. When you decide on the channel you want to use, drag the other channels to the trashcan icon at the bottom of the Channels palette.

Figure 34-3 shows the three channels that make up the Arches National Park photograph. I like the green channel best, so I'll discard the other channels. Notice how fine the channel detail is in the green channel in Figure 34-3 when compared to the grayscale conversion in Figure 34-1. Also, the overall cast of the green grayscale channel is brighter than the grayscale conversion.

Red channel

Green channel

Blue channel

• **Figure 34-3: The three channels that make up the Arches National Park photograph.**

Applying the Color Blending Mode

You can also convert a color image to grayscale using the Color blending mode. This method of conversion tends to produce the finest results. Details remain crisp and dark areas don't lose definition like they do when an image is converted using color modes.

The following directions show how to apply the color blending mode using a fill layer. You can also just fill a regular layer with black using the Paint Bucket tool, and then change the blending.

Here's how:

1. **Open the image you want to convert to grayscale.**

2. **Select the layer containing the image in the Layers palette.**

3. **Click the Create New Fill or Adjustment Layer button at the bottom of the Layers palette and choose Solid from the menu.**

4. **Select black in the Color Picker.**

5. **Click OK to close the Color Picker and create the fill layer.**

   The fill layer appears in the Layers palette, as shown in Figure 34-4. Your image in the image window disappears behind the solid black fill layer.

6. **Use the Blending Mode drop-down list at the top of the Layers palette to choose Color.**

   The image colors blend with the black fill layer to create a grayscale image, as shown in Figure 34-5.

 You can now flatten the layers, if you want, and convert the image to grayscale color mode by choosing Image➪Mode➪Grayscale. None of the fine quality of the image is lost during the color conversion.

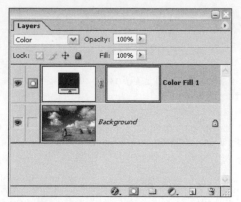

• **Figure 34-4:** The solid black fill layer appears in the Layers palette.

• **Figure 34-5:** An image converted to grayscale using the Color blending mode retains its fine detail.

Coloring and Tinting Black and White Photographs

Save Time By

- Tinting photographs
- Brushing in color using history
- Creating duotones

Ever since photography was created, folks have been painting or *tinting* black and white photographs to make them look like they were in color or to emphasize particular elements. With Photoshop, you can tint black and white photographs to add color or make color photographs look like tinted black and whites. Any way you want it, you can do it.

This technique focuses on how to add color to black and white (or grayscale as they are called in Photoshop) images. You find out how to layer color on top of a grayscale photo, apply overall tints using photo filters and the Hue/Saturation command, and paint in color using the History palette. Then, you explore the world of duotones, tritones, and quadtones, which mix two, three, or four colors to create the necessary range of tones — shadows, midtones, and highlights — for your image while creating a special look.

Because these pages are printed in black and white, I can't show these tinting and painting techniques here. However, look at Figure 35-1 here and then at Color Plate 35-1. Figure 35-1 shows the original grayscale image and Color Plate 35-1 shows several of the coloring techniques that I describe here.

• **Figure 35-1:** This photograph was originally in color. Here it's reproduced as a grayscale image.

Layering with Color

Superimposing layers of transparent color images over a grayscale image can be quite effective and easy to boot. Open the grayscale image you want to use and be sure to convert it to RGB color mode by choosing Image➪Mode➪RGB. That way, the image is ready to accept color. Open other color images containing the colored elements that you want to layer over the grayscale image, and copy and paste them onto new layers above the grayscale image. Lower the Opacity setting of the colored layers and *voila!* The grayscale image now contains interesting colorful elements.

Tinting Photographs

Two ways you can apply an overall tint to black and white photographs is to apply either the Photo Filter or Hue/Saturation commands. You can apply both of these commands directly to the layer containing the grayscale image or as adjustment layers. I discuss each of these tinting methods in detail in Technique 33.

Here's a quick rundown for applying the Hue/Saturation command as an adjustment layer:

1. **Open the grayscale photograph you want to use.**

2. **Choose Image➪Mode➪RGB.**

   This command sets the photograph up for accepting color.

3. **Select the layer containing the grayscale photograph.**

4. **Click the Create New Fill or Adjustment Layer button at the bottom of the Layers palette and choose Hue/Saturation from the menu.**

   The Hue/Saturation dialog box, shown in Figure 35-2, opens.

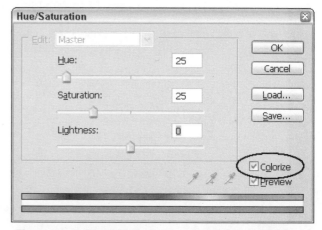

• **Figure 35-2:** The Hue/Saturation dialog box is used to colorize the black and white photograph.

5. Put a check in the Colorize check box.

6. Adjust the Hue and Saturation sliders to the color you want to use.

Some settings you can use are (with the Saturation set to 25): Hue at 25 for sepia, Hue at 130 for cyan, Hue at 225 for blue, and Hue at 300 for magenta. Of course, these settings are approximate and may need to be slightly different for your photograph.

7. Click OK to close the Hue/Saturation dialog box and apply the tinting to the photograph.

 Another way to tint a photograph is to apply a gradient map as an adjustment layer and then try different blending mode and opacity settings using the Layers palette. To find out how to apply a gradient map, turn to Technique 27.

Painting in Color with History

You can paint color back into a grayscale photograph using history only if you start with a color photograph. The History Brush uses a previous history state as the source to paint. For this example, I show you how to create a snapshot of the original color image to use as the color source. (If you want to find out more about snapshots, turn to Technique 7.)

Here's how:

1. Open the color photograph you want to use.

2. Open the History palette by choosing Window⇨ History.

By default, the History palette is grouped with the Actions palette at the right of the program window.

3. Click the Create New Snapshot button at the bottom of the History palette.

A new snapshot labeled Snapshot 1 appears in the History palette, as shown in Figure 35-3.

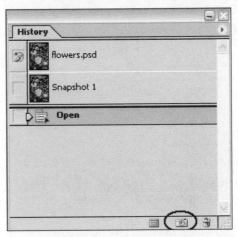

• **Figure 35-3: Click the Create New Snapshot button.**

4. Double-click the snapshot's name and rename it Color.

 Making a duplicate of the image before converting it to grayscale is always a good idea. That way, you have the color image to refer to when painting the colors back into the grayscale image. (How many times have I thought to myself, "Which leaves do I want to paint? I can't remember!") To create a duplicate of the image, choose Edit⇨Duplicate.

5. Choose Image⇨Mode⇨Grayscale.

This command converts the color photograph to black and white.

6. Choose Image⇨Mode⇨RGB Color.

This command sets the black and white photograph to accepting color (but it doesn't revert the photograph back to color).

7. In the History palette, click in the left column next to the Color snapshot you created in Step 3, as shown in Figure 35-4.

Don't select the snapshot because that reverts the photograph to the previous color state.

• **Figure 35-4:** Click the column to the left of the Color snapshot.

8. Select the History Brush tool from the Toolbox.

9. Use the Mode drop-down list on the Options bar to select a blending mode.

If you're trying this technique for the first time, select Normal. To find out more about blending modes, turn to Technique 17.

10. Use the Opacity and Flow sliders to select those settings.

For a first try, set both options to 100%.

11. Use the Brush Preset picker to select a brush tip.

12. Stroke the color back into the black and white photograph in the areas you want to emphasize.

If you're worried about painting beyond an area when you don't mean to, use the selection tools to select the area you are going to paint in before actually painting. That way, the selection limits your painting to only the selected area.

Creating Duotones

A *duotone* is a grayscale image or photograph printed with two different colored inks. Actually, if you think about it, a grayscale (or black and white) image is a *monotone* because it's printed with only one color, usually black (though you can always print with any other color). You can add a third ink color to create a *tritone,* and then also add a fourth ink color to create a *quadtone*.

Printing an image with two (or more) specific inks gives the image more depth because the two ink colors combine to heighten highlights, midtones, and shadows. The image in Figure 35-5 shows stone arches reproduced in grayscale. Now compare Figure 35-5 to Color Plate 35-2 to see the same image reproduced as a duotone, tritone, and quadtone.

• **Figure 35-5:** This grayscale image is ready for transformation into a duotone.

Here's how to create a duotone, tritone, or quadtone:

1. **If the image isn't already converted to grayscale, choose Image⇨Mode⇨Grayscale.**

2. **Choose Image⇨Mode⇨Duotone.**

   The Duotone Options dialog box opens, showing that the image is currently set as a monotone. (See Figure 35-6.)

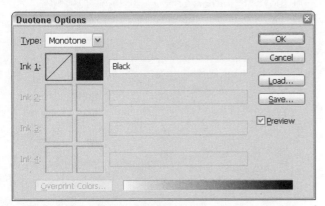

• **Figure 35-6:** Use the Duotone Options dialog box to select ink colors.

3. **Use the Type drop-down list to select Duotone, Tritone, or Quadtone.**

   Depending upon which type you choose, 2, 3, or 4 ink swatches become available in the Duotone Options dialog box.

4. **Click the ink color swatch next to each available ink option.**

   The Color Picker opens.

5. **Use the Color Picker to select a color.**

   Or click Custom in the Color Picker to switch to the Custom Colors dialog box and select a matching system color swatch, such as Pantone Yellow 012C. (To find out more about custom color systems, turn to Technique 14.)

   As you select ink colors, you can preview the color combinations in the image window.

 If you choose custom inks, such as Pantone, Trumatch, or TOYO, what you see on-screen may not exactly match the ink color. To be sure you are selecting the ink colors you need, select them from a color swatch book. You can buy swatch books from the ink manufacturers or better art supply stores. Or if you are working with a commercial printer, the printer may have a swatch book you can borrow.

6. **Click OK to close the Color Picker and return to the Duotone Options dialog box.**

7. **Repeat Steps 4 through 6 for each ink color.**

8. **Click the Curve box to the left of the ink color swatch to set how the inks blend together.**

   The Duotone Curve dialog box opens as shown in Figure 35-7.

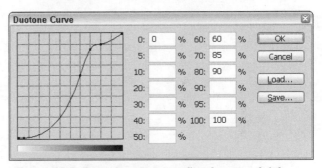

• **Figure 35-7:** Drag the curve to adjust how much ink prints on the shadows, midtones, and highlights.

9. **Drag the line on the graph to adjust how much ink prints on the shadows, midtones, and highlights.**

   To find out more about curves, take a look at Technique 30.

10. **Click OK to close the Duotone Curve dialog box and return to the Duotone Options dialog box.**

11. **Repeat Steps 8 through 10 to set the curves for each ink color.**

12. Click OK to close the Duotone Options dialog box.

 After creating a duotone (or tritone or quad-tone), you can always change the ink colors or curves settings by choosing Image⇨Mode⇨Duotone. Photoshop doesn't reconvert the image; it just gives access to the Duotone Options dialog box.

Creating "full color" duotones

Powertone 2.0 by Creo is a Photoshop plug-in that creates "full color" duotones. Using an RGB or CMYK image and two ink colors that you select, Powertone creates the best match it can based on the original colors in the image. The duotones created by Powertone have more color depth than duotones created with the Photoshop Duotone color mode. If you're going to use a duotone for any commercial job, such as a brochure or advertisement, visit www.creo.com and download a trial version of Powertone.

Technique 36

Stitching Photos to Create Panoramas

Have you ever taken several photographs across a wide panorama and wanted to seamlessly put them together? If you ever tried this in previous versions of Photoshop, matching the photos and then blending them together took time and a bit of skill. This process is called photo *stitching*. It's kind of like piecing a quilt together.

Well, no more tedious stitching! Photoshop CS has a completely amazing plug-in that does most of the work for you. The first time I ever used the Photomerge command, I was astounded, "Geez, this thing is smart!" It put all my photos together into a single image without too much fuss or bother — no need to blend between spliced photos. What a timesaver!

This technique shows you how to use this great plug-in. If you've been to the Grand Canyon and want to put a whole canyon's worth of photos together, give this a try. Or, take your digital camera outside and snap a few pictures across the horizon, import the photos into Photoshop, and then use Photomerge to put them all together.

Getting to Know Photomerge

Photomerge attempts to match similar areas from different photographs and then puts them all together into one large panorama or photomural. I use the word "attempts" because while Photomerge does give it a good try, sometimes it can't match areas. But, anything Photomerge cannot match, it leaves for you to place in the correct area. This placement is really easy. As soon as you drag and drop a photograph onto a matching area, Photomerge snaps the two together. So no exact matching skill is needed.

 You can also use Photomerge to create photomontages. For instance, you can create a great grouping of family photos using Photomerge.

Stitching Photos

I just ran outside with my digital camera and took five photos of a camphor tree growing next to my house. As shown in Figure 36-1, the five photographs all contain portions of the tree.

• **Figure 36-1:** Five photographs of the camphor tree outside my house.

Using the Photomerge command, I'm putting them all together into one giant tree image:

1. **Open the photographs you want to merge into a panorama or photomontage.**

Or, if you like you can use the Photomerge dialog box to select files or folders later.

2. **Choose File➪Automate➪Photomerge.**

The Photomerge dialog box, shown in Figure 36-2, appears.

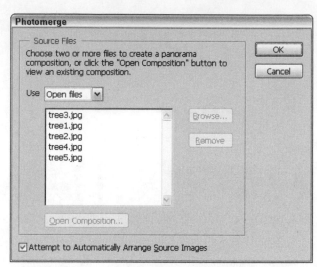

• **Figure 36-2: Use this Photomerge dialog box to select the photos for the panorama.**

3. **Choose a source for the image files with the Use drop-down list.**

Select from:

▶ **Open Files:** Automatically places all files open in Photoshop into the file list.

▶ **Files:** Lets you select individual image files.

▶ **Folder:** Lets you select an entire folder full of image files.

4. **If you chose Files or Folder in Step 3, click Browse to locate the files or folders you want to use.**

5. **Click OK after you select all the image files you want to use.**

The large Photomerge dialog box opens displaying all the image files you selected, as shown in Figure 36-3. Photomerge places any images it can't match together in the lightbox area.

If you do choose Perspective, select the Vanishing Point tool from the left side of the Photomerge dialog box. In the workspace, click the image you want to use as the vanishing point. Photoshop goes to work adjusting the perspective as shown in Figure 36-4.

Set vanishing point

Rotate image

Select image   Lightbox

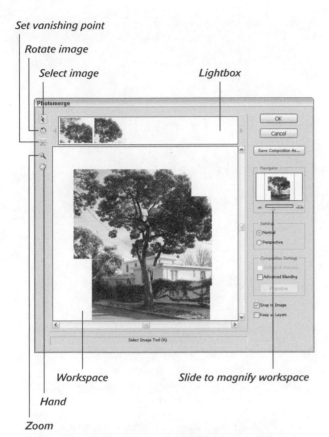

Workspace   Slide to magnify workspace

Hand

Zoom

• **Figure 36-3:** The Photomerge dialog box attempts to match all the selected images together.

• **Figure 36-4:** Photomerge adds perspective to shape the combined photographs.

6. Drag images from the lightbox down into the workspace, trying to match the photographs together as best as possible. (Don't worry; you don't have to be perfect!)

When you release the mouse, Photoshop detects where the photographs are the same and automatically snaps the photographs together. (Isn't that great?!)

7. Select Perspective in the Settings area, if you want to change the perspective of the image and add a vanishing point.

8. Put a check in the Cylindrical Mapping check box to remove the stretched distortion that can occur when creating a panorama, if you want.

Cylindrical Mapping is available only if you select the Perspective option in Step 7.

9. Put a check in the Advanced Blending check box to set Photomerge to reduce the color inconsistencies from photo to photo.

10. Click Preview.

Photomerge recolors and blends the photos together, adding perspective and cylindrical mapping if you selected it.

11. **Click Exit Preview.**

12. **Put a check in the Keep As Layers check box if you want to place each photograph on a separate layer.**

If you don't select this option, Photomerge automatically places all the photos together onto one layer.

13. **If you want, you can save the panorama or photomontage by clicking the Save Composition As button and using the Save dialog box to select a folder and enter a filename.**

14. **Click OK.**

The Photomerge dialog box closes and Photoshop goes to work placing the new panorama or photo montage in a new image window, as shown in Figure 36-5.

• **Figure 36–5: Photomerge is one smart plug-in! It combined my tree photos into one giant tree mural.**

Part VI

Amazing Fast Filter Effects

The 5th Wave   By Rich Tennant

"Hey- let's put scanned photos of ourselves through a ripple filter and see if we can make ourselves look weird."

37

Technique

Accenting with Sharpening or Blurring

Folks are always surprised when I suggest blurring portions of an image to bring out a specific detail. Sure, sharpening makes sense. After all, it adds to the detail. But, blurring? Trust me; sometimes a technique that you think of as a complete opposite can create your desired effect.

In this technique, you use the powerful Unsharp Mask filter to precisely sharpen images. You also experiment with the Unsharp Mask to increase the detail in an image until the edges start to glow. This can be used to create interesting effects. From there, you use the Blur filters to selectively blur portions of an image in order to emphasize the sharp areas. This technique has been used since the invention of photography and film.

Sharpening Effects

Four sharpening filters dwell on the Filter⇨Sharpen menu, but the first three (Sharpen, Sharpen Edges, and Sharpen More) don't give you any control over the sharpening process. All they do is click and sharpen. Sometimes you can use them sparingly as a quick fix, but I don't really recommend them. The sharpening filter to use is the fourth item down on the menu, Unsharp Mask.

The Unsharp Mask works by accenting the differences at the edges of elements in an image. These edges are usually high-contrast areas — for instance, the sudden shift from dark pixels to light pixels which the edge of an object can create. To see the Unsharp Mask filter at work, take a look at Color Plate 37-1.

If it sharpens so well, why is it called the "Unsharp" Mask?

The name seems like a contradiction, doesn't it? The best sharpener in Photoshop is termed *unsharp*. Hmph. The term *unsharp mask* actually comes from photography, where a negative and a faint positive created by using a special film (called *masking film*) are sandwiched together to increase contrast and sharpness. The faint positive created by using masking film is called an *unsharp mask*. I guess some of the programmers at Adobe are real photography buffs.

Here's how to use the Unsharp Mask filter:

1. **Open the image that you want to sharpen.**

For this example, I'm using the wagon wheel pasta shown in Figure 37-1. As you can see, the photograph is distinctly blurry.

• **Figure 37-1: This blurry pasta is going to become clearer.**

2. **Choose Filter⇨Sharpen⇨Unsharp Mask.**

The Unsharp Mask dialog box opens, as shown in Figure 37-2.

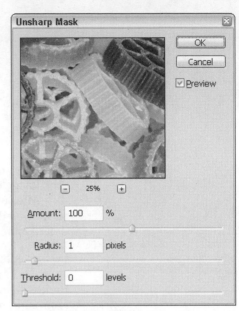

• **Figure 37-2: The Unsharp Mask dialog box is your key to sharper images.**

3. **Use the sliders to set the Amount, Radius, and Threshold.**

▶ The **Amount** sets how much the edges in the image are enhanced and defined (that is, sharpened). The higher the setting, the more sharpening.

▶ The **Radius** sets how contrast is increased from the edges. Higher settings make thicker edges.

▶ The **Threshold** sets how precisely the edges are recognized. Lower settings sharpen more pixels. Higher settings sharpen fewer pixels.

Experiment especially with the Amount and Radius settings. Find out where the settings go off the charts and create an undesired effect for you. Take a look at Figure 37-3, which shows the image from Figure 37-1 sharpened with various settings.

Amount: 100%, Radius: 1

Amount: 100%, Radius: 3

Amount: 200%, Radius: 3

Amount: 500%, Radius: 5

• **Figure 37-3:** Different settings create more contrast at the edges.

4. **Click OK when you finish adjusting the sliders to apply the sharpening to the image.**

After applying the Unsharp Mask, you can always apply other filters to accentuate the edges. Figure 37-4 shows two filters applied to the pasta wheels after extreme sharpening with the Amount set at 500% and the Radius set at 5. First, the Plastic Wrap filter was applied (top). Then, the Glowing Edges filter was applied (bottom).

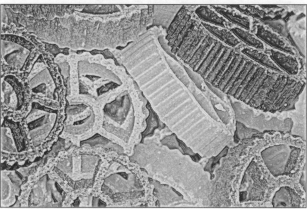

Plastic Wrap

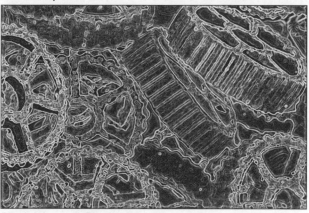

Plastic Wrap and Glowing Edges

• **Figure 37-4:** Applying filters after sharpening can increase the effects of the filters.

You can also apply the Unsharp Mask to individual channels. Experiment with this and see how sharpened channels can create colored edge glows. (For that matter, you can apply any filter to individual channels.) Take a look at Technique 52 to find out more about working with channels. Turn to Color Plate 37-1 to see these channel effects.

 Sometimes applying the Unsharp Mask several times with lower settings works better than applying the filter once with higher settings.

Blurring for Emphasis

Blurring portions of a photograph makes the viewer's eye immediately travel to the sharp areas of the picture. This technique has been used for years in photography and motion pictures.

Photoshop has eight different blur filters (count 'em!). The first three blur commands on the menu — Average, Blur, and Blur More — give you no control. They are one-shot filters that let you only click and blur. I don't use them very often. Instead, I usually head for the Gaussian Blur command, which gives control over the amount and quality of a blur.

Here's how to create a slight blur around a face to emphasize it:

1. **Open the image to which you want to add a blur.**

   For this example, I'm using the photo of the girl shown in Figure 37-5.

2. **Use any of the selection tools to select the face or faces in the photograph whose details you want to preserve.**

   For this example, I'm using the Lasso tool to select the girl's face.

• **Figure 37-5: I'm blurring the bicycle area to make the viewer immediately look at the girls face.**

3. **Choose Select➪Inverse or press Ctrl+Shift+I/ ⌘+Shift+I.**

   This inverts the selection to select the area of the photograph that you want to blur. For my example, this selects the bicycles shown behind the girl.

4. **Choose Filter➪Blur➪Gaussian Blur.**

5. **Use the Radius slider to set the amount of blur, as shown in Figure 37-6.**

   Radius can be set from 0.1 to 250. A Radius setting below 1 creates a very slight softening blur. Radius values between 1 and 5 create moderate blurs. Values above 5 blur the areas so much that they become unrecognizable. Experiment with the slider and see which results you like best.

   For my example, I chose a Radius setting of 3.

6. **Click OK to close the Gaussian Blur dialog box and apply the blur.**

   Take a look at Figure 37-7. Notice how the girl's face is really the focus of attention.

• **Figure 37-6:** Move the Radius slider to adjust the blur.

• **Figure 37-7:** Instead of just being another part of the photograph, the girl's face is really the focal point now.

Instead of blurring the entire background of an image as I did with the preceding example, you could select a channel and blur only that channel. This method can create a blurring effect that creates a slight glow around objects, almost like a very subdued star filter. Figure 37-8 shows the photograph of the girl with only the Red channel sharpened using a Radius setting of 10. Compare it to the blurring in Figure 37-7. The effect is rather subtle, but can be quite nice.

• **Figure 37-8:** Blurring only one channel creates the effect of a slight glow.

Painting Watercolors with Filters

Filters are one of Photoshop's great features. They give you so much with just a few clicks of the mouse. When I started using Photoshop (I won't tell you *how* long ago!), I was immediately enchanted with filters, and those early impressions still remain.

Photoshop CS comes with more than 100 filters that you can combine to create interesting and beautiful results. This technique takes a look at creating watercolor paintings by using filters. No painting is involved (unless you want to add a few highlights or details). Of course, you use the Watercolor filter, but this technique doesn't stop there. You use two other filters, the Underpainting and Note Paper filters, to enhance the results of the Watercolor filter, highlighting detail and adding luminosity.

So, open a photograph or an image that would make a good watercolor and have a go. If you want to use a photograph that isn't saved in digital form, turn to Technique 10 to find out all about scanning images and importing them into Photoshop. Color Plate 38-1 shows how the Watercolor filter looks when applied to a photograph.

Creating an Enhanced Watercolor

This method of creating a watercolor painting uses three filters: the Watercolor, Underpainting, and Note Paper filters. You apply each filter to a separate layer. Then, you adjust the layers' blending modes and opacities to blend them together.

1. **Open the image that you want to change into a watercolor painting.**

For this example, I'm using the photograph of a Maine coastal town shown in Figure 38-1.

2. **Select the layer containing the image in the Layers palette.**

3. **Press Ctrl+J/⌘+J or choose Layer➪New➪Layer via Copy *two times*.**

This creates two copies of the selected layer. So, you should have three identical layers, as shown in Figure 38-2.

• **Figure 38-1:** This photograph could certainly make a nice watercolor painting.

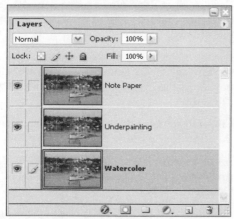

• **Figure 38-2:** You should have three identical layers in the Layers palette.

• **Figure 38-3:** Use the settings at the right side of the dialog box to adjust the Watercolor filter.

4. **In the Layers palette, rename the layers.**

I've renamed the layer at the top of the list Note Paper, the second layer down Underpainting, and the bottom layer Watercolor, as shown in Figure 38-2. I'm using these names to identify the different layers throughout the rest of the steps.

5. **Select the Watercolor layer in the Layers palette.**

6. **Choose Filter➪Artistic➪Watercolor.**

The Filter Gallery opens with the Watercolor filter selected, as shown in Figure 38-3. Notice that the settings for the filter are located at the right side of the dialog box.

7. **Move the sliders to adjust the Watercolor settings.**

▶ **Brush Detail** sets the width of the brush being used to create the watercolor. The lower the setting, the smaller the brush and the greater the detail. For my example, I set it to 12.

▶ **Shadow Intensity** deepens shadows in the image. The higher the setting, the more shadows. This option can darken the image considerably, so keep the setting low. For the example, I set it to 0.

▶ **Texture** enhances edges and adds more water droplets. The higher the setting, the more texture. For this example, I set it to 1.

8. **Click OK to close the Filter Gallery and apply the Watercolor filter to the Watercolor layer.**

You don't see the effect of the Watercolor filter unless you hide the two layers above the Watercolor layer. If you want to take a peek, Alt+click/Option+click the eye icon to the left of the Watercolor layer. (The other layers are hidden.) Afterwards, Alt+click/Option+click the eye icon to make the other layers visible again.

Figure 38-4 shows the Watercolor layer of the Maine town with the Watercolor filter applied. Notice that although the Watercolor filter did its job, the photograph is rather dark and a lot of the detail has been lost. This detail is returned in the following steps.

• **Figure 38-4: Now that I have a watercolor "base," I'll use other filters to restore the detail.**

9. Select the Underpainting layer in the Layers palette.

10. Choose Filter➪Artistic➪Underpainting.

    The Filter Gallery opens showing the Underpainting settings at the right of the dialog box. These settings are shown in Figure 38-5. The Underpainting filter is going to be used to add saturation and depth to the image.

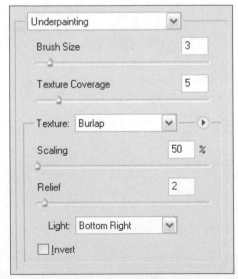

• **Figure 38-5: Use the settings to adjust the Underpainting filter.**

11. Use the Brush Size and Texture Coverage sliders to adjust these settings.

    ▶ **Brush Size** sets the width of the brush. Lower settings create more detail. For this example, I set it to 3.

    ▶ **Texture Coverage** sets how much texture is applied to the image. Higher settings make for more texture, but lower the amount of detail. So, for my example, I set it to a pretty low setting of 5.

12. Use the Texture drop-down list to select Burlap.

    Burlap texture imitates watercolor paper.

13. Set Scaling to 50% and Relief to 2.

14. Use the Light drop-down list to select the direction that the light is coming from for your image.

    For the Maine coast photograph, the light from the setting sun is coming from the lower-right portion of the photo. So, I chose Lower Right as the setting.

15. Click OK to close the Filter Gallery and apply the filter to the Underpainting layer.

16. In the Layers palette, use the Blending Mode drop-down list to select Soft Light and set the Opacity to 50%.

    You may need to fiddle with the Opacity slider to get this setting just right. If you hide the upper Note Paper layer and view the other two layers, you see that much of the detail is restored, as shown in Figure 38-6. (If you hide the Note Paper layer, don't forget to make it visible again.)

17. Select the Note Paper layer in the Layers palette.

18. Choose Filter➪Sketch➪Note Paper.

    The Filter Gallery opens with the Note Paper filter selected. Figure 38-7 shows the settings for this filter. The Note Paper filter adds more texture and detail and lightens the image overall.

• **Figure 38-6:** The Watercolor and Underpainting layers blended together with the Soft Light blending mode.

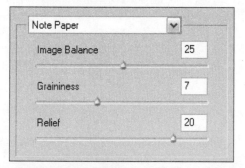

• **Figure 38-7:** Use these settings to adjust the effects of the Note Paper filter.

19. Set the Image Balance to 25.

You may need to play with this slider a bit to get the best results for your image. Lower settings show more highlight area; higher settings show more relief area. The balance between the highlights and relief shows the most details.

20. Set Graininess to 7 and Relief to 20.

21. Click OK to close the Filter Gallery and apply the filter to the Note Paper layer.

22. With the Note Paper layer still selected in the Layers palette, use the Blending Mode drop-down list to select Soft Light.

Your watercolor painting is now complete! As shown in Figure 38-8, the texture and detail in the Maine photograph looks really good.

• **Figure 38-8:** The completed watercolor painting.

Adding Highlights to Your Painting

If you want to add some highlights, select the Brush tool in the Toolbox, pick a watercolor brush tip by using the Brush Preset picker, and use either the Eyedropper tool or Color Picker to select colors. You can paint highlights on a separate, empty layer. That way, if you make a mistake, it doesn't affect any of the filtered layers.

For more about selecting brushes, turn to Technique 23.

Technique 39

Making Images Look Like Pressed Tin

Back in the early part of the previous century, pressed tin ceilings were very popular. Sometimes they were left their natural silver color; other times they were painted white or other colors.

This technique shows you how to filter an image so that it takes on the appearance of silvery pressed tin. You use the Emboss and Bas Relief filters blended by using the Overlay blending mode to achieve these results. This technique may look a bit tricky because of the many steps, but don't worry! It's really quite simple. Just follow along and you can be pressing tin in no time.

Pressing Tin

Though you can turn any image into pressed tin, simple images or homey ones are the most appropriate. Fleur-de-lis, hearts, and household objects really come to mind. For this example, I'm using a scan of the handmade doily shown in Figure 39-1.

• **Figure 39-1:** This lace doily is going to become pressed tin.

Here's how to turn images into pressed tin:

1. **Open the image that you want to use.**

2. **Select the layer containing the image in the Layers palette.**

3. **Press Ctrl+J/⌘+J or choose Layer⇨New⇨ Layer via Copy.**

   This creates a copy of the selected layer.

4. **Rename the copied layer and the bottom layer.**

   I've renamed the copied layer Bas Relief and the bottom layer Emboss, as shown in Figure 39-2. I'm using these names to identify the different layers for the rest of the directions.

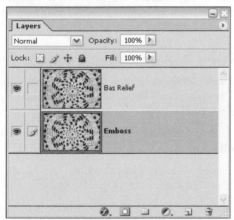

• **Figure 39-2:** You should have two identical layers in the Layers palette.

5. **Select the Emboss layer in the Layers palette.**

6. **Choose Filter⇨Stylize⇨Emboss.**

   The Emboss dialog box opens, as shown in Figure 39-3. The Emboss filter is used to create the raised areas for the pressed tin.

7. **Enter a degree in the Angle text box or drag the pointer around the circle to set where the light source is coming from.**

   For this example, I set the Angle at 135°.

8. **Set the Height to 5 and the Amount to 100%.**

9. **Click OK to close the Emboss dialog box and apply the filter to the Emboss layer.**

   If you hide the upper layer, you can see the results of the emboss filter, as shown in Figure 39-4. (Be sure to make the other layer visible again.)

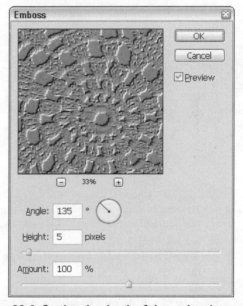

• **Figure 39-3:** Setting the depth of the embossing.

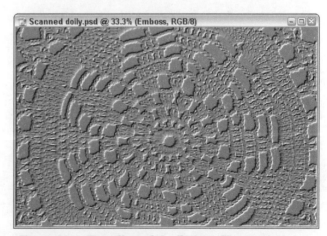

• **Figure 39-4:** The effect of the Emboss filter on the Emboss layer.

10. Select the Bas Relief layer in the Layers palette.

11. Choose Filter⇨Sketch⇨Bas Relief.

The Filter Gallery opens with the Bas Relief filter selected, as shown in Figure 39-5. Notice that the settings for the filter are at the right side of the dialog box. The Bas Relief filter adds detail.

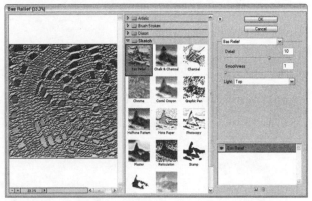

• **Figure 39-5:** Use the settings at the right side of the dialog box to adjust the Bas Relief filter.

12. Set the Detail to 10 and the Smoothness to 1.

13. Choose Top from the Light drop-down list.

14. Click OK to close the Filter Gallery and apply the filter to the Bas Relief layer.

15. With the Bas Relief layer still selected, choose Overlay from the Blending Mode drop-down list in the Layers palette.

The results so far are shown in Figure 39-6.

16. Click the Create New Layer button at the bottom of the Layers palette.

An empty layer appears at the top of the Layers palette. This layer is going to be used to brighten the image with a white overlay.

17. Make sure that the empty layer is selected in the Layers palette.

18. Select white as the Foreground color.

The quick way to do this is to press D and then press X.

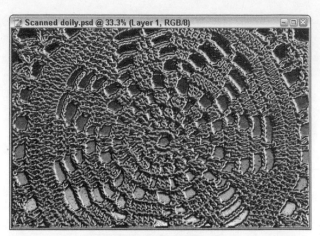

• **Figure 39-6:** The Emboss and Bas Relief layers blended together by using the Overlay blending mode.

19. Choose the Paint Bucket tool from the Toolbox.

20. On the Options bar, make sure that Fill is set to Foreground, Mode is set to Normal, and Opacity is set to 100%.

21. Click in the image window to fill the entire layer with white.

22. Choose Overlay from the Blending Mode drop-down list and set the Opacity to 50%.

You may need to fiddle with the Opacity setting to get the whiter look of pressed tin. The results of all this filtering are shown in Figure 39-7.

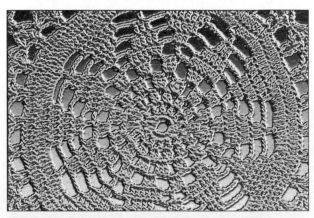

• **Figure 39-7:** The lace doily turned into pressed tin.

Technique 40

Creating Photo Silkscreens

Save Time By

- Equalizing the Green and Blue channels
- Applying the High Pass and Median filters

Andy Warhol created a revolution in the art world when he took the photo silkscreen process, normally used for commercial mass printing, and used it to create fine art. You may be familiar with his Campbell's Soup series, the Gumby silkscreens, and perhaps the best-known Marilyn Monroe photo silkscreens.

This technique takes you step-by-step through the entire process of creating your own silkscreens in a virtual Photoshop fashion. So pull out an image (perhaps a photo of Marilyn?) and create your own photo silkscreens. Color Plate 40-1 shows the colorful results of this technique.

How Did Andy Do It?

Photo silkscreens are produced by taking a high-contrast photograph and transferring the image onto silk fabric that is stretched over a frame. The silk is first coated with a light-sensitive solution. The photograph is projected onto the solution-covered silk, and the solution hardens where it is exposed to light. To produce a print, ink is pushed through the silk onto paper by using a squeegee. Any solution-hardened areas don't let the ink pass through.

Even though you don't use silk and ink in Photoshop, you can create really interesting photo silkscreens by using the High Pass and Median filters applied to individual channels.

Making Your Silkscreen

The steps here are pretty straightforward, but they do take some knowledge of the Channels palette. For instance, you need to know how to select multiple channels. If you need a refresher on channels, turn to Technique 52.

 Several of the steps involve selecting a specific channel, but you may want to experiment with a different channel depending on the colors in your image. Run through the steps a few times, selecting a different series of channels each time.

Here's how to turn your image into a photo silkscreen:

1. **Open the image that you want to use.**

For this example, I'm using the four lizards shown in Figure 40-1.

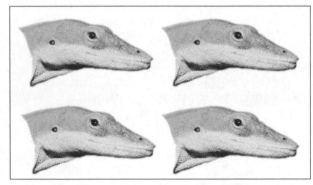

• **Figure 40-1:** These lizards are going to be silkscreened.

2. **In the Channels palette, choose the Green and Blue channels.**

3. **Choose Image⇨Adjustments⇨Equalize.**

4. **In the Channels palette, choose the Red channel.**

5. **Choose Filter⇨Other⇨High Pass.**

6. **In the High Pass dialog box, set the Radius to 3, as shown in Figure 40-2.**

7. **Click OK to close the High Pass dialog box and apply the High Pass filter to the Red channel.**

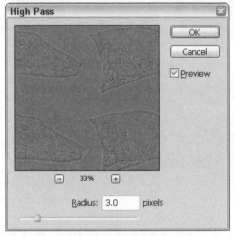

• **Figure 40-2:** Set the Radius to 3 in the High Pass dialog box.

8. **With the Red channel still selected, choose Image⇨Adjustments⇨Threshold.**

9. **In the Threshold dialog box, set the Threshold Level to 125, as shown in Figure 40-3.**

You may need to fiddle a little with this setting to get the best balance between black and white.

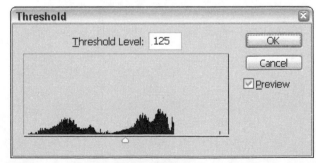

• **Figure 40-3:** In the Threshold dialog box, set the Threshold Level to 125.

10. **Click OK to close the Threshold dialog box and apply the command to the Red channel.**

The four lizards now look like those shown in Figure 40-4.

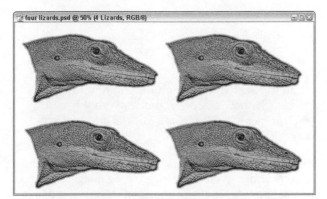

• **Figure 40-4:** After applying the Threshold command to the Red channel, the lizards are starting to look like a silkscreen.

11. **In the Channels palette, select the Blue channel.**

12. **Choose Filter⇨Noise⇨Median.**

13. **In the Median dialog box, set the Radius to 5, as shown in Figure 40-5.**

Setting the radius to 4 makes the Blue channel very smooth looking.

14. **With the Blue channel still selected, choose Image⇨Adjustments⇨Threshold.**

15. **In the Threshold dialog box, set the Threshold Level to 40.**

You may need to play with this setting to get a good balance between black and white.

After adding a black background, the four lizards look just like a Warhol silkscreen, as shown in Figure 40-6 and Color Plate 40-1.

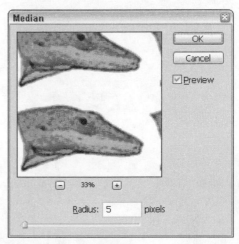

• **Figure 40-5:** Set the Radius to 5.

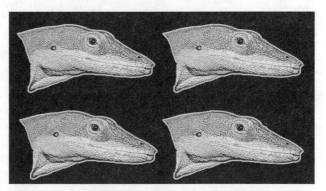

• **Figure 40-6:** The lizards definitely look reminiscent of a Warhol silkscreen.

Another way to create a photo silkscreen effect is to apply the Stamp filter to one of the channels. If you want to experiment, open an image and apply the Stamp filter to the Red channel first and see what kind of results you get.

Technique 41

Sketching with Filters

Several of the filters on the Sketch menu imitate different drawing media, including charcoal, chalk and charcoal, and graphic pen. These filters work surprisingly well, turning images into black and white sketched renditions.

When layered with the original image and blended together with a blending mode, these filters can produce even more interesting images: colored sketches. Another appealing method that produces an interesting image is to apply color to a sketch by using gradient maps, photo filters, or the Hue/Saturation command. (Take a look at Techniques 33 and 35 to find out more about these features.)

This technique is going to explore these areas. First, you find out how to use the Charcoal, Chalk and Charcoal, and Graphic Pen filters. Then you experiment with blending sketched layers and also apply color to a sketch. These techniques are quite straightforward, so have some fun and try them out! Take a look at Color Plate 41-1 to see what these colored sketches look like.

Applying Sketch Filters

The three sketch filters that I discuss here — Charcoal, Chalk and Charcoal, and Graphic Pen — all work in the same fashion. Before you even select one of these filters from the Filter⇨Sketch menu, be sure to select Foreground and Background colors in the Toolbox. These colors are the ones that will be used by the sketch filters. The Background setting determines the color of the "paper" that the sketch is done on, and the Foreground setting determines the color that is used for the actual "ink" of the sketching.

When the colors are set, you can access the Charcoal, Chalk and Charcoal, and Graphic Pen filters. To do so, open the Filter Gallery by choosing Filter⇨Sketch⇨Charcoal, Chalk and Charcoal, or Graphic Pen. The

Filter Gallery shows you a preview of the sketch on the left and various settings on the right. (See Figure 41-1.)

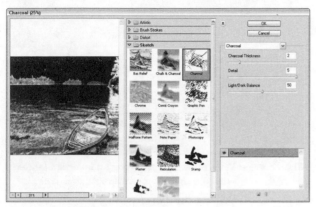

• **Figure 41-1: The settings for each Sketch filter are pretty much the same.**

The settings for each filter are pretty much the same. They include Thickness, Detail, Light/Dark Balance, and possibly Light Direction. Adjust these settings as you like to achieve a good balance between the light and dark elements. Figure 41-2 shows an original photograph and the rendering by each of the three filters.

Overall, these filters do a great job of creating charcoal and graphic pen sketches by using different drawing methods. The following sections show you how to enhance the filter effects by layering or recoloring.

Blending Layers

Using layer techniques, you can create beautiful colored sketches. Think of them as *mixed media* — for instance, a graphic pen sketch colored with watercolors, or a pastel sketch outlined and defined with charcoal.

Original photograph

Chalk & Charcoal filter

Charcoal filter

Graphic Pen filter

• **Figure 41-2: The Sketch filters in action.**

The following directions show you how to filter layers and then blend them. Which filters you use is up to you. Use your imagination when combining filtered layers. You may be surprised at some of the great results that you get. If you're trying these steps for the first time, stick to the directions so that you can get an idea of what's going on.

1. **Open the image that you're going to use.**

   For this example, I'm using the boat photograph shown in Figure 41-2.

2. **Select the layer containing the image in the Layers palette.**

3. **Press Ctrl+J/⌘+J or choose Layer⇨New⇨ Layer via Copy.**

   A copy of the selected layer appears in the Layers palette.

4. **With the copied layer selected, choose Filter⇨ Sketch⇨Charcoal (or one of the other two filters).**

5. **Use the Filter Gallery dialog box that appears to adjust the filter settings.**

   For the boat photograph, I set Charcoal Thickness to 3, Detail to 5, and Light/Dark Balance to 62. You may need to adjust these settings to suit your image.

6. **Click OK to close the Filter Gallery and apply the filter to the copied layer.**

7. **In the Layers palette, select an option from the Blending Mode drop-down list.**

   For my image, I selected the Soft Light option.

   You may also want to try the Overlay blending mode. As shown in Figure 41-3, the upper charcoal filtered layer blends with the lower layer to fill in detail and color. Use your imagination because this book is in black and white!

• **Figure 41-3:** When the Charcoal filtered layer is blended with the original photograph, the result is quite lovely.

If you want to experiment, choose the Graphic Pen filter in Step 4 to get the blended results shown in Figure 41-4.

• **Figure 41-4:** The same photo with the Graphic Pen filter applied to the upper layer instead and the layer's Opacity set to 60%.

You can apply a filter to the lower layer (the original photograph) to create a mixed media illustration. Figure 41-5 shows a blend of the Charcoal filtered layer on the top with the Rough Pastels filter applied to the lower layer.

• **Figure 41-5:** When the Rough Pastel filter is applied to the lower layer, the blended layers create a really stunning drawing.

Applying Color to Sketches

You can apply color to sketches by using the commands on the Image⇨Adjustments menu. In particular, the Gradient Map, Hue/Saturation, and Photo Filter commands work really well.

When applying any of the adjustment commands to a sketch, I recommend applying them as adjustment layers. Adjustment layers are infinitely flexible. You don't change any pixels on the sketch layer, and you can change the command's settings at any time. If you want to find out more about adjustment layers, take a look at Technique 22.

Use the following directions to apply any of the adjustment commands by using an adjustment layer:

1. Use one of the sketch filters to turn an image into a sketch.

Refer to the earlier section, "Applying Sketch Filters."

2. In the Layers palette, select the layer containing the sketch.

3. Click the Create New Fill or Adjustment Layer button at the bottom of the Layers palette.

4. Choose either Hue/Saturation, Gradient Map, or Photo Filter from the menu.

The dialog box for the command that you selected opens. (To find out more about gradient maps, take a look at Technique 27; for photo filters and Hue/Saturation, turn to Technique 33.)

5. Use the dialog box to adjust settings, and then click OK.

The selected color is applied to the sketch layer.

 You can always change the settings of the adjustment layer by double-clicking the adjustment layer's thumbnail in the Layers palette.

Technique 42

I've Been Framed!

Frames add the finishing touch to any image, be it a real-world photograph or painting, or a Photoshop image. Frames smooth out the edges, and add focus and definition to any image.

Creating frames in Photoshop is really quite easy. In this technique, you use a layer mask to delineate the area that you want to frame and then apply a filter to the layer mask to blur edges, add texture, or create some other effect. In addition, you use a fill layer to color the frame with a solid color, gradient, or pattern.

 If the terms *fill layer* and *layer mask* are completely new to you, take a look at Technique 21 to find out about fill layers, and see Technique 49 to read about layer masks. If you have some familiarity with these Photoshop features, just follow the steps; I tell you exactly what you need to do.

Creating Frames

When you create the selection that becomes the layer mask (and eventually the frame) in Step 4, remember that not all frames are rectangular. They can be elliptical, triangular, or even shaped like a heart. Besides using the selection tools as I describe in Step 4, think about what other tools you could use to create interesting selections. For instance, you could use the Custom Shape tool to create a path in the shape of a star or musical note, and then change the path into a selection by clicking the Load Path as Selection button at the bottom of the Paths palette. You could also use the Type Mask tool to create a type-shaped selection. The shape of the frame can be anything — use your imagination!

Here's how to create a frame with a layer mask:

1. Open the image that you want to put a frame around.

For this example, I'm using the photograph of the sock monkeys shown in Figure 42-1. If the image is contained on the Background layer, convert the Background to a regular layer by selecting Layer➪New➪Layer from Background.

• **Figure 42-1:** These sock monkeys are going to be framed.

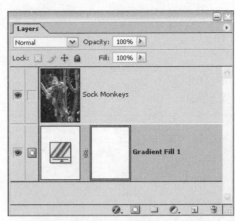

• **Figure 42-2:** Two layers should be in the Layers palette: the image layer on top and the fill layer on the bottom.

2. **Click the Create New Fill or Adjustment Layer button at the bottom of the Layers palette and choose either Solid, Gradient, or Pattern from the menu.**

This fill layer is going to be used to color the frame. If you select Solid, use the Color Picker to select a color. If you select Gradient, use the Gradient picker in the Gradient Fill dialog box to select a gradient. If you select Pattern, use the Pattern picker in the Pattern Fill dialog box to select a pattern.

If you decide later that you don't like the color, pattern, or gradient that you select in this step, you can always change it. Just double-click the layer thumbnail to access the dialog box. To find out more about how flexible fill layers are, turn to Technique 21.

3. **In the Layers palette, drag the new fill layer that you just created to *below* the layer containing the image that you want to frame.**

You should now have two layers, the fill layer on the bottom and the image layer on the top, as shown in Figure 42-2.

4. **Use any of the selection tools to select the area that you want to place the frame around.**

You could use the Rectangular Marquee tool to create a rectangular selection, the Elliptical Marquee tool to create an oval selection, or even the Lasso tool to create a freeform selection around the image area. Figure 42-3 shows the sock monkeys selected. If the selection isn't centered, don't worry about it. You can correct that later.

5. **At the bottom of the Layers palette, click Add Layer Mask.**

A layer mask appears linked to the layer containing the image in the Layers palette, as shown in Figure 42-4.

6. **In the Layers palette, click the layer mask to select it.**

7. **Choose Filter⇨Blur⇨Gaussian Blur.**

Using the Gaussian Blur filter creates a blurred edge around the image. You could also use many other filters, including those on the Filter⇨Distort and Filter⇨Texture menus, to create different frame edges (a few are shown in Figure 42-6).

• **Figure 42-3:** The selected area is going to create the layer mask.

Layer mask

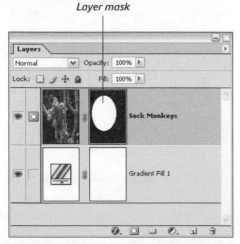

• **Figure 42-4:** You're using the linked layer mask to create the frame.

8. Use the Gaussian Blur dialog box to set the Radius to 50.

Depending on the size of the image, you may want to fiddle with this setting. Lower settings create thinner blurred edges; higher settings create wider blurred edges.

9. Click OK to close the Gaussian Blur dialog box and apply the blur to the layer mask.

As shown in Figure 42-5, the sock monkeys are surrounded by a blurred gradient frame. However, they aren't centered yet.

• **Figure 42-5:** The Gaussian Blur filter creates a soft blurred frame.

10. If the framed image isn't centered, use the Rectangular Marquee tool to select around both the image and the frame.

Make sure the frame and image are centered in the selection.

11. **Choose Image➪Crop.**

The image is cropped down to the selected area and the image is centered, as shown in Figure 42-6. In Figure 42-6, you can also see the effects created by applying different filters in Step 7.

Gaussian Blur filter

Glass filter

Mosaic filter

• **Figure 42-6:** The finished, framed sock monkeys.

Creating Frames with Auto FX Photo/Graphic Edges 6.0

Photo/Graphic Edges 6.0 by Auto FX is a great program for quickly surrounding your images with many different kinds of frames. This program can run as a standalone or it can be accessed on the Photoshop Filter menu. Figure 42-7 shows two frames that I added around the sock monkey photograph in less than a minute. Take a look at Technique 63 to find out more about other great software available from Auto FX. If you want to check out its Web site, visit www.autofx.com.

• **Figure 42-7:** Photo/Graphic Edges 6.0 by Auto FX is a really great framing tool.

Technique 43

Dunking Images in Liquid

Save Time By

- ✔ Creating liquid by using filters
- ✔ Using the Hard Light blending mode

Here it is. The big kahuna of filter techniques. You have to get through lots of steps, but it's worth it! This technique uses the Channels and Layers palettes, levels and curves, and the Gaussian Blur, Emboss, and Plastic Wrap filters to submerge an image in liquid. Don't think that this effect is only for images; you can create some type and drop it in water, too.

If the number of steps seems daunting, don't freak out! All the steps are really pretty simple, so you shouldn't have any trouble with them. Because this technique does use the Layers and Channels palettes, you may want to brush up on them by visiting Technique 15 (for layers) and Technique 52 (for channels).

Create an action

Because this technique involves a long series of steps, repeating it over and over when you want to use it can be quite tedious and time consuming. If you like the effect and want to use it again, why not create an *action* — a mini-program that does all the steps for you? To find out how to record an action, turn to Technique 8.

Ready, Get Set, Dunk!

This technique works best on simple images containing an object or type layer. For the demonstration here, I'm using a photograph of an old key, shown in Figure 43-1. Complex images add too much in the way of shadows and detail, detracting from the finished effect.

This technique uses many steps, so I've broken them up into three sections. The first section sets up a custom "Liquid" channel. Section two builds on section one and shows you how to create a "Water" layer. The third and final section takes you through putting the custom channel and layer together to create the full liquid effect. Make your way sequentially through each section and soon your image will be dripping with liquid!

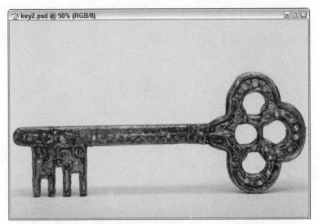

• **Figure 43-1:** For this example, I'm making this key look like liquid.

Making a "Liquid" Channel

1. Open the image that you want to submerge.

2. In the Channels palette, select the Blue channel, right-click/Option+click the channel, and choose Duplicate Channel from the menu, as shown in Figure 43-2.

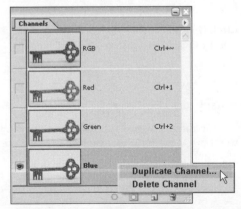

• **Figure 43-2:** Choose Duplicate Channel from the menu.

3. In the Duplicate Channel dialog box, type something in the As text box, as shown in Figure 43-3.

This names the copied channel whatever you type in the As text box. I've named my copied channel Liquid. I'm calling this channel the Liquid channel for the rest of the directions.

• **Figure 43-3:** Type the name for the copied channel.

4. Select the Invert check box.

5. Click OK to close the Duplicate Channel dialog box.

    The inverted copied channel appears at the bottom of the list of channels in the Channels palette, as shown in Figure 43-4.

6. Select the Liquid channel in the Channels palette.

    The Liquid channel appears in the image window.

7. Choose Filter⇨Blur⇨Gaussian Blur.

8. In the Gaussian Blur dialog box, set the Radius to 5.

9. Click OK to close the Gaussian Blur dialog box and apply the blur to the Liquid channel.

10. Choose Image⇨Adjustments⇨Levels or press Ctrl+L/⌘+L.

11. In the Levels dialog box, set the Input Levels by typing 35 in the Shadows text box, 1 in the Midtones text box, and 65 in the Highlights text box, as shown in Figure 43-5.

    These settings remove most of the grays and make the channel smoother.

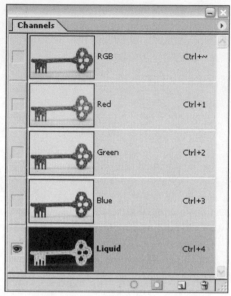

• **Figure 43-4: The inverted Liquid channel appears at the bottom of the Channels palette.**

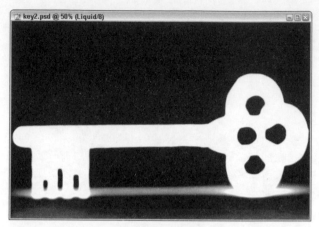

• **Figure 43-6: The Liquid channel with grays reduced.**

Creating the "Water" Layer

This section builds on the work you finished in the preceding section, "Making a 'Liquid' Channel." After completing those steps, continue with the steps here. You're well on your way to dipping your image in liquid!

1. **In the Layers palette, select the layer containing the image.**

2. **Click the Create New Layer button at the bottom of the Layers palette.**

   A new empty layer appears above the selected layer.

3. **Rename the new layer.**

   I've renamed it Water. I'm using the name Water to refer to this layer for the rest of the steps.

4. **Select white as the Foreground color.**

   An easy way to do this is to press D, and then press X.

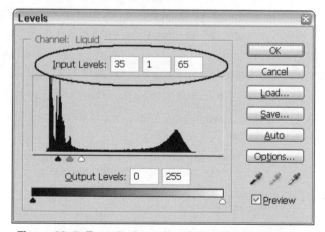

• **Figure 43-5: Type the Input Levels into the text boxes.**

12. **Click OK to close the Levels dialog box and apply the settings to the Liquid channel.**

   Your Liquid channel should look something like the one shown in Figure 43-6.

5. **Press Alt+Backspace/Option+Backspace to fill the Water layer with white.**

6. In the Channels palette, select the Liquid channel and click the Load Channel as Selection button at the bottom of the palette.

7. In the Layers palette, select the Water layer.

8. Select black as the Foreground color.

A quick way to do this is to press D.

9. Press Alt+Backspace/Option+Backspace to fill the selection with the Foreground color.

The selected area on the Water layer fills with black, as shown in Figure 43-7.

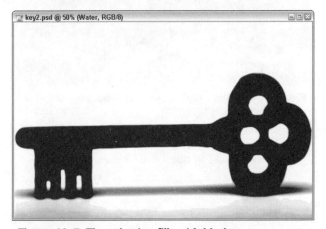

• **Figure 43-7: The selection fills with black.**

10. Press Ctrl+D/⌘+D to remove the selection marquee from the Water layer.

11. With the Water layer still selected in the Layers palette, choose Filter➪Blur➪Gaussian Blur.

12. In the Gaussian Blur dialog box, set the Radius to 5, and then click OK.

13. Choose Filter➪Stylize➪Emboss.

14. Set the Angle to the direction where the light source is coming from in your image.

For my example, 135 degrees works best because that's where the light source seems to be coming from, as shown in Figure 43-8.

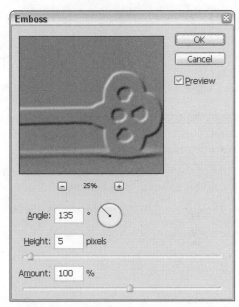

• **Figure 43-8: Set the angle to match the light source in your image.**

15. Set the Height to 5 pixels and the Amount to 100%.

16. Click OK to close the Emboss dialog box and apply the settings to the Water layer.

Your Water layer should look similar to the one shown in Figure 43-9.

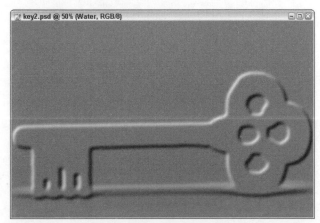

• **Figure 43-9: After applying the Emboss filter, the Water layer should look like this.**

Putting It All Together

This final section takes the "Liquid" channel and "Water" layer and shows you how to put them together to finish this cool liquid effect.

1. **In the Channels palette, select the Liquid channel and then click the Load Channel as Selection button at the bottom of the palette.**

2. **Choose Select➪Inverse or press Ctrl+Shift+I/ ⌘+Shift+I to invert the selection.**

3. **In the Layers palette, select the Water layer.**

4. **Choose Select➪Feather.**

5. **Set the Feather Radius to 2 in the Feather Selection dialog box.**

This smoothes and softens the selection.

6. **Set the Foreground color to black.**

A quick way to do this is to press D.

7. **Press Alt+Backspace/Option+Backspace to fill the selected area with black.**

8. **Choose Edit➪Fade Fill.**

9. **In the Fade dialog box, set the Opacity to 50% and select Normal from the Mode drop-down list, as shown in Figure 43-10.**

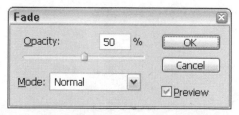

• Figure 43-10: Use the Fade dialog box to fade the black fill.

10. **Click OK to close the Fade dialog box and apply the settings.**

11. **Press Ctrl+D/⌘+D to remove the selection.**

The Water layer should now look something like the one shown in Figure 43-11.

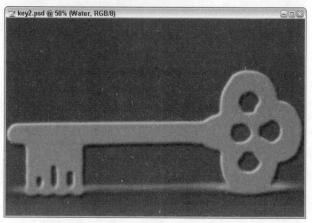

• Figure 43-11: The Water layer is an embossed gray on gray layer.

12. **Choose Image➪Adjustments➪Curves or press Ctrl+M/⌘+M to open the Curves dialog box.**

You're using curves to make the Water layer look more like liquid. (If you want to find out more about curves, turn to Technique 30.)

13. **In the Curves dialog box, click the line five times to create five evenly spaced points, as shown in Figure 43-12.**

It doesn't matter exactly where you place the points, but one point should roughly be in the center and two more should be on either side of the center point.

14. **Drag the second point up and the fourth point down until the plotted line resembles the one shown in Figure 43-13.**

Don't worry; it doesn't have to exactly match the figure. Just get it close.

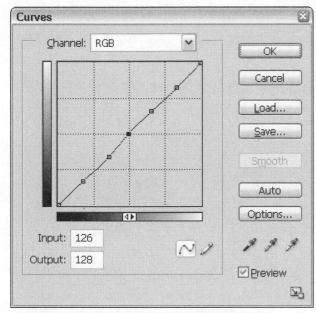

• **Figure 43-12:** Click the line to add five points.

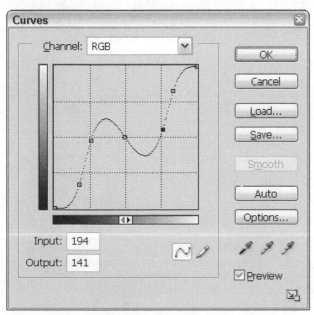

• **Figure 43-13:** Drag the second point up and the fourth point down.

15. **Click OK to close the Curves dialog box and apply the settings.**

The Water layer should now appear like the one shown in Figure 43-14.

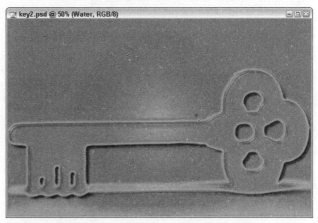

• **Figure 43-14:** The Water layer is looking more and more like liquid.

16. **With the Water layer still selected, choose Filter⇨Artistic⇨Plastic Wrap.**

The Plastic Wrap filter adds more highlights and drippy qualities to the Water layer.

17. **In the Filter Gallery, set the Plastic Wrap settings: Highlight Strength to 20, Detail to 10, and Smoothness to 10, as shown in Figure 43-15.**

• **Figure 43-15:** Set the Plastic Wrap filter settings.

18. Click OK to close the Filter Gallery and apply the filter to the Water layer.

19. Choose Edit⇨Fade Plastic Wrap.

20. In the Fade dialog box, set the Opacity to 30% and then click OK.

The Water layer now has some highlights and quite a liquid edge.

21. In the Channels palette, select the Liquid channel and then click the Load Channel as Selection button at the bottom of the palette.

22. In the Layers palette, select the Water layer.

23. Choose Select⇨Inverse or press Ctrl+Shift+I/ ⌘+Shift+I.

This inverts the selected area. The inverted selection removes the background behind the liquid areas of the layer.

24. Press Delete to remove the background behind the liquid areas.

25. Press Ctrl+D/⌘+D to remove the selection marquee.

26. In the Layers palette, choose Hard Light from the Blending Mode drop-down list.

This blends the Water layer with the image layer below. The Water layer does look like water, but it's a bit too light to really be noticeable.

27. Choose Layer⇨New⇨Layer via Copy or press Ctrl+J/⌘+J.

A copy of the Water layer (named Water Copy) appears above the Water layer in the Layers palette.

28. Add a drop shadow to the Water Copy layer by clicking the Add Layer Style button at the bottom of the Layers palette and choosing Drop Shadow from the menu.

29. In the Layer Style dialog box, set the Angle to the direction where the light source in your image is coming from. (This should be the same setting that you used in Step 14 in the "Creating the 'Water' Layer" section.)

For my key example, I used 135 degrees.

30. Set the Distance to 20 pixels, Spread to 0%, and Size to 5 pixels, as shown in Figure 43-16.

You may need to fiddle with these settings to get the best look for your liquid image.

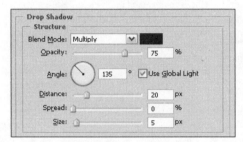

• **Figure 43-16:** Use the sliders to set the drop shadow settings.

31. Click OK to close the Layer Style dialog box and apply the drop shadow to the Water Copy layer.

You made it! Your image should now look like liquid, like the key in Figure 43-17. Congratulations!

• **Figure 43-17:** The liquid key with the drop shadow applied.

You could also delete the layer containing the image and add a solid fill layer below the two Water layers to just show the liquid effect. Figure 43-18 shows a white fill layer behind the two Water layers.

 To change the color of the liquid, add a solid fill layer above the Water Copy layer and select any color that you want. Then, set the fill layer's blending mode to Color by using the Layers palette. (To find out how to add fill layers, take a look at Technique 21.)

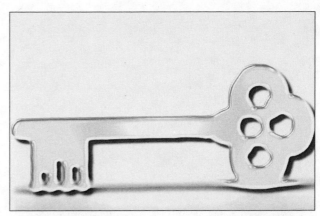

• **Figure 43-18:** The two Water layers shown with a white fill layer.

Part VII

Super Type Effects

The 5th Wave   By Rich Tennant

Shadow Type

Save Time By

- Using inner and drop shadows to define the type
- Lowering the Fill opacity to 0%

When you see type on a page or in an image, it's often filled with some color, perhaps red or black. It may have a drop shadow to give it a three-dimensional look, but usually it's the color inside the type that defines each character's shape.

This morning I woke up and thought to myself, "What if the type is transparent? How could I read it?" Then the answer came to me: Define the shape of the type's outline by using a drop shadow and an inner shadow. And, *voilà*, here you are.

This technique works really well on any image because the type itself is transparent — no color matching is needed to fill the type because the shadows do all the work. This method works best when an image displays a lot of contrast. In the following steps, I use black for the drop shadow and white for the inner shadow, which works well on any area that isn't too dark. But if you want to use this method on a black area, for instance, you should change the drop shadow's color to red or white. The shadows' contrasts are the key to defining the shape of the type.

Shadow Dancing

Creating type by using shadows is really easy thanks to layer styles and the Fill slider on the Layers palette. What you need to do is create some type, which automatically appears on its own type layer, and then apply a drop shadow and an inner shadow using layer styles. The final step is to lower the type layer's Fill opacity to 0% making the type's fill (but not the shadows) transparent. Here's how:

1. Open the image that you want to add type to.

For this example, I'm using the hearts image shown in Figure 44-1.

• **Figure 44-1:** I'm adding some love to these hearts.

• **Figure 44-2:** The type appears on a type layer in the Layers palette.

2. Select the Horizontal Type tool from the Toolbox.

3. Use the Options bar to select the type font and size.

For this example, I'm using ComicSans MS set at 100 points.

4. Click in the image window and type some text.

5. Click the Commit button on the Options bar (it looks like a check mark) to apply the type.

The type appears on its own type layer in the layers palette, as shown in Figure 44-2. If you need to, you can use the Move tool to position the type in the image window.

6. With the type layer selected in the Layers palette, click the Add Layer Style button at the bottom of the palette and choose Drop Shadow from the menu, as shown in Figure 44-3.

If you've never used Layer Styles before, you might want to take a quick look at Technique 20.

7. In the Structure area in the Layer Styles dialog box, set the options for the drop shadow, as shown in Figure 44-4.

► Set the **Opacity** to 100%.

► Set the **Distance** to 20 pixels.

► Move the **Spread** slider to 5%.

► Set the **Size** to 10 pixels.

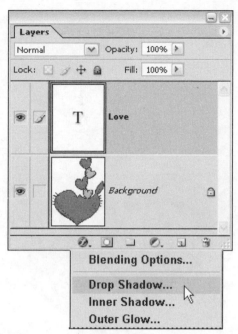

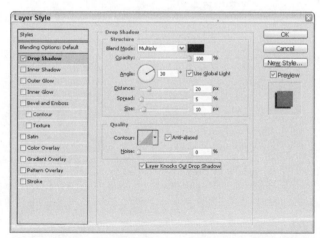

• **Figure 44-3:** Choose Drop Shadow from the Add Layer Style menu.

• **Figure 44-4:** In the Structure area, select settings for the drop shadow.

The settings listed are good basic settings. You may want to fiddle with these settings to get them just the way you want them. Just make sure that the shadow doesn't spread too far or you'll lose letter definition.

8. In the Effects column on the left of the Layer Styles dialog box, put a check mark next to Inner Shadow and click the words Inner Shadow to view those settings.

9. In the Structure area, use the Blend Mode drop-down list to select Normal, as shown in Figure 44-5.

• **Figure 44-5:** Use the Blend Mode drop-down list to select the Normal blending mode.

10. Click the color square next to the Blend Mode drop-down list to select an inner shadow color by using the Color Picker.

For this example, I selected white.

11. Set the Opacity to 100%.

12. Set the Distance to 5 pixels and the Size to 5 pixels.

13. Click OK to close the Layer Styles dialog box and apply the shadows to the type.

14. With the type layer still selected in the Layers palette, drag the Fill slider at the top of the palette to 0%.

The type's fill color becomes transparent, leaving the shadows to define the type, as shown in Figure 44-6.

• Figure 44-6: Lowering the **Fill** opacity to 0% leaves shadow type.

• Figure 44-7: Adding a pattern overlay can jazz up the type.

Jazzing Up Your Shadow Type

Experiment with the other layer styles that are available. For instance, you could add a bevel to the type or an inner glow. I took the shadow type created in the preceding steps and added a pattern overlay with the Multiply blending mode, as shown in Figure 44-7. The pattern picks up the red of the hearts underneath and adds a fun touch to the type.

Technique 45

Knock-Out Type

Save Time By

- Using the Type Mask tools
- Applying layer masks

I'm sure that you've seen advertisements in newspapers or magazines where some large type looks like it is filled with an image, pattern, or texture. This effect is really easy to create by using a layer mask. (I give you a quick run-down here of how a layer mask works, but to find out the full score, turn to Technique 49.)

Imagine that you have an image with two layers. The lower layer contains a photograph of trees, and the upper layer is filled with a solid color. Both layers are set at 100% opacity. This means that you can see the upper, solid color layer, but you can't see the tree layer below it. Now, you link a layer mask to the solid color layer and paint with black on the layer mask. The black areas of the layer mask hide the corresponding areas of the solid color layer, letting you see the tree layer underneath. The white areas of the layer mask leave the corresponding areas of the solid color layer visible. Basically, a layer mask is used to hide portions of the layer that it's linked to, revealing the layer underneath.

In this technique, you find out how to use a layer mask to create *knock-out* type — type shapes filled with an image or color. What really makes this easy are the Type Mask tools, which create type-shaped selections. After creating your knock-out type with a layer mask, why not experiment with applying a filter to the layer mask to enhance the type effect? Using filters, you can come up with some really interesting results. For starters, try applying the Sponge or Craquelure filter.

Cookie Cutting and Knock-Outs

I was making cookies with my kids the other day, using alphabet-shaped cookie cutters, when I realized that we were creating type knock-outs. After pressing down with the cookie cutter and removing the cut out letter, we were left with a letter-shape cut on the sheet of cookie dough that let the table underneath show. Nothing like life imitating art.

Creating type knock-outs is really easy even if you've never worked with layer masks before. Just follow the directions and you can have knock-outs in no time. (I've avoided the urge to be a punster and include "Your type will be a knock-out" or "Your type will be able to go five rounds with Mohammed Ali, ready for a knock-out." Real groaners, huh?)

Here's how:

1. **Open an image that you want to use as the fill for the knock-out type.**

You could also create a new document and fill it with a solid color, gradient, or pattern. Whatever you want. For this example, I'm using the zebra photograph shown in Figure 45-1.

• **Figure 45-1: For this example, I'm using a zebra photo for the knock-out type filler.**

2. **Click the Create New Layer button at the bottom of the Layers palette.**

A new layer appears selected above the fill layer.

3. **Rename the new layer.**

I've renamed mine Type Cut-Out. This is what I call this layer for the rest of the directions.

4. **Fill the new layer with a solid color.**

For my example, I've filled the layer with brick red.

5. **Change the Foreground color to black.**

A fast way to do this is to press D, and then press X.

6. **Click the Add Layer Mask button at the bottom of the Layers palette.**

A layer mask appears linked to the Type Cut-Out layer, as shown in Figure 45-2. (If you're unfamiliar with working with layer masks, take a look at Technique 49.)

Layer mask

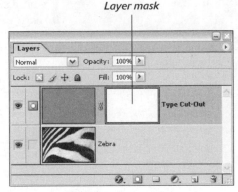

• **Figure 45-2: You should now have two layers, the upper one with a linked layer mask.**

7. **In the Layers palette, click the layer mask to make sure that it's active.**

8. **Select the Horizontal Type Mask tool from the Toolbox.**

9. **Use the Options bar to select a type font and size.**

For this example, I'm using Bard set at 65 points.

10. **Click in the image window and type some text.**

Because you're using the Horizontal Type Mask tool, Photoshop automatically switches you to quickmask mode, and a translucent red overlay appears on your screen. This overlay disappears when you're finished using the tool.

11. **Click the Commit button (the check mark) on the Options bar.**

The characters that you typed become a type-shaped selection, as shown in Figure 45-3.

You can reposition the type-shaped selection with the Rectangular Marquee tool.

• **Figure 45-4:** The black type-shaped areas on the layer mask hide the Type Cut-Out layer and let the zebra layer show through.

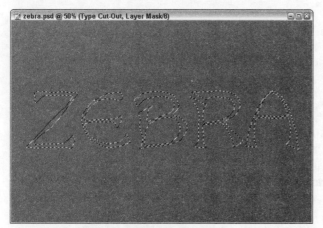

• **Figure 45-3:** The Horizontal Type Mask tool creates type-shaped selections.

12. **Press Alt+Backspace/Option+Backspace.**

This fills the type-shaped selection with black on the layer mask, creating a text knock-out, as shown in Figure 45-4.

You can apply a gradient to the layer mask to create a fade out effect above and below the type, as shown in Figure 45-5. To find out how to create fade outs, turn to Technique 50.

• **Figure 45-5:** Adding fade outs above and below the text lets more of the zebra layer show.

Technique 46

Pouring Liquid Metals

Save Time By

- Using extreme curves
- Applying filters

Real world metal is shiny, reflective, and lustrous. It has depth and can even look heavy. How do you create the appearance of metal when you're dealing with a two-dimensional object like a type character on a flat screen?

The real trick to making a two-dimensional object look like metal is in the extreme contrast of lights and darks that give the impression of reflection, shine, and depth. This technique focuses on two different methods for creating metals. The first method shows you how to create what I call *super chrome* by using a custom gradient and curves. The second method takes you into pouring molten copper into type with the Bas Relief filter, curves, layer styles, and the Chrome filter.

 Even though this technique uses type as the object for these liquid metal effects, you can use any kind of simple image (such as a stylized company logo or nav bar) for a Web site.

Creating Super Chrome

I've seen lots of techniques that create the look of chrome, but many fall short when it comes to the shininess and reflective qualities of highly polished chrome. The secret to this super chrome method is applying two curves adjustment layers at the end. Here's how:

1. **Choose File⇨New to create a new document.**

Make it rather large, say 3 inches high by 5 inches wide, and set it in RGB color mode with a white background.

2. **Set the Foreground color to light gray and the Background color to white.**

For this example, I used the Color Picker to set the HSB text boxes to H: 0%, S: 0%, and B: 70% for the light gray Foreground color.

3. **Use the Horizontal Type tool to create some type.**

The type needs to be large for this effect to work best. For my example, I'm using the Wingdings font set at 250 points, as shown in Figure 46-1. You should now have two layers: a white Background layer and a type layer.

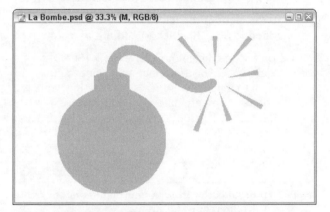

• **Figure 46-1:** I'm turning this bomb into chrome.

4. **With the type layer selected in the Layers palette, click the Add Layer Style button at the bottom of the palette and choose Bevel and Emboss from the menu.**

5. **In the Structure area of the Layer Style dialog box, use the drop-down lists and sliders to select settings, as shown in Figure 46-2.**

▶ Use the **Style** drop-down list to select Inner Bevel.

▶ Use the **Technique** drop-down list to select Chisel Hard.

▶ Set the **Depth** slider to 100%.

▶ Select the Up **Direction** radio button.

▶ Set the **Size** to 10 pixels.

▶ Set **Soften** to 0 pixels.

6. **Click the words Gradient Overlay to view those layer style settings and put a check mark in the Gradient Overlay check box.**

The default settings shown in Figure 46-3 work fine, but you need to create a custom gradient for this effect (not hard!).

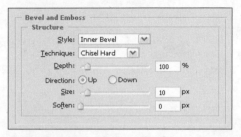

• **Figure 46-2:** Use the settings in the Structure area to create the bevel.

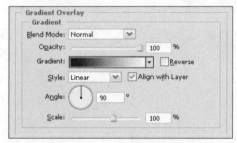

• **Figure 46-3:** Use the default Gradient Overlay settings, but create a custom gradient.

7. **Click the gradient swatch to open the Gradient Editor shown in Figure 46-4.**

8. **In the Presets swatch area at the top of the dialog box, click the Foreground to Background gradient swatch. (It's the first swatch in the upper left.)**

You use this swatch to create the custom gradient. Figure 46-5 shows the Custom Gradient Bar (below the Smoothness text box) that you use to create the custom gradient. At the bottom of the bar are *color stops.* Notice that the color stop on the left contains the Foreground color (gray), and the color stop on the right contains the Background color (white). You're going to add more gray and white color stops.

Foreground to background gradient

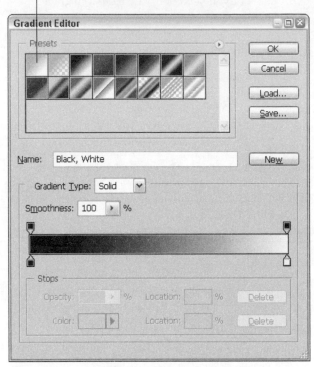

• **Figure 46-4:** You use the Gradient Editor to create a custom gradient for this effect.

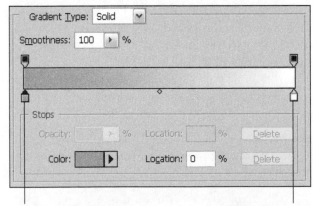

Foreground color stop   *Background color stop*

• **Figure 46-5:** The color stops are on the bottom of the Custom Gradient Bar.

9. Click the color square on the right end containing the Background color to select it.

10. At the left side of the Custom Gradient Bar, click about a quarter of the way down the bar to add a white color stop.

11. Click the color square on the left end containing the Foreground color to select it.

12. To the right of the white color stop that you added in Step 10, click to add a gray color stop.

Don't space the color stops evenly. (See Figure 46-6.) For this effect, you want to add seven to nine color squares, alternating white and gray to create different width stripes.

• **Figure 46-6:** Add color stops at uneven intervals to create different width stripes.

13. Continue adding gray and white color stops until the Custom Gradient Bar looks something like the one in Figure 46-6.

14. Type a name for the custom gradient in the Name text box, and then click New.

Your custom gradient appears at the bottom of the Presets swatch area.

> If you like this effect and want to use it again, you can now select the custom gradient that you created instead of creating a new one every time.

15. Click OK to close the Gradient Editor and return to the Layer Style dialog box.

16. Click OK to close the Layer Style dialog box.

Your type should now have horizontal gray and white stripes and a bevel, as shown in Figure 46-7.

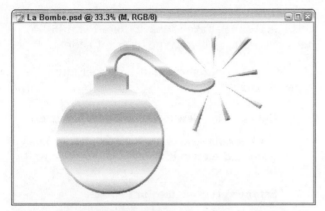

• **Figure 46-7:** The type is beveled and striped with a gray and white gradient.

17. **With the type layer selected in the Layers palette, click the Create New Fill or Adjustment Layer button at the bottom of the palette and choose Curves from the menu.**

The Curves dialog box opens, as shown in Figure 46-8. Notice that a straight line runs from the bottom-left corner of the grid to the upper-right corner of the grid.

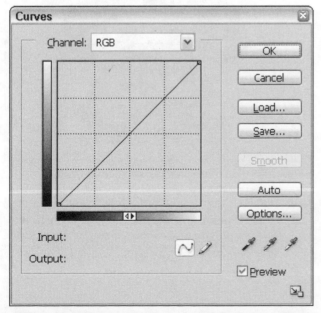

• **Figure 46-8:** You use curves to create the chrome effect.

18. **Click on the line in four places from left to right to create four evenly spaced points.**

19. **Drag the first point up, the second point down, the third point up, and the fourth point down.**

The plotted line should look something like the one in Figure 46-9. Don't worry if it isn't exactly the same.

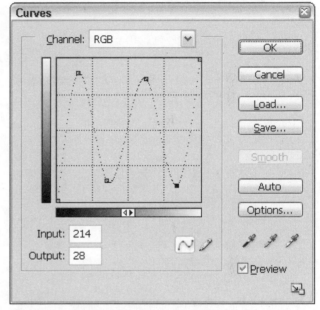

• **Figure 46-9:** Create a curve with steep mountains and deep valleys.

20. **Click OK to close the Curves dialog box and apply the curves to the adjustment layer.**

The gray and white stripes now look like chrome, as shown in Figure 46-10.

21. **With the adjustment layer selected in the Layers palette, choose Layer➪New➪Layer via Copy or press Ctrl+J/⌘+J.**

This copies the adjustment layer and makes the chrome turn into super chrome, as shown in Figure 46-11.

La Bombe.psd @ 33.3% (Curves 2, Layer Mask/8)

• **Figure 46-10:** Using curves, the gray and white stripes turn into chrome.

• **Figure 46-11:** Adding a second curves adjustment layer turns the chrome into super chrome.

 If you want to rasterize the type layer and permanently apply the layer styles and adjustment layers, click the eye icon next to the Background layer to hide it. Then, choose Layer➪Merge Visible.

Molten Copper

Copper can be red, yellow, sometimes even silvery white. Real world polished copper has a shine and depth that this technique duplicates rather well. The

final application of the Chrome filter really makes this metal shine. Take a look at Color Plate 46-1 to see how ordinary black type turns into copper type.

Here's how to pour some molten copper into your type or logo:

1. **Choose File➪New to create a new document.**

   Make it rather large, say 3 inches high by 5 inches wide, and set it in RGB color mode with a white background.

2. **Set the Foreground color to black.**

   The quick way to do this is to press D.

3. **Use the Horizontal Type tool to create some type.**

   The type should be large for this effect to work best. For my example, I'm using the Wingdings font set at 250 points, as shown in Figure 46-12. You should now have two layers: a white Background layer and a type layer.

Copper.psd @ 33.3% ((, RGB/8)

• **Figure 46-12:** I'm turning this phone from black to copper.

4. **Right+click/Control+click the type layer in the Layers palette and choose Rasterize Layer from the menu.**

5. **Rename the layer, if you want.**

For this example, I've named the layer Telephone. That's how I refer to the layer for the rest of the steps.

6. Choose Filter⇨Sketch⇨Bas Relief.

7. Use the sliders to select settings in the Filter Gallery, as shown in Figure 46-13.

▶ Move the **Detail** slider to 10.

▶ Set **Smoothness** to 1.

▶ Use the **Light** drop-down list to select Top Left.

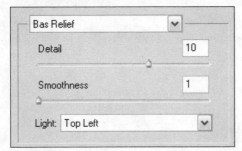

• **Figure 46-13: Use the sliders to set the Bas Relief filter.**

8. Click OK to close the Filter Gallery and apply the filter to the Telephone layer.

9. Click the Add Layer Style button at the bottom of the Layers palette and choose Drop Shadow from the menu.

10. In the Drop Shadow Structure area, select Normal from the Blend Mode drop-down list and set the Distance to 20 pixels, as shown in Figure 46-14.

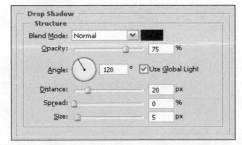

• **Figure 46-14: Use the settings in the Structure area to shape the drop shadow.**

11. Select the Inner Shadow check box in the Effects column.

The default Inner Shadow settings work just fine, so there's nothing to change there.

12. Click the words Color Overlay to view those settings and put a check mark in the Color Overlay check box.

13. Select Overlay from the Blend Mode drop-down list and set the Opacity to 75%, as shown in Figure 46-15.

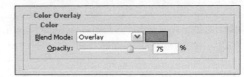

• **Figure 46-15: Set the Color Overlay to look like copper.**

14. Click the color square to open the Color Picker and select a coppery color.

For my example, I created a coppery red-orange by setting R=208, G=111, and B=52.

 If you want to create a different metal, use a different color overlay. For instance, you can use a medium blue to create the look of steel or yellow for the appearance of gold.

15. Click OK to close the Color Picker and return to the Layer Style dialog box.

16. Click OK to close the Layer Style dialog box and apply the styles to the Telephone layer.

The image now looks coppery, but it doesn't shine. (See Figure 46-16.) You can fix that with the curves and the Chrome filter.

17. Choose Image⇨Adjustments⇨Curves or press Ctrl+M/⌘+M.

The Curves dialog box opens. (Refer to Figure 46-8.) Notice that a straight line runs from the bottom-left corner of the grid to the upper-right corner of the grid.

• **Figure 46-16:** The image looks copper-colored, but it doesn't shine — yet.

18. Click on the line in four places from left to right to create four evenly spaced points.

19. Drag the first point up, the second point down, the third point up, and the fourth point down.

The plotted line should look something like the one shown previously in Figure 46-9. Don't worry if it isn't exactly the same.

20. Click OK to close the Curves dialog box and apply the curves Telephone layer.

21. Choose Filter⇨Sketch⇨Chrome.

22. In the Filter Gallery, set the Detail to 5 and the Smoothness to 5.

23. Click OK to close the Filter Gallery and apply the Chrome filter.

Your image should now look like shiny copper, as shown in Figure 46-17.

• **Figure 46-17:** The telephone now looks like molten copper.

Technique 47

Going Up in Flames

Save Time By

- Applying filters
- Liquifying type

Burn, baby, burn! Fire is such a primeval force. Volcanoes erupt spewing rock that's so hot it's literally on fire. Lava and fire glow red and yellow; they radiate heat. Lava drips, oozes, and melts things.

What can you do to create type that looks like it's on fire or dripping with lava? You can't make type literally radiate heat (unless your computer CPU is having a meltdown!), but you can make the type glow and look like it's flickering like flames.

This technique takes a look at creating two kinds of hot type: type that looks like it's on fire and type that appears to be melting under the heat of dripping lava. First, you create fiery type by applying the Neon Glow and Sprayed Strokes filters, and then you add a red glow by using layer styles. Next, you move on to creating type that drips and oozes with lava. You use the Liquify filter to stretch the type, and then add a lava layer by creating a path with the Freeform Pen tool. After filling the path with red, you apply layer styles to make the lava lumpy and the type glow. To see the full effect in color, take a look at Color Plate 47-1.

So pull out your fireproof mitts and start handling burning type!

 This technique isn't only for type — you can also use it to light up graphic logos and images. After seeing what you can do with type, open an image and experiment with it!

Setting Your Type on Fire

You don't have to sing as well as the Doors to set your type on fire. This method is really quite simple and easy. All you use are filters and the Outer Glow layer style, so just follow the steps and you won't get burned!

Here's how to heat things up:

1. **Choose File⇨New or press Ctrl+N/⌘+N to create a new document.**

Make it rather large, say 3 inches high by 5 inches wide, and set it in RGB color mode with a white background.

2. **Select black as the Foreground color.**

A quick way to do this is to press D.

3. **Use the Horizontal Type tool to create some black type.**

For this example, I used the John Handy LET font set at 150 points to create the Fire! type shown in Figure 47-1.

• **Figure 47-1: Use the Horizontal Type tool to create some type.**

4. **Right-click/Control+click the type layer in the Layers palette and choose Rasterize Type from the menu.**

5. **Rename the rasterized type layer if you want.**

For this example, I named the layer Fire. That's how I refer to the layer for the rest of the steps.

6. **Choose Filter⇨Artistic⇨Neon Glow.**

7. **In the Filter Gallery, set the settings for the glow, as shown in Figure 47-2.**

▶ Move the **Glow Size** slider to -7.

▶ Set the **Glow Brightness** to 50.

▶ Click the **Glow Color** square and use the Color Picker to select bright red.

You may need to fiddle with the Glow Size setting to size the glow for the type you're using.

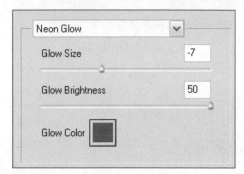

• **Figure 47-2: Use the sliders and color square to set the Neon Glow filter.**

8. **Click OK to close the Filter Gallery and apply the filter to the Fire layer.**

Your text should look something like the one shown in Figure 47-3.

• **Figure 47-3: The type is starting to glow like smoldering embers.**

9. **Choose Filter⇨Brush Strokes⇨Sprayed Strokes.**

10. **In the Filter Gallery, set the Stroke Length to 12, the Spray Radius to 7, and use the Stroke Direction drop-down list to select Right Diagonal.**

11. **Click OK to close the Filter Gallery and apply the Sprayed Strokes filter.**

The text now appears to waver like flames, as shown in Figure 47-4.

• **Figure 47-4: The Sprayed Strokes filter makes the text appear to move like flames.**

12. **Click the Add Layer Style button at the bottom of the Layers palette and choose Outer Glow from the menu.**

13. **In the Outer Glow Structure area of the Layer Style dialog box, set the options for the Outer Glow. (See Figure 47-5.)**

▶ Use the **Blend Mode** drop-down list to select Normal.

▶ Set the **Opacity** to 90%.

▶ Click the **color square** and use the Color Picker to select bright red.

14. **In the Elements area, set the Spread to 11% and the Size to 49 pixels.**

15. **Click OK to close the Layer Style dialog box and apply the Outer Glow.**

After adding a black background, the text really looks like it's on fire. (See Figure 47-6.)

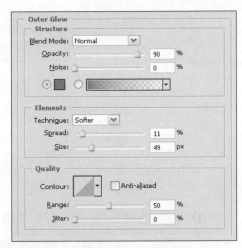

• **Figure 47-5: Set the Outer Glow to bright red.**

• **Figure 47-6: The Outer Glow makes the text look like it's on fire.**

Melting Lava Type

This method of enhancing your type is a bit more involved than the previous technique, "Setting Your Type on Fire." Even so, you don't have to lava or leave it to make your type melt and ooze.

In order to make the type look like it's melting, you need to use the Liquify filter, which is accessible by choosing Filter⇨Liquify. If you haven't used it before, don't be intimidated by the huge dialog box and many controls. All you really need to know about the dialog box is that the tools are located along the left side, the Work Area in the middle is where you stretch and pull the type, and the settings at the upper-right control the size of the brush tip that you're using. If you have a few minutes, play with Liquify before trying this technique. If you don't have a few minutes, just follow the steps — I'm sure you'll do great!

1. **Choose File⇨New or press Ctrl+N/⌘+N to create a new document.**

Make it rather large, say 3 inches high by 5 inches wide, and set it in RGB color mode with a white background.

2. **Use the Horizontal Type tool to create some black type.**

For this example, I used the Impact font set at 150 points to create the Lava! type shown in Figure 47-7.

• **Figure 47-7:** Use the Horizontal Type tool to create some type.

3. **Right-click/Control+click the type layer in the Layers palette and choose Rasterize Type from the menu.**

4. **Rename the rasterized type layer if you want.**

For this example, I named the layer Text. That's how I refer to the layer for the rest of the steps.

5. **Choose Filter⇨Liquify.**

6. **Use the Liquify filter to make the type look like it's melting, as shown in Figure 47-8.**

When working in the Liquify dialog box, I used the Forward Warp and Pucker tools with a 100 pixel diameter brush to make the type drip.

• **Figure 47-8:** Use the Liquify filter to make the type look like it's melting.

7. **With the Text layer still selected, click the Create New Layer button at the bottom of the Layers palette.**

A new, empty layer appears selected above the Text layer.

8. **Name this new layer.**

I've named it Lava, the name that I use to refer to the layer for the rest of the directions.

9. **Select the Freeform Pen tool from the Toolbox.**

10. **On the Options bar, click the Paths button.**

11. **Use the Freeform Pen tool to draw lava-shaped drips over the type.**

Follow the drippy shape of the liquified text as you draw. Figure 47-9 shows the path that I drew. Notice how I made the path a closed shape by drawing over the top of the type.

When you finish your path, take a look at the Paths palette. There, you see your path labeled Work Path, as shown in Figure 47-10.

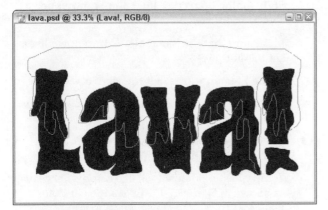

• **Figure 47-9: Use the Freeform Pen tool to draw lava-shaped drips.**

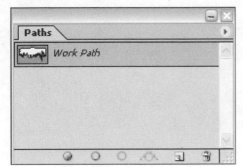

• **Figure 47-10: The lava drips that you drew are temporarily saved as a Work Path in the Paths palette.**

12. **Double-click the name Work Path in the Paths palette and rename the path to save it.**

For this example, I named the path Lava.

13. **Use the Foreground color square in the Toolbox to select bright red.**

14. **Click the Fill Path with Foreground Color button at the bottom of the Paths palette.**

The Lava path fills with bright red, as shown in Figure 47-11.

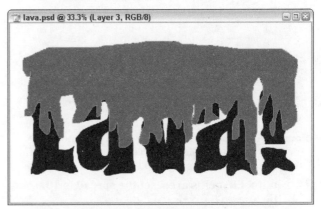

• **Figure 47-11: Fill the path with bright red.**

15. **Ctrl+click/⌘+click the Text layer's thumbnail. (*Don't* select the Text layer.)**

This creates text-shaped selection marquees. Make sure that the Lava layer is still selected.

16. **Choose Select⇨Inverse.**

17. **Press Backspace/Delete.**

This removes the extra red lava that extends beyond the letters.

18. **Press Ctrl+D/⌘+D to remove the selection marquee.**

19. **With the Lava layer still selected, click the Add Layer style button at the bottom of the Layers palette and choose Outer Glow from the menu.**

20. **In the Outer Glow Structure area in the Layer Style dialog box (see Figure 47-12), click the color square and select bright yellow by using the Color Picker.**

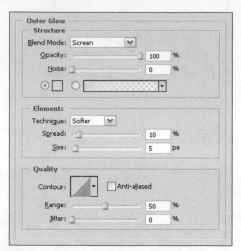

• **Figure 47-12:** Use the settings to select how the Outer Glow is applied.

21. In the Elements area, set the spread to 10% and the Size to 5 pixels.

22. Select the Bevel and Emboss check box in the Effects column.

The default settings work just fine, so there's nothing to change.

23. Select the Contour check box in the Effects column.

The Linear contour that is selected by default works great, so there aren't any settings to change.

24. Click the word Texture to put a check mark in the Texture check box and view those settings, as shown in Figure 47-13.

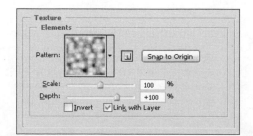

• **Figure 47-13:** Select a Texture to make the lava lumpy.

25. In the Texture Elements area, use the Pattern picker to select the Molecular pattern.

26. Click OK to close the Layer Style dialog box and apply the settings to the Lava layer.

27. Select the Text layer.

28. Click the Add Layer Style button at the bottom of the Layers palette and choose Outer Glow.

29. In the Outer Glow Structure area of the Layer Style dialog box, click the color square and select bright red.

Make sure that the Blend Mode drop-down list is set to Multiply.

30. In the Elements area, set the size to 45 pixels.

You may need to fiddle with this setting to adjust it for your type.

31. Click OK to close the Layer Style dialog box and apply the Outer Glow.

Your type should now look like drippy, fiery lava, as shown in Figure 47-14. Take a look at Color Plate 47-1 to see the glowing lava in color.

• **Figure 47-14:** The lava type really burns!

Technique 48

Going Translucent: Clear Type and Jelly Type

Some of the most powerful graphic effects with type involve manipulating clear — or translucent — effects. Undoubtedly, you've seen many examples of type or graphics such as logos created by using these effects in magazines and other print media.

The great thing is that it's really easy to create powerful and smashing translucent type effects with Photoshop. As a general matter, creating these effects involves using layer styles and a few select filters.

In this technique, first I show you how to create generic clear type. This is the basic form of the translucent type effect. After you see how it works, you can use it as the springboard for more elaborate effects. Try adding another layer and applying a filter or adding a little color to the type by using a layer style such as Color Overlay.

Next, you find out how to create type that looks like jelly. Have you looked at a bowl of gelatin lately? (I have; my kids are 6 and 2!) It wiggles, it jiggles, and I'm not sure how appetizing it is, but it certainly has a distinctive graphic appearance. You can pretty easily create type that looks like gelatin by using layer styles. Best of all, you don't even have to eat it. You can see each of these effects in full living color if you turn to Color Plate 48-1.

 This technique also works for graphic logos and simple images. For instance, you can create buttons for a Web page. So don't feel limited because the title says "type." Use your imagination and try applying these great effects to a special image.

Creating Clear Type

The trick to clear type is defining it with shadows, highlights, and bevels. Because if the type is really clear, how can you see it?

This type effect is most visible with an image or patterned background behind it. The shape of the type is initially defined by using Inner Shadow and Drop Shadow layer styles. Then, it's given a three-dimensional shape by applying a Bevel and Emboss layer style. Finally, a second layer is added above the type layer and the Plaster filter is applied to give the appearance of thickness.

Here's how to jellify your type:

1. **Open the image that you want to use as the background for the type.**

For this example, I'm using the pink stone background shown in Figure 48-1.

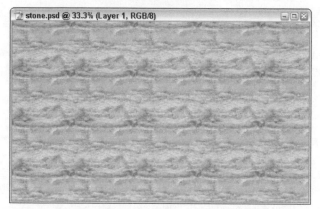

• **Figure 48-1:** Select a background image or pattern for the type.

2. **Use the Horizontal Type tool to create some type, as shown in Figure 48-2.**

The type appears on its own type layer above the background image. For this example, I selected AdLib BT set at 110 points.

3. **With the type layer selected, click the Add Layer Style button at the bottom of the Layers palette and choose Drop Shadow from the menu.**

For this effect, you're using the Drop Shadow, Inner Shadow, and Bevel and Emboss layer styles.

4. **In the Drop Shadow Structure area, use the Blend Mode drop-down list to select Soft Light.**

The rest of the default settings work just fine, so there's no need to change them.

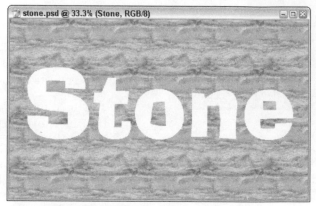

• **Figure 48-2:** The type layer appears above the background image.

5. **Click the words Inner Shadow to select the Inner Shadow check box and to view those settings.**

6. **In the Inner Shadow Structure area, use the Blend Mode drop-down list to select Pin Light.**

The rest of the default settings work well, so there's no more fiddling here.

7. **Click the words Bevel and Emboss to select the Bevel and Emboss check box and to view those settings.**

8. **In the Bevel and Emboss Structure area, move the Depth slider to 50% and set the Size to 40 pixels, as shown in Figure 48-3.**

This sets the shape of the bevel. You may need to fiddle a bit to get the best results for the type that you're using. Ultimately, you're looking for a pretty rounded shape.

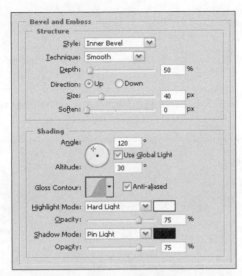

• **Figure 48-3:** Select the Bevel and Emboss settings so that the clear type stands out from the background image.

9. In the Bevel and Emboss Shading area, use the Highlight Mode drop-down list to select Hard Light and the Shadow Mode drop-down list to select Pin Light.

The settings affect how the highlights and shadows blend with the background image layer.

10. In the Shading area, click the down arrow next to the Gloss Contour swatch to open the Contour picker, as shown in Figure 48-4.

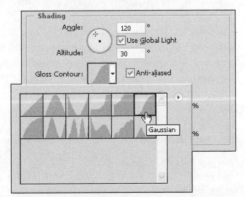

• **Figure 48-4:** The Gloss Contour affects how the highlights and shadows are shaped on the letters.

11. Select the Gaussian contour in the Contour picker.

12. Click OK to close the Layer Style dialog box and apply the effects to the type.

13. With the type layer still selected, lower the Fill Opacity to 0% in the Layers palette.

The fill disappears and the type becomes clear, as shown in Figure 48-5.

• **Figure 48-5:** The clear type looks really great.

And that's it — you've created clear type. If you want, you can stop after completing the preceding 13 steps. However, if you want to add extra definition to the shape of the type, continue with these steps:

1. With the type layer still active, click the Create New Layer button at the bottom of the Layers palette.

A new empty layer appears selected above the type layer.

2. Rename the new layer if you want.

For this example, I've named the layer Definition. I refer to the layer by this name for the rest of the steps.

3. Ctrl+click/⌘+click the type layer's thumbnail to create a selection shaped like the type.

Don't select the type layer. The Definition layer should still be selected.

4. Select white as the Foreground color.

A quick way to do this is to press D, and then press X.

5. Choose Select⇨Modify⇨Contract.

6. In the Contract Selection dialog box, enter 10 in the text box, as shown in Figure 48-6, and then click OK.

This makes the selection areas smaller by 10 pixels.

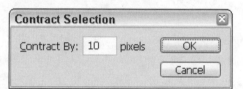

• **Figure 48-6:** Enter 10 pixels in the Contract Selection dialog box.

7. Press Alt+Backspace/Option+Backspace to fill the selected area with the Foreground color.

8. Choose Filter⇨Sketch⇨Plaster.

9. In the Filter Gallery, set the Image Balance to 50 and the Smoothness to 5, as shown in Figure 48-7.

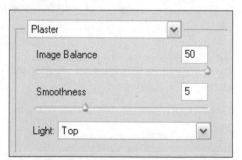

• **Figure 48-7:** Use the sliders to select Plaster filter settings.

10. Use the Light drop-down list to select Top.

11. Click OK to close the Filter Gallery and apply the Plaster filter to the Definition layer.

12. In the Layers palette, use the Blending Mode drop-down list to select Overlay.

13. Use the Fill slider to lower the Definition layer's fill opacity to 40%.

You may need to fiddle with this setting to get the Definition layer to blend just right with the background image that you're using. The finished clear type should look like the type shown in Figure 48-8.

• **Figure 48-8:** The clear type has a slight white sheen for added clarity.

Making That Jelly Roll

This technique is *the* layer style blowout! You use six layer styles to create jelly-like type, and then add a layer on top that adds brightness and shine with the Chrome filter. Take a look at Color Plate 48-1 to see the metamorphosis from flat type to red jelly.

The steps may look rather complicated, but they're not! Even if you've never used layer styles before, you can use these directions to create some super type. Just follow along and you can have jelly type in no time. (If you want to find out more about layer styles, take a look at Technique 20.)

1. Choose File⇨New to create a new document.

Make it rather large, say 3 inches high by 5 inches wide, and set it in RGB color mode with a white background.

2. Use the Horizontal Type tool to create some type.

It doesn't matter what color the type is. For this example, I created some black type set in the Brush455 BT font at 180 points. (See Figure 48-9.)

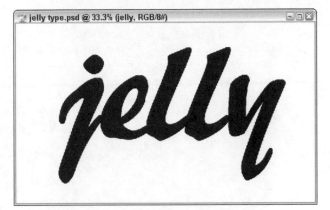

• **Figure 48-9:** Create some type in a nifty font.

3. **With the type layer selected in the Layers palette, click the Add Layer Style button at the bottom of the palette and choose Color Overlay.**

You're using six layer styles, but the first one that you need to set up is Color Overlay. This overlay is the color of the type.

4. **In the Color Overlay area in the Layer Styles dialog box, select Normal from the Blend Mode drop-down list, as shown in Figure 48-10.**

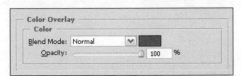

• **Figure 48-10:** Use the Color Overlay to select a color for the type.

5. **Click the color square to select a color by using the Color Picker and set the Opacity to 100%.**

My kids like cherry gelatin, so they told me to use red.

6. **In the Effects column of the Layer Style dialog box, click the words Blending Options: Default to view those settings.**

7. **In the Advance Blending area, select the Blend Interior Effects as a Group check box.**

8. **Click the words Drop Shadow to select the Drop Shadow check box and to view the settings shown in Figure 48-11.**

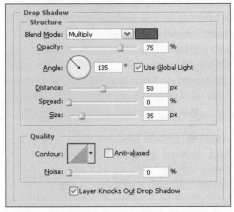

• **Figure 48-11:** Use the Drop Shadow options to set the color and size of the drop shadow.

9. **In the Drop Shadow Structure area, set the options for the shape and color of the drop shadow.**

▶ Select Multiply from the **Blend Mode** drop-down list.

▶ Click the **color square** to select a shadow color that's darker than the color that you selected for the Color Overlay. Because the color that I selected for the Color Overlay is bright red, I chose a dark brick red for the shadow.

▶ Set the **Angle** to 135° and select the Global Light check box. (Selecting Global Light automatically sets the Angle option available in any other layer style to 135°. So if you change the Angle in one layer style, the Angle changes for all the layer styles.)

▶ Move the **Distance** slider to 50 pixels.

▶ Set the **Size** to 35 pixels.

10. **Click the words Inner Shadow to select the Inner Shadow check box and to view the settings shown in Figure 48-12.**

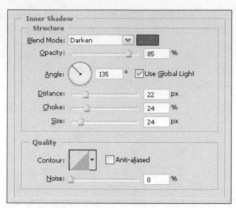

• **Figure 48-12:** Select a color and blending mode for the Inner Shadow.

11. In the Inner Shadow Structure area, select the settings for the shape and color of the inner shadow.

▶ Select Darken from the **Blend Mode** drop-down list.

▶ Click the **color square** and select an inner shadow color by using the Color Picker. This should be the same color that you selected for the Drop Shadow.

▶ Set the **Distance** to 25 pixels, the **Choke** to 25%, and the **Size** to 25 pixels.

12. Click the words Outer Glow to select the Outer Glow check box and to view the settings shown in Figure 48-13.

13. In the Outer Glow Structure area, set the options for the shape and color of the glow.

▶ Select Screen from the **Blend Mode** drop-down list.

▶ Set the **Opacity** to 70%.

▶ Click the **color square** and use the Color Picker to select the same color that you used for the Color Overlay in Step 5. (I'm using bright red.)

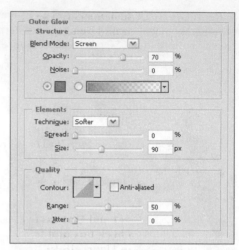

• **Figure 48-13:** Select a color and blending mode for the Outer Glow.

14. In the Outer Glow Elements area, set the Size to 90 pixels.

15. Click the words Inner Glow to select the Inner Glow check box and to view the settings shown in Figure 48-14.

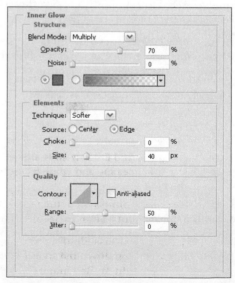

• **Figure 48-14:** Use the Inner Glow settings to add extra brightness.

16. In the Inner Glow Structure area set the options for the color and opacity.

▶ Use the **Blend Mode** drop-down list to select Multiply.

▶ Set the **Opacity** to 70%.

▶ Click the **color square** and use the Color Picker to select the same color that you used for the Drop Shadow in Step 9. (I'm using dark brick red.)

17. In the Inner Glow Elements area, set the Size to 40 pixels.

18. Click the words Bevel and Emboss to select the Bevel and Emboss check box and to view those settings, as shown in Figure 48-15.

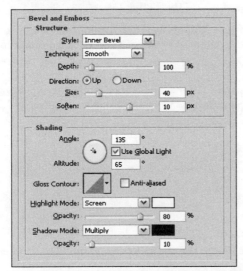

• **Figure 48-15:** The Bevel and Emboss adds a rounded shape to the type and white highlights.

19. In the Bevel and Emboss Structure area, set the Size to 40 pixels and Soften to 10 pixels.

20. In the Bevel and Emboss Shading area, use the Highlight Mode drop-down list to select Screen, and set the Highlight Mode Opacity to 80%.

21. Also in the Bevel and Emboss Shading area, use the Shadow Mode drop-down list to select Multiply, and set the Shadow Mode Opacity to 10%.

22. Click the word Contour to select the Contour check box and to view those settings, as shown in Figure 48-16.

• **Figure 48-16:** The Contour adds extra shape to the Bevel and Emboss.

23. In the Contour Elements area, open the Contour Picker and select the Gaussian contour, and then set the Range to 90%.

24. Click the word Satin to select the Satin check box and to view those settings, as shown in Figure 48-17.

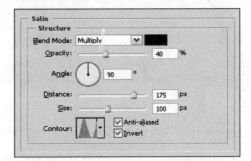

• **Figure 48-17:** The Satin layer style is going to add a mottled effect.

25. In the Satin Structure area, set the options to create a shiny mottled effect:

▶ Move the **Opacity** slider to 40%.

▶ Set the **Angle** to 90°.

▶ Move the **Distance** slider to 175 pixels.

▶ Set the **Size** to 100 pixels.

▶ Open the **Contour** picker and select the Ring contour.

▶ Select the **Anti-Aliased** and **Invert** check boxes.

Using this layer style is optional. Try viewing your type with and without Satin to see which effect you like best.

26. **Click OK to close the Layer Style dialog box and apply the effects to your type.**

Congratulations! At this point, your type should look something like the type shown in Figure 48-18.

• **Figure 48-18: The jelly type is looking pretty wiggly at this point.**

 Because the type is contained on a type layer, you can still edit it! If you want, you can change its font or size, and the layer effects automatically adjust to accommodate changes.

If you like the effect the way it is, you can stop after completing the preceding steps. If you want to add extra brightness by using the Chrome filter, however, continue with these steps:

1. **Click the Create New Layer button at the bottom of the Layers palette.**

A new empty layer appears selected above the type layer.

2. **Rename this layer if you want.**

For this example, I named the layer Chrome. That's how I refer to the layer for the rest of the steps.

3. **Set the Foreground color to light gray.**

For my example, I used the Color Picker to set H=0%, S=0%, and B=70%.

4. **Ctrl+click/⌘+click the type layer's thumbnail to create a type-shaped selection.**

5. **Make sure that the Chrome layer is still selected.**

6. **Choose Select⇨Modify⇨Contract.**

7. **In the Contract Selection dialog box, enter 5 pixels and then click OK.**

8. **Press Alt+Backspace/Option+Backspace to fill the selected area with the Foreground color.**

9. **Choose Filter⇨Sketch⇨Chrome.**

10. **In the Filter Gallery, set the Detail to 10 and the Smoothness to 10, as shown in Figure 48-19.**

• **Figure 48-19: Use the sliders to set the Chrome filter.**

11. **Click OK to close the Filter Gallery and apply the filter to the Chrome layer.**

12. **Press Ctrl+D/⌘+D to remove the selection marquee.**

13. **In the Layers palette, use the Blending Mode drop-down list to select Soft Light.**

Your wiggly jelly type is finished! Figure 48-20 shows the jelly type.

If you like this effect and want to use it again on other type, save the effect as a preset in the Styles palette. Then, you can apply the effect without having to run through all the steps again. Turn to Technique 20 for directions on creating a preset.

• **Figure 48-20:** The type really looks like jelly.

Part VIII

Transforming Images Using Channels and Masks (It's not as hard as you think!)

The 5th Wave   By Rich Tennant

"Well, well! Guess who just lost 9 pixels?"

Technique 49

Working with Layer Masks

Save Time By

✔ Creating layer masks

✔ Editing layer masks

Layer masks are great! They're simple to use and very powerful, but people don't use them enough. For some reason, many Photoshop users tend to think that layer masks are hard to use or that they somehow work by magic. Not so! This technique is here to debunk the myths — I condense years of explaining layer masks into a couple pages.

Here's the definition: *A layer mask hides or reveals parts of a layer.* Period. End of mystery. I've heard so many confusing, over-complicated explanations about layer masks that I'm setting it all out in black and white (literally) with clear, simple explanations.

So open Photoshop, grab an image to play with, and try your hand at layer masks. At first, they may seem a bit counterintuitive, but after you get a handle on layer masks, you won't be able to live without them!

Layer Masks 101: How They Work

I'm sure that you've worked with layer opacity by now. For instance, if you move the Opacity slider on the Layers palette down from 100%, the layer starts to become translucent. Lower the Opacity slider all the way to 0%, and the layer disappears altogether.

But, how to you hide one part of the layer and leave another part of the same layer visible? Do it with layer masks.

For my demonstration today, the friendly looking alien in Figure 49-1 has volunteered to help me. (Cute, isn't he? I especially like the jaunty hat over one eye.)

• **Figure 49-1:** This happy looking fellow is going to help with the layer mask demonstration.

Here's the layer mask demonstration:

1. In the Layers palette, click Create New Layer and fill the layer with white.

A quick way to do this is to press D, and then press X, and then press Alt+Backspace/Option+Backspace. A new layer appears above the layer containing the alien, so the alien disappears, and all you can see is the white layer. (I omit the figure here because I'm sure that you can imagine a white layer.)

2. In the Layers palette, select the layer that you want to add the layer mask to.

For this example, select the white layer.

3. Click the Add Layer Mask button at the bottom of the Layers palette.

A layer mask appears linked to the layer, as shown in Figure 49-2.

 A layer mask can be added to any layer except the Background layer.

 The tiny link icon that appears to the left of the layer mask thumbnail indicates that if you move or transform the layer, the layer mask will be transformed at the same time.

Layer mask

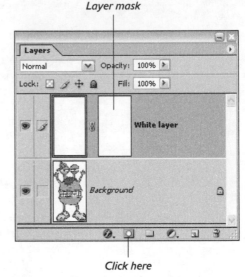

Click here

• **Figure 49-2:** The layer mask appears linked to the layer.

4. Select black as the Foreground color.

A quick way to do this is to press D.

5. Select the Brush tool from the Toolbox and select a simple brush tip from the Brush Preset picker on the Options bar.

For this example, I'm using a brush tip with a 50 pixel diameter and a 100% Hardness setting.

6. In the Layers palette, click the layer mask to select it.

7. **Stroke with the Brush in the image window.**

As you paint with black on the layer mask, the areas that you cover hide the white layer that the layer mask is attached to and reveal the alien below, as shown in Figure 49-3.

Area of layer mask painted with black

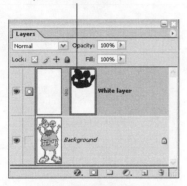

Revealed layer underneath

• **Figure 49-3:** Painting with black reveals the layer below. Notice where the black area is on the layer mask and the corresponding area in the image window.

Following the preceding steps, you discover that

✔ White on a layer mask leaves the attached layer visible, hiding the layer underneath.

✔ Black on a layer mask hides the attached layer, revealing the layer underneath.

But, what about gray? Painting on a layer mask with gray is like using the Opacity slider on the Layer palette. Gray makes a layer mask translucent. You can vary the opacity by using lighter or darker grays. Lighter grays leave the layer mask more opaque, and darker grays make the layer mask more transparent, as shown in Figure 49-4.

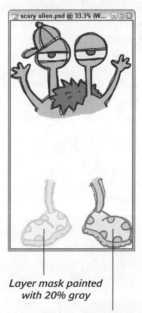

Layer mask painted with 20% gray

60% gray

• **Figure 49-4:** Painting with different shades of gray makes the layer mask more or less transparent.

Another way to make the layer mask translucent is to use the Opacity slider on the Options bar. You can use just black or white (instead of gray) and lower the Opacity to partially reveal or hide portions of a layer. The advantage is that you don't need to select different shades of gray, and Opacity percentages are absolute and easy to replicate.

Layer Masks 102: What Are They Really?

Under the hood, a layer mask is actually a grayscale channel. If you take a look at the bottom of the list in the Channels palette, you see the layer mask you create in the previous section, "Layer Masks 101: How They Work," as shown in Figure 49-5. If you click the layer mask channel in the Channels palette, it's displayed in the image window.

Because the layer mask is a channel, it gives you all the flexibility of a channel. You can use the channel to create a mask-shaped selection, you can edit the layer mask to reshape it, and you can view the layer mask either by itself in the image window (where it appears in grayscale) or as a colored overlay superimposed on the image. (To find out more about channels and what they're capable of, turn to Technique 52.)

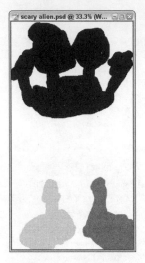

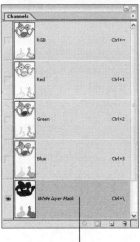

Layer mask channel

• **Figure 49-5: Under the hood, a layer mask is really a grayscale channel.**

Creating Layer Masks by Using Selections

Layer masks can also be created by using a selection. Of course, you can create the selection by using any of the selection tools available in the Toolbox. However, you have another way to create very precise selections: using the Pen tool.

With the Pen tool, you can create an exact path around the object that you want to select. For instance, take a look at Figure 49-6. I selected the woman's face and hair with the Pen tool. Because the Pen tool uses Bezier curves with points and direction points, you can shape the path exactly the way that you want it. After that, all you need to do is turn the path into a selection by clicking the Load Path as Selection button at the bottom of the Paths palette.

• **Figure 49-6:** The Pen tool can be used to create precise selections.

 Layer masks can't be added to the Background layer. You must first convert the Background layer to a regular layer by choosing Layer➪ New➪Layer from Background. Then you can use the Pen or selection tools to create a selection and turn the selection into a layer mask.

Here are the rest of the directions for turning a selection into a layer mask:

1. **Create a selection by using any of the selection tools or the Pen tool.**

Figure 49-7 shows the woman's face selected.

 You can feather the selection by choosing Select➪Feather. This softens the transition from the selected area to the unselected area.

2. **Choose Layer➪Add Layer Mask to open the Add Layer Mask menu.**

• **Figure 49-7:** Select the area that you want to mask.

3. **Choose one of the Add Layer Mask menu items.**

> ▶ **Reveal Selection** creates a layer mask that fills the selected area with white and the unselected area with black. This hides the unselected area of the layer and leaves the selected area visible.

> ▶ **Hide Selection** creates a layer mask that fills the selected area with black and the unselected area with white. This hides the selected area of the layer and leaves the unselected area visible.

Figure 49-8 shows the woman's face after Layer⇨ Add Layer Mask⇨Reveal Selection is chosen.

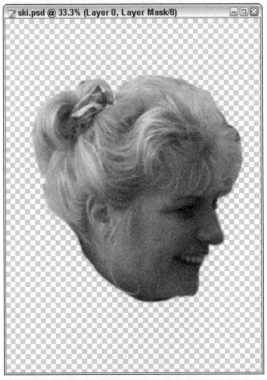

• **Figure 49-8: After choosing Reveal Selection, only the woman's face is visible.**

Corel KnockOut 2

KnockOut 2 by Corel is an amazing product. It helps you quickly create complicated masks that include difficult areas — such as hair, eyelashes, and shadows — in a selection. When you install KnockOut 2, it's automatically loaded onto the Filter menu. To access KnockOut, choose Filter⇨ KnockOut 2⇨Load Working Layer. The KnockOut 2 program loads, showing the selected layer in the Work Area.

All you need to do to create a selection is to use the Inside Object and Outside Object tools to quickly create rough outlines that indicate to KnockOut where the inside and the outside areas are. (KnockOut also provides Inside Shadow Object and Outside Shadow Object tools to roughly outline shadowed areas to include in the selection.)

From there, choose Edit⇨Process and KnockOut creates the complex selection for you, as shown in the following figure. (Notice how the strands of hair are selected!)

If you need to create complicated masks, I highly recommend KnockOut 2. You can find it at www.corel.com; choose Products⇨All Products.

Editing Layer Masks

You can change the shape of a layer mask if you need to. For instance, suppose you decide that the layer linked to the layer mask doesn't show enough of a face down in the left corner. You can paint with white on the layer mask to reveal more of the layer and the face.

You can edit a layer mask in three ways:

✔ Display the layer mask by itself in the image window and modify it that way.

✔ Select the layer mask thumbnail in the Layers palette and modify the layer mask by painting on the image in the image window. (The layer mask isn't visible.)

✔ Display the layer mask as a color overlay super-imposed on the layer's image and modify the layer mask by using the image as your guide.

Although all three of these options are useful at some time or another, I find myself selecting Door Number 3 — displaying the layer mask as an overlay — the most often. This method is handy because you can see the layer mask on the layer and use the layer as a guide.

Here's how to edit a layer mask:

1. Select an editing tool, such as the Brush tool, from the Toolbox.

For a complete list of tools that you can use to edit layer masks, take a look at the sidebar "What tools can you use to modify layer masks?"

2. Display the layer mask to edit it.

▶ Alt+click/Option+click the layer mask thumb-nail in the Layers palette to view only the layer mask in the image window. (If you want to use the shape tools to edit the layer mask, you need to use this method.)

▶ Click the layer mask thumbnail in the Layers palette to select it (but not to view it).

▶ Alt+Shift+Click/Option+Shift+Click the layer mask thumbnail to view the layer mask as a

color overlay superimposed on the layer. Figure 49-9 shows this method. In the figure, the overlay appears as light gray.

3. On the Options bar, choose Normal from the Mode drop-down list and set the Opacity to 100%.

If you want to partially hide or reveal a layer, use a lower Opacity setting.

Masked area

Color overlay

• **Figure 49-9: Viewing the layer mask as an overlay lets you see exactly what is masked.**

4. **Paint in the image window with black, white, and/or gray.**

- ▶ Select black as the Foreground color and paint with it to hide the layer (revealing more of the layer underneath).

- ▶ Select white as the Foreground color and paint with it to view more of the layer (hiding more of the layer underneath).

- ▶ Select gray as the Foreground color to make the layer mask translucent, partially revealing the layer underneath.

Some Layer Mask Tricks

You can do a few more things with layer masks to enhance your Photoshop prowess:

- ✔ Ctrl+click/⌘+click the layer mask thumbnail in the Layers palette to create a layer mask-shaped selection.

- ✔ Click the layer mask thumbnail in the Layers palette to select it, and then choose Image➪ Adjustments➪Invert to reverse the effects of the layer mask. Visible areas become hidden and hidden areas revealed.

- ✔ Select the layer mask in the Channels palette and apply a filter to the layer mask to create a special effect. For instance, you could use the Gaussian Blur filter to soften the edges of the mask.

- ✔ Disable the effect of a layer mask by Shift+clicking the layer mask thumbnail in the Layers palette. To restore the layer mask, Shift+click again.

Final Thoughts

To cap off this technique, I created a multi-layer image to show you several layer masks in action. Figure 49-10 shows the individual layers in the image in their order in the Layers palette from top to bottom.

My idea with this image is to place the Morning Glory layer on the moon in the background image. This means that I need to use a layer mask to hide the areas of the morning glory that would go beyond the edges of the moon. Then, I want to place the goats among the alien landscape, as if they were just walking around there. This also requires a layer mask to hide the shrubs around the goats.

After adding the layer masks and using the Soft Light blending mode on the Morning Glory layer to blend it into the moon, the goats look pretty happy in their new environment. (See Figure 49-11.)

You can see the goats in color by turning to Color Plate 49-1.

• **Figure 49-11:** The goats look pretty happy — they don't even need extra oxygen.

• **Figure 49-10:** These separate layers are going to be combined into one image with layer masks.

Using Layer Masks to Create Fade Ins and Outs

U sing the Opacity or Fill slider on the Layers palette can make an entire layer translucent or even invisible. But, how do you make only part of a layer fade out? By using layer masks, of course!

This technique is a quick study in adding gradients to layer masks to create fade outs (or fade ins depending on how you look at it). The outlined steps are really simple, so open an image and give this a go. After you get the hang of it, I guarantee that you can find interesting ways to employ this method in your images.

Checking Out Layer Masks

If you've worked with layer masks before, you know that white areas of a layer mask leave the attached layer visible, hiding the layer underneath. Black areas on a layer mask hide the attached layer, revealing the layer underneath. Gray areas make the layer mask translucent, partially revealing the attached layer and the layer underneath. (If you've never used layer masks, take a look at Technique 49 for a complete demonstration.)

So, if you apply a gradient made up of white and black (with a gray transition area) to a layer mask, the image on the layer linked to the layer mask fades out.

Fading Away

Because layer masks work only in grayscale, the gradients that you use to create the fade out effect have to be in grayscale also. Grayscale includes 256 levels of gray. Black and white are part of the grayscale spectrum in Photoshop because they're at the extreme opposite ends of the spectrum. (Black is designated as 0, and white is designated as 255.)

Here's how to create a fade out by using a gradient:

1. **Open the image that you want to use.**

For this example, I'm using the statue shown in Figure 50-1.

 A layer mask cannot be added to the Background layer. If your image is contained on the Background, convert the Background layer to a regular layer by choosing Layer⇨ New⇨Layer Via Background.

• **Figure 50-1:** I plan to use a layer mask to fade out this image.

2. **With the image layer selected in the Layers palette, click the Add Layer Mask button at the bottom of the palette.**

A layer mask appears linked to the image layer.

3. **Click the Create New Layer button at the bottom of the Layers palette.**

4. **Move this new layer below your image layer and fill it with white.**

You should now have two layers, and the upper one should have an attached layer mask, as shown in Figure 50-2.

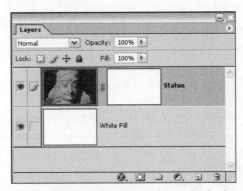

• **Figure 50-2:** You should have two layers in the Layers palette.

5. **Click the layer mask thumbnail in the Layers palette to select it.**

6. **Select white as the Foreground color and black as the Background color.**

The quick way to do this is to press D, and then press X.

7. **Select the Gradient tool from the Toolbox.**

8. **On the Options bar, use the Gradient picker to select the Foreground to Background gradient (the first option in the swatch list).**

9. **On the Options bar, select Normal from the Mode drop-down list and set the Opacity to 100%.**

10. **In the image window, click and drag from left to right to create the gradient on the layer mask.**

When you release the mouse button, the image in the image window fades out to white, as shown in Figure 50-3. Take a look at the layer mask thumbnail in the Layers palette to see the gradient. Notice how the white area on the layer mask corresponds to the area in the image window where you can see the image.

 Of course, the gradient doesn't have to be drawn from left to right. It can be drawn in any direction. Experiment with gradients on a layer mask, remembering that you can use selections to limit the area where the gradient is applied.

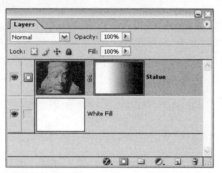

• **Figure 50-3: The gradient on the layer mask makes the image layer fade out.**

Technique 51

Grouping Layers into Clipping Masks

Save Time By

✔ Creating clipping masks by using shapes

✔ Creating clipping masks by using type

You've probably seen a matted picture in a frame. The opening in the matting can be shaped like a rectangle, or if it's fancy, like an oval or heart. When the mat is placed over the image in the frame, it limits the area of the image that you can see. The matting acts like a mask.

Clipping masks (formerly called clipping groups) work in the same way. A clipping mask contains several layers, and the bottom layer acts like the matting. The outline of the bottom layer clips the other layers in the group, so only the pixels contained within the outline are shown in the image window. The finished effect actually looks like a knock-out.

This may seem a bit counterintuitive because the matting layer is on the bottom (it would make more sense if this layer were above, right?), but after you've used clipping masks a couple of times, it will seem natural.

This technique shows you how to create clipping masks. You can use any kind of shape for the masking layer, including type. First, you create a clipping mask by using a shape on a layer to define the clipped area, and then you create a clipping mask with type to define the clipped area.

Creating a clipping mask is easier than it may seem in the steps that follow. After you've created a few clipping masks, you'll see how it works and get the hang of it. What other ways can you think of to incorporate clipping masks into your projects?

 You need to know one thing when using a shape to clip the other layers in the clipping mask: The area around the shape outline needs to be transparent. So as you follow the steps, notice how the area around the heart is transparent. If it were filled, the clipping mask effect wouldn't work because the other layers wouldn't be clipped. (This transparency issue doesn't apply when a type layer is used to clip the other layers.)

Using a Shape to Define Your Knock-Out

Here's how to use a shape to define the knock-out:

1. **Open a multi-layered image.**

For this example, I'm using a heart shape as the lower clipping layer and a photograph of tulips for the upper layer, as shown in Figure 51-1. Notice that the area around the heart is transparent. This is represented by the checkerboard pattern in the Heart layer thumbnail.

 Layers joined together in the clipping mask must be listed consecutively in the Layers palette.

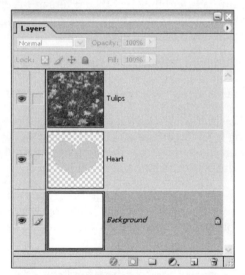

• **Figure 51-1:** To create a clipping mask, you need at least two layers.

2. Click the upper layer to select it.

3. Press Ctrl+G/⌘+G or choose Layer➪Create Clipping Mask.

The two layers are combined into a clipping mask, as shown in Figure 51-2. Notice that in the Layers palette the upper layer in the clipping mask is indented and a tiny down-pointing arrow points to the layer below.

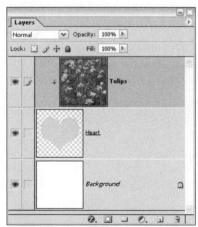

• **Figure 51-2:** When two layers are combined in a clipping mask, the lower layer acts as a mask.

4. If you want to add another layer to the clipping mask, select the layer in the Layers palette, and then press Ctrl+G/⌘+G again.

Continue adding as many layers as you want.

You can remove a layer from a clipping mask by choosing Layer➪Release Clipping Mask.

Even though layers are combined in a clipping mask, you can still select the lower layer in the clipping mask and apply layer styles, as shown in Figure 51-3.

• **Figure 51-3:** Applying layer styles to the lower layer in the clipping mask can add a finishing touch.

Using Type to Define Your Knock-Out

Here's how to use a type layer to define the knock-out:

1. **Open an image that you want to use in a clipping mask.**

2. **Use the Horizontal Type tool to create some type.**

   It doesn't matter what color the type is. For this example, I'm using type set in Lithograph Bold at 90 points, as shown in Figure 51-4.

• **Figure 51-4:** Create the type that you want to use as the mask when the layers are grouped together.

3. **In the Layers palette, move the type layer below the image layer, as shown in Figure 51-5.**

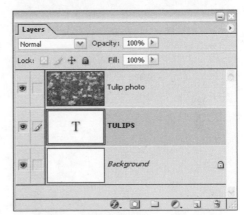

• **Figure 51-5:** Be sure that the type layer is below the image layer.

4. **Select the upper image layer.**

5. **Press Ctrl+G/⌘+G to combine the image layer and type layer into a clipping mask.**

   The type layer acts as a mask, creating the type cut-out shown in Figure 51-6.

 Because the type is still contained on a type layer, you can always edit it and apply layer styles.

• **Figure 51-6:** When a type layer is combined with an image layer in a clipping mask, the type acts as a cut-out.

Technique 52

Working with Channels

Save Time By

✔ Using the Channels palette

✔ Viewing and correcting individual channels

Many folks who use Photoshop think that channels are somehow mysterious, dangerous, and not for them. You may not know it, but you use channels all the time. Here's a secret: Even though Photoshop can create gorgeous, rich colors in fabulous images, those colors are actually created by using grayscale pixels in channels. "What?!" you exclaim. It's true.

Depending on the color mode that an image is set in, each pixel in an image can contain up to four grayscale *color channels* — channels that contain the information that colors images. Any selections or masks that you create are saved as *alpha channels*.

Often forgotten, many times ignored, channels can give you more control over your image editing. This technique focuses on how channels work, where you can find them, and how you can use them to improve your images. So, if you're ready for a mind-expanding session that will definitely increase your knowledge of Photoshop and its capabilities, check out channels. They're worth the time!

Understanding Channels

Three types of channels can store information in Photoshop. *Color channels* contain the color information for an image, *alpha channels* store masks or selections that are used to edit parts of an image, and *spot color channels* store ink color information for high-end color printing. (You can find out how to create and use spot color channels in Technique 14.)

Color channels

Color channels are actually grayscale images that store specific color information. Each channel can contain up to 256 shades of gray — black and white are at the opposite ends of this grayscale spectrum. Channels can be viewed with the Channels palette, which is shown in Figure 52-1.

Saved selection (alpha channel)

Layer mask (alpha channel)

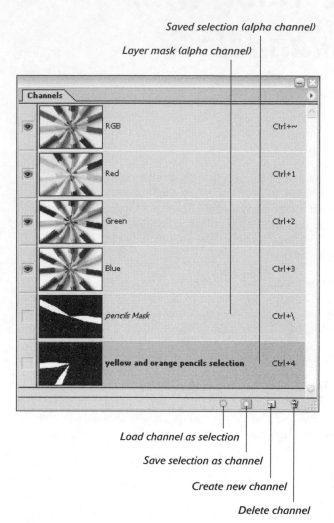

Load channel as selection

Save selection as channel

Create new channel

Delete channel

• **Figure 52-1: Color channels are listed first in the Channels palette.**

In Figure 52-1, notice that the individual color channels (Red, Green, and Blue for an RGB image, or Cyan, Magenta, Yellow, and Black for a CMYK image) are listed first along with a composite color channel that shows all the color channels mixed together. Figure 52-2 shows an RGB image of colored pencils separated out into its individual color channels.

Composite RGB image

Red channel

Green channel

Blue channel

• **Figure 52-2: An RGB image is made up of three color channels.**

Every pixel in an image can contain up to four color channels depending on the color mode that the image is set in.

By default, color channels are viewed in grayscale in Photoshop. For an experiment, you can take a look at the color channels in their respective color by choosing Edit/Photoshop⇨Preferences⇨Display & Cursors, and then selecting the Color Channels in Color check box in the Preferences dialog box.

 Viewing the channels in color can be educational. However, when you're finished checking them out in color, be sure to return them to the default grayscale. If you apply any filters or tonal adjustments to individual channels, it can be very hard to see the effects when the channels are shown in color.

You may be wondering how a grayscale image fits into this channel scheme. Any image with less than 256 colors is displayed as a single channel. So, a grayscale image contains only one channel.

Table 52-1 shows how many channels exist per color mode.

TABLE 52-1: HOW MANY CHANNELS IN A COLOR MODE?

One Channel	Three Channels	Four Channels
Bitmap	RGB	CMYK
Grayscale	LAB	
Duotone	Multichannel	
Indexed Color		

Multichannel mode is a bit of an oddball because it can have from one to four channels depending on the color mode conversion. If an RGB image is converted to Multichannel mode, it still has three channels. A CMYK image that's converted to Multichannel mode still has four channels. Likewise, when a color channel is deleted from an RGB or CMYK image, the image is automatically converted to Multichannel mode.

Alpha channels

Just like color channels that store the color information for an image, alpha channels are also grayscale images. However, alpha channels are used to store layer masks or selections. They're located at the bottom of the list in the Channels palette. (Refer to Figure 52-1.)

You can view an alpha channel at any time in two ways: as an overlay superimposed on the image or load it as a selection.

 Saving a complicated selection as an alpha channel is *so* handy. You can always reload the selection in an instant instead of having to create it from scratch.

Using any shade from the grayscale spectrum (including black and white), you can paint on an alpha channel to enlarge or reduce the protected (selected or masked) areas. (If you want to find out how to work with and edit layer masks, turn to Technique 49.)

Using the Channels Palette

You can apply any filters or tonal adjustments to individual channels. What does this mean for you? You get super control over the various color elements in an image. In fact, many filters work better when they're applied to each channel individually, instead of to all the channels at the same time as a composite image. (Technique 53 delves into this interesting topic.)

If you've never really used the Channels palette before, the following list can give you an idea of (and the directions for!) working with the channels in the Channels palette:

✔ **Select an individual channel** by clicking the channel's name. When a channel is active, you can apply tonal adjustments such as levels or curves, or filters effects to the individual channel.

✔ **Select more than one channel at a time** by holding down the Shift key and clicking the channels' names.

✔ **Hide a specific channel** by clicking the eye icon in the column to the left of the channel. View the channel again by clicking in the column.

✔ **Rename an alpha channel** by double-clicking the alpha channel's name and typing a new name. (Color channels cannot be renamed.)

✔ **Create a copy of a channel** by right-clicking/Control+clicking the channel and then choosing Duplicate Channel from the menu. In the Duplicate Channel dialog box that opens, enter a name for the copy and choose whether it appears in the image that it was copied from or as a new image.

✔ **Delete a channel** by dragging it to the trashcan icon at the bottom of the palette. If you delete a color channel, the image automatically converts to Multichannel mode. Multichannel mode is typically used for specialized offset printing.

Individual Channel Adjustments

Save Time By

- Adjusting color and tone channel by channel
- Applying filters channel by channel

Sometimes adjusting the tone or color in an image just doesn't seem to work no matter what you do. In many such cases, if you tackle each channel individually (instead of applying the adjustment to all the channels at the same time), you can achieve superior results. The same goes for filters: Applying filters channel by channel can create a sharper overall image with much cleaner results.

This technique shows you how to improve images by modifying channels individually. You find out what typically needs to be adjusted when tone or color is off. Also, I show you the difference that applying a filter to each channel can make.

I've got one more tantalizing treat for this technique: Because you can apply adjustments and filters to channels individually, why not try creating some interesting effects by modifying only one channel (instead of all of them)? You may be surprised at the cool looks that you achieve when you quickly apply a filter to just one channel.

Performing Individual Channel Adjustments

Suppose that your Aunt Marge hands you a disk containing a digital photograph of your cousin Eddy, and she asks you to pretty it up for a holiday card. Because Aunt Marge is a nice lady and also has included you in her multi-million dollar will, you say, "Sure, no problem." You take the file home (how hard can this be?), open it in Photoshop and find . . . a mess. The photo has too much blue, the flash created some nasty reflections that make highlighted areas look white hot, and little Eddy's nose looks a bit like a squashed tomato.

So you get to work trying to adjust the tone by using Levels, apply the Unsharp mask in an attempt to add definition to Eddy's nose, and even try adjusting the image by using the Brightness/Contrast command (always a mistake — that command has wrecked more images than it ever helped). You start to get a bit nervous because sharpening the nose also added to the white hot highlight mess, and even though the blue is out of the photo, Eddy's skin has taken on a sun-burnt hue. You don't want to get written out of Aunt Marge's will, so what can you do?

Upon reflection (and some serious use of the History palette to undo all the previous attempts at correction) you think to yourself, "Hmm, too much blue, what about the Blue channel?" That leads you to take a look at the Blue channel in the Channels palette. You find that the Blue channel looks horrible — the edges aren't sharp, some odd pixels are hanging around, and overall it's *way* too dark. (This is a typical result when photographs are taken with lower-end digital cameras.)

You start adjusting the photograph channel by channel, and *voilà!* Little Eddy's picture (and your place in Aunt Marge's will) is restored.

Adjusting the channels individually in an image gives you several advantages:

- ✔ If a particular tonal area is off (for instance, the blue mentioned in the Aunt Marge story), you can target the problem color by using a specific channel — there's no need to correct the Red and Green channels when the Blue channel is off.

- ✔ Adjustments are more precise because you correct each channel's problem individually, not the collective problems of the combined channels, which are different.

- ✔ You control how the tonal values mix when the image is viewed with its composite channels. You can adjust the colors that you think need correction (instead of letting Photoshop do this for you automatically, which can lead to poor results).

The color and tonal adjustments commands (found on the Image⇨Adjustments menu) that you can apply to individual channels include Levels, Curves, Brightness/Contrast, Shadows/Highlights, and all the one shot tonal commands: Invert, Equalize, Threshold, and Posterize.

For example, Figure 53-1 is an interesting photograph of the Brooklyn Bridge. The photograph is way too dark — the bridge columns in the background are almost indistinguishable from the shadows, and the sky looks murky.

• **Figure 53-1: An interesting photograph of the Brooklyn Bridge needs some adjustments.**

If I apply Levels to all the channels at once (the composite), the best results that I can get without over-brightening the highlights are shown in Figure 53-2. To my eye, the photograph looks a bit washed out and it doesn't have enough definition.

I went back to the starting board and adjusted the Levels of each channel individually. After fiddling for only five minutes, I was able to adjust the shadows and add the definition that I was looking for. As shown in Figure 53-3, the texture of the footpath has more definition and the bridge columns aren't lost in the background anymore.

So anytime that you're looking at a photograph and it just doesn't have the clear quality that you want, the colors are dull, or overall it looks washed out, try adjusting each channel individually. You may be surprised at the great results that you get.

• **Figure 53-2:** Although the Levels adjustment helps, it doesn't add enough definition.

• **Figure 53-3:** Applying Levels to each individual channel adds the definition that I'm looking for.

Filtering Individual Channels

If you need to apply a filter to an image (for instance the Unsharp Mask filter), and the correction that you are going to make is very slight, you may want to try applying the filter to each channel individually. This can give you more precise and satisfactory results.

For an example, I'm using this great photograph of a Manhattan office building under construction, shown in Figure 53-4. As you look at the photograph, notice how it looks a bit blurry. The edges can really use a good sharpening.

• **Figure 53-4:** This photograph looks a little blurry.

After applying the Unsharp Mask filter to all the channels at once, Figure 53-5 shows the best results that I can get. (You may have to look closely because these filter corrections are very slight.)

• **Figure 53-5: The photograph is better, but it's not good enough.**

So instead of sharpening all the channels at once, I turned to applying the Unsharp Mask filter to each channel individually. Figure 53-6 shows the great results with sharp edges.

• **Figure 53-6: Applying the Unsharp Mask to each channel really sharpens the photograph.**

You can also create some really cool effects by applying a filter to only one channel. Take a look at Figures 53-7 and 53-8. In each figure, the upper image shows the filter applied to the entire photograph. In the lower image, the same filter has been applied to only one channel.

Filter applied to all channels

Filter applied to all channels

Filter applied to red channel only

Filter applied to green channel only

• **Figure 53-7:** The Filter⇨Stylize⇨Glowing Edges filter applied to the entire image (top) and to only the red channel (bottom).

• **Figure 53-8:** The Filter⇨Artistic⇨Sponge filter applied to the entire image (top) and to only the green channel (bottom).

54 Technique

Mixing Color with Channels

Save Time By

✔ Replacing color channels

✔ Applying the Channel Mixer command

If you ever wanted to recolor an image but found that you lost detail when using the Photo Filter, Gradient Map, or Hue/Saturation commands, recoloring an image by using channels may work for you.

This technique focuses on recoloring images by using two channel methods. First, you swap channel information by copying and pasting from one channel to another. Although the results of this method can be unpredictable, they can also be excellent — a true case of "you never know until you try." Details are preserved as some colors are pumped up and other colors are toned down. The second method involves changing how the channels blend together by using the Channel Mixer command. The Channel Mixer adjusts the output of each channel by making the grayscale image in a channel whiter or blacker. The whiter a channel is, the more output color from that channel.

Recoloring images by using channels is really unpredictable. The results can be wild or subtle depending on how much adjustment you make. If other methods of recoloring haven't worked to your satisfaction, give channels a try. You may be surprised at the great results. Take a look at Color Plate 54-1 to see the effects — in color — of channel swapping and channel mixing.

Swapping Channels

You can use a fantastic channel technique to recolor an image: Simply swap the contents of the color channels. It works by literally copying and pasting the contents of one color channel to another. Open an image and experiment with this. Some of the results may be wild, but others may be downright lovely.

The following directions swap the contents of the Red and Green channels, but you can exchange any combination:

1. Open the image that you want to recolor.

For this example, I'm using the photograph of a white peacock, shown in Figure 54-1.

• **Figure 54-1:** This white peacock is going to have his feathers recolored.

2. In the Channels palette right-click/Control+click the Red channel and choose Duplicate Channel from the menu.

3. Click OK in the Duplicate Channel dialog box that opens.

A duplicate of the Red channel, named Red Copy, appears at the bottom of the Channels palette.

4. In the Channels palette right-click/Control+click the Green channel and choose Duplicate Channel from the menu.

5. Click OK in the Duplicate Channel dialog box that opens.

A duplicate of the Green channel, named Green Copy, appears at the bottom of the Channels palette. You should now have two duplicated channels, as shown in Figure 54-2.

6. Select the Red Copy channel in the Channels palette.

7. Choose Select⇨All or press Ctrl+A/⌘+A.

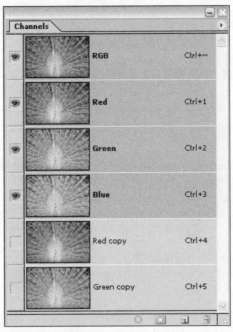

• **Figure 54-2:** You should have two copied channels at the bottom of the Channels palette.

8. Choose Edit⇨Copy or press Ctrl+C/⌘+C.

9. Select the Green channel in the Channels palette.

10. Choose Edit⇨Paste or press Ctrl+V/⌘+V.

This copies the contents of the Red Copy channel to the Green channel.

11. Select the Green Copy channel in the Channels palette.

12. Choose Select⇨All or press Ctrl+A/⌘+A.

13. Choose Edit⇨Copy or press Ctrl+C/⌘+C.

14. Select the Red channel in the Channels palette.

15. Choose Edit⇨Paste or press Ctrl+V/⌘+V.

This copies the contents of the Green Copy channel to the Red channel. You've now swapped the contents of the Red and Green channels. How did the colors change in your image? In the peacock photograph, the peacock's feathers changed to a bright violet.

You can see the results of some channel swapping in Color Plate 54-1.

Working with the Channel Mixer

By adjusting channel output with the Channel Mixer command, you can quickly recolor an image without losing any detail.

The Channel Mixer command can be used in two ways. It can be applied directly to a layer by choosing Image⇨Adjustments⇨Channel Mixer or it can be applied as an adjustment layer. Adjustment layers don't permanently change a layer's pixels and are very flexible. For instance, you can always come back later and adjust the Channel Mixer settings if you need to. When I have the choice, I always use an adjustment layer. (Turn to Technique 22 to find out more about adjustment layers.)

Here's how to use the Channel Mixer:

1. **In the Layers palette, select the layer that you want to recolor.**

2. **Make sure that the composite color channel is selected in the Channels palette.**

3. **Apply the Channel Mixer command by using an adjustment layer. At the bottom of the Layers palette, click the Create New Fill or Adjustment Layer button and choose Channel Mixer from the menu.**

   or

   Apply the Channel Mixer command to the selected layer. Choose Image⇨Adjustments⇨ Channel Mixer.

   The Channel Mixer dialog box opens, as shown in Figure 54-3. Notice the Output Channel drop-down list at the top of the dialog box. This is where you select the channel that you want to modify. The sliders adjust the brightness of the grayscale image in each channel. Higher settings make a channel lighter and whiter; lower settings make a channel darker and blacker.

• **Figure 54-3:** Use the sliders in the Channel Mixer dialog box to recolor an image.

4. **Use the Output Channel drop-down list to select the channel that you want to adjust.**

5. **In the Source Channels area, use the sliders to adjust the blend of the channels and recolor the image to get the results that you need.**

   Notice that when one color channel (say, Red) is selected in the Output Channel drop-down list, that color is set to 100%, and the other two colors (for this example, Blue and Green) are set to 0%.

6. **When you're finished adjusting the color of your image, click OK to close the Channel Mixer dialog box and apply the color modifications.**

 You can also use the Channel Mixer to create fine grayscale images. With the Channel Mixer dialog box open, select the Monochrome check box to convert the image to grayscale. Then, use the sliders to adjust the amount of detail and contrast in the image.

Part IX

Creating Flashy, Professional Web Graphics

The 5th Wave   By Rich Tennant

"Oh, we're doing just great. Philip and I are selling decorative jelly jars on the Web. I run the Web site and Philip sort of controls the inventory."

Technique 55

Getting to Know ImageReady

ImageReady, Photoshop's sister program, is the place to go when you want to create and save Web graphics. With the introduction of the Creative Suite, ImageReady cs and Photoshop cs are much more tightly integrated than before. You can create graphics in Photoshop, jump to ImageReady to get them ready for the Web, and jump back to Photoshop for any last minute touch-ups.

This technique is a quick introduction to ImageReady. You find out about the program interface, along with available tools and palettes. Then, I show you how to preview your graphics in ImageReady or a browser to see how they look in the environment in which you'll really use them. Finally, you take a look at saving your Web graphics with the best balance between small file size and good visual quality.

If you've never used ImageReady before or you need a refresher, take a look at this technique before moving on to the other Web techniques in this part. After you're acclimated, you'll be creating super Web graphics in no time!

Looking at the Program Window

Launch ImageReady and take a look around the program environment. The ImageReady program environment is organized just like the Photoshop environment. You find a Menu bar and Options bar at the top of the screen, the Toolbox is on the left side, and palettes are located on the right side. Figure 55-1 shows the ImageReady environment with the various items labeled for quick reference.

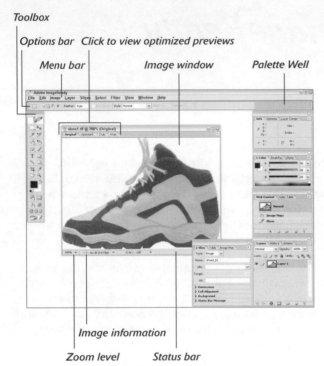

• **Figure 55-1:** ImageReady's program window looks a lot like Photoshop's.

Checking Out the Toolbox

When looking closer at the Toolbox, you'll see some familiar tools (such as the Move, Paintbrush, Hand, and Zoom tools) and some Web graphic specific tools — including the Image Map Select, Rectangle Image Map, Slice, and Slice Select tools. Figure 55-2 shows the Toolbox with the Web tools and buttons labeled.

Following is a list of the tools in the ImageReady Toolbox that may be a bit unfamiliar. I briefly explain what each tool does. The letter in the parentheses is the keyboard shortcut for the tool.

- ✔ **Slice (K):** Creates slice divisions.
- ✔ **Slice Select (O):** Selects slices.
- ✔ **Image Map Select (J):** Selects image map areas.

- ✔ **Rectangle Image Map (P):** Creates rectangular image map areas.
- ✔ **Tab Rectangle (R):** Creates rectangular shapes with rounded corners.
- ✔ **Toggle Image Map (A):** Shows/hides hotspot boundaries.
- ✔ **Preview Document (Y):** Quickly shows how the image will look in a browser environment.
- ✔ **Toggle Slice Visibility (Q):** Shows/hides slice boundaries.
- ✔ **Preview in Default Browser (Ctrl+Alt+P/ ⌘+Option+P):** Displays your document in your favorite Web browser.
- ✔ **Jump to Photoshop (Shift+Ctrl+M/Shift+⌘+M):** Quickly jumps to Photoshop to make adjustments to your image.

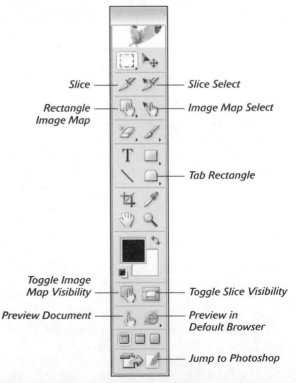

• **Figure 55-2:** The ImageReady Toolbox contains Web-specific tools and buttons.

As you expect, just as in Photoshop, any time a tool is selected in ImageReady, the Options bar changes to display that tool's settings.

Tear-off toolbars

A super feature of the ImageReady toolbar is the ability to *tear off* toolbars from the Toolbox. If you open a fly-out menu on the ImageReady toolbar, you notice that a tiny downward-pointing arrow is at the bottom of the fly-out, as shown in Figure 55-3.

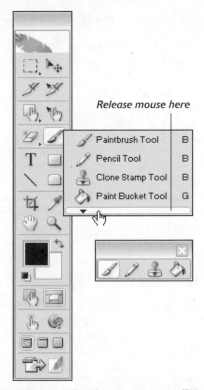

Release mouse here

• **Figure 55-3: In ImageReady you can tear off the Toolbox fly-out menus to create mini-toolbars.**

If you drag the mouse down over that arrow, and then release the mouse button, a mini-toolbar containing the tools of the fly-out menu appears. You can drag the mini-toolbar anywhere you need it in the program window. When you finish with the mini-toolbar, just click the Close button to make it disappear.

Jumping back and forth between ImageReady and Photoshop

When you're working on Web graphics, you can leave both Photoshop and ImageReady open. That way, you can quickly jump back and forth, making changes to the same open file.

To jump between the programs, just click the Jump To button at the bottom of the Toolbox, or select File⇨Edit in Photoshop or File⇨Edit in ImageReady (depending upon the program you're using).

When you jump to Photoshop from ImageReady, perform some edits, then jump back to ImageReady, the Photoshop edits are shown in the ImageReady History palette as a history state named "Update from Photoshop." Likewise, when you jump to Photoshop, any changes made in ImageReady are listed in Photoshop's History palette as "Update from ImageReady." Because these "Updates" are history states, you can undo them at any time by selecting an earlier history state.

Picking Palettes

ImageReady contains several palettes that you already use in Photoshop, including the Layers, Swatches, Colors, and History palettes (just to name a few). These palettes work, of course, just like they do in Photoshop. So, if you're unsure of any palette, turn to the appropriate technique in this book that covers it.

ImageReady also includes several Web graphic palettes that are used to create animations, manage image maps and slices, and optimize file size and quality. Figure 55-4 shows some of the ImageReady palettes that you'll be using in the Web techniques included in this part.

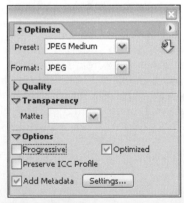

• **Figure 55-4: These palettes are just for working with Web graphics.**

Previewing Your Graphics

ImageReady provides several features you can use to view file size, estimated download time, and preview what an image will look like if it's saved in a specific way.

You can access these features using either the Status bar at the bottom of the image window or the Preview tabs at the top of the image window.

Viewing image size and download times

If you've ever surfed to a Web site and found yourself going nuts waiting for images to appear (also called *build*) on-screen, then you have an idea of how important managing image file size and figuring out how long images will take to load is.

Using ImageReady's Status bar, you can find out estimated times based on file size and connection speeds. Figure 55-5 shows two slots on the Status bar that you can use to view image size and download times. You can use these slots to compare two possible download scenarios and see how long each image takes to load depending upon the connection speed.

Using ImageReady previews

At the top of the ImageReady image window are four tabs: Original, Optimized, 2-Up, and 4-Up. These tabs show different views of the Web graphic you're working on, as shown in Figure 55-6.

Here's a quick look at what the tabs do:

✔ The **Original** tab displays the image without any *optimization*. Optimization is the process that saves files with specific file sizes and formats.

✔ The **Optimized** tab shows the image using the current settings in the Optimize palette. The Optimized preview updates every time a setting on the Optimize palette changes. To find out more about optimizing files and using the Optimize palette, turn to Technique 57.

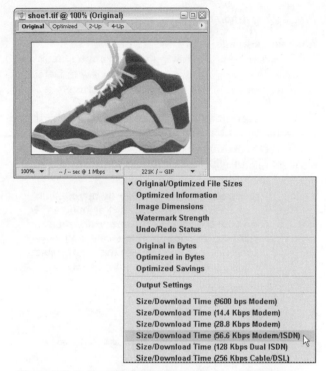

• **Figure 55-5:** Use the Status bar to find out estimated download times.

✔ The **2-Up** tab displays two versions of an image. The left image shows the original image that you would view if you selected the Original tab. The left image shows the optimized image that you would see if you selected the Optimized tab.

✔ The **4-Up** tab shows the original image, an optimized image based on the settings in the Optimize palette, and two other previews based on setting variations from the Optimize palette.

Previewing your graphics in a browser

You can preview your Web graphics right from Image-Ready. You can check out image maps, rollovers, or any animations that you create to make sure that they're working without leaving ImageReady. Previewing your images is great for checking out things and making any necessary adjustments.

• **Figure 55-6:** The four views of an image using the Preview tabs in the image window.

Adding browsers

When you launch ImageReady for the first time, ImageReady finds the default browser installed on your computer and uses this browser to generate the preview. But, if you want to view your graphics in other browsers to see how they look (and they can look quite different from browser to browser), you need to add the browsers to the Browser List.

Here's how:

1. **Choose File➪Preview In➪Edit Browser List.**

   The Edit Browser List dialog box opens (shown in Figure 55-7).

2. **Click the Find All button.**

   ImageReady automatically locates and loads all the available browsers it can find that are installed on your computer.

3. **Select the browser you want to use as the default browser from the Browser List on the left side of the dialog box.**

4. **Click the Set As Default button.**

5. **When you finish adding browsers, click OK to close the Edit Browser List dialog box.**

   After setting a default browser, the Preview in Default Browser button in the Toolbox will have changed to the icon of the default browser you selected.

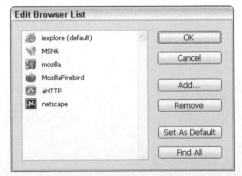

• **Figure 55-7: Click Find All to let ImageReady find the browsers installed on your computer.**

Previewing graphics

After you add all the browsers you want to use to the Browser List, previewing your graphics in a browser is easy. Simply click the Preview in Default Browser button in the ImageReady Toolbox.

To view a graphic in another browser, click the tiny arrow next to the Preview in Default Browser button and select a browser from the fly-out menu, as shown in Figure 55-8.

 At the bottom of the browser fly-out menu in Figure 55-8 is a tiny downward-pointing arrow. Drag your mouse over the arrow, and then release the mouse button to create a mini-browser toolbar. You can use this mini-toolbar for quick previews in different browsers.

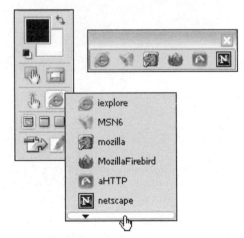

• **Figure 55-8: Choose a browser from the fly-out menu.**

Technique 56

Slicing Web Graphics

Save Time By

✔ Creating slices

✔ Converting and resizing slices

Slices are a really important part of creating Web graphics using ImageReady. You can use slices to speed up image load time, create image maps, and other fancy graphics such as rollovers and animations.

This technique tells you about the kinds of slices that you can create in ImageReady. Then I show you how to create slices manually, using layers or guides, and even automatically. From there, you find out how to convert slices, divide them, assign Web addresses to them, and even delete them.

If you want to create great Web graphics, start slicing up your images because slices are the springboard from which most Web graphics are made.

I'll Take a Slice

A slice of pizza, a slice of cherry pie, a slice of life — a lot of slices are out there. The type of slice that ImageReady and Photoshop creates is a mechanism for dividing up graphics for the Web.

Depending upon what you're going to do with an image, dividing it into slices has different benefits and uses. Some of the ways you can use slices include the following:

✔ **Speeding up load time:** By dividing a large image into many smaller sections, a graphic is processed by browsers as many small images instead of one huge one. Slices can let you put large images on the Web without making folks who visit your Web page wait too long.

✔ **Creating image maps:** Image maps allow users to click an area of an image and be transported to another specified Web location. (Take a look at Technique 58 to find out how to create image maps.)

✔ **Creating rollovers:** *Rollovers* are areas of a Web page that change when the mouse passes over them or performs an action such as clicking. (Technique 59 shows you how to create rollovers.)

✔ **Creating animated GIFs:** If you surf the Web, no doubt you've seen some type of animation — a penguin hops across the Web page, a volcano appears to blow up — you can create animations using ImageReady. (Turn to Technique 60 to find out how to make animated GIFs.)

Slices are really an integral part of creating many types of Web graphics using ImageReady.

You can create three different types of slices: user slices, auto slices, and layer-based slices. User slices are created manually using the Slice tool. Layer-based slices are created by using (what else?) layers. And, auto slices are the left over areas that Photoshop or ImageReady automatically turn into slices when user or layer-based slices are created. If an area isn't included in a user or layer-based slice, it is automatically turned into one or more auto slices.

 You can create, select, and edit slices in Photoshop, but ImageReady offers more slice options. Thus, creating and managing slices in ImageReady is usually best. But, if you do use the Slice tool in Photoshop to create slices, you can jump to ImageReady and be assured that all slices and slice settings are preserved.

Figure 56-1 shows the three different types of slices in use. Notice that each slice is numbered and has a special icon marking it as a user slice, auto slice, or layer-based slice.

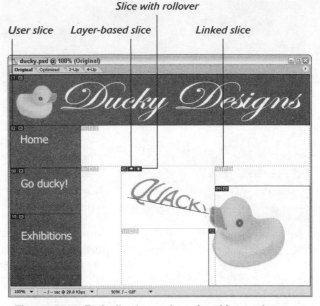

• **Figure 56-1:** Each slice is numbered and has an icon marking it as a user slice, auto slice, or layer-based slice.

Slicing and Dicing

You can create slices in a graphic in ImageReady several ways:

✔ Let ImageReady automatically create a specified number of horizontal and/or vertical slices

✔ Create slices using layers

✔ Manually slice an image using the Slice tool

✔ Generate slices using guides

 When you finish slicing an image and you want to publish it to the Web, save the image using the optimization directions in Technique 57. Then, upload the image *and* associated HTML file that ImageReady creates to your Web service provider. This HTML file contains the code that slices the image. If you don't upload the HTML file, your image won't be sliced.

Automatically creating slices

Automatically creating slices works especially well if you have a large image that you want to slice up for quicker downloading in Web pages. Using this method, you specify how many vertical and/or horizontal slices you want, and ImageReady does the work for you.

Here's how:

1. **Open the image to which you want to add slices in ImageReady.**

2. **Choose Slices⇨Divide Slice.**

   The Divide Slice dialog box opens, as shown in Figure 56-2.

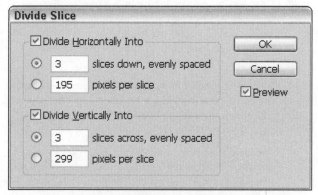

• **Figure 56-2: Use the Divide Slice dialog box to create horizontal and/or vertical slices.**

3. **Select the Divide Horizontally Into check box if you want to create horizontal slices.**

   If you select this option, enter the desired number of horizontal slices in the Slices Down, Evenly Spaced text box, or enter a pixel value in the Pixels Per Slice text box. When you enter a value in either text box, the horizontal slices appear as a preview in the image window.

4. **Select the Divide Vertically Into check box if you want to create vertical slices.**

   If you select this option, enter the desired number of vertical slices in the Slices Across, Evenly Spaced text box, or enter a pixel value in the Pixels Per Slice text box.

5. **Click OK.**

   A user slice label appears in the upper-left corner of each slice, as shown in Figure 56-3.

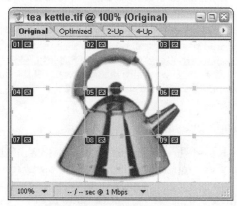

• **Figure 56-3: The number of vertical and horizontal slices you entered appears in the image window.**

 After creating slices using the Divide Slice dialog box, all the slices are selected. To select only one slice, choose the Slice Select tool in the Toolbox, and then click the slice you want to select. You can then reshape the slice, if necessary, or assign a URL to the slice, which I describe in "Working with Slices."

Manually slicing an image

The Slice tool works just like the Rectangular Marquee tool in Photoshop. Drag the tool to enclose a rectangular area to create a slice (instead of a selection). As you create user slices, ImageReady automatically generates auto slices, dividing up the leftover area.

1. **Open the image to which you want to add slices in ImageReady.**

2. **Select the Slice tool from the Toolbox.**

3. **Position the mouse where you want to start the slice, press the mouse button, and then drag diagonally to create the slice.**

When you release the mouse button, a numbered user slice label appears in the upper-left corner of the slice.

4. **Continue to create as many slices as you need.**

 If you need to divide an auto slice or user slice into smaller slices, select the slice using the Slice Select tool, and then choose Slices⇨Divide Slice. Use the Divide Slice dialog box to set the number of slices, and then click OK.

Creating slices using layers

A layer-based slice contains all the visible pixels on a layer. If you modify the layer in some way (move, transform, add layer effects to the layer, and so on) then the layer-based slice automatically resizes to include any new pixels. Layer-based slices work very well for creating rollovers that contain effects, such as a drop shadow, which may increase layer size. (Technique 59 shows you how to create rollovers.)

To create a layer-based slice, select the layer you want to turn into a slice in the Layers palette in ImageReady, and then choose Layer⇨New Layer Based Slice.

Generating slices using guides

Using guides to create slices lets you plot out where the slices are before you create them. Be a bit cautious when creating slices using this method, however, because any slices you previously created are deleted.

1. **Open the image you want to add slices to in ImageReady.**

2. **Choose View⇨Rulers or press Ctrl+R/⌘+R to display the rulers.**

3. **Drag guides from the rulers into the positions you want to use for the edges of the slices.**

4. **Choose Slices⇨Create Slices from Guides.**

Working with Slices

After you create slices, you can resize them, link them together, align and distribute them, put them into slice sets, and much more. Also, you can optimize individual slices based on the needs of the image contained within the slice. For instance, one slice on a Web page could contain a photograph optimized as a JPEG. Another slice on the same Web page could contain an animated figure optimized in that file format. (Turn to Technique 57 to find directions.)

Here's a kitchen sink list of things you can do with slices:

- ✔ **Convert an auto slice or layer-based slice into a user slice:** Choose the Slice Select tool from the Toolbox and select the slice you want to convert in the image window. Then, choose Slices⇨Promote to User Slice.

- ✔ **Combine auto slices and/or user slices into a larger user slice:** Select two or more slices in the image window using the Slice Select tool, and then choose Slices⇨Combine Slices.

- ✔ **Resize a user slice:** Select the Slice Select tool from the Toolbox, select the slice in the image window, and then drag the slice boundary handles.

- ✔ **Optimize a slice in a specific file format:** Use the Slice Select tool to select the slice in the image window; then use the Optimize palette to select optimization settings. Turn to Technique 57 for more about optimization.

- ✔ **Copy optimization settings from one slice to another:** Use the Slice Select tool to select the slice whose optimization settings you want to copy, and then drag the Create Droplet button from the Optimization palette onto the slice you want to copy the settings to. Take a look at Technique 57 for details.

- ✔ **Link slices together for optimization:** Use the Slice Select tool to select a slice in the image window. Then, Shift+click to select other slices that you want to link together. Choose Slices⇨Link Slices for Optimization.

✔ **Unlink slices:** Use the Slice Select tool to select the linked slice you want to unlink, and then choose Slices➪Unlink Slice.

✔ **Assign a URL to a slice:** Use the Slice Select tool to select the slice in the image window, and then enter a Web address in the URL text box in the Slice palette, as shown in Figure 56-4. When the slice loads on a Web page, any user who clicks the slice is redirected to that Web address.

✔ **Align slices:** Select the slices you want to line up using the Slice Select tool, and then click one of the alignment buttons on the Options bar. You can align slices vertically by their upper or lower edges or centers, or horizontally by their left or right edges or centers. When you align slices, only the slices move, not the images inside them.

✔ **Distribute slices:** Select the slices you want to distribute using the Slice Select tool, and then click one of the distribution buttons on the Options bar.

✔ **Delete a slice:** Select the slice by using the Slice Select tool, and then choose Slices➪ Delete Slice. This command deletes only the slice, not the image inside the slice.

• **Figure 56-4:** In the Slice palette, type a Web address in the URL text box.

57 Technique

Optimizing and Saving Images for the Web

Save Time By

- Optimizing images in GIF or JPEG file format
- Creating Droplets to speed optimization

When you create an image that you want to save for the Web, you need to keep several key issues in mind: image dimensions, the number of colors that an image has (including the image's color depth), and the file format that the image is saved in.

Working with each of these is like balancing on a tightrope. (Well, maybe it's not *quite* that perilous.) When dealing with the number of colors in an image and color depth, there's a balance between reducing the number of colors (thus reducing the file size) and maintaining image quality. When considering what file format you should use for an image, remember that not all file types are created equal. The GIF file format is great for saving animations; JPEG is great for saving photographs, but loses a bit of image data each time it's saved; and the PNG file format can handle transparency like a GIF file and can save photographs like a JPEG, but it doesn't compress as much.

This balancing act is called *optimization,* which basically translates to getting as much visual quality as you can out of as little file size as possible.

What's a Web graphic artist to do? ImageReady can help you make the right choice when saving graphics for the Web and even lets you preview the image before saving.

This technique discusses the ins and outs of saving Web graphics — what's important, what's not, and how to squeeze an extra smidgen of image quality out of the last compressed file bit. You find out what type of file format works with what kind of image and how to use these formats to create great quality graphics. Then, you find out exactly how to optimize and save your Web images.

Web Graphics Considerations

When creating an image for the Web, I use a basic formula:

1. Create an RGB image in Photoshop by using all the great tools and features that Photoshop has to offer.

2. Save the image in Photoshop. (Who wants to lose work?)

3. Jump to ImageReady and create any special animations or effects that you need.

4. Save the image for Web output by using the Optimize palette settings.

So, when I create an image for the Web, I keep a couple things in mind: What dimensions should I make the image, how few colors can I get away with (before the image quality starts degrading), and in which Web file format is it best to save the image?

Image size

The first consideration is purely practical and based on real world measurements. What are the maximum dimensions of the computer screen area? After all, you don't want to create a graphic (or a Web page) that's too large. If you do, your users have to scroll around to see it all.

Here's a formula that you can use to figure out how large the image area is that you can design for:

View area width ÷ image resolution = Max pixel width

View area height ÷ image resolution = Max pixel height

When selecting view area width and height measurements, use the most common computer monitor resolution setting: 800 x 600 pixels. Then consider that a browser takes up some screen real estate, so the width and height of the viewing area should be reduced by about an inch to 720 x 530 pixels.

Graphics created for the Web should be set at 96 ppi. A higher image resolution just makes for bigger file size and it doesn't increase image quality.

 Mac monitors view images at 72 ppi, and Windows monitors view images at 96 ppi. Creating Web graphics set at 96 ppi lets both types of monitors view the graphics equally well and doesn't increase file size by very much (only a few bits).

So, if you plug the numbers into the formula:

720 pixels wide ÷ 96 ppi = 7.5 inches wide

530 pixels high ÷ 96 ppi = 5.5 pixels high

So, what does this all mean for you as a Web graphics designer? The most important thing to remember is that the combined widths and heights of the design elements on a Web page have to be smaller than these dimensions. For instance, suppose that you want to create a navigation bar that runs across the top of your Web page. From the formula, you know that the nav bar should be less than 720 pixels wide (and even smaller than that if you want to center the bar and have a bit of space on each end).

Color depth

Color depth (also called bit-depth) sets how much color information is available in each pixel in an image. The lower the color depth, the fewer colors available to the image. Fewer colors and a smaller color depth translates to reduced file sizes, which make the Web graphics load faster.

 Drastically reducing the number of colors and the color depth in an image can result in grainy-looking edges and colors that are less vibrant. So, when you reduce the number of colors that an image has, you have to keep in mind the balance between file size and image display quality.

You can reduce the number of colors and the color depth in an image by using the ImageReady Optimize palette. When reducing the number of colors, ImageReady lets you see a preview, letting you decide whether the image quality is good enough before saving the image. I discuss the Optimize palette and color reduction in detail in "Optimizing Web Graphics."

Dithering and anti-aliasing

The terms that you see used when reducing colors in an image are *dithering* and *anti-aliasing*:

- ✔ **Dithering:** Mixes two available colors from an image's color palette to create an approximation of a color that isn't available in the color palette. Dithering is used to make images with fewer colors look like they have more colors and shades.

- ✔ **Anti-aliasing:** Describes the blending that occurs between an object's edges and the background in an image. When an image is anti-aliased, increasingly transparent pixels are added to edges to help smooth transitions.

Web-safe colors

ImageReady and Photoshop offer a Web Safe Color palette that's made up of the 216 colors that Windows and Mac browsers have in common. When selecting colors for a Web graphic, I surely recommend using this palette. That way, your graphics end up looking just as colorful in a browser as they did when you designed them.

Loading the Web Safe Color palette is easy: In either Photoshop or ImageReady, choose Window⇨Swatches to open the Swatches palette. Open the Swatches palette menu and choose Web Safe Colors.

Web file formats and compression

Three Web graphic file formats exist: GIF, JPEG, and PNG. Each format uses a mathematical compression formula to reduce the file size of an image and make it load faster on the Web.

GIF file format

The GIF file format can contain up to 256 colors. This format is best for high-contrast images with sharp edges including type. The GIF file format is used to retain transparency and save animations. (Turn to Technique 60 to find out how to create GIF animations. Fun!)

JPEG file format

The JPEG file format can contain millions of colors. This format works best with photographs and continuous tone images that display subtle color changes such as lighting effects.

You should know about two trade-offs when using this file format:

- ✔ The compression formula that the JPEG format uses can compress a huge file way down. However, when a JPEG file is loaded into a browser, the file has to be decompressed, which can take time.

- ✔ This format uses *lossy* compression, meaning that tiny bits of file information are lost every time a JPEG is opened, edited, saved, and closed in ImageReady. So, when creating an image for JPEG format, finish all the editing and save the file as a PSD or TIFF image. Then create a copy of the original and save it as a JPEG.

PNG file format

The PNG file format was originally created to replace the GIF format because of patent disputes. It is actually an improvement on the old GIF standard, but it does have a few drawbacks.

Two PNG file formats exist: PNG-8 and PNG-24. PNG-8 can contain up to a maximum of 256 colors, and PNG-24 can contain millions of colors. In addition, the PNG format can save transparent pixels. Because both PNG formats use *lossless* compression, no data is lost when images are saved and resaved.

Here's the downside of the PNG file format:

- ✔ You can't save animations in PNG format.

- ✔ PNG-24 files don't compress as much as JPEG files, so the file size is bigger.

- ✔ The PNG format is supported only by later file browsers: Microsoft Internet Explorer 4.0 and later, Netscape Navigator 6 and later, and Mac's standard browser, Safari.

Optimizing Web Graphics

The ImageReady Optimize palette lets you select from an array of Web file formats and settings to suit the needs of your Web projects. Using the Optimize palette, you can compare different optimized versions of an image side-by-side to maximize display quality while minimizing file size.

Save for Web command

Photoshop does offer the File⇨Save for Web command, which uses a slightly stripped-down version of the Optimize palette in ImageReady. Because you're saving an image for the Web, I really recommend using the full features that the Optimize palette has to offer in ImageReady. Also, working in ImageReady has the fringe benefit of all those great Web tools and features.

Optimizing a GIF

The steps in this section walk you through optimizing an image in the GIF file format with the ImageReady Optimize palette:

1. **Open the image that you want to optimize and save in ImageReady.**

2. **Choose Window⇨Optimize to view the Optimize palette, as shown in Figure 57-1.**

   Take a few seconds to look over the Optimize palette. It's packed with settings!

3. **Click the 2-Up tab in the image window, as shown in Figure 57-2.**

   This view displays the original image on the left, and the preview of the optimized image on the right. As you select optimization settings, the optimized preview changes to reflect the settings that you've selected.

4. **Use the Preset drop-down list to select an optimized GIF preset combination.**

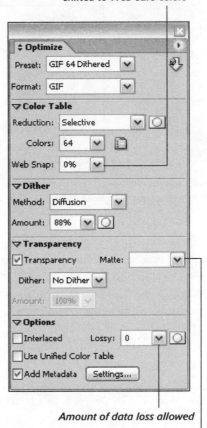

Percentage of colors shifted to Web-safe colors

Amount of data loss allowed

Transparent pixel blending

Figure 57-1: The Optimize palette contains optimized presets.

Even if you want to select custom settings, start with a preset combination to get you going.

If you like the preset as it is, stop here and move on to the later section "Saving Your Graphics." To select custom settings, continue with Step 5.

5. **Use the Reduction drop-down list to select a color reduction method.**

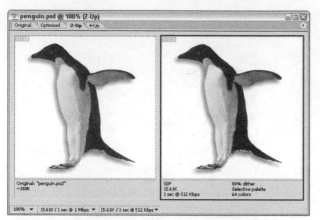

• **Figure 57-2:** View your image as a 2-Up so that you can see the original and optimized versions.

The GIF file format uses mathematical formulas to reduce the number of colors (and the file size). Here are the settings that you can choose from:

▶ **Perceptual:** Creates a color table based on the colors in the image and how the eye perceives color.

▶ **Selective:** Creates a color table by using the flat colors and Web-safe colors in the image.

▶ **Adaptive:** Creates a color table based on the part of the color spectrum that contains most of the colors in the image.

▶ **Restrictive:** Creates a color table that shifts the colors in the image to the 216 standard Web-safe colors that Windows and Mac Web browsers have in common.

The Web Snap slider is used to set how wide a range of colors is automatically set to their Web-safe equivalents. The higher the percentage, the more Web-safe colors are used. Higher settings can result in more dithering and graininess.

6. Use the Method drop-down list in the Dither area to select a dithering method.

You can choose from four options: No Dither, Diffusion, Pattern, or Noise. The Diffusion option creates the most subtle results. (To find out more about dithering, turn to "Dithering and anti-aliasing" earlier in this technique.)

In addition, you can increase the amount of dithering by using the Amount slider in the Dither area.

7. Select the Transparency check box to preserve any transparent pixels in the image.

If Transparency is left unchecked, any transparent pixels are colored with the currently selected Matte color. You can select a Matte color in the next step, if you need to.

8. Select a Matte color in the Transparency area to control how partially transparent pixels along the edge of an image blend with the background of the Web page.

If you know the color of the Web page's background, you can use the Matte drop-down list to select the color. Other options that you can select include None, Foreground Color, and Background Color.

9. In the Options area, select the Interlaced check box if you want to display the image in successively greater detail as it downloads on the Web page.

You can now save your Web graphic as described in "Saving Your Graphics."

Optimizing a JPEG

These steps take you through optimizing an image in the JPEG file format with the ImageReady Optimize palette:

1. Open the image that you want to optimize as a JPEG in ImageReady.

2. Choose Window⇨Optimize.

The Optimize palette shown in Figure 57-3 opens. If you haven't used this palette before, take a look at it. It has lots of settings, but it helps you to quickly optimize your image.

3. Click the 2-Up tab in the image window, as shown in Figure 57-4.

Applies blur to remove graininess

Compression quality

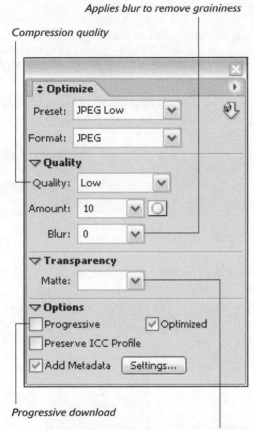

Progressive download

Transparent pixel blending

• **Figure 57-3:** Select a preset JPEG setting for starters even if you want to select custom options.

This view displays the original image on the left and the preview of the optimized image on the right. As you select optimization settings, the optimized preview changes to reflect the settings that you've selected.

4. Select an optimized JPEG preset combination from the Preset drop-down list.

Even if you want to select custom settings, start with a preset to give yourself basic settings to work with.

If you like the preset as it is, stop here and move on to "Saving Your Graphics." To select custom settings, continue with Step 5.

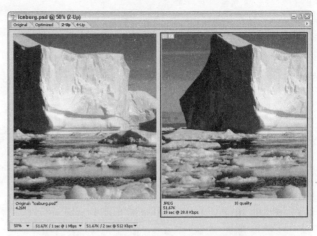

• **Figure 57-4:** The 2-Up view lets you see both the original image (left) and the optimized version (right).

5. Use the Quality drop-down list to select a compression quality for the optimized image.

You can also use the Amount slider to set the exact amount of compression.

The higher the Quality setting, the lower the compression. This means that you end up with a higher display quality and a larger file size. Fiddle with the settings to see how low you can go before the image quality starts to degrade.

6. In the Transparency area, select a Matte color to set how partially transparent pixels blend with the background of the Web page.

The JPEG format doesn't support transparency, so if you know the color of the Web page background, use the Matte drop-down list to select the color. If the None setting is selected, transparent pixels are automatically colored white.

7. In the Options area, select the Progressive check box if you want to display the image in successively greater detail as it downloads on the Web page.

You can now save your Web graphic as described in "Saving Your Graphics," later in this technique.

Optimizing a Web page that contains both GIFs and JPEGs

With ImageReady, you can optimize GIFs and JPEGs separately even if they are contained within the same Web page.

In order to do this, you must create slices around the different graphic elements on the Web page, select the slices that you want to optimize as GIFs or JPEGs, and then perform the optimization. (To find out how to create slices, turn to Technique 56.)

1. **Shift+click with the Slice Select tool to select the slices containing the graphical elements that you want to optimize.**

You should select only slices containing graphic elements that need to be optimized as GIFs or only the graphical elements that you want to optimize as JPEGs. (You can optimize only one type of graphic at a time.)

2. **If you're optimizing the selected graphics as GIFs, turn to the section "Optimizing a GIF," earlier in this technique, and follow the directions. If you're optimizing the selected graphics as JPEGs, turn to "Optimizing a JPEG," earlier in this technique, and follow the directions.**

Working with Droplets

Droplets are handy little mini-programs that you can quickly create to automate the optimization process.

 A Droplet saves the settings that you select in the Optimization palette. You can then drag an image or a folder of images over the Droplet icon in order to apply the optimization settings. If you need to optimize many Web graphics with the same optimization settings, Droplets can be a real timesaver.

Droplets can also be used to quickly copy optimization settings from one slice to another.

Here's how to create a Droplet:

1. **Use the directions in either "Optimizing a GIF" or "Optimizing a JPEG," earlier in this technique, to select the optimization settings that you need.**

2. **Drag the Droplet icon from the Optimize palette onto the desktop, as shown in Figure 57-5, or into a folder window.**

Alternatively, you can double-click the Droplet icon and use the Save Optimized Settings As Droplet dialog box to enter a name for the Droplet and select a folder where you want the Droplet to reside.

The Droplet is now ready for use.

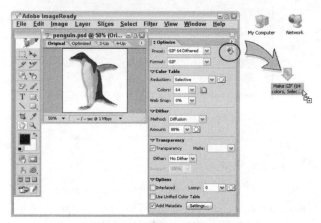

• **Figure 57-5: Drag the Droplet from the Optimize palette onto the desktop.**

After you create Droplets, you can use them to optimize individual files or a folder of files. Simply drag an image file or folder onto the Droplet icon on the desktop. If ImageReady isn't running when you use the Droplet, the Droplet automatically launches ImageReady and opens the file(s) in the program.

You can also copy optimization settings from one slice to another. Here's how:

1. **Select the slice containing the optimization settings that you want to copy with the Slice Select tool.**

2. **In the Optimization palette, drag the Droplet icon onto the slice to which you want to copy the settings.**

The settings are automatically copied to that slice.

Droplets and platform compatibility

Droplets are cross-platform compatible. Any Droplet created on a Mac can be used on a Windows machine and vice versa. However, a little conversion needs to be performed before a Droplet created on one platform can be used on the other.

✔ When a Droplet created on a Windows machine is copied to a Mac, drag the Droplet onto the ImageReady program icon. ImageReady launches (if it isn't running already) and opens a dialog box asking whether you want to convert it to a Mac Droplet (see the following figure). Click Yes.

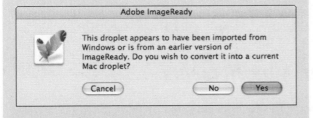

✔ After copying a Droplet created on the Mac to a Windows machine, rename the Droplet with an .exe extension. Then, drag the Droplet onto the ImageReady program icon. ImageReady launches (if it isn't already running) and opens a dialog box asking whether you want to convert it for Windows use. Click Yes.

Saving Your Graphics

After you optimize your Web graphics, it's time to save them and publish them to your Web site.

Here's how to save Web graphics in ImageReady:

1. **After optimizing your image, choose File⇨ Save Optimized As to save the file.**

2. **In the Save Optimized As dialog box, enter a name for the image in the File Name/Save As text box and select a location where you want to store the file.**

3. **Click Save.**

 When you save images in ImageReady by using the File⇨Save Optimized As dialog box, ImageReady also generates HTML files associated with the image files. These HTML files are necessary for making Web graphics, such as rollovers and image maps, work. To find out more about these HTML files, take a look at the sidebar "ImageReady and HTML."

ImageReady and HTML

By default, ImageReady saves HTML files along with graphic files for the Web. These files contain the HTML and JavaScript code necessary to make features, such as rollovers and image maps, work.

When you use the File⇨Save Optimized As command in ImageReady, the program also creates a folder structure where the image files referenced by the HTML are placed. By default, the folder for image files is named `images`.

Take a look at the structure that ImageReady creates when you publish these files to a Web site or when you want to combine the HTML created by ImageReady with your own HTML code. When you publish image maps and rollovers to a Web site, you must also upload the accompanying HTML files. Otherwise, the image maps and rollovers don't work.

In the Save As Type drop-down list in the Save Optimized As dialog box, you can tell ImageReady to save only image files (as opposed to HTML and image files, which is the default).

In addition, you can use the various dialog boxes associated with the File⇨Output Settings command to change the way that HTML files are saved and named. You can also use these same dialog boxes to set the names of the folders where image and HTML files are stored.

Creating Image Maps

Image maps designate where specially selected areas, or *hotspots,* appear on an image in a Web page. Each hotspot is linked to a URL. When folks browse a Web page that contains an image map, they can click a hotspot and be redirected to the assigned URL.

ImageReady includes tools and commands that make it easy for you to create image maps containing hotspots. This technique shows you how to create image maps with tools that enable you to create hotspots by hand. Then, you find out how to create image maps with layers.

So grab a Web image and add an image map! This type of Web functionality is sure to make your Web site more professional and easy to use.

Using Tools to Map Hotspots

Creating an image map with the tools supplied by ImageReady is really quite simple. The Rectangle Image Map and Circle Image Map tools work just like the marquee selection tools in Photoshop. And the Polygon Image Map tool works in a fashion similar to the Pen Tool — just click to create the hotspot boundary.

Here's the lowdown on designating hotspots by hand:

1. **Select either the Rectangle Image Map, Circle Image Map, or Polygon Image Map tool from the Toolbox.**

2. **Create the hotspot around the area.**

If you selected the Rectangle Image Map tool or Circle Image Map tool, click and drag a rectangular or circular area in the image window.

If you selected the Polygon Image Map tool, click where you want the hotspot boundary to start, and then continue clicking around the contour of the area. When the area is surrounded, double-click to close the image map, or click the starting point to close the boundary.

Figure 58-1 shows the Polygon Image Map tool in action, creating an irregularly shaped hotspot around the middle fish.

• Figure 58-1: Use the image map tools to create hotspots around Web page elements. In this figure, the middle fish has been mapped.

3. **In the Image Map palette, enter a Web address in the URL text box, as shown in Figure 58-2.**

When you enter the Web address, be sure to type **http://** before the Web address. Also, enter the alternate text in the Alt text box. This text appears when someone browsing the Web page passes the mouse over the hotspot. It also appears as a placeholder while the viewer waits for graphics to load.

• Figure 58-2: Enter the Web address in the URL text box.

4. **Repeat Steps 1 through 3 to create another image map hotspot.**

If you preview the image in a browser by clicking the Preview in Browser button in the Toolbox, you can test the image hotspots that you've created.

You can also optimize and save the image with its image map as described in Technique 57. Be sure to upload the image and associated HTML file that ImageReady generates to your Web service provider. Without the HTML file, your image doesn't have an image map.

Creating an Image Map by Using Layers

When you create an image map by using layers, ImageReady does most of the work for you, creating a hotspot around the colored pixels on each selected layer. In addition, if you ever edit a layer containing a layer-based hotspot — if you move the layer, transform it, or edit it in any way — ImageReady automatically updates the layer-based image map.

1. **In ImageReady, use the Layers palette to select a layer.**

> The layer that you use to create a layer-based image map must contain transparent areas. Otherwise, the entire layer will be turned into one giant hotspot.

2. **Choose Layer⇨New Layer Based Image Map Area.**

3. **In the Image Map palette, use the Shape drop-down list to select a shape for the hotspots.**

You can choose from Square, Circular, or Polygonal hotspots. Figure 58-3 shows polygonal hotspots around the fish.

• **Figure 58-3:** The fish on the layer are surrounded by polygonal hotspots.

4. **In the Image Map palette, enter a Web address in the URL text box. (Refer to Figure 58-2.)**

When you enter the Web address, be sure to type **http://** before the Web address. Also, enter the alternate text in the Alt text box. This text appears when someone browsing the Web page passes the mouse over the hotspot. It also appears as a placeholder while the viewer waits for graphics to load.

When the URL is entered in the Image Map palette, a tiny pointing finger icon appears near the layer name in the Layers palette, as shown in Figure 58-4. This pointing finger icon indicates that the layer contains a layer-based image map.

5. **Repeat Steps 1 through 4 to create hotspots on any other layers.**

Preview the image in a browser by clicking the Preview in Browser button in the Toolbox. Previewing the image lets you test the hotspots that you've created.

When you're happy with the image map, you can optimize and save the layered image with its image map, as described in Technique 57. Be sure to upload the image and associated HTML

file that ImageReady generates to your Web service provider. Without the HTML file, the layer-based image map doesn't work.

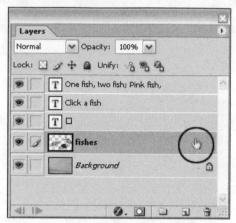

• **Figure 58-4:** The pointing finger icon indicates that the layer contains a layer-based image map.

Working with Image Maps

After you create image maps, you can reshape hotspots, convert layer-based image maps to tool-based image maps, hide image maps if you need to work on another aspect of a Web page, or (of course) delete the image maps. Here's the list from the kitchen sink:

✔ **Reshape tool-based hotspots** by choosing the Image Map Select tool from the Toolbox. Then, select the hotspot that you want to reshape in the image window and drag the hotspot boundary handles to reshape the hotspot.

✔ **Convert a layer-based image map to a tool-based image map** by using the Image Map Select tool to select the image map that you want to convert. Then, choose Promote Layer Based Image Map Area from the Image Map palette menu, as shown in Figure 58-5. Because only tool-based hotspots can be reshaped, you must convert a layer-based image map before you can reshape hotspots.

✔ **Duplicate an image map** by using the Image Map Select tool to select the image map that you want to copy. Open the Image Map palette menu and choose Duplicate Image Map Area. A copy of the image map appears in the image window. You can then use the Image Map Select tool to move the duplicate image map to the place where you need it.

✔ **Hide image maps in the image window** by choosing View➪Show➪Image Maps. Choose the Image Maps command again to view the image maps.

✔ **Delete an image map** by using the Image Map Select tool to select the image map that you want to delete. Then, press Backspace/Delete.

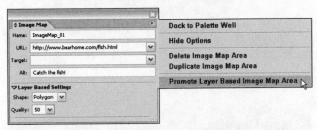

• **Figure 58-5:** Choose Promote Layer Based Image Map Area from the Image Map palette menu.

Technique 59

Making Your Graphics Rollover

Almost any Web page that you visit on the World Wide Web these days has some kind of *rollover*. A rollover is a Web page event that happens when the mouse moves over a graphic or clicks an area of a Web page. (For instance, when the mouse passes over a button, the button changes from gray to another color.) Rollovers make a Web site look professional and add interactivity for viewers.

Creating super rollovers with ImageReady is easy. Image Ready gives you all the tools that you need. Follow the directions in this technique to create a few rollovers, and then let your imagination take over. After you get the hang of creating rollover Web effects, use any of the Photoshop filters, effects, transformations, or other features to create your own custom rollovers.

Getting to Know Rollovers

If you've surfed the Web, no doubt you've seen rollovers. When your mouse passes over a button or a hotspot on a Web page, the appearance of the graphic changes. For instance, a button changes from gray to another color, or a light bulb appears to turn on. These rollovers are created by using *rollover states*.

The six rollover states are associated with the six actions that a mouse can perform. The mouse actions work as triggers, activating the rollover state. The six rollover states are

- ✔ **Over:** Activates when the user passes the mouse over a slice or image map area. In the Over state, the mouse button is not pressed.

- ✔ **Down:** Activates when the user clicks and holds down the mouse button over a slice or image map area. This state is active as long as the user keeps the mouse button pressed down and doesn't release it.

✔ **Click:** Activates when the user clicks the mouse button while the mouse is over a slice or image map area.

✔ **Selected:** Activates when the user selects a slice or image map area. The rollover remains active until the user selects another slice or image map area. For instance, a button changes color because the user selects it. The button doesn't change back to its original color until the user selects another button.

✔ **Out:** Activates when the user moves the mouse out of the slice or image map area.

✔ **Up:** Activates when the user releases the mouse button while the mouse is over a slice or image map.

The default sequence of rollover states that ImageReady assigns is Over, Down, and Click. First, the user passes the mouse over the slice or image map, activating the Over state. Then, the user presses the mouse button down, activating the Down state. Finally, the user releases the mouse button, triggering the Click state.

You can use the following three ways to create rollovers by using rollover states:

✔ **Change an image area.** For instance, a color changes or a drop shadow appears. In Figure 59-1, a drop shadow appears.

✔ **Substitute one image for another.** In Figure 59-2, a new image is substituted for the original image.

✔ **Make text or another image appear in a different area of the browser window.** In Figure 59-3, text appears in a nearby area of the browser window.

Mouse Off

Mouse Over

• **Figure 59-1: Changing the image area.**

To create a rollover, an image must be divided into slices first. Only user slices and layer-based slices can be assigned rollover states. If ImageReady has automatically generated auto slices surrounding an area that you want to use in a rollover, you need to convert the auto slices to user slices by using the Slices⇨Promote to User Slices command. (To find out more about creating slices and converting them, turn to Technique 56.)

Mouse Off

Mouse Over

• **Figure 59-2:** Substituting a new image for the original image.

Mouse Off

Mouse Over

• **Figure 59-3:** Making text appear in a different area of the browser window.

 In version 7 of ImageReady, rollovers were created by using the Rollover palette. With ImageReady CS, the Rollovers palette is gone and the new Web Content palette has all the functionality of the old Rollovers palette. So, to create rollovers in ImageReady CS, you use the Web Content palette to assign rollover states and the Layers palette to hide and display layers.

Creating a Rollover by Using Slices

When creating a rollover by using a slice, you use the Web Content palette to create the rollover states and the Layers palette to hide and display the layers associated with the rollover states. This example uses only the Over state. When the example is complete, a mouse passing over the slice triggers the Over state, changing the way the sliced area looks.

The following steps show how to create a rollover by using slices:

1. **In ImageReady, open the image that you want to use for the rollover.**

   Take a look at the Web Content palette shown in Figure 59-4. At the top of the palette, a thumbnail of the image is labeled Normal. ImageReady uses the Normal state to display the entire image without any slices or rollover states. Along the bottom of the palette are five buttons (from left to right): Create Layer-Based Rollover, Group Slices into Tabs, New Slice Set, Create Rollover State, and Delete.

   To make the rollover, you create a slice to let ImageReady know which area to assign to a rollover state.

• **Figure 59-4:** When you first open an image, a thumbnail of the image appears in the Web Content palette.

2. **Select the Slice tool from the Toolbox.**

3. **Create a slice around the area that you want to use to make the rollover.**

   As shown in Figure 59-5, a slice is created around the top of the glass. Notice that a thumbnail of the slice appears in the Web Content palette.

• **Figure 59-5:** When you create a slice, a thumbnail of the slice appears in the Web Content palette.

4. **Choose Select➪Create Selection from Slice.**

   A selection marquee appears around the slice boundary.

5. **Choose Layer➪New➪Layer via Copy or press Ctrl+J/⌘+J.**

   A copy of the selected area is pasted into a new layer. The new layer appears in the Layers palette above the original layer.

6. Rename the copied layer.

You can name the layer anything you want, but I'm using Cup in this example. You modify this layer to make the image look different when the mouse passes over the rollover.

7. Choose Layer⇨Duplicate Layer or Press Ctrl+J/⌘+J.

A duplicate of the new layer created in Step 5 appears in the Layer palette, as shown in Figure 59-6.

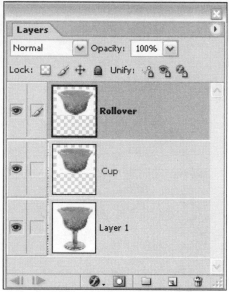

• **Figure 59-6:** The duplicated layer appears at the top of the stack in the Layers palette.

8. Rename the duplicate layer that you created in Step 7.

You can name the layer anything you want, but for this example I'm using the name Rollover.

Before performing the next step, make sure that the Rollover layer is selected in the Layers palette and the slice that you created in Step 3 is selected in the Web Content palette.

9. Click the Create Rollover State button at the bottom of the Web Content palette.

When you click the button, the rollover state labeled Over appears in the Web Content palette below the original slice, as shown in Figure 59-7.

Over is the default rollover state. If you want to change to a different rollover state, double-click the word Over and select a state from the Rollover State Options dialog box. For this example, I use the Over state.

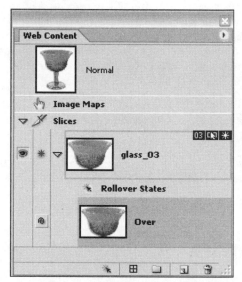

• **Figure 59-7:** The Over rollover state appears with a thumbnail below the slice in the Web Content palette.

10. In the Layers palette, click the eye icon next to the Rollover layer to hide it.

11. Select the Cup layer.

This is the layer that you need to modify to make the image look different when the mouse passes over the sliced area.

12. Use a filter, layer effect, or other feature to modify the appearance of the selected Cup layer.

In this example, the Watercolor filter is applied to the Cup layer.

Notice that when you alter the Cup layer, the layer thumbnail in the Layers palette changes to reflect the modification, and the thumbnail next to the Over state in the Web Content palette changes also.

Congratulations! You just created a rollover. To preview the rollover in ImageReady, click the Preview Document button in the Toolbox. To preview the rollover in a browser, click the Preview in Browser button in the Toolbox. Figure 59-8 shows the rollover in a browser window.

• **Figure 59-8:** The image before the mouse passes over the slice (top) and after (bottom).

Creating a Rollover by Using Layers

Using the Create Layer-Based Rollover button at the bottom of the Web Content palette, you can quickly turn a layer into a layer-based slice and create a new rollover state all with the click of one button. When you create a rollover by using a layer, the only way that you can create changes between the rollover states is to use layer styles.

1. In the Layers palette, select a layer.

2. At the bottom of the Web Content palette, click the Create Layer-Based Rollover button.

The layer is instantly turned into a layer-based slice. This change is indicated in the Layers palette by the tiny Slice tool icon that appears next to the layer's name. Simultaneously, the Over rollover state is generated by using the slice in the Web Content palette, as shown in Figure 59-9.

Over is the default rollover state. If you want to change to a different rollover state, double-click the word Over and select a state from the Rollover State Options dialog box. For this example, I use the Over state.

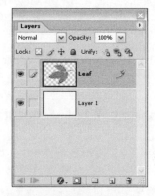

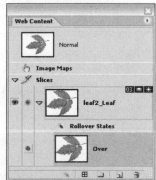

• **Figure 59-9:** When you click the Create Layer-Based Rollover button, the selected layer is used to create a layer-based slice, and the Over rollover state is assigned to the slice in the Web Context palette.

3. **In the Layers palette, click the Add layer style button at the bottom of the palette, and then choose an effect from the menu.**

Use the Layer Style dialog box to create an interesting effect, such as a drop shadow, bevel, or gradient overlay. In this example, I used a drop shadow. To find out more about layer styles, take a look at Technique 20.

When you're finished creating the layer effect, click OK to close the Layer Style dialog box. Notice that the rollover state thumbnail in the Web Content palette changes to reflect the layer style that you applied.

That's all there is to it! You just created a rollover by using a layer style. To preview the rollover in ImageReady, click the Preview Document button in the Toolbox. To preview the rollover in a browser, click the Preview in Browser button in the Toolbox. Figure 59-10 shows the rollover in a browser window.

• **Figure 59-10: The leaf before the mouse passes over it (top) and during (bottom).**

Creating a Rollover by Using a Layer Style

When you create a rollover by using a layer style, you don't have to duplicate layers and assign them to rollover states like you do when creating a rollover by using a slice. Instead, different layer styles can be applied to the same layer for each rollover state.

1. **Open the image that you want to use for the rollover.**

2. **Use the Slice tool to create a slice around the rollover area.**

3. **In the Web Content palette, click the Create Rollover State button.**

Creating preset rollover styles

If you come up with a layer-based rollover effect that you really like, you can save it as a preset, and (here's the great part) apply the rollover effect to any other layer with just one click!

Here's how to save your preset:

1. Create a layer-based rollover following the steps in the section "Creating a Rollover by Using Layers."

2. Make sure that the layer that was used to create the layer-based slice is selected in the Layers palette.

3. In the Swatches palette, choose New Style from the palette menu.

4. Enter a name for your rollover style in the Style Options dialog box and make sure to select the Include Rollover States check box.

5. Click OK to close the Style Options dialog box.

   Your custom rollover style appears as a swatch at the bottom of the Swatches palette.

To apply your custom rollover style to another layer, just select the layer, and then click the swatch. Preview the rollover in a browser. Cool!

The Over rollover state automatically appears with a thumbnail of the sliced area in the Web Content palette.

Over is the default rollover state. If you want to change to a different rollover state, double-click the word Over and select a state from the Rollover State Options dialog box. For this example, I use the Over state.

4. **Make sure that the rollover state that you just created in Step 3 is selected.**

5. **In the Layers palette, click the Add Layer Style button at the bottom of the palette, and then choose an effect from the menu.**

Use the Layer Style dialog box to create a fun effect, such as a drop shadow, bevel, or gradient overlay. I used a texture for this example. To find out more about layer effects, turn to Technique 20.

When you're finished creating the layer effect, click OK to close the Layer Style dialog box. Notice that the rollover state thumbnail changes to reflect the layer style that you applied.

Preview the rollover in ImageReady by clicking the Preview Document button in the Toolbox, or preview the rollover in a browser by clicking the Preview in Browser button in the Toolbox.

Substituting Another Image

Creating a substitution rollover is easy. All you need is two layers containing different images. One image is active in the Normal state, when the mouse is off the image. The other image is the substitution image, which replaces the original image when the Over state is triggered by a mouse action, such as passing over the slice area.

Use the following steps to create a substitution rollover:

1. **Create a document with two layers.**

On one layer is the original image, which you'll attach to the Normal state. The user sees this image when the mouse is off the sliced area. The other layer contains the substitution image. The user sees the substitution image when the mouse passes over the sliced area. (It doesn't matter which layer is on top in the stacking order.)

Figure 59-11 shows two penguin layers, one labeled Standing and the second labeled Flying.

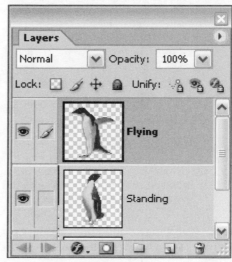

• **Figure 59-11:** I'm using two penguin layers, Standing and Flying, to create a substitution rollover.

2. **Select the Slice tool from the Toolbox.**

3. **Create a slice that encompasses the larger of the two layers.**

Notice that when you create the slice, it appears in the Web Content palette.

4. **In the Layers palette, select the layer that you want to use as the Normal state (when the mouse is off the image).**

For my example, the Standing layer is selected, as shown in Figure 59-12.

5. **In the Layers palette, hide the substitute layer (in my example, the Flying layer) by clicking the eye icon.**

Figure 59-12 shows that the Flying layer is hidden.

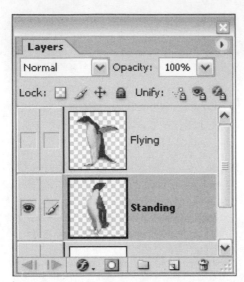

• **Figure 59-12:** Use the Layers palette to hide the layer that you don't want to see when the mouse is not over the image.

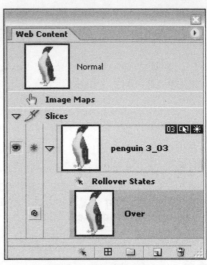

• **Figure 59-13:** When you create the Over rollover state, the thumbnail contains the same image as the Slice thumbnail.

6. In the Web Content palette, click the Create Rollover State button at the bottom of the palette.

The Over rollover state appears below the slice with the same image in the thumbnail as the slice, as shown in Figure 59-13.

7. With the Over rollover state selected in the Web Content palette, use the Layers palette to make the substitution image visible and the Normal state image hidden.

In this example, the eye icon next to the Flying penguin layer is clicked to make it visible and the Standing penguin layer eye icon is clicked to hide the layer, as shown in Figure 59-14.

When you hide one layer and make the other layer visible, the Over state thumbnail in the Web Content palette changes to display the visible layer.

And that's it! Try out the rollover by previewing it in ImageReady or in a browser.

• **Figure 59-14:** When you make the substitution image visible, it appears in the Over rollover state thumbnail in the Web Content palette.

Technique 60

Making GIF Animations

When you make a GIF animation, images contained in frames play back in a specific order and speed, creating the impression of motion. It's just like creating a mini-movie. You see many types of animations, but you can create two basic types easily with ImageReady: text or an image moves across a Web page, and text or an image fades in or out.

Create animations in ImageReady using the Animation palette shown in Figure 60-1. This palette contains all the tools necessary to mark the first and last frames of the animation, create the frames in between (called *tweening*), and play back the animation for testing.

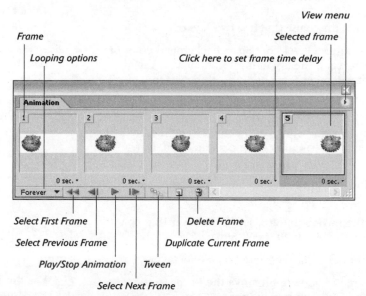

Frame

Looping options

View menu

Selected frame

Click here to set frame time delay

Select First Frame

Select Previous Frame

Play/Stop Animation

Tween

Select Next Frame

Delete Frame

Duplicate Current Frame

• **Figure 60-1: The Animations palette contains all the tools you need to create great animations.**

This technique takes you through creating two types of GIF animations: The first uses layers to create the animation, and the second uses the Layer palette's opacity slider to make text fade in and out. So, pull out a Web graphic, launch ImageReady, and create an animation. Animations are really quite easy. After you get the hang of it, use your imagination to come up with variations and your own ideas.

Creating an Animation Using Layers

When you run the animation created with the following steps, it looks like an image is moving from one side of the browser window to the other side. This type of GIF animation uses an image on a transparent layer with another layer behind it that contains a background color or background texture. Here's what you need to do:

1. **Create an image that has two layers.**

   The bottom layer contains a background color or texture and the upper layer contains the image that will move from one side of the window to the other.

   For my example, shown in Figure 60-2, the image contains a White layer that is used for the background and a Puffer layer containing an ornery looking puffer fish.

2. **Choose Window⇨Animation to display the Animation palette.**

3. **In the Layers palette, select the layer that contains the image that will move.**

   In this example, I selected the Puffer layer.

4. **Using the Move tool, move the image to the left side of the image window.**

   In the Animation palette, Frame 1 updates to display the moved image.

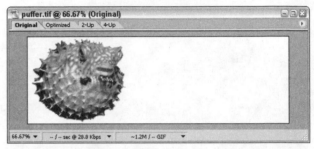

• **Figure 60-2: Using the Animation palette, this puffer fish is going to swim from left to right in the image window.**

5. **Click the Duplicate Current Frame button at the bottom of the Animation palette.**

   A new frame labeled 2 appears selected in the palette.

6. **With Frame 2 still selected in the Animation palette, use the Move tool to move the image to the right side of the image window.**

   Frame 2 in the Animation palette updates to display the moved image, as shown in Figure 60-3.

7. **With Frame 2 still selected, click the Tween button at the bottom of the Animation palette.**

   Use the Tween dialog box to create the frames in between the selected frames in the Animation palette. In this example, I add three frames between Frame 1 and Frame 2.

8. **Use the Tween With drop-down list to select Previous Frame.**

   This option sets ImageReady to create frames with progressive motion across the image window.

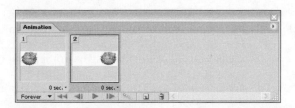

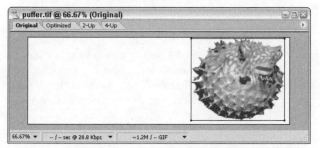

• **Figure 60-3:** After you move the image to the right side of the image window, the Frame 2 thumbnail in the Animation palette updates to display the moved image.

9. **Enter a number of frames in the animation in the Frames to Add text box.**

> ▶ In the Layers area, select whether to copy **All Layers** (even layers that don't change) or only copy **Selected Layers** to copy pixels from the currently selected layers.

> ▶ In the Parameters area, select the items that the frames in between modify: **Position**, **Opacity**, and/or **Effects**. (Effects are layer styles applied to the image. For more about applying layer styles to an image, turn to Technique 20.)

10. **Click OK to close the Tween dialog box.**

ImageReady automatically generates the frames in between Frame 1 and Frame 2. In this example, I added three frames, so Frame 2 is automatically renumbered Frame 5, as shown in Figure 60-4.

That's it! You've just created an animation. Click the Play button on the Animation palette to watch your animation in action.

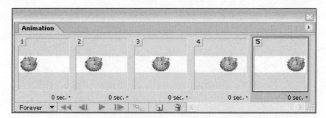

• **Figure 60-4:** ImageReady creates frames between Frame 1 and Frame 2. Because three frames were added between Frame 1 and Frame 2 in this example, Frame 2 is renumbered Frame 5.

Making Text Fade In and Out

You can use ImageReady to create animations that make text fade in and fade out. The way to do this animation is to set the opacity for the text using two frames. Using the following steps, the first frame opacity is set to 0% and the second frame opacity is set to 100%. Then using the Tween dialog box, add frames between the two frames that step the opacity first up, and then back down.

1. **Create a new image that you will use to make the text fade in and out or open an image that you want to add text to.**

2. **Using the Text tool, add type to the image.**

When you create the type, it appears in the Layers palette on its own type layer. In this example, I added type around the teakettle, as shown in Figure 60-5.

• **Figure 60-5:** I added type on either side of the teakettle.

3. **With the type layer selected in the Layers palette, set the layer's opacity to 0%.**

When you set the type layer opacity to 0%, the type becomes invisible. Notice that type in the Frame 1 thumbnail in the Animation palette updates also become invisible.

4. **With the type layer still selected, click the Duplicate Current Frame button on the Animation palette.**

You now have two frames in the Animation palette with invisible text with Frame 2 currently selected.

5. **In the Layers palette, set the type layer's opacity to 100% to make the type visible.**

The Frame 2 thumbnail updates, showing the text, as shown in Figure 60-6.

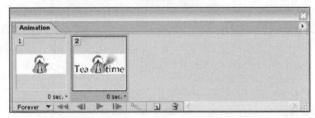

• **Figure 60-6:** You now have two frames in the Animation palette. The type in Frame 1 is invisible and the type in Frame 2 is visible.

6. **With Frame 2 still selected, click the Tween button at the bottom of the Animation palette.**

Use the Tween dialog box to create the frames in between selected frames in the Animation palette. In this example, I added three frames between Frame 1 and Frame 2.

▶ Use the Tween With drop-down list to select **Previous Frame**. This option sets ImageReady to create frames with progressive opacity from invisible to visible.

▶ Enter a number of frames in the animation in the **Frames to Add** text box. In the Layers area, select whether to copy **All Layers** (even layers that don't change) or to copy **Selected Layers** to copy pixels from the currently selected layers.

▶ In the Parameters area, select the items that the frames in between will modify: **Position**, **Opacity**, and/or **Effects**. (*Effects* are layer styles applied to the image. For more about applying layer styles to an image, turn to Technique 20.) For this example, I made sure that Opacity is checked.

7. **Click OK to close the Tween dialog box.**

ImageReady automatically generates the frames in between Frame 1 and Frame 2. In this example, I added three frames, so Frame 2 is automatically renumbered as Frame 5, as shown in Figure 60-7. Notice that the type becomes more visible as the frames progress.

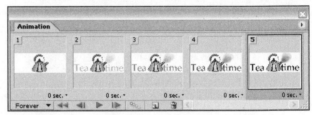

• **Figure 60-7:** As the frames progress, the type becomes more opaque and visible.

Great work! You've created the fade in for the first part of the animation. For the second part of the animation, you need to add more frames to make the type fade out again. Using the Tween dialog box makes this task easy.

8. **With the last frame still selected, click the Tween button at the bottom of the Animation palette.**

In the Tween dialog box, use the Tween With drop-down list to select First Frame. Enter the number of frames you want to add after the selected frame.

9. **Click OK to close the Tween dialog box.**

ImageReady automatically generates frames and places them after the selected frames. Notice that the new frames fade out the type, as shown in Figure 60-8.

Check out your fading type by clicking the Play button at the bottom of the Animation palette or by clicking the Preview in Browser button in the Toolbox to preview the animation in a browser.

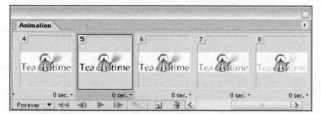

• **Figure 60-8:** After adding the final set of frames, the type fades out again.

 Another great text effect is creating warped text. To create a warped text animation, create the regular type as the first frame, and then warp the type for the second frame. Use the Tween dialog box to add frames between the two frames and, *voilà!* You have an animation using warped text.

Working with Animations

After creating an animation, you can set how long each frame plays and how many times the animation loops. Also, you can copy frames, move them around in the Animation palette to change their order, reverse the entire frame order, and even delete a frame or an entire animation. Here's the lowdown:

✔ **Set frame play time:** Click the tiny downward-pointing triangle below the frame you want to change in the Animation palette, as shown in Figure 60-9. Select a preset amount of time from the menu or click Other to specify the number of seconds in the Set Frame Delay dialog box.

✔ **Set how many times an animation loops:** Click the Select Looping Options button at the bottom left of the Animation palette, and then select Once, Forever, or Other from the menu. If you select Other, use the Set Loop Count dialog box to enter the number of times you want the animation to loop.

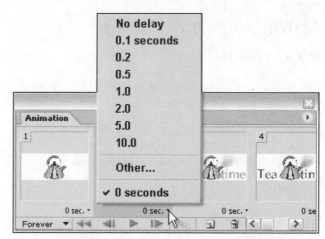

• **Figure 60-9:** After clicking the tiny arrow under the frame, select an amount of time delay using the menu.

✔ **Copy a frame:** Select the frame you want to copy in the Animation palette, and then click the Duplicate Current Frame button at the bottom of the palette.

✔ **Move a frame to another position in the Animation palette:** Drag the frame across the palette to a new location. As you drag, a dark line appears between the frames indicating the position.

✔ **Reverse frame order in the Animation palette:** Select the frames you want to reverse by Shift+clicking. Alternatively, you can select one frame to reverse all the frames. Open the palette menu and choose Reverse Frames.

✔ **Delete a frame:** Select the frame you want to delete, and then drag it to the trashcan icon at the bottom of the Animation palette.

✔ **Delete an entire animation:** Choose Delete Animation from the palette menu.

Optimizing and Saving an Animation

ImageReady is set up to quickly optimize animations and save them in GIF format.

To optimize an animation, follow these steps:

1. **Choose Optimize Animation from the Animation palette menu.**

The Optimize Animation dialog box opens.

2. **Make sure the Bounding Box and Redundant Pixel Removal check boxes are selected.**

The Bounding Box option saves the first frame and the Redundant Pixel Removal reduces file size by removing any pixels that don't change during an animation.

3. **Click OK to close the dialog box and optimize the animation.**

To save an animation in GIF file format, follow these steps:

1. **Choose File⇨Save Optimized As.**

The Save Optimized As dialog box opens.

2. **Enter a name for the animation and select a folder location where the animation will be stored.**

3. **Choose Images Only (*.gif) from the Save As Type drop-down list (Format pop-up menu on a Mac).**

4. **Click Save to save the animation and close the dialog box.**

Technique 61

Creating Background Tiling for Web Pages

When you use a tile to create a background in a Web page, the small tiles are placed next to one another in a checkerboard pattern, creating a seamless background. Background tiles are frequently used on Web pages as decoration and for added visual interest. Because it consists of only one small tile, whose file size is quite small, a tiled background loads very quickly on a Web page.

This quick little technique shows you how to create a background tile using the Tile Maker filter and how to view the tile as a Web page background right in ImageReady. Grab an image, pull out your virtual trowel, and get tiling!

Creating Tiling

You need to be aware that when creating background tiling, you should use a tile that is rather plain with little color change or texture. A background made from a tile that has a lot of color makes any text on a Web page hard to read. Also, any text you add to a Web page with a background should be created using a color that contrasts sharply with the background. For instance, text on a dark gray background should be rather light, perhaps cream or white. (Imagine how hard it would be to read black text placed on a dark gray background!)

 Using a small tile for a background instead of one large image really pays off because the small tile loads much faster. In addition, a tiled background fills a user's entire browser window no matter how large or small the browser window is.

Here's how to create a tile for a background:

1. **In ImageReady, open an image that you want to use to create a background tile.**

   I'm using the image in Figure 61-1 to create a tile for a tiled background.

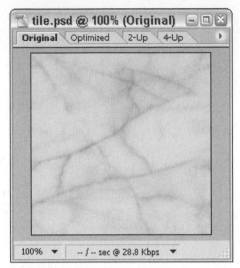

• **Figure 61-1:** This little marble tile will be used to create an entire tiled background.

2. **If the image contains slices, remove the slices by choosing Slices⇨Delete All.**

If you want to use only a portion of the image to create the tile, use the Marquee tool to select the area you want to use, and then choose Image⇨Crop.

3. **Choose Filter⇨Other⇨Tile Maker.**

The Tile Maker dialog box opens.

4. **Select the Blend Edges check box to make the edges of each tile overlap.**

5. **Enter a percentage in the Width text box to set how much the edges overlap.**

6. **Select the Resize Tile to Fill Image check box.**

This setting resizes the tile to fill the entire image window. If it isn't selected, a border appears around the tile when it is used as a tiled background.

7. **Click OK to close the dialog box.**

8. **Choose File⇨Save Optimized.**

The Save Optimized dialog box opens.

9. **Enter a name for the file and select a folder location where the tile will be stored.**

10. **Click Save to save the tile and close the dialog box.**

Previewing Your Tiling Handiwork

To view the tile you just created as a background in ImageReady, follow these steps:

1. **Choose File⇨Output Settings⇨Background.**

2. **Select Background in the View Document As area in the Output Settings dialog box.**

3. **Click OK to close the dialog box.**

4. **Click the Preview in Browser button in the Toolbox.**

The tile is used for the tiled background in the browser window, as shown in Figure 61-2.

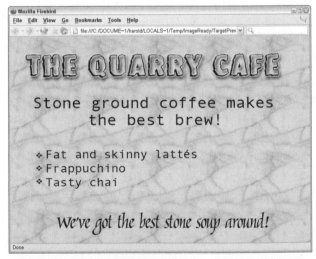

Figure 61-2: The marble tile becomes a tiled background in the browser window.

 Don't forget to choose File⇨Output Settings⇨ Background again and select Image in the View Document As area. Otherwise, anything you preview in a browser appears in the background.

Part X

The Scary (or Fun) Stuff

Installing Plug-Ins

Save Time By

🖊 Installing plug-ins

🖊 Using plug-ins

Plug-ins extend the functionality of Photoshop in a seamless way. Plug-ins are integrated right into the Photoshop environment and are activated from within Photoshop. In fact, you have probably already used plug-ins many times, even if you didn't know it. Filters are the most common plug-in type, the same filters that you find on the Filter menu. Other plug-ins include all the commands on the File⇨Import, Export, Automate, and Scripts menus — such as PDF Presentation, Contact Sheet II, and Picture Package.

This technique takes a look at where you can find plug-ins on the Web and where you need to install them on your computer so that you can access them in Photoshop. Plug-ins are really easy to install, so if you need to create a special effect, but none of the filters that come with Photoshop quite do it for you, download some plug-in filters and give them a spin.

Finding Plug-Ins on the Web

Oodles of Web sites offer plug-ins. Typically, plug-ins are filters. Some plug-ins are freeware, but others are available for a fee.

I mention several plug-ins offered by third-party vendors throughout this book. They include

🖊 **KnockOut 2** by Corel, a super, easy-to-use masking interface (Technique 49)

🖊 **penPalette** by nik multimedia, used for recoloring and enhancing images (Technique 12)

🖊 **Color Efex Pro** by nik multimedia, which offers many filters that create special effects such as imitating an old photo, adding saturation, and converting images to black and white (Technique 30)

🖊 **Dfine 1.0** by nik multimedia, which reduces noise and other imperfections in images (Technique 31)

🖊 **Powertone 1.5** by Creo, a duotone image enhancer (Technique 35)

🖊 **Photo/Graphic Edges** by Auto FX, which quickly lets you create super frames and borders around any image (Technique 42)

✔ **Mystical Lighting** by Auto FX, which enhances lighting and tone (Technique 63)

✔ **Mystical Tint, Tone, Color** by Auto FX, which lets you adjust color and tone, and add special hand painting techniques (Technique 63)

The following is a list of Web sites that offer plug-ins. These sites should get you started. To find more resources, just go to your favorite search engine on the Web, such as Google or Yahoo!, and type in **Photoshop plug-ins**.

✔ Adobe Studio Exchange, share.studio.adobe.com

✔ Alien Skin Software, www.alienskin.com

✔ BoxTop Software, www.boxtopsoft.com

✔ Extensis, www.extensis.com

✔ Flaming Pear Software, www.flamingpear.com

✔ Free Photoshop, www.freephotoshop.com

✔ Redfield Plugins, www.redfieldplugins.com

✔ The Plugin Site, www.thepluginsite.com

Downloading and Installing Plug-Ins

When you find a plug-in that you want to download from a Web page, most often you can simply click a link to download the file, as shown in Figure 62-1.

Because plug-in files can be rather large, they're usually compressed as .Zip (Windows) or .Sit (Mac) files.

After downloading the compressed file, double-click it to decompress it. Your computer takes you through the decompression steps, as shown in Figure 62-2.

 Decompression software comes with Mac OS X. If you're running a Windows machine and you need the WinZip decompression software, you can download it from www.winzip.com.

• **Figure 62-1:** Click the link to download the plug-in file.

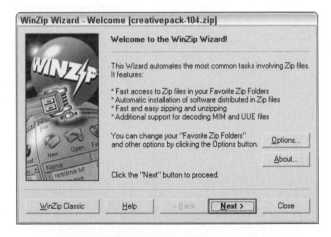

• **Figure 62-2:** Decompress the .Zip (top) or .Sit file (bottom).

Next, place the file in the proper folder, as listed in Table 62-1.

 I list the default folder for actions, which you can also download from the Web. Actions are mini-programs that perform long series of commands that modify images. (To find out more about actions, turn to Technique 8.)

TABLE 62-1: FOLDER LOCATIONS FOR PLUG-INS, SCRIPTS, AND ACTIONS

If You Downloaded a(n) . . .	Place It Here
Action	`C:\Program Files\ Adobe\Photoshop CS\ Presets\Photoshop Actions` (Windows) or `Applications:Adobe Photoshop CS:Presets: Photoshop Actions` (Mac)
Filter	`C:\Program Files\ Adobe\Photoshop CS\ Plug-Ins` (Windows) or `Applications:Adobe Photoshop CS:Plug-Ins` (Mac)
Script	`C:\Program Files\ Adobe\Photoshop CS\ Presets\Scripts` (Windows) or `Applications:Adobe Photoshop CS:Presets: Scripts` (Mac)

After you place the new filter or script in the appropriate folder, close Photoshop (if it's running) and relaunch it. Then, look on the Filter menu for the new filter (see Figure 62-3) or on the File⇨Scripts menu. (Actions can be found by using the Actions palette.)

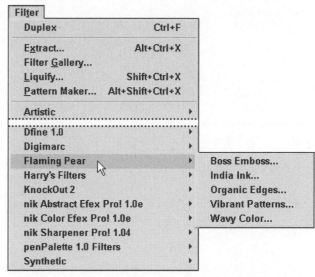

• **Figure 62-3: The new filter is located on the Filter menu.**

Creating your own filters

If you like a good challenge and are mathematically inclined, you might want to try your hand at creating your own custom filters.

You can create custom filters by using Filter Factory, a plug-in created by Joe Ternasky. Using a programming language that resembles C, you can create your own filters and effects and compile them into filter files.

One of the best resources for the Filter Factory is Werner D. Streidt's Filter Factory Web site at `mitglied.lycos.de/ filterfactory`. There you can find an extensive Filter Factory manual and other resources.

Technique 63

Enhancing Your Images with Auto FX Software

Auto FX Software has created some amazing products that you can use to expand Photoshop's capabilities. These software programs work as standalone applications or as filters inside Photoshop. After you install them, they're a dream to use. So many presets are available that you can start with one and modify it for your needs.

This technique takes a look at two Auto FX Software programs: Mystical Lighting; and Mystical Tint, Tone, Color. (I discuss another great Auto FX program, Photo/Graphic Edges, in Technique 42.)

If you like the effects you see here (and I can only show a morsel of the entire feast!), then check out the great software offered by Auto FX at its Web site, www.autofx.com. You can download free trial versions of many Auto FX products.

Installing the full version software isn't a problem; just insert the CD-ROM and follow the installation instructions. After the installation is complete, a handy shortcut (Windows) or alias (Mac) is automatically placed on the desktop. Double-click the shortcut/alias to launch the standalone program. To access the programs within Photoshop, open the Filter menu and look at the bottom of the list, where you find the programs listed on an Auto FX submenu.

Applying Mystical Lighting

Mystical Lighting is used to enhance the lighting in your Photoshop images. You can choose from softening effects, modifying color casts, and adding edge lighting to rainbows, fairy dust, and sunrays.

The program comes with many presets, so you can experiment with different looks to get as close as you can to the results you want. Then you can use various controls to adjust the settings and get the mystical lighting effect just right.

Here's a quick demo of Mystical Lighting:

1. **In Photoshop, open an image you want to add lighting effects to.**

For this example, I'm using the photograph of Arches National Park shown in Figure 63-1.

• **Figure 63-1:** I'm adding a ray of sunlight to this photograph.

2. **Choose Filter⇨Auto FX Software⇨Mystical.**

The Mystical Lighting program dialog box opens, as shown in Figure 63-2. (Depending upon the speed of your computer, the program may take a minute to load.)

Take a minute to look around the program window. On the left are File, Edit, View, and Special Effects buttons. On the right is a floating Layer Options palette that lets you choose from layer presets, create new layers, and clone and delete layers.

3. **Click the Special Effects button to choose from the menu of effects, as shown in Figure 63-3.**

For this example, I'm using LightCaster to add a ray of sunlight to the photograph.

Depending upon the special effect you select, a set of tools and settings appears at the left side of the program window, as shown in Figure 63-4.

• **Figure 63-2:** The Mystical Lighting program window opens full screen.

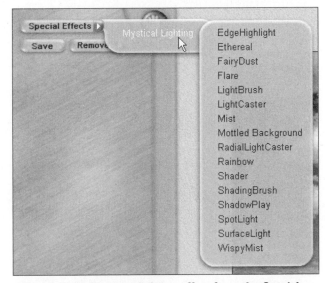

• **Figure 63-3:** Choose a lighting effect from the Special Effects menu.

4. **For the LightCaster effect, drag the T-shaped path to set the width and direction of the light cast on the image, as shown in Figure 63-5.**

5. **Using the sliders at the left side of the program window, set the Cast Color, Spread, and Fade Out of the sunbeam.**

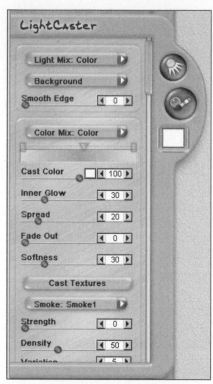

• **Figure 63-4:** The LightCaster tools and settings appear at the left side of the program window.

• **Figure 63-5:** Drag the T-shaped path to set the width and direction of the sunbeam.

6. **Click OK to apply the lighting effect to the image and return to Photoshop.**

As shown in Figure 63-6, the LightCaster adds a lovely sunbeam to Delicate Arch.

• **Figure 63-6:** The sunbeam adds a glow to Delicate Arch.

Adjusting Tint and Tone

Mystical Tint, Tone, Color is used to modify the tint and tone of images to give them special looks, such as antique photographs, bleaching (to create a sun blasted look), cooling, and increasing color depth and saturation.

You can apply most effects in this program in two ways: over the entire image or brushed onto specific areas.

Color tint and tone corrections can be applied using Effect layers or Correction layers. Both of these layer types work like Photoshop adjustment layers, recoloring the pixels of the original image, but not permanently changing them. You can also apply masking layers to protect areas of an image that you don't want to modify.

Here's a brief look into adjusting tint and tone using Mystical Tint, Tone, Color:

1. **In Photoshop, open the image you want to modify.**

   For this example, I'm using the cottage shown in Figure 63-7.

• **Figure 63-7:** I'm giving this picture of a cottage the appearance of an old photograph.

2. **Choose Filter⇨Auto FX Software⇨Mystical TTC.**

   The Mystical Tint, Tone, Color program window opens, as shown in Figure 63-8. (Depending upon the speed of your computer, you might need to wait a minute.)

   Take a minute to look around the program window. On the left are File, Edit, View, and Special Effects buttons. On the right is a floating Layer Options palette that lets you choose from layer presets, create new layers, and clone and delete layers.

3. **Click the Special Effects button to choose from the menu of effects shown in Figure 63-9.**

   For this example, I'm using Antique Photo to make the cottage image look old.

   Depending upon the special effect you select, a set of tools and settings appears at the left side of the program window, as shown in Figure 63-10.

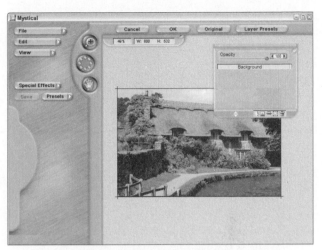

• **Figure 63-8:** The Mystical Tint, Tone, Color program window includes a Work Area showing the image.

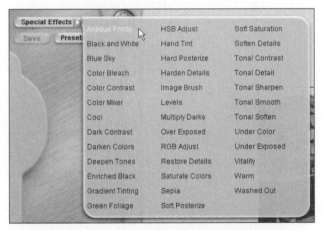

• **Figure 63-9:** Choose a special effect from the menu.

4. **Using the drop-down lists and sliders at the left side of the program window, select the Antique Style, Sepia Tone, Brightness, and Contrast.**

   The Dreamy slider controls the Sepia setting's highlights, giving the image a softer appearance.

• **Figure 63-10:** The Antique Photo tools and settings appear at the left side of the program window.

5. **Click OK to apply the settings and return to Photoshop.**

Figure 63-11 shows the results of antiquing the cottage photo.

• **Figure 63-11:** The cottage photo now has an old, diffused appearance.

Loading New Libraries

Technique 64

Photoshop ships with many libraries — such as brushes, styles, and gradients — that aren't automatically loaded into the appropriate palette or picker. Adding and using these libraries while working in Photoshop can really enhance your ability to modify images and effects. In addition, many Photoshop artists have created custom libraries that are available on the Web. Downloading these libraries and using them in Photoshop is easy and fun.

This technique takes you through the ins and outs of loading libraries by using palettes and pickers. I reveal how the Preset Manager — the ultimate Photoshop library clearinghouse — loads and even creates libraries. Also, I list a few Web sites that offer libraries for download to get you started. From there, you can use your favorite Web search engine, such as Google, Yahoo!, or AltaVista, to quickly find more.

Loading Libraries by Using Palettes or Pickers

You can load libraries by using either palettes or pickers. No matter which palette or picker you use to load a library, they all fundamentally work in the same way. Here's how:

1. **Depending on the tool you're using, open the appropriate palette or picker.**

For instance, if you're working with the Gradient tool, open the Gradient picker on the Options bar, as shown in Figure 64-1. Or, if you're working with the Horizontal Type tool, open the Tool Preset picker on the Options bar.

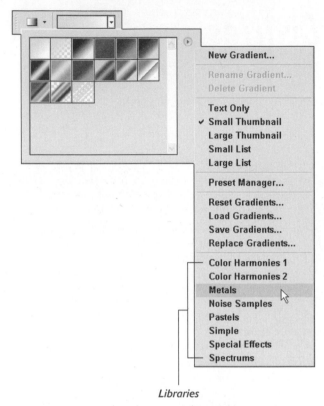

Libraries

• **Figure 64-1:** Many extra gradient libraries ship with Photoshop.

2. **Click the tiny arrow button at the upper-right corner of the palette or picker. A menu opens.**

3. **Choose a library from the bottom of the menu, as shown in Figure 64-1.**

Photoshop opens a dialog box that asks whether you want to append the new library to the presets already shown in the picker or palette. (See Figure 64-2.)

 If you don't see a library at the bottom of the menu but you know that it's available on your computer (perhaps you downloaded it from the Web), choose Load from the menu to view the Load dialog box. Then locate the library in the folder where you saved it, and click Load.

• **Figure 64-2:** Click Append or OK depending on what you want to view.

4. **Click Append to add the new library presets to those currently available or click OK to delete the currently listed presets and view only the new presets.**

The library that you selected appears in the palette or picker.

 You can always restore the default presets to any palette or picker by choosing Reset from the picker or palette menu and then clicking OK.

Working with the Preset Manager

The Preset Manager works like a big filing cabinet for all the available tool presets. Using the Preset Manager, you can load new libraries, create your own libraries, and delete libraries that you don't want anymore.

Here's how to load new libraries by using the Preset Manager:

1. **Choose Edit⇨Preset Manager.**

The Preset Manager opens, as shown in Figure 64-3.

2. **Use the Preset Type drop-down list to select the type of preset library that you want to add.**

Your choices are Brushes, Swatches, Gradients, Styles, Patterns, Contours, Custom Shapes, and Tools.

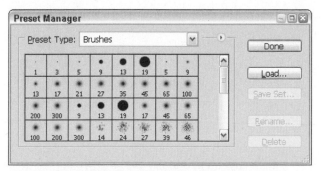

• **Figure 64-3:** The Preset Manager is used to organize, load, save, and delete preset libraries.

3. Click the tiny right-pointing arrow button to the right of the Preset Type drop-down list to open the menu, as shown in Figure 64-4, and choose the library you want to load from the bottom of the menu.

 If you don't see a library at the bottom of the menu but you know that it's available on your computer (perhaps you downloaded it from the Web), choose Load from the menu to view the Load dialog box. Then, locate the library in the folder where you saved it, and click Load.

• **Figure 64-4:** Choose a new library from the bottom of the menu.

 If you create your own presets and want to save them in a custom library for later use, you can use the Preset Manager to create libraries. Also, after you create a library you can always e-mail it to friends or colleagues.

To save your custom presets in a library, follow these steps:

1. Choose Edit➪Preset Manager.

The Preset Manager opens. (Refer to Figure 64-3.)

2. Use the Preset Type drop-down list to select the type of preset library that you want to create.

3. Ctrl+click the presets in the list to select the presets that you want to save in a custom library. (See Figure 64-5.)

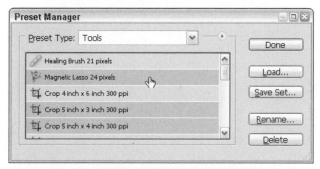

• **Figure 64-5:** Ctrl+click to select the presets that you want to include in your custom library.

4. Click Save Set.

5. Use the Save dialog box to enter a name for the custom library in the File Name (Windows) or Save As (Mac) text box, and then click Save.

Your custom library is now ready for use.

 If you want to load your newly created custom library by using a palette or picker, you need to exit Photoshop and relaunch before you can view the custom library on the palette or picker menu.

Downloading libraries from the Web

Many commercial and hobbyist sites offer great libraries for download. The following are just a few sites that offer libraries:

- Adobe Studio (studio.adobe.com)

- Design Spice (www.designspice.com/main/ free/free_downloads.php)

- Software-X (www.software-x.com)

- Free Photoshop (www.freephotoshop.com/html/ downloadables.html)

- Nocturna (http://nocturna.net/brushes/)

You can find more libraries for download by using your favorite Web search engine.

Index

Numbers & Symbols

Z

Notes

Notes

Notes

Notes

Notes

FOR DUMMIES

The easy way to get more done and have more fun

FOR DUMMIES®

A world of resources to help you grow

TRAVEL

0-7645-5453-0

0-7645-5438-7

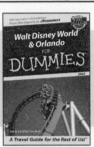

0-7645-5444-1

Also available:

America's National Parks
For Dummies
(0-7645-6204-5)

Caribbean For Dummies
(0-7645-5445-X)

Cruise Vacations
For Dummies 2003
(0-7645-5459-X)

Europe For Dummies
(0-7645-5456-5)

Ireland For Dummies
(0-7645-6199-5)

France For Dummies
(0-7645-6292-4)

Las Vegas For Dummies
(0-7645-5448-4)

London For Dummies
(0-7645-5416-6)

Mexico's Beach Resorts
For Dummies
(0-7645-6262-2)

Paris For Dummies
(0-7645-5494-8)

RV Vacations For Dummies
(0-7645-5443-3)

EDUCATION & TEST PREPARATION

0-7645-5194-9

0-7645-5325-9

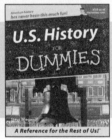

0-7645-5249-X

Also available:

The ACT For Dummies
(0-7645-5210-4)

Chemistry For Dummies
(0-7645-5430-1)

English Grammar For Dummies
(0-7645-5322-4)

French For Dummies
(0-7645-5193-0)

GMAT For Dummies
(0-7645-5251-1)

Inglés Para Dummies
(0-7645-5427-1)

Italian For Dummies
(0-7645-5196-5)

Research Papers For Dummies
(0-7645-5426-3)

SAT I For Dummies
(0-7645-5472-7)

U.S. History For Dummies
(0-7645-5249-X)

World History For Dummies
(0-7645-5242-2)

HEALTH, SELF-HELP & SPIRITUALITY

0-7645-5154-X

0-7645-5302-X

0-7645-5418-2

Also available:

The Bible For Dummies
(0-7645-5296-1)

Controlling Cholesterol
For Dummies
(0-7645-5440-9)

Dating For Dummies
(0-7645-5072-1)

Dieting For Dummies
(0-7645-5126-4)

High Blood Pressure For
Dummies
(0-7645-5424-7)

Judaism For Dummies
(0-7645-5299-6)

Menopause For Dummies
(0-7645-5458-1)

Nutrition For Dummies
(0-7645-5180-9)

Potty Training For Dummies
(0-7645-5417-4)

Pregnancy For Dummies
(0-7645-5074-8)

Rekindling Romance For
Dummies
(0-7645-5303-8)

Religion For Dummies
(0-7645-5264-3)

Available wherever books are sold. Go to www.dummies.com or call 1-877-762-2974 to order direct

FOR DUMMIES®

Plain-English solutions for everyday challenges

HOME & BUSINESS COMPUTER BASICS

0-7645-0838-5

0-7645-1663-9

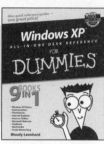

0-7645-1548-9

Also available:

Excel 2002 All-in-One Desk Reference For Dummies (0-7645-1794-5)

Office XP 9-in-1 Desk Reference For Dummies (0-7645-0819-9)

PCs All-in-One Desk Reference For Dummies (0-7645-0791-5)

Troubleshooting Your PC For Dummies (0-7645-1669-8)

Upgrading & Fixing PCs For Dummies (0-7645-1665-5)

Windows XP For Dummies (0-7645-0893-8)

Windows XP For Dummies Quick Reference (0-7645-0897-0)

Word 2002 For Dummies (0-7645-0839-3)

INTERNET & DIGITAL MEDIA

0-7645-0894-6

0-7645-1642-6

0-7645-1664-7

Also available:

CD and DVD Recording For Dummies (0-7645-1627-2)

Digital Photography All-in-One Desk Reference For Dummies (0-7645-1800-3)

eBay For Dummies (0-7645-1642-6)

Genealogy Online For Dummies (0-7645-0807-5)

Internet All-in-One Desk Reference For Dummies (0-7645-1659-0)

Internet For Dummies Quick Reference (0-7645-1645-0)

Internet Privacy For Dummies (0-7645-0846-6)

Paint Shop Pro For Dummies (0-7645-2440-2)

Photo Retouching & Restoration For Dummies (0-7645-1662-0)

Photoshop Elements For Dummies (0-7645-1675-2)

Scanners For Dummies (0-7645-0783-4)

Get smart! Visit www.dummies.com

- **Find listings of even more Dummies titles**

- **Browse online articles, excerpts, and how-to's**

- **Sign up for daily or weekly e-mail tips**

- **Check out Dummies fitness videos and other products**

- **Order from our online bookstore**

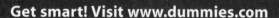

Available wherever books are sold. Go to www.dummies.com or call 1-877-762-2974 to order direct

FOR DUMMIES®

Helping you expand your horizons and realize your potential

GRAPHICS & WEB SITE DEVELOPMENT

0-7645-1651-5

0-7645-1643-4

0-7645-0895-4

Also available:

Adobe Acrobat 5 PDF
For Dummies
(0-7645-1652-3)

ASP.NET For Dummies
(0-7645-0866-0)

ColdFusion MX For Dummies
(0-7645-1672-8)

Dreamweaver MX For Dummies
(0-7645-1630-2)

FrontPage 2002 For Dummies
(0-7645-0821-0)

HTML 4 For Dummies
(0-7645-0723-0)

Illustrator 10 For Dummies
(0-7645-3636-2)

PowerPoint 2002 For Dummies
(0-7645-0817-2)

Web Design For Dummies
(0-7645-0823-7)

PROGRAMMING & DATABASES

0-7645-0746-X

0-7645-1626-4

0-7645-1657-4

Also available:

Access 2002 For Dummies
(0-7645-0818-0)

Beginning Programming
For Dummies
(0-7645-0835-0)

Crystal Reports 9 For Dummies
(0-7645-1641-8)

Java & XML For Dummies
(0-7645-1658-2)

Java 2 For Dummies
(0-7645-0765-6)

JavaScript For Dummies
(0-7645-0633-1)

Oracle9i For Dummies
(0-7645-0880-6)

Perl For Dummies
(0-7645-0776-1)

PHP and MySQL For Dummies
(0-7645-1650-7)

SQL For Dummies
(0-7645-0737-0)

Visual Basic .NET For Dummies
(0-7645-0867-9)

LINUX, NETWORKING & CERTIFICATION

0-7645-1545-4

0-7645-1760-0

0-7645-0772-9

Also available:

A+ Certification For Dummies
(0-7645-0812-1)

CCNP All-in-One Certification For
Dummies
(0-7645-1648-5)

Cisco Networking For Dummies
(0-7645-1668-X)

CISSP For Dummies
(0-7645-1670-1)

CIW Foundations For Dummies
(0-7645-1635-3)

Firewalls For Dummies
(0-7645-0884-9)

Home Networking For Dummies
(0-7645-0857-1)

Red Hat Linux All-in-One Desk
Reference For Dummies
(0-7645-2442-9)

UNIX For Dummies
(0-7645-0419-3)

Available wherever books are sold.
Go to www.dummies.com or call 1-877-762-2974 to order direct